T0213260

The Enterprise Engineering Series

Explorations

More information about this series at http://www.springer.com/series/8371

Henderik A. Proper • Robert Winter •
Stephan Aier • Sybren de Kinderen
Editors

Architectural Coordination of Enterprise Transformation

 Springer

Editors
Henderik A. Proper
Luxembourg Institute of Science
and Technology
Esch-sur-Alzette, Luxembourg

Robert Winter
Institute for Information Management
University of St. Gallen
St. Gallen, Switzerland

Stephan Aier
Institute for Information Management
University of St. Gallen
St. Gallen, Switzerland

Sybren de Kinderen
University of Duisburg-Essen
Essen, Germany

ISSN 1867-8920   ISSN 1867-8939   (electronic)
The Enterprise Engineering Series
ISBN 978-3-030-09900-8   ISBN 978-3-319-69584-6   (eBook)
https://doi.org/10.1007/978-3-319-69584-6

Printed on acid-free paper

This Springer imprint is published by the registered company Springer International Publishing AG part of Springer Nature.
The registered company address is: Gewerbestrasse 11, 6330 Cham, Switzerland

In writing this book, the authors were kindly supported by:

Institute of Information Management

The Enterprise Engineering Network
informed design and operation of enterprises

Preface

Enterprises frequently engage in transformations. Typical examples of such enterprise transformations include changes of the business model, mergers and acquisitions, large-scale outsourcing, and the introduction and/or replacement of core enterprise information systems. Due to their strategic character, their complexity, and the amount of effort, enterprise transformations significantly impact the competitiveness of enterprises, their economic success, and the people that are involved or affected. As a consequence, they are a phenomenon of great significance for society, economy, and business informatics.

The complexity of enterprise transformations creates challenges for its coordinated planning as well as for the many concurrent projects involved in its implementation. Enterprises, and senior management in particular, struggle with the question to steer and/or coordinate enterprise transformations. In complex organisations, enterprise-wide changes imply that a wide variety of actors are involved in the design and implementation of a large number of local changes. To make large enterprise transformations feasible and manageable, they are typically split into programmes and eventually into projects. Even more, larger enterprises typically do not just conduct one transformation programme at a time, but conduct multiple in parallel, which all need to be coordinated with the enterprise's strategy. Local changes, as made in the projects that collectively make up the transformation programme(s), are not always in line with overall objectives because not only subunit-specific concerns "pull" or "tug" the direction taken by the transformation, but also perceived direction may deviate from intended direction. Thus, local changes need to be coordinated in order to constitute a purposefully engineered and coherently implemented intervention to the enterprise instead of an "emergent" change process. There is a need to guard the coherence between the different concerns and aspects of an enterprise across programme(s).

These challenges have triggered us to initiate a broad research programme on *architectural coordination of enterprise transformation* (ACET (A list of frequently used acronyms is provided on page xxiii)) involving a collaboration between researchers from Luxembourg, Switzerland, as well as the Netherlands. The ACET programme involved four applied research projects: the core ACET project, the *general enterprise architecting* (GEA) project, the Corporate Intelligence project, and the Rational Architecture project, involving different constellations of the University of St. Gallen in Switzerland, the Luxembourg Institute of Science and Technology in Luxembourg, the Radboud University in the Netherlands, the University of Luxembourg, and several industrial partners such as Ordina and SAP.

Each of these applied research projects focussed on different aspects of enterprise transformations and different strategies to use enterprise architecture to steer the direction of such transformations. The ACET project formed the integrative core of these four research projects, also leading to the general focus of this book on architectural coordination of enterprise transformation.

The resulting book brings together the work of ten PhD researchers and six senior researchers. While this book is built around individual contributions of the researchers involved, the final result goes beyond being a mere collection of disconnected chapters. As the work involved four related research projects, the different results are well connected to each other, while some terminological and theoretical integration across the different researchers has also been achieved. At the same time, it should be said that this book can only provide a humble beginning towards the creation of a more complete understanding of architectural coordination of enterprise transformation and the development of an integrated set of instruments supporting ACET in practice.

The ambitions at the start of the ACET research programme were high. It was, indeed, the ambition to develop an integrated design theory for ACET. However, the early stages of the projects involved in the programme provided the insight that the heterogeneity and multifacetedness of the domain of ACET was so high that the development of an integrated design theory for ACET would be too ambitious. A choice had to be made between the creation of a "superficial" overall method for ACET or, for the moment, a set of disconnected and partial, yet well-founded, elements/components towards a more comprehensive method for ACET. We made a choice for the latter, where the research efforts were compartmentalised, in the sense that each of the involved researchers focussed on a specific (set of related) aspect(s), with the aim to develop an initial explanatory theory covering the aspect.

Finally, we would like to thank our primary sponsors, the FNR (Fonds National de la Recherche) in Luxembourg and the SNSF (Swiss National Science Foundation) in Switzerland. We would also like to explicitly thank Dirk van der Linden, who helped in converting different Word sources into LaTeX. Using a mix of Word and LaTeX across the team requires a technical integration at some stage, and Dirk was very helpful in achieving this. We would also like to express our gratitude to the proofreaders of this book, which, next to the co-authors of the different chapters, included Bas van Gils.

Looking back on developing and shaping the content of this book, two important events come to our mind. The first event was a writing workshop of the core team on Crete. As it turned out, it was more cost efficient for the entire core team to meet there, as opposed to either gathering in full in St. Gallen or in Luxembourg. The result was a very productive, and enjoyable, workshop. The second event involved the final push in structuring the book. Two of the editors worked closely together for almost a week, being hosted by our dear friend José Tribolet in Lisbon, Portugal. This allowed us to "hide away" from day-to-day activities and focus on structuring the book.

As editors, we sincerely hope you will enjoy reading this book, while exploring the richness of the architectural coordination of enterprise transformation playing field and gaining more insights into both its practical and theoretical aspects.

Belval, Luxembourg	Henderik A. Proper
St. Gallen, Switzerland	Robert Winter
St. Gallen, Switzerland	Stephan Aier
Essen, Germany	Sybren de Kinderen

Contents

1 Introduction 1
    1.1   Enterprise Transformation 1
    1.2   The Need for Coordination 3
    1.3   Enterprise Architecture Management 5
    1.4   Architectural Coordination of Enterprise Transformation 7
    1.5   Outline of This Book 9

Part I Observing Architectural Coordination in Practice

2 A Major Transformation at a Global Insurance Company 15
    2.1   The Organisation 15
    2.2   The Enterprise Transformation 16
    2.3   Structuring the Enterprise Architecture Management Function ... 17
    2.4   The Role of Enterprise Architecture Management 19
    2.5   Reflection 20

3 Centralised Monitoring of Pensions in Greece 21
    3.1   A Fragmented Social Security Landscape 21
    3.2   The Enterprise Transformation 22
        3.2.1   Baseline Architecture 23
        3.2.2   Target Architecture 24
        3.2.3   Scenario 1: Fully Consolidated Architecture 25
        3.2.4   Scenario 2: Aggregation of Pension Payments Files ... 25
    3.3   Reflection 29

4 Enterprise Coherence in the Public Sector 31
    4.1   The Organisation 32
    4.2   The Enterprise Transformation 32
    4.3   The Used Approach 33
    4.4   The Management Dashboard for DGA 34
    4.5   Answering the Business Issue 37

4.6   Results of the Programme.................................   40
4.7   Reflection...   41

5   Public Services Opening Up To Innovation   43
5.1   The Organisation...   43
5.2   The Enterprise Transformation............................   44
       5.2.1   Introduction of Architecture Board..................   45
       5.2.2   Introduction of Innovation Department...............   46
       5.2.3   Introduction of New Project Types...................   46
5.3   Challenges...   47
       5.3.1   Unclear Role of the Architecture Board..............   47
       5.3.2   Legitimacy of the Architecture Board................   47
       5.3.3   Long Communication Lines...........................   48
       5.3.4   Innovation as an Addition..........................   49
       5.3.5   Double Role of Architects..........................   49
       5.3.6   The Pace of the Enterprise Transformation...........   50
       5.3.7   Change in Mindsets.................................   50
5.4   Reflection...   51

Part II Exploring Architectural Coordination of Enterprise Transformation

6   Degrees of Change in Enterprises   57
6.1   Introduction...   57
6.2   Domains of Work..   58
       6.2.1   Added-Value Domain................................   58
       6.2.2   Innovation Domain.................................   59
       6.2.3   Value Systems Domain..............................   60
6.3   Causal Texture of the Environment.........................   61
       6.3.1   Placid, Randomised Environment.....................   62
       6.3.2   Placid, Clustered Environment......................   62
       6.3.3   Disturbed-Reactive Environment.....................   63
       6.3.4   Turbulent Field...................................   63
6.4   Types of Change Interventions.............................   64
       6.4.1   Restructuring.....................................   64
       6.4.2   Reengineering.....................................   64
       6.4.3   Rethinking..   65
6.5   Three Information Technology Realms.......................   65
6.6   Three Degrees of Enterprise Change........................   66
       6.6.1   Scope of Change...................................   67
       6.6.2   Environmental Contingency..........................   68
       6.6.3   Type of Change Interventions.......................   68
       6.6.4   The Role of Information Technology..................   69
6.7   Conclusion...   70

7   Enterprise Transformation from a Social Perspective 71
  7.1   Introduction.. 71
      7.1.1   Structuration-Foundation........................... 73
      7.1.2   Origin.. 73
      7.1.3   Type.. 74
      7.1.4   Momentum....................................... 74
      7.1.5   Trajectory....................................... 74
  7.2   Applying the Structuration-Foundation....................... 75
  7.3   Conclusions.. 75

8   More than Engineering: The Role of Subcultures 77
  8.1   Introduction.. 77
  8.2   What is an Organisational Subculture?....................... 78
  8.3   Relevance of Organisational Subcultures in ACET............. 79
  8.4   Potential Consequences if Cultural Differences Are Ignored..... 82
  8.5   Conclusion... 85

9   The Need for a Use Perspective on Architectural Coordination 87
  9.1   Introduction: The Importance of a Use Perspective on ACET.... 87
  9.2   Importance of the Use of Architectural Coordination........... 88
  9.3   ACET Artefacts from the Users' Perspective................... 90
  9.4   Relevant State of the Art of Use-Centricity in Literature........ 91
  9.5   Managerial Implications for Architectural Artefacts............ 95
  9.6   Conclusion... 96

**10 Enterprise Coherence Governance: Involving the Right
Stakeholders**... 99
  10.1 Introduction.. 99
  10.2 Beyond Engineering... 100
  10.3 Stakeholder Fragmentation in Enterprise Transformation........ 101
      10.3.1 Social Complexity................................ 101
      10.3.2 Wickedness...................................... 102
  10.4 The Need to Govern Enterprise Coherence..................... 103
      10.4.1 Enterprise Coherence Governance.................... 103
      10.4.2 Beyond Blue-Print Thinking........................ 104
      10.4.3 Engaging Stakeholders............................. 105
  10.5 Requirements for Enterprise Coherence Governance............ 106
      10.5.1 Stakeholder Involvement........................... 106
      10.5.2 Management Control............................... 107
      10.5.3 Change Management............................... 108
      10.5.4 General Systems Theory............................ 109
  10.6 Conclusion... 110

11 Information Requirements for Enterprise Transformation 111
  11.1 Introduction.. 111
  11.2 State of the Art... 112

11.3   Dimensions of Information Requirements...................... 113
        11.3.1   People: Consumers of Information.................... 114
        11.3.2   Structure: Organisational Scope of Information....... 115
        11.3.3   Task: Purpose of Information........................ 115
        11.3.4   Technology: Detail of Information................... 116
11.4   Information Processing During Enterprise Transformation...... 116
11.5   Information Provision in the Context of ACET................. 118
11.6   Conclusion.. 121

12   **Institutionalisation of ACET: Needs and Foundations** 123
12.1   Introduction.. 123
12.2   Theoretical Perspectives on the Effective Anchoring of ACET... 126
12.3   An Institutional Theory Perspective on ACET................. 129
        12.3.1   Institutional Theory Foundations.................... 129
        12.3.2   Application of Institutional Theory Concepts
                  to ACET.. 132
12.4   Conclusion.. 135

13   **The Need for Model Engineering**.............................. 137
13.1   Introduction.. 137
13.2   Limits to One-Size-Fits-All Languages....................... 138
13.3   Research Questions.. 140
13.4   Candidate Existing Approaches............................... 140
        13.4.1   Expressing Architectural Concerns by Language
                  Federation 141
        13.4.2   Situational Method Engineering..................... 142
        13.4.3   Domain-Specific Language Design.................... 143
13.5   Our Approach: Component-Based Language Composition...... 144
13.6   Conclusion.. 144

14   **Steering Transformations with Architecture Principles** 147
14.1   Introduction.. 147
14.2   Challenges in Using and Evaluating Architecture Principles..... 150
14.3   Conclusion.. 151

15   **The Need for Explicit Decision-Making Strategies** 153
15.1   Introduction.. 153
15.2   Design Rationale.. 155
        15.2.1   What is Design Rationale?.......................... 155
        15.2.2   Design Rationale Fundamentals...................... 156
        15.2.3   Types of Design Rationale Approaches............... 156
        15.2.4   Design Rationale Approaches and Related Work...... 159
15.3   Design Rationale and Enterprise Architecture................. 160
15.4   Objectives of a Rationale Management System................. 161
15.5   Conclusion.. 162

Part III Harvesting Components of an ACET Design Theory

16 ACET Constructs 169
16.1 General ACET Constructs.................................... 169
16.1.1 Enterprise Transformation.......................... 169
16.1.2 Architecture...................................... 170
16.1.3 Enterprise Architecture............................ 170
16.1.4 Enterprise Architecture Management................. 170
16.1.5 Coordination...................................... 170
16.1.6 Method Fragment/Method Chunk.................... 171
16.1.7 Model.. 171
16.1.8 Stakeholder....................................... 171
16.2 Key Constructs for ACET Method Fragments.................. 171
16.2.1 Value.. 171
16.2.2 Organisational Subculture......................... 172
16.2.3 Decision.. 172
16.2.4 Architecture Principles............................ 172
16.2.5 Information Systems Model......................... 172
16.2.6 Reference Model................................... 173
16.2.7 Community of Practice............................. 173
16.2.8 Boundary Object.................................. 173
16.2.9 Institution.. 173
16.2.10 Institutionalisation................................ 173

17 Transformation Intelligence Capability Catalogue 175
17.1 Role of the Capability Catalogue for ACET.................... 177
17.2 Method Fragments of the Capabilities Catalogue............... 178

18 Coherence Management Dashboard for ACET 183
18.1 Introduction.. 183
18.2 The Enterprise Coherence Framework........................ 184
18.2.1 Coherence at the Strategic Level.................... 185
18.2.2 Coherence at the Design Level...................... 187
18.2.3 Coherence Between the Levels...................... 190
18.3 Coherence Management Dashboard........................... 191
18.4 Case studies.. 191

19 Guidelines for Architecture Models as Boundary Objects 193
19.1 Introduction.. 193
19.2 Boundary Objects... 195
19.2.1 Boundary Object Properties........................ 196
19.2.2 Enterprise Architecture Models as Boundary
Objects... 197
19.3 Semantic Boundary Object Capacities........................ 198
19.3.1 Visualisation..................................... 199
19.3.2 Experimental Setup................................ 199

19.3.3   Experimental Results.............................. 202
19.3.4   Modularity....................................... 204
19.3.5   Abstraction/Concreteness......................... 205
19.3.6   Stability.. 206
19.3.7   Development of Boundary Object Design Principles... 206
19.4   Discussion... 209

20   The ACET Information Requirements Reference Model 211
20.1   Introduction... 211
20.2   Research Approach.. 212
20.3   ACET Information Requirements Reference Model............. 213
20.3.1   Strategy... 215
20.3.2   Goals.. 215
20.3.3   Business Structure............................... 215
20.3.4   Project Portfolio................................ 216
20.3.5   Design Options................................... 217
20.3.6   Methods.. 217
20.3.7   Social Factors................................... 217
20.3.8   Performance...................................... 218
20.3.9   Stakeholders..................................... 218
20.3.10   Risks.. 219
20.3.11   IT Structure..................................... 219
20.4   Discussion... 219

21   Model Bundling: Componential Language Engineering 221
21.1   Introduction... 221
21.2   Model Bundling.. 222
21.2.1   The e^3RoME Model Bundling Artefact............... 222
21.2.2   Adapting a Value-Based Service Bundling
         Mechanism.. 223
21.3   Experiment: Integrating e^3Value and ArchiMate via DEMO..... 223
21.4   Two e^3RoME Ontologies.................................... 224
21.4.1   The Stakeholder Perspective Ontology............... 225
21.4.2   The Catalogue Perspective Ontology................. 228
21.5   Generating Model Bundles................................. 229
21.5.1   Creating an Initial Model Bundle................... 230
21.5.2   Modifying a Model Bundle......................... 232
21.6   Discussion... 233

22   Principle-Based Goal-Oriented Requirements Language 235
22.1   Introduction... 235
22.2   Guidelines for the Formulation of Architecture Principles....... 237
22.3   Semiformal Representation of Architecture Principles.......... 239
22.4   Constraints for Architecture Principle Representation........... 242

22.5   Relevance and Consequences for ACET   244
      22.5.1   Support for Formulation of Architecture Principles   244
      22.5.2   Supporting Design Decisions Based on Architecture
               Principles   244
      22.5.3   Supporting Consistency Checks   245
      22.5.4   Evaluate Consistency with Architecture Principles   245
22.6   Discussion   247

23   The EA Anamnesis Approach   249
23.1   Introduction   249
23.2   Decision Properties   249
23.3   Decision-Making Process Concepts   252
23.4   Enterprise Architecture Decision Relationships   254
23.5   Discussion   255

24   Formalising Enterprise Architecture Decision Models   257
24.1   Introduction   257
24.2   Preliminaries   259
      24.2.1   Meta-model and Decision Design Graphs   259
      24.2.2   Reflection   262
24.3   A Formal Model for Architectural Decision Modelling   263
      24.3.1   Elementary Definitions for Architectural Decision
               Modelling   263
      24.3.2   Layered Decision Model and Logical Relations   265
24.4   Case Study: ArchiSurance   269
      24.4.1   Introduction   269
      24.4.2   Validation   270
24.5   Related Work   273
24.6   Discussion   274

25   Situational Adaptations of ACET   277
25.1   Introduction   277
25.2   Situational Method Engineering   278
25.3   Classifying Enterprise Architecture Management Approaches . . .   278
25.4   Classification of Transformation Types   282
      25.4.1   Configurable Reference Models   282
      25.4.2   Design of an Enterprise Transformation
               Information Model   285
25.5   Situations in ACET   286
25.6   Discussion   289

Part IV   Epilogue

26   Conclusion and Reflections   293
26.1   Introduction   293
26.2   Summary of Results   294

26.3   Reflections on the Development of Large-Scale Methods........   295
          26.3.1   Change of Programme Strategy....................   295
          26.3.2   A Method as a Design Theory.....................   296
          26.3.3   Complexity and Uncertainty for the Use of Methods...   297
          26.3.4   Research Methodological Guidance.................   297
   26.4   Suggestions for Future Research............................   300
          26.4.1   Sociocultural Context of ACET...................   301
          26.4.2   Enterprises Are in Motion.......................   301
          26.4.3   Enterprise Architecture Modelling...............   302
          26.4.4   Enterprise Architecture Principles..............   303
          26.4.5   Architectural Decision-Making...................   303
          26.4.6   Integrated Method for ACET......................   304
   26.5   Conclusion..   304

References   305

About the Authors

Ralf Abraham During the ACET programme, Dr. Ralf Abraham worked as a PhD researcher at the Institute of Information Management, University of St. Gallen, in Switzerland. Currently, Ralf works at DATEV eG in Nürnberg, Germany.

Stephan Aier Prof. Dr. Stephan Aier is an Assistant Professor at the Institute of Information Management, University of St. Gallen, in Switzerland. His research interests are in architecture, integration, and transformation management. He heads the Architectural Coordination Group at the Institute of Information Management and is responsible for fundamental research funded by public research organisations, such as the Swiss National Science Foundation, and for applied research funded by industry partners.

Stefan Bischoff During the ACET programme, Dr. Stefan Bischoff worked as a PhD researcher at the Institute of Information Management, University of St. Gallen, in Switzerland.

Sybren de Kinderen During the ACET programme, Dr. Sybren de Kinderen worked as a postdoctoral research fellow at the Luxembourg Institute of Science and Technology (LIST) in Luxembourg. Currently, he is an Assistant Professor at the University of Duisburg-Essen, in Germany.

Hella Faller During the ACET programme, Dr. Hella Faller worked as a PhD researcher at the Luxembourg Institute of Science and Technology (LIST) in Luxembourg. In March 2016, she received her PhD from the Radboud University, Nijmegen, in the Netherlands.

Sepideh Ghanavati During the ACET programme, Dr. Sepideh Ghanavati worked as a postdoctoral research fellow at the Luxembourg Institute of Science and Technology (LIST) in Luxembourg. Currently, she is an Assistant Professor in the Department of Computer Science at Texas Tech University, in Lubbock, Texas, USA.

Janne J. Korhonen During the ACET programme, Janne J. Korhonen was a visiting researcher at the Luxembourg Institute of Science and Technology (LIST) in Luxembourg, while being enrolled as a PhD candidate at the Aalto University in Finland.

Nils Labusch During the ACET programme, Dr. Nils Labusch worked as a PhD researcher at the Institute of Information Management, University of St. Gallen, in Switzerland.

Diana Marosin During the ACET programme, Diana Marosin worked as a PhD researcher at the Luxembourg Institute of Science and Technology (LIST) in Luxembourg. She expects to defend her doctoral thesis at Radboud University, Nijmegen, the Netherlands, by the end of 2017. Currently, she is working at Sopra Steria Luxembourg as a Solution Building Engineer.

Wolfgang A. Molnar Dr. Wolfgang Molnar currently works as a researcher at Warwick Business School and practitioner in the automotive industry for ZF in Germany. Previously, he was a Research Fellow at the Luxembourg Institute of Science and Technology. He earned his PhD in Information Systems and Management from the Warwick Business School, University of Warwick. His research expertise focuses on socio-technical aspects in developing information systems.

Georgios Plataniotis During the ACET programme, Dr. Georgios Plataniotis worked as a PhD researcher at the Luxembourg Institute of Science and Technology (LIST) in Luxembourg. In April 2017, he received his PhD from the Radboud University, Nijmegen, in the Netherlands. Georgios is currently working as a scientific officer at the e-Government Center for Social Security (IDIKA), Greece.

Hend*erik* A. Proper Prof. Dr. Hend*erik* A. Proper, Erik to friends, is Head of Academic Affairs at the Luxembourg Institute of Science and Technology (LIST) in Luxembourg and Senior Research Manager within its IT for Innovative Services (ITIS) Department. Since 2003, he has been a Professor at the Radboud University, Nijmegen, the Netherlands. Since May 2017, he is also an Adjunct Professor at the University of Luxembourg, in Luxembourg. Professor Proper is the editor-in-chief of Springer's *Organisational Design & Enterprise Engineering* journal as well as an editor of Springer's Enterprise Engineering series. He serves as Associate Editor, or is member of the editorial board, for several journals, including the *Business & Information Systems Engineering* journal, the *International Journal of Cooperative Information Systems*, and *Enterprise Modelling and Information Systems Architectures*.

Marc van Zee During the ACET programme, Dr. Marc van Zee worked as a PhD researcher at the University of Luxembourg, in Luxembourg. Currently, Marc is a researcher at Google Research in Zurich, Switzerland.

Roel Wagter During the ACET programme, Dr. Roel Wagter was enrolled as a PhD candidate at the Radboud University, Nijmegen, the Netherlands, while also being a principal consultant at Ordina Consulting in the Netherlands. Currently, Roel is Associate Partner at Solventa in the Netherlands, while also being Senior Lecturer at the Antwerp Management School in Antwerp, Belgium.

Simon Weiss During the ACET programme, Dr. Simon Weiss worked as a PhD researcher at the Institute of Information Management, University of St. Gallen, in Switzerland.

Robert Winter Prof. Dr. Robert Winter is Full Professor of Business & Information Systems Engineering at the University of St. Gallen (HSG) and Director of HSG's Institute of Information Management. He was vice editor-in-chief of the *Business & Information Systems Engineering* journal and currently serves as Senior Associate Editor of the *European Journal of Information Systems* and member of the editorial boards of several journals including *Enterprise Modelling and Information Systems Architectures* and *MIS Quarterly Executive*. His research interests include design science research methodology, enterprise architecture management, transformation management, and the management of very large IT projects/programmes.

List of Acronyms

ACET	Architectural coordination of enterprise transformation
GEA	General enterprise architecting
IT	Information technology
KPI	Key performance indicator
OCL	Object constraint language
TOGAF	The Open Group Architecture Framework
UCM	Use case maps
URN	User requirements notation

Chapter 1
Introduction

Hend*erik* A. Proper, Robert Winter, Stephan Aier, and Sybren de Kinderen

Abstract In this chapter, we introduce the phenomenon of enterprise transformation, its enterprise-wide character and the challenges that result from the co-existence of top-down design of transformations and decentralised implementation of change activities. We introduce *architectural coordination of enterprise transformation* [ACET (A list of frequently used acronyms is provided on page xxiii)] as an approach that addresses these challenges and outline the playing field of contributions to the ACET body of knowledge.

1.1 Enterprise Transformation

An *enterprise* is understood as being "*any collection of organisations that have a common set of goals*" (The Open Group 2011), for example, a company, a network organisation, or a government agency. In the context of business informatics, the common set of goals is usually related to economic value creation in a specific context—such as offering certain services, addressing certain markets, or exploiting certain capabilities or resources.

Enterprises are dynamic systems which are constantly changing and evolving. There is a distinction, though not always a clear one, between what constitutes routine change or optimisation and what can be regarded as *transformation*. Hammer

H.A. Proper (✉)
Luxembourg Institute of Science and Technology, Esch-sur-Alzette, Luxembourg
e-mail: e.proper@acm.org

R. Winter • S. Aier
Institute of Information Management, University of St. Gallen, St. Gallen, Switzerland

S. de Kinderen
University of Duisburg-Essen, Duisburg, Germany

© Springer International Publishing AG, part of Springer Nature 2017
H.A. Proper et al. (eds.), *Architectural Coordination of Enterprise Transformation*,
The Enterprise Engineering Series, https://doi.org/10.1007/978-3-319-69584-6_1

and Champy (1993) characterise transformation as fundamental change regarding an enterprise's products, markets or cost structures, whereas Winter (2010) concludes that the distinction between optimisation, on the one hand, and "small" transformations, on the other hand, is fluent. Optimisation is regarded as a gradual, continuous process that evolves existing structures step-by-step. Transformation, on the other hand, is seen as taking place in unique and context-specific programmes and being wider in scope (Winter 2010). In line with Rouse (2005), we define enterprise transformation as a fundamental change that *"substantially alters an [. . .] [enterprise's] relationships with one or more key constituencies, e.g., customers, employees, suppliers, and investors. Enterprise transformation can involve new value propositions in terms of products and services, how these offerings are delivered and supported, and / or how the enterprise is organised to provide these offerings"* (Rouse 2005). As such, the concept of enterprise transformation is thus concerned with generally top-down initiated, and governed, change.

Typical exemplars of enterprise transformations include changes of the business model (Aspara et al. 2011), mergers and acquisitions (Johnston and Madura 2000), large-scale outsourcing (Loh and Venkatraman 1992), and introductions and replacements of core enterprise information systems (Sarker and Lee 1999; Proper 2001; Bhattacharya et al. 2010; Hock-Hai Teo et al. 1997).

Due to their strategic character, their complexity, and their consumption of resources, enterprise transformations significantly impact the competitiveness of enterprises, their economic success, and the people that are involved or affected. As a consequence, enterprise transformations are a phenomenon of great significance for society and economy, and thus also for business informatics focusing on the role of information systems in these transformations. Enterprise transformations may be triggered by internal drivers (e.g. strategic repositioning, efficiency enhancement programmes) or by external drivers (e.g. market changes, technology disruptions). Due to the related effort and risks, organisations only once in a while undergo enterprise transformations. Enterprise transformation is about fundamentally *changing* the business, not about *running* the business. As a consequence, organisations often lack well-tested and established enterprise transformation approaches, and most of the standard management approaches are not sufficient to successfully plan and implement enterprise transformations. Enterprise transformations entail fundamental changes that do not only affect individual processes, organisational units, *information technology* (IT) systems, or products, etc., but rather touch upon several aspects of an enterprise simultaneously. They require cross-cutting, *enterprise-wide* perspectives to successfully deliver on the goals of the overall enterprise transformation.

The complexity of enterprise transformations creates challenges for its coordinated planning as well as for the many concurrent projects for its implementation. One of the challenges of *planning* enterprise transformations is to provide the relevant information regarding drivers, stakeholders, their goals and benefits, possible solutions, and contingencies of the transformation to the respective stakeholders. Insufficient information may for example lead to the underestimation of the transformation's complexity and to setting too ambitious and unrealistic targets. One of the challenges of *implementing* enterprise transformations is to consistently refine and implement the transformation plans locally by division of labour. Locally managed implementation projects may lead to inconsistent designs, conflicting goals, local project teams working against each other, and finally to inconsistent or inferior solutions.

1.2 The Need for Coordination

Despite the relevance of enterprise transformation, industrial reports indicate failure rates ranging from 70% to 90%, across a broad range of domains (CHAOS 1999, 2001). Dietz and Hoogervorst (2008) name a lack of coordination in enterprise transformation projects as one key reason for the high rates of *inadequate strategy implementations*.

In complex organisations, enterprise-wide changes imply that a wide variety of actors are involved in the design and implementation of a large number of local changes. To make large enterprise transformations feasible and manageable, they are typically split into programmes and eventually into projects. Even more, larger enterprises typically do not just conduct one transformation programme at a time, but conduct multiple in parallel, which all need to be aligned with the enterprise's strategy. Local changes, as made in the set of projects that collectively make up the transformation programme(s), are not always in line with overall objectives because not only sub-unit specific concerns "pull" or "tug" the direction taken by the transformation, but also the perceived direction may deviate from the intended direction. Thus, local changes need to be coordinated in order to constitute a purposefully engineered and coherently implemented intervention to the enterprise instead of an "emergent" change process. There is a need to guard the coherence between the different concerns and aspects of an enterprise across programme(s) (Op 't Land et al. 2008; Wagter et al. 2005; The Open Group 2009).

Traditionally, project management and programme management are put forward as being responsible for these coordination tasks (Axelos 2009; PMI 2001). However, these approaches focus primarily on the management of typical project parameters such as budgets, resource use, and deadlines. When indeed only considering the typical project parameters, one runs the risk of conducting "local optimisations" at the level of specific projects.

For example, when making design decisions that have an impact that transcends a specific project, projects are likely to aim for solutions that provide the best cost/benefits ratio within the scope of that specific project, while not taking the overall picture into account. Regretfully, however, in practice such local optimisations do not just remain a potential risk. The risk actually materialises, and consequently damages the overall quality of the transformation result (Op 't Land et al. 2008). This type of risk generally occurs when stakes regarding general infrastructural elements of an enterprise collide with local short-term interests. This especially endangers the needed coherence/alignment between different aspects within an enterprise (such as business and IT, but also human resources, physical infrastructures, etc.).

Table 1.1 Overview of coordination mechanisms (reprinted by permission from Martinez and Jarillo 1989)

Structural	Informal
(1) Departmentalisation or grouping of organisational units, shaping the formal structure	(6) Lateral or cross-departmental relations: direct managerial contact, temporary or permanent teams, task forces, committees, integrators, and integrative departments
(2) Centralisation or decentralisation of decision-making through the hierarchy of formal authority	(7) Informal communication: personal contacts among managers, management trips, meetings, conferences, transfer of managers, etc.
(3) Formalisation and standardisation: written policies, rules, job descriptions, and standard procedures, through instruments such as manuals and charts	(8) Socialisation: building an organisational culture of known and shared strategic objectives and values by training, transfer of managers, career path management, measurement and reward systems, etc.
(4) Planning: strategic planning, budgeting, functional plans, scheduling, etc.	
(5) Output and behaviour control: financial performance, technical reports, sales and marketing data, etc., and direct supervision	

As a result, more often than not (CHAOS 1999, 2001; Op 't Land et al. 2008), enterprises fail to actually realise the desired transformation even though it might be the case that all projects are finished on time, within budget, and delivering the specified (local) quality.

Malone and Crowston (1990) define coordination as the "*act of working together harmoniously*" and as "*managing dependencies between activities*". Coordination can be achieved through different mechanisms. Several scholars (March and Simon 1958; Thompson 1967; Mintzberg 1983) have identified coordination mechanisms in organisations and provide classification systems for these mechanisms (Abraham et al. 2012a).

Martinez and Jarillo (1989) provide an extensive review of literature on coordination mechanisms. They discuss two classes of coordination mechanisms. The first class is comprised of structural mechanisms that represent a formally defined part of an organisation, while the second class is comprised of informal mechanisms that are not formally decided upon but that may evolve over time. Table 1.1 provides an overview of the classification.

The numerical order of the mechanisms, from 1 through 8, indicates both the level of *rising effort in implementation* and the level of increasing *complexity level of strategies* they are able to support. While simple strategies can be coordinated using structural mechanisms only, more complex strategies demand the additional use of informal mechanisms of coordination. Informal coordination mechanisms are more costly, but at the same time capable of supporting more complex strategies than structural coordination mechanisms (Chan 2002; Martinez and Jarillo 1989).

Although coordination is often interpreted as an intra-organisational issue, more and more enterprise transformations involve enterprises across organisational boundaries (e.g. a value creation network) so that we understand coordination also as an inter-organisational issue.

A number of disciplines intend to provide means to achieve coordination. *Leadership* aims at influencing an actor's behaviour in a certain way, *HR management* guides actors' behaviour by defining personal goal and reward systems, *budgeting and financial control* allocate an enterprise's resources in a distinct way, or enterprise architecture management restricts the way certain artefacts are designed. The above mentioned disciplines have in common that they have a potentially cross-cutting, that is, enterprise-wide, coordinating effect. They implement some of the coordination mechanisms listed in Table 1.1 to different degrees. Thus, they provide different lenses, that is, methods and models, for implementing these coordination mechanisms.

In this book, we focus specifically on the methods and models of enterprise architecture management as a starting point for improving the coordination of enterprise transformations.

1.3 Enterprise Architecture Management

One of the most often cited publications on the definition of *architecture* is the IEEE standard 1471-2000 (IEEE 2000)[1] and its adaptation to enterprise architecture by The Open Group (2011). Architecture is defined there as (1) "*[t]he fundamental organisation of a system embodied in its components, their relationships to each other, and to the environment*", and as (2) "*the principles guiding its design and evolution*" (IEEE 2000). In the field of enterprise architecture, "system" is then specialised to "enterprise". As enterprises are social systems with a purpose and typically use technological artefacts to (better) achieve their purpose, enterprise architecture covers a diverse set of artefacts ranging from social constructs (e.g. shared objectives, valuations) all the way to technical constructs (e.g. software, IT infrastructure). The (1) *fundamental organisation* (the "what") of enterprise architecture can be represented by models of its as-is state and/or possible to-be states. The (2) *principles guiding an EA's design and evolution* (the "how") are related to enterprise architecture management, which is concerned with the establishment and development of enterprise architecture in order to consistently respond to business and IT goals, opportunities, and necessities (Abraham et al. 2013a). Enterprise architecture intends to represent a holistic perspective on an enterprise as a socio-technical system.

"Managing", the M in enterprise architecture management, therefore, is not only concerned with describing and envisioning aggregate representations of a diverse set of artefacts, their dependencies, and their evolution, but is also concerned with the task of reaching, and maintaining, consensus among stakeholders about the current status and the desired future development of the enterprise.

---

[1] As well as its later versions in ISO/IEC 42010:2007 and ISO/IEC/IEEE 42010:2011.

The "holistic" perspective of enterprise architecture spans at least three dimensions of the enterprise (Jonkers et al. 2006; Lankhorst 2012; Winter and Fischer 2007; van't Wout et al. 2010):

1. Enterprise architecture covers the entirety of artefacts of a specific type in an enterprise, for example, all objectives or all applications or all processes or all projects.
2. Enterprise architecture covers the entirety of aspects/concerns that stakeholders have in an enterprise, for example, strategic concerns, operational business concerns, IT implementation concerns, or social concerns (company culture, company politics, leadership style).
3. Enterprise architecture covers at least a complete transformation cycle, for example, the entire lifecycle (from requirements analysis, via design to decommissioning) of all affected artefacts.

Due to complexity limitations, no management discipline can be holistic and cover all details at the same time. Enterprise architecture management looks at the enterprise from a holistic, but aggregate, perspective. This differentiates enterprise architecture management approaches from other management disciplines like business process management or IT project management, which have a more focused perspective and, as a consequence, can cover more detail. Please note that enterprise architecture may of course be applied with more focus [e.g. positioned towards project management or portfolio management (Op 't Land et al. 2008)]—but in this book we take an enterprise-wide perspective and therefore use enterprise architecture management in a holistic way.

If enterprise architecture covers an enterprise transformation holistically, then enterprise architecture management is expected to identify and leverage potential synergies (or detect incoherence) that cannot be detected or handled by a single project, in a single process, or a single organisational unit. Hence, enterprise architecture management appears to enable appropriate coordination mechanisms for enterprise transformation. The enablement can be achieved by providing the necessary transparency throughout the business-to-IT stack and over the planning horizon as a basis to support discourse and decision-making for diverse stakeholder groups in organisations, thereby implementing some of the coordination mechanisms presented in Table 1.1 by, for example, enterprise architecture planning or enterprise architecture principles. Enterprise architecture planning contributes to coordination by deriving local transformation activities from and/or fitting local transformation activities to a consistent overall plan that describes the preferred to-be state of the enterprise architecture as well as the projects or programmes necessary to achieve this state. Enterprise architecture principles do not describe the preferred to-be state; they rather guide the design decisions in the enterprise transformation in a consistent way. Therefore, enterprise architecture management supports the constant (re-)alignment of an organisation's resources internally as well as with the changing requirements of its environment (Abraham et al. 2012b).

This understanding of enterprise architecture management, however, is only one aspect of *architecting*. Plans and principles are, in a top-down manner, *a restriction of design freedom* of affected actors/actor groups (Dietz 2008; Hoogervorst 2004, 2009; Greefhorst and Proper 2011). This traditional way of implementing enterprise architecture management makes establishing it in a given organisation's governance structure a key challenge. Although an enterprise as a whole is expected to benefit from EAM (Schmidt and Buxmann 2011; Tamm et al. 2011b), individuals or groups in the enterprise are often hesitant or openly refuse to adopt enterprise architecture management or its consequences (Aier and Weiss 2012).

In the face of the necessity to be accepted by a large number of actors that need to be coordinated in an enterprise transformation, the traditional, stipulative, and governance-enforced implementation of enterprise architecture management therefore needs to evolve. Supportive elements that specifically address the large number of local decision-makers, such as informing design, visualising dependencies, and simulating indirect impacts, need to complement the traditional, often centralised toolbox of enterprise architecture management in order to create an effective means for architectural coordination.

1.4 Architectural Coordination of Enterprise Transformation

ACET utilises the holistic perspective of enterprise architecture management to support the coordination of enterprise transformations. The core purpose of ACET is to inform decision-makers with local concerns as well as decision-makers with more enterprise-wide concerns in a way that overall transformation goals can be successfully pursued, that is, that inconsistencies are reduced and local decisions contribute to overarching goals. Therefore, ACET integrates and aggregates local information and provides different viewpoints, such as financial, structural, or skill perspectives to the respective stakeholder groups. ACET aims at creating a shared understanding and consensus among the stakeholders of an enterprise transformation—often such a shared understanding is only needed among a few stakeholders and only with regard to a selection of concepts.

ACET, therefore, does not aim to perform direct steering of enterprise transformation, but rather focuses on providing the actors who *are* responsible for steering an enterprise transformation with the relevant information in order to increase the efficiency and effectiveness of their action. ACET will indeed take the diversity of enterprise transformations into account and provide configuration mechanisms for adapting ACET to transformation types.

The focus of ACET is to provide coherency and alignment at an architectural level. It does not focus the implementation on a project level. More specifically, as also summarised in Table 1.2:

- ACET is global, not local—ACET is enterprise-wide, instead of concentrating on local (e.g. project/programme/department level) optimisations.
- ACET is long-term oriented, instead of short to mid-term oriented— Architecture is concerned with that part of the enterprise that remains stable over a long time, and with translating this long-term view into short-term actions. This is opposed to operational change management programmes, which

Table 1.2 What ACET is, and what it is not

	ACET is	ACET is not
Nature of time horizon	Long-term oriented	Short- to medium-term oriented
Span of control	Global, across projects or programmes	Local, project specific
Intentionality of change	Purposeful	Emergent
Type of change	Fundamental	Routine change, continuous improvement
Essentiality	Based on the consensus of key stakeholders	No explicit consensus required
Planning of change	Planned	Unplanned, bricolage, or improvisation

focus on the short to medium-term perspectives without considering the long-term strategic perspective.

- ACET is purposeful and planned, not emergent and improvised. ACET concentrates on engineering oriented change: purposeful, planned, and employing a defined set of methods. This is opposed to emergent/evolutionary change. From the point of view of emergence, change just happens and, as a result, responses to change are improvised on the fly rather than a priori planned.

ACET approaches the integration of enterprise transformation and enterprise architecture management approaches from two directions. First, ACET identifies those aspects of enterprise transformations that potentially benefit from architectural coordination. Second, ACET translates and extends EAM's methods and models in a way to make them accessible and valuable to enterprise transformation managers.

From a functional perspective, ACET should be specified in terms of its goals, products, and resources. From a constructional perspective, ACET should be specified in terms of its constructs and their dependencies, its processes, capabilities, and principles. These specifications can partially be adopted from existing enterprise architecture management approaches (for overviews, see Aier et al. 2008; Mykhashchuk et al. 2011; Schelp and Winter 2009; Schönherr 2009; Simon et al. 2013) and existing enterprise transformation approaches (e.g. Rouse 2006; Uhl and Gollenia 2012), but need to be adapted, integrated, and extended by configuration mechanisms as enterprise transformation is largely contextual and a "one size fits all" approach would not be able to exploit the full potential of ACET.

Compared to existing proposals to apply enterprise architecture management for supporting enterprise transformations (see Lankhorst 2012; Ross et al. 2006; Op 't Land et al. 2008; Pulkkinen et al. 2007; Greefhorst and Proper 2011), the approach outlined in this book (a) goes far beyond the IT perspective of enterprise transformations (Asfaw et al. 2009) and (b) is conceptually "outside in", that is, develops the approach based on context and stakeholder analysis instead of being driven by a collection of models and methods that have been developed in a different domain.

Scientifically, ACET can be approached from fundamentally different directions. Descriptive research would aim at understanding ACET as a phenomenon in the real world, identifying relevant constructs, hypothesising and validating cause—

effect relations. Design research would aim at understanding ACET as a problem (i.e. a gap between a—to be determined—desired state and observed state in the real world) and proposing effective means that address important aspects of that problem. The ACET initiative summarised in this book adopts the latter approach, that is, aims at understanding ACET as a situated design problem and ultimately proposing effective configurable solution components.

1.5 Outline of This Book

These challenges have triggered us to initiate a broad research programme on ACET, involving a collaboration between researchers from Luxembourg, Switzerland, as well as the Netherlands. The ACET programme involved four applied research projects: the core ACET project, the GEA project, the Corporate Intelligence project, and the Rational Architecture project, involving different constellations of the University of St. Gallen in Switzerland, the Luxembourg Institute of Science and Technology in Luxembourg, the Radboud University in the Netherlands, the University of Luxembourg, and several industrial partners such as Ordina and SAP.

Each of these applied research projects focused on different aspects of enterprise transformations, and different strategies to use enterprise architecture to steer the direction of such transformations. The ACET project formed the integrative core of these four research projects, also leading to the general focus of this book on architectural coordination of enterprise transformation.

The resulting book brings together the work of ten PhD researchers and six senior researchers. While this book is built around individual contributions of the researchers involved, the final result goes beyond being a mere collection of disconnected chapters. As the work involved four collaborative projects, the different results are well connected to each other, while some terminological and theoretical integration across the different researchers has also been achieved. At the same time, it should be said that this book can only provide a humble beginning towards the creation of a more complete understanding of architectural coordination of enterprise transformation and the development of an integrated set of instruments supporting ACET in practice.

The ambitions at the start of the ACET research programme were higher. It was, indeed, the ambition to develop an integrated design theory for ACET. However, the early stages of the projects involved in the programme, provided the insight that the heterogeneity and multifacetedness of the domain of ACET was so high that the development of an integrated design theory for ACET would be too ambitious. A choice had to be made between the creation of a "superficial" overall method for ACET, or a, for the moment, set of disconnected and partial, yet well-founded, elements/components towards a more comprehensive method for ACET. We made a choice for the latter, where the research efforts were compartmentalised, in the sense that each of the involved researchers focused on a specific (set of related) aspects, with the aim to develop an initial explanatory theory covering the aspect.

Regardless of whether their concerns are primarily local or enterprise-wide, decision-makers will accept and use ACET solutions only as long as the perceived specific characteristics of the enterprise and of the transformation are considered. As a consequence, we adopt a clear outside-in approach in this book. Starting with an analysis of the current state of corporate ACET practice (Part I), we continue with an exploration (Part II) of the challenges facing ACET from a more theoretical perspective.

In Part III, we propose a collection of concrete components for "doing" ACET. These components have been "harvested" from the work of the individual researchers in the programme. This collection of components, one could say method fragments, can be arranged and/or tuned in different ways depending on the specific situation, in particular, the actual enterprise architecture management approach used, the enterprise transformation type, and the transformation's context.

Chapter 26 concludes the book with a brief review on the results presented in this book, as well as a reflection on the use of design science in the development of a large-scale design theory as the ACET programme set out to do at the start, and finally a discussion of what could/should be the next steps in future research.

Part I
Observing Architectural Coordination in Practice

To gain a better appreciation of the issues involved in actual enterprise transformations, as well as the possible role of architectural coordination, and the associated challenges, this Part reports on real world situations involving architectural coordination. Each of these situations will touch upon challenges facing architectural coordination.

Chapter 2
A Major Transformation at a Global Insurance Company

Nils Labusch, Stephan Aier, and Robert Winter

Abstract In this chapter, we report on the case of a globally operating insurance company that has leverage enterprise architecture management to support business transformations. In order to do so, the company has developed enterprise architecture management capabilities that help the business structure the business transformation, particularly in the early stages before handing over respective responsibilities to more specialised corporate functions later on. This case is interesting for understanding ACET because it is one of the rare cases where enterprise architecture management truly bridges the business–IT gap.

2.1 The Organisation

GlobalSurance[1] is a globally operating insurance company with more than 10,000 employees, who are employed across a large number of countries. The company mostly deals with corporate solutions. In a volatile and changing environment, GlobalSurance needs to be flexible and open-minded concerning changes—a capability that was not necessary for insurance companies in the past.

To contribute to that goal, GlobalSurance has established enterprise architecture management as a strong and business-focused function within the organisation. More specifically, the enterprise architecture management function was assigned

---

[1] An actual Switzerland-based insurance company. However, the corporate communications department of GlobalSurance prefers the actual name not to be used.

N. Labusch (✉) • S. Aier • R. Winter
Institute of Information Management, University of St.Gallen, St. Gallen, Switzerland
e-mail: nils.labusch@gmail.com

© Springer International Publishing AG, part of Springer Nature 2017
H.A. Proper et al. (eds.), *Architectural Coordination of Enterprise Transformation*,
The Enterprise Engineering Series, https://doi.org/10.1007/978-3-319-69584-6_2

to a central "business engineering" unit that, in addition to enterprise architecture management, also centralised other functions that are relevant to enterprise transformations, such as project management (keeping track on deliverables and financial aspects) and change management (keeping track on people aspects). Although the enterprise architecture management function was recently moved to the IT department, close relations to the "business" (in the sense of senior management) were maintained.

In more specific terms, the enterprise architecture management function at GlobalSurance involves four major tasks:

1. Adhere to the implementation of the corporate strategy by leveraging governance bodies, providing a common architecture framework, and managing enterprise-wide architecture communities.
2. Manage an "architecture heat map", particularly concerning integration topics and thus deal with existing requirements for change.
3. Provide resources to projects, drive the reuse of existing architectural themes, and resolve cross-domain integration issues.
4. Achieve business benefit realisation by measuring and steering the architecture health and assessing the maturity of shared business capabilities.

As a result, the enterprise architecture management function provides a clear value proposition by enabling long-term business agility, using a common language, strengthening shared capabilities, and enabling effective end-to-end change.

2.2 The Enterprise Transformation

Based on this mission statement, enterprise architecture management is involved in major transformations at GlobalSurance. One of the transformations conducted at GlobalSurance is the "Transform" programme. This programme affects almost 7000 employees in one of the major business lines of GlobalSurance. It aims at realising three major goals:

1. Increase client centricity.
2. Increase operational excellence.
3. Increase revenues.

Transform is, therefore, not merely an IT-driven transformation, but clearly a business-driven transformation. It involves major changes and consolidations in the business processes, information flows, and the information system landscape. Connected to the aforementioned goals, the business transformation needs to address the following problems:

1. Ease of doing business needs to be improved and the response time to clients has to become faster.
2. Administrative work creates too much overhead and administrative systems are cumbersome.

3. Overly complex processes and low available capacity need to be handled at no additional costs.

Based on an analysis of the value chain, especially the client offering and contract management areas were identified as opportunities for change. Transform is planned to take 4 years and involves an investment of more than 20 million Euro.

In general, enterprise architecture management has to ensure that the planning and realisation of the business transformation fits to the proposed, and signed-off, goals and designs of business processes and IT solutions. Thus, its general roles involve, on the one hand, being the *trusted advisor* to senior business management, and, on the other hand, overseeing the IT implementation. With these two major roles, the architects involved in the enterprise architecture management function, find themselves involved in many of the activities of the Transform programme.

2.3 Structuring the Enterprise Architecture Management Function

The enterprise architecture management function at GlobalSurance uses a "capability catalogue" to structure its activities. The goal of this "capability catalogue" is to provide guidance to architects regarding the scope of their target transformation support capabilities. As such, it primarily provides a reference model for the capabilities that could be supported by enterprise architecture management, and are considered necessary to conduct successful business transformations. Thus, the catalogue comprises not necessarily all capabilities that are necessary for business transformations, but rather focuses on those that could be effectively supported by a state-of-the-art corporate enterprise architecture management function. The capability catalogue is illustrated in Fig. 2.1.

The capability catalogue is structured in terms of five major perspectives that deliver coordination support to the overall transformation management function. From a strategy perspective, the general goals of the transformation need to be agreed upon, while a common understanding and stakeholder buy-in also needs to be achieved. The value and risk perspective aims at identifying and safeguarding benefits that justify the transformation, as well as at achieving transparency about the related risks. Transparency about both benefits and risks is regarded as being important in communicating the transformation in a credible manner. The goal of the design perspective is to develop the future processes, organisational structures, and IT landscape, on an essential level. The transition from the current state ("as-is" architecture) to this future state ("to-be" architecture) needs to address the identified benefits and risks. The implementation perspective covers the actual realisation of the developed design ("to-be" architecture). Thus, a main part of the perspective is the coordination of activity streams, sub-projects, or projects of the transformation as much as their harmonisation with existing architectures, processes, and cultural

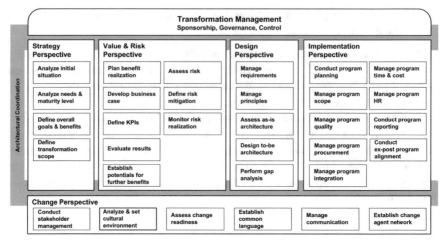

Fig. 2.1 Capability catalogue

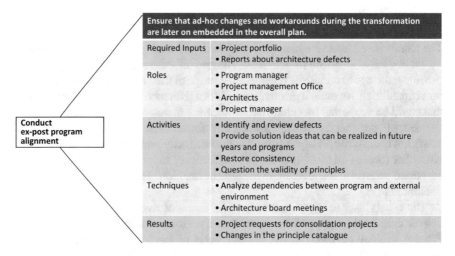

Fig. 2.2 Exemplary capability description

aspects. The change perspective addresses the people involved in and/or affected by a transformation.

The capability catalogue should not be understood as a process model of transformation support. It rather defines different perspectives on business transformation that exist simultaneously. For each of the perspectives, different capabilities are considered important. For all of them, the required inputs, involved roles, conducted activities, applied techniques, and typical results, have been documented. An exemplary capability description is illustrated in Fig. 2.2.

2.4 The Role of Enterprise Architecture Management

From the *strategy perspective*, enterprise architecture management is involved in gathering the expectations of the different managers involved in the Transform programme. This means that the architects conduct interviews with executives, and top-managers in general, to gather their perceptions of the business transformation. The architects afterwards analyse and consolidate the results, and discuss these with various stakeholders. In many cases, the challenge is to identify the actual meaning of statements made. This leads to a definition of the transformation's scope. This, in turn, provides the foundation of a more detailed definition of goals and benefits. In this stage of the business transformation, the architect takes the role of a consultant: providing expertise concerning specific topics but also being able to structure the overall consolidation process.

In the Transform business transformation, the architects are also involved in the *value and risk perspective*. They take the lead in the planning of benefits realisation, as well as the consolidation of the business case. Important *key performance indicators* (KPIs) are defined together with the major business stakeholders. The risks that have been analysed at the start of the transformation programme differ from those that are analysed by enterprise architecture management during the transformation. While in the beginning the risk analysis was concerned with the "*risk of doing or not doing the transformation*", during the transformation this shifted towards more operational risks such as "*when doing X what might happen*". In general, many of the tasks that needed to be done from the value and risk perspective have been conducted first by architects and have later on been transferred to more specific functions in the governance of the transformation programme. For example, while architects did the first iteration of benefits identification, this task was transferred to a dedicated corporate centre of excellence for the following iterations. Thus, architects describe their role in the business transformation support as "*building the machine in such a way that it can run*".

The *design perspective* is considered to be "*the most classical perspective*". However, the scope of the capabilities at GlobalSurance differs from that of many other architects in other organisations. Architecture here does not cover IT infrastructure and applications only. Instead, architects also have responsibility concerning processes and information. Partially, also external constraints belong to the architects' responsibility.

In the *implementation perspective*, the architects at GlobalSurance are only partially involved. Managing programme time and cost, HR, and reporting are usually done by the respective programme functions. Concerning procurement, the architects are only involved in technology decisions. When it comes to programme scoping and planning, the architects are strongly involved again. Enterprise architecture management usually is not involved in the day-to-day planning of the programme, but instead focuses on subsequent iterations. Their main focus, however, is on programme integration. This capability especially includes the identification and realisation of common tasks among projects. An example from the Transform programme is the integration of different work streams. A new target front-end working model was introduced and enterprise architecture management found that different work streams identified the same input channel of a customer requests (e.g. mail). By identifying this matter, one common solution for all work streams could be set up—instead of three individual and possibly inconsistent solutions.

The *change perspective* is also considered by the GlobalSurance architects. Stakeholder management is considered a major part of their job. Analysing the cultural environment is understood as finding resistances and understanding how statements by the diverse stakeholders are meant and need to be addressed. Assessing the change readiness was part of the enterprise architecture management work in the beginning of Transform. However, these tasks have been shifted to the formal programme organisation during the transformation. Establishing a common language was also considered especially important in the beginning of the programme. This also includes creating a common understanding. Communication was partially conducted by the architects in the beginning of the programme, but later shifted to more specialised functions in the programme. The same is true for the establishment of change agent networks.

2.5 Reflection

In this chapter, we have reported on the capability catalogue we have developed together with partners, where these partners consider enterprise architecture management as a valuable means to support business transformation. The above brief description of the case study indicates that GlobalSurance makes more use of enterprise architecture management in the steering of business transformation than other companies tend to do. Architects who are involved at GlobalSurance and who also worked for other companies before, also confirm this perception of the researchers. From our point of view, it is especially interesting how enterprise architecture management shifts its role during the transformation: while being heavily involved in structuring and performing many tasks in the beginning in the role of a consultant, these tasks are shifted to more specialised functions later on—once those corporate functions are established.

GlobalSurance also learned that positioning the enterprise architecture management function purely within the business domain also brings some disadvantages, in particular in terms of the perception of business stakeholders regarding IT knowledge of the architects. After shifting the enterprise architecture management function from the business domain to the IT domain, the architects receive more trust regarding their IT knowledge from business stakeholders—they are now perceived to be better able to consult on IT-related matters.

Chapter 3
Centralised Monitoring of Pensions in Greece

Georgios Plataniotis

Abstract In this chapter, we present an enterprise transformation of the Greek social security system. More specifically, we present the incorporation of a centralised monitoring system for pension payments in Greece. This monitoring system enabled the Greek government to have an overview of the amount of budget that was spent for pension payments across the various social security institutions.

3.1 A Fragmented Social Security Landscape

The financial crisis that started in the late 2000s forced the Greek government to implement, in a very short period of time, major structural reforms. One of the most important reforms was the establishment of the national register of pensioners and pension payments.

In the past years, social insurance policies were developed in a fragmented way (OECD 2002) through the establishment of social insurance institutions per different socio-professional categories. For example, doctors have their own social security institution, engineers a different one, etc. Greece had, by the end of 2002, a total of 170 different social security institutions (OECD 2002). In the following years, consecutive Greek governments initiated a series of mergers. As a result, the number of the institutions was significantly reduced. However, the number of these institutions is still high compared to the average number of institutions in other EU member states. Furthermore, the mergers were not executed at a deep level in terms

G. Plataniotis
e-Government Center for Social Security (IDIKA), Likourgou 10, 105 51 Athens, Greece
e-mail: georgeplataniotis@gmail.com

© Springer International Publishing AG, part of Springer Nature 2017
H.A. Proper et al. (eds.), *Architectural Coordination of Enterprise Transformation*,
The Enterprise Engineering Series, https://doi.org/10.1007/978-3-319-69584-6_3

of the organisational structure of the institutions. As a result, there are cases where these merged social security institutions have departments with overlapping activities and information systems.

The fragmented landscape of social insurance institutions caused a variety of problems. One of the largest problems was the lack of a centralised control regarding the money spent on pension payments, and the huge delays in the initial awarding of pension payments. The problems were getting even worse when the same person had worked in two or more different types of professions during their career. For example, someone that had worked 10 years as a professional driver and the rest of their career as an employee in a company had to wait more than 2 years to have an accurate estimation and award of their pension payment. This was due to the fact that different social insurance institutions had to exchange in paper the social security information for this person and then make a common decision regarding the amount of pension that each institution had to pay to this person. Even the pension payment was fragmented among the institutions. Each institution was sending separate payment notices, per pensioner, to the bank.

As a result of the increased number of social security institutions and the lack of a standardised process on the pension payment calculation, as well as the actual payment, in each of these institutions, there was a lack of *central monitoring* of the aggregate amount of budget that was spent nationally on pension payments. On the one hand, the government was not able to make projections regarding the money spent on pension payments, while, on the other hand, there were cases where citizens were cheating the system in a variety of ways (receiving double allowances, etc.).

To address these issues, the Greek government established a centralised system for pensions and their payment. The planning, design and operation of this project was assigned to the Social Security e-government centre of the Ministry of Labour (e-gov centre). The agency had to deliver in a short period of time a system that would provide a unified report of the pension payments by the Greek government.

3.2 The Enterprise Transformation

We now provide the description of the enterprise transformation by means of enterprise architecture models. In our analysis, we used the ArchiMate modelling language. We do not provide the enterprise architecture models for every social security institution. Instead, we use the abbreviation "*SSI01*" to refer to the first social security institution of our study and "*SSI...n*" to signify that we have more than one institution in our analysis. By doing so, we reduce the complexity of the enterprise architecture models. Moreover, for simplicity reasons, in our models we do not use architecture elements that have a supportive role in the current setup like network infrastructure, etc.

3.2.1 Baseline Architecture

Figure 3.1 presents the enterprise architecture model of the baseline architecture (i.e. the architecture of the pre-existing situation) before the incorporation of the pension report system. Each of the institutions has, independently of the others, the business role *"Pension administrator"*. Two business services support the *"Pension administrator"* business role, the *"Pension salary invoice"* and *"Pension payment SSI"*. These business services are subsequently realised by the business processes *"Pension calculation SSI"* and *"Pension payment SSI"*. The institution calculates the amount of pension payment to be made, based on:

1. The years that each citizen was insured in the specific institution
2. The special legal regulations that are applied for each profession

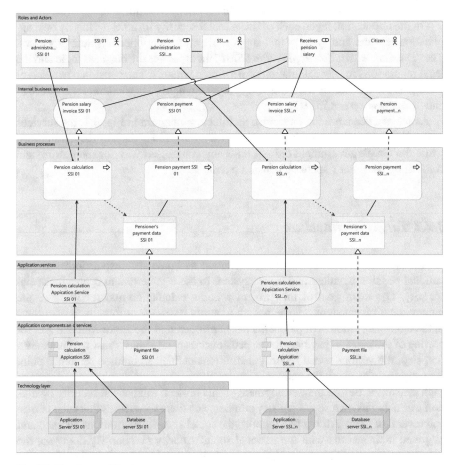

Fig. 3.1 Baseline architecture

During the lifetime of a citizen's pension, several calculations are performed to determine the correct payment. This is because the amount to be paid has to be adapted to several factors like inflation, new regulations, etc. After the calculation of the pension payment, a salary statement is issued and forwarded to the pensioner. Moreover, the pension payment information is forwarded through the business object *"Pensioner's payment data"* to the business process *"Pension payment SSI"* in order to execute the payment order of a pension payment through the banking system. It is worthwhile to mention again that due to the high number of social security institutions, there are cases that a pensioner receives pension payments from more than one institution. This situation is depicted in the enterprise architecture model by the multiple links between the citizen's role *"Receives pension salary"* and the business services *"Pension salary invoice SSI01"*, *"Pension payment SSI01"*, *"Pension salary invoice SSI...n"* and *"Pension payment SSI...n"*. In other words, a pensioner instead of receiving an aggregate pension payment was still receiving separate parts of pension payments by the different social security institutions.

On the application layer, each of these social security institutions has its own application services and systems that support the aforementioned business processes. The *"Pension calculation application SSI01"* incorporates the business logic and the legal regulations for the calculation of pension payments. The pension payment applications are realised by the Technology layer elements *"Application server SSI01"* and *"Database server SSI01"*.

As we can see from the enterprise architecture diagram in Fig. 3.1, the services of the different social security institutions were mirrored at each of the institutions, while the Greek government did not have any centralised way for monitoring and controlling the money spent on pension payments.

3.2.2 Target Architecture

As mentioned before, the Greek government assigned the responsibility of the national pension payment and report system to the e-government centre for social security. The main goal of this project was the calculation and reporting of the money spent on pensions payments on a monthly basis, the enforcement of cutouts in the aggregate amount of payments per pensioner, and the apportionment and reporting of the pension payment to the pensioner's social security institution(s). As a first step, the various social security institutions defined a common reference point for pensioners by using the national security number (unique number per citizen) of each pensioner. Before the development of this project, each social security institution was using its own social registry numbers and there were cases that each person had several of them. After a few months, the social security institutions adopted and migrated their records with the national social security number. By doing so, the e-gov centre responsible for making the cutouts was able to collect data from the different institutions and make mappings across the different pensioner's records.

Below, we provide two alternative enterprise architecture scenarios that were considered as solutions for the national pension payment and report registry. The first scenario is the *"Fully consolidated architecture"* and the second is the *"Aggregation of social security institutions' pension reports"*. The two scenarios have commonalities only in the provision of the requested business services.

3.2.3 Scenario 1: Fully Consolidated Architecture

Figure 3.2 presents a candidate architecture scenario where the national payment report business service is provided by the unification of the individual business processes and information systems. The business process *"Unified pension calculation"* which realises the business service *"Unified pension salary invoice"* would be created by establishing a common business process for the calculation of the pension payments. Moreover, the *"Unified pension payments"* business process would be created by the integration of the individual Pension payments' business processes of the social security institutions. Through this integration, the e-gov centre responsible for making the cutouts, would also be able to provide the *"National payment report"* business service to the government. In other words, the national pension payment and report project would be used as an opportunity for the unification of the individual business processes among the various social security institutions and this implies that the e-gov centre would be the responsible authority not only for the reporting of pension payments, but also for the calculation of the pensions, as well as their actual payment.

On the information systems side, the aforementioned business processes would be supported by the corresponding application and technology artefacts. One of the biggest challenges in this transformation scenario was the migration of the individual pension calculation applications into a new *"Migrated Pension Application"* that would incorporate a core business logic for the calculation of the pension payments and in parallel it would take into account the different pension calculation specificities among the various social security institutions. The application architecture team should coordinate a migration procedure where the characteristics of the individual pension calculation application per institution would be taken into account. In parallel, the application architecture team should coordinate a data migration procedure in order to integrate the pensioner's data into a common database based on the national social security number. The e-gov centre should also provide *"Application servers"* that would host the *"Migrated pension application"* and *"Database servers for the migrated pensioners"* data.

3.2.4 Scenario 2: Aggregation of Pension Payments Files

Figure 3.3 presents the alternative enterprise architecture scenario which was actually selected by the architecture team. At first glance, we can see that the business

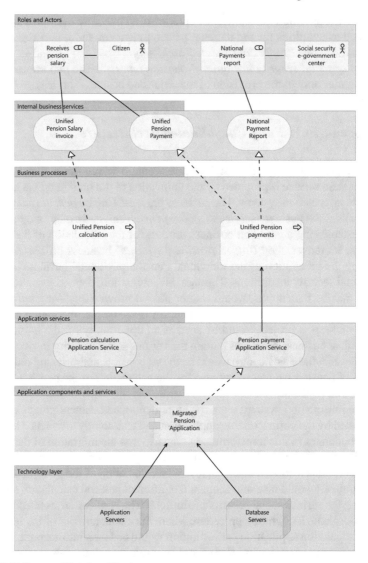

Fig. 3.2 Fully consolidated architecture

services "*Unified pension salary invoice*", "*Unified pension payment*" and "*National payment report*" are provided in a completely different way. The main difference is that the pension payment calculations are still kept under the authority of the individual social security institutions, while the pension payments and national payment reports is the responsibility of the e-gov centre. More specifically, we can observe that the business process "*Pension calculation*" is still maintained in every social security institution and, moreover, each social institution has to provide a business object "*Pension payment data*" to the e-gov centre. Therefore, the social security

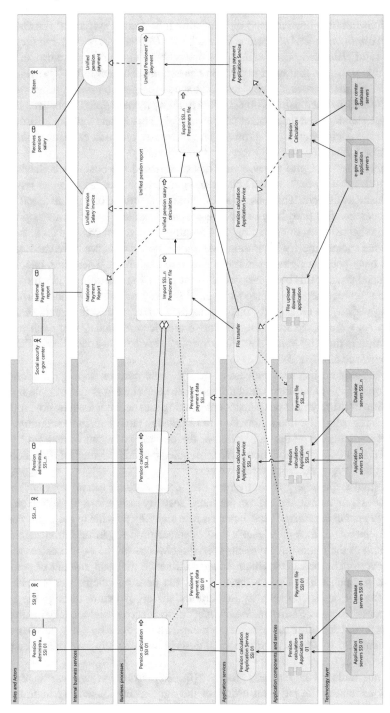

Fig. 3.3 National pension report by aggregation of pension payments files

institutions not only have to keep their existing information systems ("*Pension cal-culation application*", "*Application servers*" and "*Database servers*"), but they also have to send "*Pensions payment data*" business objects to the e-gov centre. In other words, this indicates that each institution has established next to the "*Pension cal-culation*" business process a new task that sends the pensioner's payment data to the e-gov centre. The business object "*Pensioner's payment data*" is realised by the use of the standardised data object "*Payment file*". This means that the information between the social security institutions and the e-gov centre is exchanged through standardised data files.

On the other side, the e-gov centre has established the business collaboration "*Unified pension report*", which acts as an aggregator of the "*Pensioners payment data*" business objects. This business collaboration consists of four different busi-ness processes. The first, "*Import SSI...n pensioner's file*", is the business process with the responsibility of collecting on a monthly base the payment data files from the various social security institutions. As mentioned earlier, we have cases where citizens have pension rights from more than one institution. Therefore, one of the most crucial tasks of this business process is the provision of a unified data file which has as a reference key the pensioner's social security number and the information from the various social security institutions that correspond to this social security number. As we can see from the enterprise architecture model, this exchange of information is done by using the "*File transfer*" service of a specialised "*File up-load/download application*".

The subsequent business process is the "*Unified pension salary calculation*". This is one of the most important business processes since it is responsible for the calculation of the payment per pensioner by taking into account the new government measures regarding the maximum amount of pension payments in the country. The business logic regarding the calculation of the pension payments is realised by the "*Pension calculation*" application. The aggregated pension payments information is stored in the "*e-gov centre database servers*".

As a final step, the e-gov centre runs the "*Export SSI...n pensioner's file*" busi-ness process. As mentioned before, the social security institutions are still in charge of their "*Pension administration*" business role and they provide to the e-gov centre (via the "*Import SSI...n pensioner's file*" business process) information regarding the amount of their pension payments spending. Moreover, the e-gov centre applies some government measures which actually influence the total amount of pension payment per pensioner. Due to the fact that the pension calculation is scattered among the various social security institutions, the e-gov centre through the busi-ness process "*Export SSI...n pensioner's file*" informs each social security institution about its actual spending on pension payments. This is done by using another type of payment file. To simplify, architectural description of this type of data exchange is not included.

Last but not least, the business process "*Unified pensioner's payment*" is respon-sible for executing the payment orders of the aggregated pension payment to the pensioner's bank.

3.3 Reflection

In this chapter, we discussed two different enterprise architecture scenarios for the national pension payment and report project. The "*National pension report by aggregation of pension payments files*" scenario was finally selected by the stakeholders' team. By just observing the enterprise architecture scenarios, it is obvious that "*Scenario 1: Fully consolidated architecture*" seems better in terms of complexity and the number of enterprise architecture elements. More specifically, we can see that each social institution maintains individually the "*Pension calculation business process*", which means that institutions spend a significant amount of budget on employees that are actually executing a quite similar task. Moreover, each of these institutions is maintaining their own information systems, which implies additional cost for IT systems and their maintenance.

The examination of the enterprise architecture models triggers questions regarding their rationalisation. For example, what made the architecture team decide on a more complicated architecture, which factors played a role in the decision-making process, etc. Without rationalisation support, these questions remain unanswered and enterprise architects and relevant stakeholders (especially newcomers) have to search through unstructured documentation in order to provide the answers. Moreover, the lack of design rationale support causes design integrity issues when architects want to maintain and further change the architecture.

In order to identify the extent to which design rationale can support practitioners, we conducted interviews with the involved stakeholders both from the business as well as the IT domain of the organisation. The purpose of these interviews was to understand how they addressed the enterprise architecture challenges from their own domain of responsibility, what were the most important design decisions for them and how they documented these design decisions. Moreover, stakeholders provided us with the documentation of the project. We analysed this documentation, we extracted design decisions, and finally compared them with those that emerged from the interviews.

Our findings indicate that practitioners found the exercise of revisiting design rationales extremely useful. They were able to make explicit the reasons behind the selection of specific design decisions and they also recalled the constraints they had during the decision-making process. For example, in most of the cases, the necessity to deliver the solution as soon as possible forced them to select less desirable alternatives.

Furthermore, practitioners recognised that capturing design rationales raises awareness for problematic situations in the enterprise. The national pension payment and report system is considered quite a successful project, especially if we take into account how quickly it was implemented. However, our analysis showed that there are a lot of malfunctions in the enterprise architecture of this project. During our study we observed that some obvious malfunctions that actually increased the operation costs of the business collaboration were not considered as open issues for further improvement. Most of the problems were disregarded since the project was providing the requested results and the key stakeholders were preoccupied with the operational support in the current architecture context. In other words, there was no time to reflect on possible improvements of the enterprise architecture. Our study helped stakeholders to realise and rethink about these problematic situations.

Last but not least, we observed that some design decisions had a high impact in the enterprise architecture, in terms of changes in the architectural design. On the other hand, we came up with design decisions which did not play a significant role in our analysis. Based on this observation, we argue that the capturing effort for a potential design rationale approach for enterprise architecture can be significantly reduced by capturing selectively the most critical design decisions.

Chapter 4
Enterprise Coherence in the Public Sector

Roel Wagter

Abstract This chapter is concerned with a real-world case study in Business/IT alignment, at the strategic level. The case study is situated in the Dutch public sector, in the context of a Dutch government agency responsible for the processing of European subsidy applications lodged by companies. The specific business issues addressed in the case are: a drive for more operational excellence, in combination with a general lack of management control. The case study will also illustrate that Business/IT alignment is not only a matter of aligning "the business" and "the IT" aspects of an enterprise. The case indicates that a more refined perspective is called for. This is also why we uses the term Enterprise Coherence, rather than Business/IT alignment, as it more explicitly stresses the need to align multiple aspects with the goal of achieving coherence among these aspects.

In the case of the Dutch government agency, the *general enterprise architecting* (GEA) method was used. This chapter will therefore take the GEA method as a given. Nevertheless, to better understand and appreciate the case study, we will also briefly review the GEA method and its background. Furthermore, we will also provide an evaluation on the GEA method, which was/is developed using a design science approach combined with case study research.

R. Wagter
Solventa B.V., 3439 ML Nieuwegein, The Netherlands
e-mail: roel.wagter@solventa.nl

© Springer International Publishing AG, part of Springer Nature 2017
H.A. Proper et al. (eds.), *Architectural Coordination of Enterprise Transformation*,
The Enterprise Engineering Series, https://doi.org/10.1007/978-3-319-69584-6_4

4.1 The Organisation

The case is situated in the Dutch public sector, involving a Dutch government agency (DGA[1]). DGA has to deal with a business issue on the subject of operational excellence and lack of management control, while carrying out a number of European subsidy arrangements. These subsidy arrangements cover thousands of companies which, to be eligible for these subsidies, submit an annual application. For a smooth execution of all this work, about 30 internal and external parties, whose contributions are interdependent and time critical, have to work together. Besides this factor of synchronicity, the complexity of the process is also increased by outsourcing factors, as well as factors pertaining to the communication channels used to lodge and process the applications. Two primary, massively batch-oriented, processes were already outsourced. Besides the traditional collection form based subsidy applications, applications are now also gathered via the Internet. The processing of these subsidies has a high level of political exposure, in the sense that a flaw, or even a drop in the performance, will immediately become public by the national press, causing serious damage to the reputation of the organisation. Furthermore, non-compliance with laws and regulations will lead to heavy financial fines.

4.2 The Enterprise Transformation

After outsourcing the batch-oriented processes, the outsourcing party remained in default with respect to the quality of their services to be provided. Partly due to the fact that these services were on the critical path, the primary processes got out of control. Some figures to substantiate this are: approximately 60% of the client dossiers had to be returned to the applicants, while about 20% of the subsidy applications resulted in submitted objections by the clients causing the statutory deadlines to be exceeded, which ultimately resulted in a threatening of a 20 million Euro fine. As a result, the existence of this government agency was put at risk, while the situation quickly raised critical questions in parliament. As a result, the core business issue that had to be investigated by the enterprise architects was: *How can the execution of the subsidy submission, evaluation, and allocation process be made more manageable and efficient?* In this regard, it was also argued that the failing outsourcing situation was not the only symptom of the real problem, and that more elements were involved that led to the current situation.

---

[1] An actual Netherlands-based government agency. However, DGA prefers the actual name not to be used.

4.3 The Used Approach

Management at DGA decided to follow the GEA method (Wagter 2009) in meeting the above business issue. The GEA method comprises three core ingredients (Wagter 2009). Next to the Enterprise Coherence Assessment (ECA), that allows organisations to assess their ability to govern coherence during enterprise transformation, it involves an enterprise coherence framework and a (situational) enterprise coherence governance approach. The latter includes the identification of specific deliverables/results to be produced, processes needed to produce these deliverables/results, as well as an articulation of the responsibilities and competences of the people involved. The enterprise coherence framework, which will be summarised below (and discussed in more detail in Chap. 18), enables enterprises to set up their own management dashboard in terms of how the enterprise coherence can be governed/improved during enterprise transformations. This, enterprise-specific dashboard enables senior management to govern the coherence between key aspects of an enterprise during transformations.

Enterprises which have never used GEA before, as was the case at DGA, will have to set up their enterprise coherence framework based dashboard before proceeding the activities of the enterprise coherence governance part of the method. Once the dashboard has been created, it can be used over and over again, and updated based on major changes to the enterprise and/or experiences.

The enterprise coherence framework (Wagter 2009) defines a series of cohesive elements and cohesive relationships, which together define the playing field for an enterprise's coherence. By making the definition of these elements explicit in a specific enterprise, a management dashboard helps one gain insight into the "state of coherence" while also being able to assess the impact of potential/ongoing transformations. This then enables a deliberate governance of enterprise coherence during transformations. The enterprise coherence framework is defined in terms of two levels and their connections: the *level of purpose* and the *level of design*. The *level of purpose* involves a description of the enterprise's strategy in commonly known concepts from strategy formulation (Balogun et al. 2003; Simons 1994), such as *mission*, *vision*, *core values*, *goals* and *strategy*. The *design level* involves concepts such as the following:

Perspective—an angle from which one wishes to govern/steer/influence enterprise transformations. The set of perspectives used in a specific enterprise depend very much on its formal and informal power structures; both internally and externally. Typical examples are culture, customer, products/services, business processes, information provision, finance, value chain, corporate governance, etc.

Core concepts—a concept, within a perspective, that plays a key role in governing the organisation from that perspective. Examples of core concepts within a perspective such as "Finance" are, for instance, "Financing" and "Budgeting".

Guiding statement—an internally agreed and published statement, which directs desirable behaviour. They only have to express a desire and/or give direction.

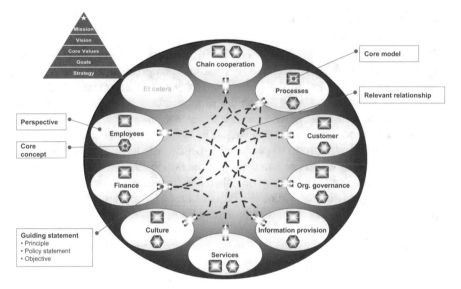

Fig. 4.1 The enterprise coherence framework

Guiding statements may therefore cover policy statements, (normative) principles (Greefhorst and Proper 2011) and objectives.

Core model—a high level view of a perspective, based on, and in line with, the
guiding statements of the corresponding perspective.

Relevant relationship—a description of the connection between two guiding statements of different perspectives.

The presence of a well-documented enterprise mission, vision, core values, goals
and strategy are preconditions to be able to determine the content of the core factors on the design level of the organisation and they are the essential resources for
this determination. The coherence elements and their relationships are illustrated in
Fig. 4.1.

4.4 The Management Dashboard for DGA

Since this was the first time for DGA to apply/use GEA, it was necessary to first
develop an organisation-specific management dashboard. To this end, the case at
DGA started with an intensive desk research activity, conducted by a small team
of architects. This team studied relevant policy documents from DGA, resulting in
the first version of the management dashboard for the agency, in terms of a list of

Table 4.1 Definitions of perspectives for DGA

Perspective	Definition
ICT	All processes, activities, people and resources for obtaining, processing and delivery of relevant information for DGA
Chain cooperation	The collaboration of the parties involved in the subsidy arrangement chain
Processes	A coherent set of activities needed to deliver results of DGA
Organisational structure	The governance and organisational structure of the DGA organisation so that desired goals are attained
Employees	All persons who execute tasks or activities within the DGA-organisation
Suppliers	Companies or organisations that supply or sell products and/or services to DGA
Culture	Explicit and implicit norms, values and behaviours within the DGA organisation
Services	All services that DGA within legal frameworks, or through agreed appointments with statutory authorities, establishes and delivers to applicants
Customer	The applicant of a service of DGA
Law and regulations	All legal frameworks that form the basis for the task performance of DGA

the cohesive elements and their definitions, covering both the purpose level and the design level. Starting point for creating this list were the strategic documents of the organisation such as the mission statement, vision notes, policy plans, business strategy, business plan, etc. In a validation workshop, this draft management dashboard was then validated with the major stakeholders and approved after some modifications. This validation workshop involved the executives of DGA, complemented with a number of (internal) opinion leaders and key stakeholders.

Table 4.1 (page 35) shows the perspectives that were selected by DGA, while as an example the core concepts of five of the perspectives are listed in Table 4.2.

This set of perspectives also illustrates the need to align more aspects of an enterprise rather than just business and IT. Several of the perspectives may put requirements towards ICT, for instance, customer followed by chain cooperation and processes being some dominant ones in this sense. However, the chosen set of perspectives shows that when it comes to alignment, the stakeholders do not simply think in terms of Business/IT alignment, but rather in a much more refined web of aspects that need alignment. During desk research at DGA, more than 200 guiding statements were derived from the aforementioned policy documents. Needless to say, presenting all guiding statements goes beyond the purpose of this chapter. Therefore, as an example Table 4.3 only shows those guiding statements that turned out to be relevant to the processes perspective.

Table 4.2 Core concepts for DGA

Organisational structure	Customer	Chain cooperation	Processes	ICT
Governance	Applicants	Collaboration	Formal checks	Standardisation
Political leadership	Third parties	Chain test	Material checks	Architecture
Responsibilities and tasks	Channel selection	Chain parties	Seasonal peaks	Integrality
Organisational division	Internet	Chain mandate	Efficiency	Security
Employership	Supply coordination	Service level agreements	Effectiveness	Facilities
Policy cores	Objections	Chain management	Predictability	Information
Programme management	Switchers	Objections	Transparency	Maintenance
Scaling up			Planning	Systems
Combined arrangements			Procedures	Ownership
Work council			Regulations	Storage

Table 4.3 Guiding statements relevant to the *processes* perspective

Processes
Execute three subsidy arrangements through one application
Execution of the subsidy arrangements should be compliant to legislation
All sub-processes should contribute to sustainability
All processes must be described and provided with work instructions
Of all the processes timely progress reports have to be delivered to the control department
Processes should be implemented more cost efficiently
Our aim for DGA is an agile, transparent and fast operation
Factory work as data entry and scanning of maps are outsourced
All process activities must be performed within the statutory time limits
The initialisation activities of the new subsidy year should start in parallel to the 3rd main 'judge' process
The processes of the various partners must connect seamlessly
Also determined by the number of subsidy applications received, we aim to compile an optimal size of batches to be processed
Batches of subsidy applications may only move to the next procedure after approval through formal and material checks
Objections should as much as possible be prevented by means of an active application of the possibility of administrative modification
As a result of far-reaching expected changes in European legislation, only the most needed process improvements should be performed

4.5 Answering the Business Issue

With the dashboard in place, the next step was to organise a workshop, where the business issue at hand was put central and analysed in terms of four questions. During the workshop, each of the ten perspectives of Table 4.1 had an explicit representative with clear (delegated) ownership of the cohesive elements (in the real organisation, i.e. not just the documentation) of that perspective.

At the start of this workshop, the owner(s) of the business issue gave a thorough introduction of the issue in terms of causes, degree of urgency, degree of interest, implications, risks, etc. This introduction gave the representatives of the perspectives a deeper insight into the associated issues of this business issue, enabling them to make a translation of the issue to their own perspective. Now the representatives of the perspectives were capable of determining jointly which perspectives were most affected by/related to the business issue at hand.

The core business issue: *"How can the execution of the subsidy submission, evaluation, and allocation process be made more manageable and efficient?"* was addressed in terms of four questions, leading to four sub-analyses of the business issue:

1. Determine the impact of the business issue on the dominant perspectives.
2. Determine the impact of the business issue on the sub-dominant perspectives.
3. Determine the solution space for the business issue from the dominant perspectives.
4. Determine the solution space for the business issue from the sub-dominant perspectives.

In the first two sub-analyses, the analyses were conducted from the viewpoint of the business issue at hand, resulting in the description of the potential impact and/or needed change initiatives, in relation to the respective perspective, in order to solve the given business issue. In the last two sub-analyses, the analyses were conducted from the viewpoint of the guiding statements of the perspectives, resulting in the possibilities and/or necessary change initiatives, but also the limitations with respect to the solution of the business issue, the so-called solution space. This creates appropriate solutions within the framework of the organisation. Conversely, it becomes clear whether and which frames as a result of a solution should be adjusted and continue to give direction to the organisation. The synthesis of the results from these sub-analyses then formed the integral solution and preferred approach to meet the business issue at hand.

Examples resulting from the four sub-analysis are shown in Table 4.4. The column *Problem* shows the sub-problems that have been expressed by the problem owners. The third column, *"Perspective"*, shows the perspectives which the representatives perceived as most relevant to a sub-problem. The impact on this perspective is expressed in terms of new or modified guiding statements in the adjacent column *"Guiding statement"* (column 4). The impacts resulting from this sub-problem on other possible perspectives (columns 5 and 7) are adjacently expressed in terms of guiding statements (columns 6 and 8). The last column shows the formulated

Table 4.4 Partial cross-perspective impact analysis

Nr.	Problem	Perspective	Guiding statement	Perspective	Guiding statement	Perspective	Guiding statement	Solution elements
1	Awareness of low change ability towards the necessary interventions	Organisational structure	New: The change ability must continually adjust to our ambitions	Chain cooperation	New: Entire chain management should be under programme control			Remove steering from the line organisation, and bring it under programme control. Organise programme management
2	Execution is insufficiently compliant with international laws	Laws and regulations	Existing: Execution should be compliant with legislation	Processes	New: Checks should be carried out at the place of execution by authorised officials	Suppliers	New: All outsourced activities shall be performed in the Netherlands	Renew the outsourcing parties and outsourcing contracts, and refocus them on legal regulations
3	ICT support is insufficient	ICT	New: ICT must support the entire chain	Chain cooperation	New: Support and control the chain at the level of file sharing	Services	New: We communicate only by e-mail, telephone and Internet	Picture the file exchange and govern this exchange. Organise multi-channel support
4	Many complaints from customers about not knowing the state of progress	Customer	New: Status of progress file logistics must always be visible to customer	Process	New: transparency per file in massive processing			Automate logistics on file level
5	Many discussions and problems with suppliers on their payments	Supplier	New: No deals with operational staff	Processes	New: Manage suppliers by supply management	Organisational structure	New: Separation of functions and performance accountability	Organise professional supply management
...	...	...	...	...	...		...	...
...	...	...	...	...	...		...	...

solutions of the sub-problems in which the representatives reached consensus as part of the integral solution.

To further illustrate the problem analysis, we will elaborate on one concrete example. Problem number 2 as listed in Table 4.4: "*The execution was not sufficiently compliant with international laws*". Every year, a number of checks are conducted by European officials on the degree of compliance with European laws and regulations. There was a need for better anticipation to these checks. This provided a further confirmation of the existing guiding statement in the perspective *Laws and regulations*, that is, "*the execution should be compliant with the international law*". In addition, a new guiding statement was created in the perspective *Processes*: *The checks have to be carried out on the place of execution by authorised officials*. Finally, a new guiding statement to the perspective *Suppliers* was added as well: "*All outsourced activities shall be performed in the Netherlands*". The reached solution for this problem was: "*Renew outsourcing parties and outsourcing contracts and refocus them on the legal regulations*". This solution meant that the involved suppliers could not re-outsource the activities to a lower wage country and that the outsourced processes could be monitored in an easier way. The detailed analysis is illustrated in terms of the coherence framework [see Fig. 4.1 (page 34)] in Fig. 4.2.

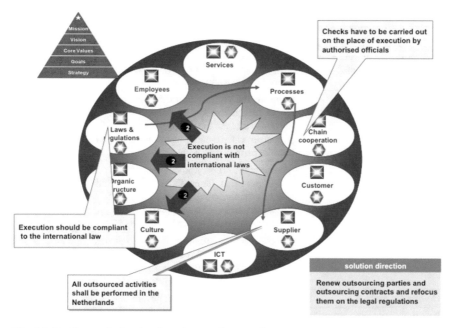

Fig. 4.2 Problem analysis using the coherence framework

4.6 Results of the Programme

As a first step in the synthesis process that followed, the participants clustered the logically belonging together sub-solutions of the four sub-analyses. This is shown on the right side of Table 4.5, which results from clustering the most right column of Table 4.4 (page 38), and the associated solution approaches for the business issue at hand, as shown on the left side of Table 4.5.

During the synthesis process, the participants could also add additional solutions. These could, on the one hand, be based on the new established guiding statements, or, on the other hand, be based on the overall insight of the integral solution and choice of approach. In Table 4.6 (page 41), some examples are provided for the clusters *Renew outsourcing* and *Govern the chain*.

The elaboration of this solution and choice of approach resulted after a final decision into a programme start architecture for controlling the subsequent change programme (Wagter et al. 2005). The resulting programme start architecture was the first part of the contract made with the designated programme manager. The execution of the change programme according to the programme start architecture led to the following results and associated benefits:

Table 4.5 Clustering sub-solutions

Clusters of the integral solution	Sub-solutions from sub-analyses
Organise supply management	Organise professional supply management Develop SLA's and sanctions
Govern the chain	Remove the steering from the line organisation and bring it under programme control Organise programme management Organise chain management including chain mandate and development of a chain-test
Redesign processes	Redesign the primary processes Insert pre-filled forms and complete printing solution at the solution *"Redesigning primary processes"* Organise multi-channel support Automate logistics on file level
Renew outsourcing	Renew the outsourcing parties and outsourcing contracts and refocus them on legal regulations Maintain the outsourcing, and govern the outsourcing professional
Govern file exchange	Picture the file exchange and govern this exchange
Renew Internet application	Redevelop the Internet application Encourage use of the internet channel, maintaining freedom of choice of channels Insert personalised website solution at the solution *"Redevelop Internet application"*
Remain combined data gathering	Proposed unbundling is not accepted, and the status quo maintained Working in multiple shifts was no longer seen as a solution

Table 4.6 Added solutions from the synthesis process

Cluster of integral solution	Solutions, source sub-analyses	Solutions added during synthesis process based on overall insight	Solutions added during synthesis process based on new guiding statements
Renew outsourcing	Renew the outsourcing parties and outsourcing contracts and refocus them on legal regulations Maintain the outsourcing, and govern the outsourcing professional	Set the existing outsourcing parties liable for damages suffered Retraining of employees	Include measurements of throughput in the contract Sanction of €5000 per lost record in the contract Suppliers carry out outsource activities under one roof
Govern the chain	Remove the steering from the line organisation and bring it under programme control Organise programme management Organise chain management including chain mandate and development of a chain-test	Organise a quality assurance project	

- The execution of the subsidy arrangements was within time and agreed budget.
- The return of application forms due to application errors was reduced from 62% to 35%, and consequently fell within the error tolerance.
- The number of objections was reduced from 22,000 to 7000 with corresponding reduction in associated costs.
- The Internet participation of applicants rose from 0.5% to 6.0%.
- The European supervisory authority and the Dutch parliament were satisfied about the results and answers on their submitted questions.
- With regard to the new outsourcing parties:
  - Their performance was in line with the agreed quality, time and budget.
  - Not one client dossier has been lost.
  - Given the good performance all contracts were subsequently prolonged.

4.7 Reflection

The case also illustrates that Business/IT alignment is not only a matter of aligning "the business" and "the IT" aspects of an enterprise. The case suggests that a more refined perspective is called for. More specifically, we see how "the business" is not just a single aspect that needs to be aligned to "the IT", but rather that it involves many more aspects that need mutual alignment just as well. This is also why we prefer to use the term enterprise coherence. It more clearly expresses the fact that it is more about achieving coherence between multiple aspects, rather than merely aligning the business and IT aspects.

Chapter 5
Public Services Opening Up To Innovation

Hella Faller

Abstract This chapter introduces an enterprise transformation taking place in the passport issuing and registration office of the Dutch government: adding innovation to the strategic agenda of a purely maintenance-focused organisation. This transformation is divided into three projects: introduction of a formal architecture board, introduction of an innovation department, and introduction of new project types (innovation projects). During the transformation, the architecture board faces different challenges linked to the institutionalisation of ACET, cultural aspects and communication defects.

5.1 The Organisation

The passport issuing and registration office of the Dutch government, called the Basisadministratie Persoonsgegevens en Reisdocumenten (BPR), belongs to the ministry of the interior in the Netherlands and is responsible for the registration and delivery of the personal data and travel documents of all Dutch citizens. As such, their core business is the maintenance of different registration systems, that is, ensuring that the systems are secure and reliable.

BPR's key stakeholders are the users of those systems: the municipalities but also non-governmental institutions such as the police, credit card institutes or insurance companies. Another key stakeholder is BPR's sponsor, which is also an agency of the ministry of the interior [Directie Burgerschap en Informatiebeleid (B&I)]. B&I is responsible for making laws concerning the registration and the use of personal data. BPR can be understood as an execution organisation, which is strongly influenced by the laws made by B&I.

H. Faller
knk Business Software AG, Darmstadt, Germany
e-mail: hella.faller@gmail.com

© Springer International Publishing AG, part of Springer Nature 2017   43
H.A. Proper et al. (eds.), *Architectural Coordination of Enterprise Transformation*,
The Enterprise Engineering Series, https://doi.org/10.1007/978-3-319-69584-6_5

Table 5.1 Characteristics of interviewees

#	Position	Department	Gender	At BPR	Experience
1	Former project leader	System knowledge and innovation	Male	0.17 years	15 years
2	System architect	System knowledge and innovation	Male	5.33 years	38 years
3	Senior project employee	Customer Relation Management	Male	12 years	45 years
4	Project leader	System knowledge and innovation	Female	14 years	25 years
5	Project architect	System knowledge and innovation	Male	12.5 years	25 years
6	Head of department	Customer Relation Management	Female	1.5 years	12 years
7	Business architect	Business Control	Male	6.5 years	25 years

In general, BPR has three kinds of tasks:

1. Their regular work of maintaining the data systems
2. Internally initiated projects concerning BPR's infrastructure
3. Projects initiated through external requests coming from B&I

In the following sections, we present an enterprise transformation taking place at BPR (Sect. 5.2) and the Enterprise Architecture (EA)-related challenges BPR is facing during that transformation (Sect. 5.3). In Sect. 5.4 we reflect on those challenges in the context of architectural coordination of enterprise transformation (ACET).

The case-related information presented in this chapter originates from multiple sources of data: we analysed some of BPR's internal documents, such as strategic documents, organisational charts and project plans, to gain information on the organisational context. Furthermore, we conducted a focus group meeting with BPR's architecture board to triangulate the data gained from the document analysis (Yin 2009). In addition, the focus group meeting provided insights into the challenges the enterprise architecture function encountered during the enterprise transformation. As a third source of information, we used qualitative interviews. In total, we conducted six semi-structured and one unstructured interview with different types of employees. Table 5.1 shows the interviewees' characteristics. The interviews lasted between 30 min and 3 h, depending on the interviewee's availability. The unstructured interview was conducted with interviewee #7.

5.2 The Enterprise Transformation

Traditionally, BPR is a maintenance organisation. However, in 2010 a new director is appointed to BPR. In 2011 she decides, together with B&I, to add innovation to BPR's strategic agenda. They want BPR to become an open, flexible and learning organisation. Thus, BPR has the task to develop from a solely maintenance organisation to an organisation that, in addition, is open and able to innovate. To this end, the new director decides to restructure the entire organisation (Fig. 5.1). Within this restructuring, two changes are particularly relevant to the introduction of innovation

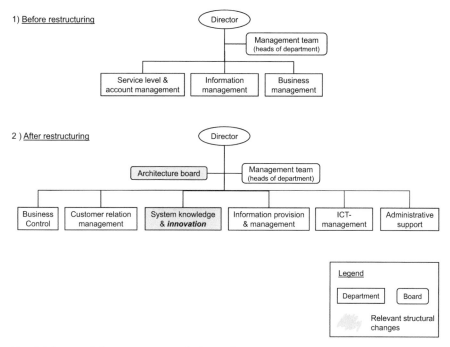

Fig. 5.1 Structural changes to open up for innovation

and will be highlighted in the following paragraphs: (1) introduction of a formal architecture board and (2) introduction of an innovation department. In addition to these two structural changes, the director also introduces a change concerning BPR's operations: (3) the introduction of new project types, namely of innovation projects.

5.2.1 Introduction of Architecture Board

Before the start of the transformation, BPR already had architects but there was no formal enterprise architecture body. By opening up to innovation, the organisation extends their scope of tasks. To ensure that this opening up does not come at the expense of achieving operational excellence,[1] BPR introduces an architecture board (Fig. 5.1). This board is responsible for helping the organisation in achieving their strategic goals, that is, in reaching operational excellence and excellence in innovation.

To this end, a new procedure concerning project plans and changes in projects is implemented: every project plan or other document that needs to be decided on by the management team of BPR has to be approved by the architecture board be-

---

[1] Given that BPR is a maintenance organisation, operational excellence, that is, providing secure and reliable services, is one of their main goals.

fore the management team takes a decision. Hence, the architecture board has an advisory function towards the management team. It is responsible for ensuring coherence among the different tasks and projects conducted in BPR and the different systems used at BPR.

The architecture board is composed of three architects coming from different departments: a business architect (business control department), a system architect (department of system knowledge and innovation) and an information and communications technology (ICT) architect (ICT management department). Furthermore, a quality manager is part of the architecture board.

5.2.2 Introduction of Innovation Department

While opening up to innovation, BPR keeps their maintenance focus. To separate these two types of tasks, BPR introduces a department dedicated to innovation: the system knowledge and innovation department (Fig. 5.1). This department is responsible for identifying and investigating new developments and for embedding them in BPR's existing structure and processes.

5.2.3 Introduction of New Project Types

To open the organisation up to innovation, new projects are started. The project requests come from B&I. These new projects do not concern the maintenance of the data systems but for instance the development of new instruments. We now introduce two example projects. We will frequently refer to these when illustrating challenges and conflicts later on.

The first example of such a new project type is the development of a self-assessment tool that can be used to check the quality of the data collected in the different systems. Before, data quality was checked for each municipality every 3 years in the context of an audit. The new tool aims at helping municipalities to continuously assess the quality of their data themselves. Thus, the self-assessment tool contributes to maintaining the quality of the data systems. That is, it supports BPR's main task. What is new is that the project of developing the self-assessment tool is conducted within BPR. Before the start of the enterprise transformation, such a project would have been conducted entirely by an external company.

Another new project is the creation of a contact centre for citizens who have become victims of identity fraud. This contact centre shall advice individual citizens regarding what to do about the fraud, that is, whom to contact and which other steps to take. One innovation of this project is that BPR has contact with individual citizens. Usually, they only communicate with other organisations, such as the municipalities and the insurance companies. This means that BPR's customer relation management (CRM) enlarges their group of stakeholders. In the context of the identity fraud project, communication channels need to be set up for the citizens to contact BPR. Furthermore, a suitable database needs to be established to collect the data BPR receives from the citizens. Also, the project employees have to be informed about what can and/or has to be done regarding different types of identity fraud.

5.3 Challenges

During the enterprise transformation, the architecture board faces the following challenges.

5.3.1 Unclear Role of the Architecture Board

To help BPR in coordinating the enterprise transformation, the architecture board has been created as a formal enterprise architecture body in the beginning of the transformation. However, within BPR the role of the architecture board is not clear. Different stakeholders have different perspectives and opinions on what the architects are supposed to do and where they should intervene. For instance, lots of project employees understand the architecture board as an advisory board that can be used when they have a problem in their project. They do not interpret the architecture board as an organ that should already be involved in the planning phase of a project to prevent potential problems.

In contrast, the architects would like to be involved in projects from the beginning on. They complain about being contacted too late: "*we are used as trouble shooters*" (interviewees #2 and #7). There are also employees who share the architects' understanding of their role. The head of the CRM department (interviewee #6) says for instance:

> I think it would be better if the architects were involved from the start. But that doesn't happen. It's difficult to reach them.

The examples show that the role of the architecture board is not clear within BPR. Different understandings exist. And even if two groups seem to have the same understanding of the role of the architecture board, the degree of the architecture board's involvement does not comply with that understanding.

5.3.2 Legitimacy of the Architecture Board

To ensure that the innovation projects are coherent with BPR's project and system landscape, a new rule has been implemented that requires every project plan, change request, etc. to be approved by the architecture board before the management team takes a decision on it. However, while this rule exists on paper it is not always followed in practice. New project requests coming from B&I are usually sent to the director of BPR or to one of the heads of department. And on some occasions the architecture board is not consulted before taking a decision regarding a project request. This behaviour raises questions regarding the legitimacy of the architecture board and makes it more difficult for the architects to fulfil their role as advisers.

5.3.3 Long Communication Lines

As illustrated in Sect. 5.2, the enterprise transformation entails that development projects are conducted within BPR. This means that BPR is the owner of the innovation projects and is therefore responsible for the project management. Yet, it does not mean that new systems and/or products are developed by BPR's employees. In many cases BPR hires an external company to develop new products. This is due to the fact that BPR's employees are often not skilled for developing new tools.

The external product development is accompanied by long communication lines, which result in a lack of communication between the external developers and BPR's architects: on the one hand, the developers do not involve the architecture board; on the other hand, the architecture board does not try to engage themselves, that is, they are not very proactive regarding external developments. This lack of communication makes it more difficult for the architecture board to monitor during the development phase if the product is coherent with BPR's enterprise architecture. Often the architecture board is confronted with the finished product, which sometimes is difficult to integrate within BPR. Also, because of long lines of communication some conflicting requirements are not identified early enough. This leads to problems that need to be solved after the product has been developed.

The following example illustrates the challenge of long communication lines. Consider the "*self-assessment tool for municipalities*" project (Sect. 5.2): currently, all the systems and applications BPR is responsible for are hosted on a Windows-based server. However, BPR plans to move them to a Linux-based server. Therefore, when the development of the self-assessment tool is outsourced, one of the requirements is that the final application needs to run on Linux. So the external company develops the tool for Linux. However, before the tool is fully implemented and can be used by all municipalities BPR wants to run a pilot with only a few municipalities. This pilot is conducted before the operating system is changed from Windows to Linux. Thus, for the pilot the application needs to run on Windows. Yet, the requirement for the pilot is only discovered when the development of the self-assessment tool is finished. So, the external company has to change the tool to make it work on Windows, which leads to an increase in costs and to delays for BPR.

In theory, these extra costs should have been avoided by using enterprise architecture management. The architecture board should have an overview over existing and planned organisational components (van der Raadt et al. 2010) and should point out inconsistencies. However, in the described project, the architecture board is not involved in the tool development. The outsourcing leads to longer communication channels, which has two consequences in the case of BPR: first, the developers do not involve the architecture board; second, the architecture board does not try to engage themselves in the development. Therefore, the outsourcing of development favours problems of integrating the respective tool/system into BPR's landscape.

5.3.4 Innovation as an Addition

At BPR, employees distinguish their "regular work" from project work. A peculiarity of BPR is that project work is usually done in addition to people's regular work. That is, employees have a larger workload when they are contributing to a project. This is particularly challenging for the opening up to innovation because, as explained in Sect. 5.2, the introduction of innovation happens to a large extent through projects. A consequence of this system is that employees do not have enough time for the innovation projects:

> One of the big issues here is the lack of capacity. It is very important that people who work here do the regular work, they have tasks and every day they do their job. But they also have to think about the new development, the project. One of the problems of projects is that they are separated from the organisation (interviewee #4).

Another challenge that is related to this double load is that most employees do not have their minds clear for innovation:

> So, if they are available and they have to think, they have a lot in mind. They are sitting next to you and they still have a lot of things in their head. So, they can't really be free in their heads to think with us (interviewee #4).

In other words, many employees do not have time for innovation and/or cannot concentrate on innovation-related tasks because they are busy with their regular work. This makes the introduction of innovation more difficult.

5.3.5 Double Role of Architects

As described in Sect. 5.2, the architecture board is composed of employees who belong to different departments. In their departments they have certain roles, which entail interests that are different from those of the architecture board. For example, the system architect (interviewee #2), who works in the system knowledge and innovation department, explains:

> the architecture board's focus is more on long term aspects. And I'm a system architect. So my focus is more towards the short term.

This quotation illustrates the problematic of holding two different roles. The system architect needs to balance the different interests:

> in the architecture board I try to keep in mind the long term aspects. But I also try to convince the other architects in the board that B&I has a wish, which we have to take into account as well, and which can also be very important.

While the variety of perspectives in the architecture board offers the advantage of not being too isolated from the rest of the organisation, it also adds some bias to the decisions made by the members of the architecture board. The double role sometimes leads to situations in which a single person has conflicting interests. In the quote above, the system architect decided to be on the side of his department and, in particular, of his manager.

5.3.6 The Pace of the Enterprise Transformation

As stated in Sect. 5.2, one measure to introduce innovation at BPR is to conduct innovation projects. Yet, the architecture board and the management team of BPR have different opinions about how many of such projects should be carried out, that is, about how fast innovation is introduced in the organisation. While the management team is more in favour of accepting most of the innovation requests B&I sends, the architecture board first wants to reach internal stability. They argue that BPR needs to optimise their internal procedures before they are able to innovate. Due to the difference in opinions about the optimal pace of the enterprise transformation, the architecture board invests a lot of time in convincing the management team of their point of view. Therefore, they have less time to spend on the coordination of the accepted innovation projects.

5.3.7 Change in Mindsets

Another challenge BPR is facing is related to the employees' mindsets. As described in Sect. 5.2, BPR's core business has traditionally been the maintenance of different data systems.

> Most of the people in our organisation are focused on maintenance. It's not a development organisation. We are a maintenance organisation (interviewee #2).

This is reflected in most employees' mindsets. Those employees are not ready for doing innovation because it requires a different way of thinking. As a solution, BPR starts hiring new employees:

> The director is trying to get more people from a different culture into the organisation. They are trying to find people who do not come from a culture like us – keeping the system up and running – but more people that think with creativity (interviewee #1).

However, new employees have to be integrated in the organisation, which means more work for BPR. Furthermore, some of the "old" employees still need to be involved in innovation projects, which means that their mindsets need to be changed.

5.4 Reflection

The challenges BPR is facing in the context of their enterprise transformation can be (partially) linked to the problem perspectives, as will be discussed in Chap. 12. For instance, BPR introduces a new rule stipulating that every change request or project plan has to be approved by the architecture board before it can be approved by the management team. Yet, this rule is not always followed, meaning that the management team sometimes accepts requests without asking the architecture board for approval (see Sect. 5.3). This challenge reveals a lack of *institutionalisation* of ACET. As will be explained in Chap. 12, it is not sufficient to introduce new tools, regulations and guidelines to institutionalise architectural coordination in an organisation. It is important that many stakeholders comply with the new rule so that ACET achieves a "*rule-like status in social thought and action*" (Meyer and Rowan 1977). This status has not (yet) been reached at BPR. Another indication for ACET not being institutionalised at BPR is the fact that the role of the architecture board is not clear. Different employees have different opinions about the architects' responsibilities. When institutionalised, the role of the architecture board should be clear to everyone. ACET should become part of BPR's culture and identity.

Among the presented challenges we also recognise a number that are related to *cultural aspects*. Organisational subculture has been defined as the aggregate "*of values, norms, and attitudes, which are adopted consciously or unconsciously by the members of an organisational subgroup, and which distinguish the members of that subgroup from those of another subgroup in the same organisation*" (Faller and de Kinderen 2014). A more elaborate discussion of the role of such subcultures in the context of ACET will be provided in Chap. 8.

One example of subculture-related challenges is the necessary change in the employees' mindsets. As illustrated in Sect. 5.3, many employees need to adapt a new way of thinking to be able to innovate. In their (sub)culture framework Detert et al. (2000), introduce the orientation to change (with the two dichotomous values: stability and change/innovation) as one culture dimension. Hence, the way of thinking about innovation is closely linked to the cultural background of an employee.

Furthermore, the challenge of architects having two roles is related to subculture, more precisely to differences between organisational subcultures: the illustration in Sect. 5.3 indicates that within BPR there are different attitudes towards time. While the architecture board focuses on the long-term perspective, the system knowledge and innovation department is predominantly short-term oriented. These two groups can be interpreted as two subcultures. The system architect has a role in both subcultures (Sect. 5.3). He tries to concentrate on the long term within the architecture board. However, he personally is more short-term than long-term oriented. This might lead to difficulties within the architecture board given that in a way he has to act in conflict with his own attitude.

In this case description, we also identify challenges related to *communication defects*, which will also be addressed in more detail in Chap. 8 [in particular Sect. 8.4 (page 82)]. For instance, the challenge that the role of the architecture board is unclear cannot only be discussed in the context of institutionalisation (see beginning of this section). We can also analyse it through the lens of communication: in Sect. 5.3 ("*Unclear role of the architecture board*"), we have introduced the example of a department head having the same understanding of the architecture board as the architects themselves. Still, the head of department complains that it is too difficult to reach the architects, which is a problem of communication. The potential cooperation between the architecture board and the head of department suffers from a lack of communication as the architects are not involved and do not seem to engage proactively.

Another example of lacking communication is the outsourcing of development tasks. In Sect. 5.3, we have illustrated that communication does not take place between external developers and the architects, which makes it difficult for the architects to coordinate the transformation. In both examples, the lack of communication results in the architects not being involved early enough.

The case of BPR shows that the ACET has to face different challenges. In this chapter, we have illustrated that such challenges can be analysed from different problem perspectives. Chapter 8 introduces theoretical solutions to overcome (some of) BPR's challenges.

Part II
Exploring Architectural Coordination of Enterprise Transformation

Where the previous part provided an analysis of the current state of corporate ACET practice, this part will continue with an exploration of the challenges facing ACET from a more theoretical perspective, in particular:

- Chapter 6 will start by exploring different types of changes and transformations as they may occur in enterprises.
- Chapter 7 then considers enterprises as social systems and explores enterprise transformation from this perspective.
- An important aspect of social systems are cultures. In particular subcultures, as they play an important role in the coordination of enterprise transformations. By their very nature, enterprise transformations will bring together different subcultures. Therefore, Chap. 8 explores the potential role of subcultures in the coordination of enterprise transformations.
- In Chap. 9, we will then continue to explore (the need for) a *use perspective* for ACET, in particular the *use* of the created architectural artefacts.
- In Chap. 10, we then zoom in on the role of stakeholders during ACET and explore a possible strategy to engage, in a controlled way, the key forces that should/will influence enterprise transformations.
- As coordination relies on the capturing and processing of information, Chap. 11 considers the information requirements for doing ACET.
- Chapter 12 is concerned with the question on how to establish a sustainable discipline of "doing ACET" in an organisation, that is, how it can be *institutionalised*.
- Architecting also involves a myriad of models and associated modelling languages, be it highly informal languages, be it languages with a precise/formally defined syntax, or even languages with a formally defined semantics. The landscape of modelling languages, and how to manage this in practical settings for ACET, is discussed in Chap. 13.
- Next to models, another key ingredient of architectures are architecture principles. Their role in ACET, particularly how one might operationalise their meaning as a restriction of design freedom, is explored in Chap. 14.
- Decisions taken at an architectural level, be they explicit or implicit, have a major impact on the enterprise architecture as it will finally materialise. In Chap. 15, we therefore explicitly consider the motivation and rationalisation of architectural design decisions.

As mentioned above, this part is concerned with an exploration only. Part III provides several elements of a design theory for ACET that address the challenges as addressed in the remainder of this part.

Chapter 6
Degrees of Change in Enterprises

Janne J. Korhonen

Abstract Enterprise change can be seen to have different degrees, each of which is progressively wider in scope and different in nature, varies in type of intervention, and absorbs an increasing amount of environmental complexity. In this chapter, three degrees of enterprise change are identified. The first degree of change is about restructuring in an operational scope with focus on reliability, cost containment, and efficiency. The second degree is broader in scope, more dynamic in nature, and focused on value creation through reengineering. The third degree of change is complex, strategic, and aimed at fundamental rethinking and value innovation. It is argued that each successive degree of change addresses a progressively more complex environmental context and calls for increasingly developed information technology capability.

6.1 Introduction

In the increasingly interconnected, complex, and dynamic environment, the unprecedented frequency and magnitude of exogenous shocks forces organisations not only to change continually, but also to reinvent their very essence. At the same time, the role of IT as the enabler and driver of enterprise change has increased in importance.

Enterprise change is not uniform in its type, scope, or environmental contingencies, but differs in its *degree* in distinct orders of magnitude. In this chapter, a typology of three degrees of enterprise change is put forward. It is suggested that each

J.J. Korhonen
Department of Computer Science, Aalto University School of Science, Konemiehentie 2,
FI-02150 Espoo, Finland
e-mail: janne.korhonen@aalto.fi

© Springer International Publishing AG, part of Springer Nature 2017
H.A. Proper et al. (eds.), *Architectural Coordination of Enterprise Transformation*,
The Enterprise Engineering Series, https://doi.org/10.1007/978-3-319-69584-6_6

successive degree is progressively wider in scope, more sophisticated in type, and absorbs an increasing amount of environmental complexity. Moreover, the nature and role of IT in these different degrees of enterprise change is discussed.

In the following, Sects. 6.2 through 6.5 provide a theoretical background for the proposed typology. In Sect. 6.2, we will review three qualitatively different yet interdependent "domains of work" as identified in the classical sociological literature (Parsons 1960; Thompson 1967) and elaborated by Hoebeke (1994) from the work levels perspective (also: Jaques 1998; Rowbottom and Billis 1987). In Sect. 6.3, we summon four "causal textures" (Emery and Trist 1965) of the environment that denote increasingly complex types of environment. And in Sect. 6.4, we review three types of enterprise change as frequently distinguished in literature (Hamel and Prahalad 1994; Keidel 1994). In Sect. 6.5, we summarise and extend our earlier work on the typology of IT Realms (Korhonen and Poutanen 2013; Korhonen and Hiekkanen 2013). Finally, in Sect. 6.6, we put forward the typology of three degrees of enterprise change, integrating the concepts introduced in the earlier sections.

6.2 Domains of Work

In the classical sociological literature (Parsons 1960; Thompson 1967), three levels of social organising are commonly identified. Parsons (1960) identifies three distinct levels of responsibility and control—technical, managerial, and institutional. The functions at these levels are interdependent and qualitatively different.

Relatedly, Hoebeke (1994) identifies recursively linked *domains of work*, each with its own language, interests, and other emergent characteristics. Each domain comprises three vertical levels, or strata (Jaques 1998), with the top and bottom level overlapping with another domain (see Table 6.1). The first three domains in Hoebeke's scheme—the added-value domain, innovation domain, and value systems domain—appear to be in line with Parson's three levels, respectively. These domains are described in more detail below.

6.2.1 Added-Value Domain

The *added-value domain* (Hoebeke 1994) spans requisite strata I–III (Jaques 1998). The focus is on efficiency of operations, operational quality and reliability, not on

Table 6.1 Levers of change at strata I–III

Stratum	Work output	Lever of change
III	Systematic provision	Linear extrapolation from current trends
II	Situational response	Continuous improvement of work
I	Prescribed output	Streamlining work; eliminating waste

the conception of new products and services. It addresses the question of "how" and is concerned with *doing*: producing, selling, or providing services (Olivier 2013). The *"requirements of a group of clients are transformed into those requirements being met"* (Hoebeke 1994). Decision-making involves accountability for existing resources. According to Olivier (2013), this is where most companies operate and where 95% of adult human work takes place.

At Stratum I, work has a *prescribed output* (Rowbottom and Billis 1987), confined by specifications, requirements, quality standards or acceptance criteria. To materialise this specified output in the most efficient way, the prescribed means are employed with a minimum of waste (Hoebeke 1994). Change at this level is therefore directed at streamlining the existing processes.

At Stratum II, *situational response* (Rowbottom and Billis 1987) to each case of work requires judgement, interpretation, and reflection of each specific situation and adjustment to the varying customer needs. The specific client requirements are moulded into minimal critical specifications on the input, output, procedures and tools for the people working at Stratum I (Hoebeke 1994). As work is continually redefined, improved and automated to increase efficiency and reliability of operations, change at this level is about continuous improvement.

The output of Stratum III work is *systematic provision* (Rowbottom and Billis 1987) that accommodates to the varying needs of today as well as those of the future. This requires developing alternative products and services, as well as alternative ways of meeting the requirements and needs of known clients (Hoebeke 1994). The kind of product or service to be provided is given, as are the people, buildings, and equipment, yet there is much room for technical improvement and innovation (Macdonald et al. 2006). At this level, the changing requirements of the as-yet-unknown but probable future are predicted by extrapolating from current trends.

Table 6.1 summarises the three strata in the added-value domain.

6.2.2 Innovation Domain

Strata III–V comprise the *innovation domain* (Hoebeke 1994). This domain shifts away from operational business-as-usual and is concerned with added value for the future: managing continuity and change, devising new means to achieve new ends, and letting go of obsolete means and ends (McMorland 2005). The domain is about asking "why" or "so what" and it entails more complex and often abstract activities that maintain the continuity of operations, while following the organisation's strategic intent (Olivier 2013).

Stratum III forms a hinge between the added-value domain and the innovation domain, as the relations between the two domains need an overlapping set of common activities (Hoebeke 1994). Work at Stratum IV entails *comprehensive provision* (Rowbottom and Billis 1987), where the means and ends of underlying added-value work systems are adjusted to reshape profitability within the overall business

Table 6.2 Levers of change at strata IV–V

Stratum	Work output	Lever of change
V	Field coverage	Whole system transformation
IV	Comprehensive provision	Pairwise comparison of known systems

purpose. The signals of change in the value systems of the major stakeholders are transformed into "*new generic products and services, which, at the same time, make this change perceptible to them*" (Hoebeke 1994). Resources need to be negotiated and reallocated between the Stratum III work systems. Change is discontinuous, but predictable, and sought through pairwise comparison of existing systems.

Field coverage (Rowbottom and Billis 1987) at Stratum V expands the scope from a range of products or services to a framework that specifies a general field of need. Changes in the value systems are sensed and reflected in the creation of whole new product/service/market/technology combinations (Hoebeke 1994). The whole system addressing a field of need is transformed, which creates a point of no return (ibid.).

A summary of the two additional strata provided by the *innovation domain* is provided in Table 6.2.

6.2.3 Value Systems Domain

Hoebeke (1994) refers to Strata V–VII as the value systems domain. This is the domain of multinational corporations and international institutions and about creating "*new languages and new descriptions and prescriptions about the world*" (Hoebeke 1994). Decisions pertain to often-global issues of resource allocation and where and in what to invest or disinvest, when and why, which requires integrated thinking across diverse fields (Olivier 2013).

Again, Stratum V forms a hinge between the innovation domain and the value systems domain. Stratum VI represents *multi-field coverage* (Rowbottom and Billis 1987), where the task is to ensure that the output covers the whole complex of fields of need in a coordinated way. Complexity is not so readily contained, but the "great organisational divide" is crossed to a "whole world" view (Jaques 1998). Stratum VI widens the perspective from an individual system, such as organisation, to the larger ecosystem. Stratum V systems are shaped from the outside. This involves articulating the relationships between the strategic business units (Cashman and Stroll 1987) and direct interaction with the external social, political, and economic environment (Macdonald et al. 2006). Development becomes non-teleological (Hoebeke 1994) and change is about creating the future rather than predicting it.

Meta-field coverage (Rowbottom and Billis 1987) at Stratum VII is concerned with managing the development, formation, and construction of various complexes or conglomerates of Stratum V organisations in order to produce an output that covers the whole model-field. Rather than responding to the needs of specific markets

Table 6.3 Levers of change at strata VI–VII

Stratum	Work output	Lever of change
VII	Meta-field coverage	Shaping conglomerates of stratum V systems
VI	Multi-field coverage	Shaping stratum V whole systems

or sections of the population, Stratum VII work is concerned with judging the needs of society, nationally and internationally, and deciding what types of business units to provide to satisfy them. Change at this level pertains to the development of language, values, and culture (Hoebeke 1994).

The summary of the two additional strata provided by the *value systems domain* is provided in Table 6.3.

6.3 Causal Texture of the Environment

Just as the complexity of biological organisms cannot be isolated from the complexity of their environment (Lineweaver et al. 2013), the complexity of the organisation is contingent on the complexity of its environment. While the organisation cannot be characterised without characterising its environment, the environment cannot be characterised without characterising the kinds of organisations for which it is an environment (cf. Emery and Trist 1973).

To analyse the exchange processes between the organisation and elements in its environment, Emery and Trist (1965) reintroduce the concept of the causal texture of the environment (Tolman and Brunswik 1935) at a social level of analysis. The causal texture refers to the processes through which interdependencies in the environment come about.

Emery and Trist (1965) identify four "ideal types" of causal texture:

1. Placid, randomised environment
2. Placid, clustered environment
3. Disturbed-reactive environment
4. Turbulent field

Emery and Trist (1973) have hinted at a possible fifth type of environmental texture, while McCann and Selsky (1984) and Babüroğlu (1988) have indeed elaborated on such a fifth type. However, this hyperturbulent (McCann and Selsky 1984), or vortical (Babüroğlu 1988), environment is a theoretically limiting case in the same vein as Type 1 environment. Thereby, it is excluded from this discussion.

The four environment types identified by Emery and Trist (1965) are discussed in more depth below.

6.3.1 Placid, Randomised Environment

The simplest type of environmental texture is the *placid, randomised environment* (Emery and Trist 1965), in which goals and noxiants ("goods" and "bads") are independent, relatively unchanging, and randomly distributed. Organisations can exist adaptively as single and small units with no need to differentiate between tactics and strategy (ibid.): "*the optimal strategy is just the simple tactic of attempting to do one's best on a purely local basis*" (Schützenberger 1954, p. 101). The survival of an organisation in this type of environment is a simple function of the availability of environmental relevancies and the response capabilities of the organisation—no complex organisational capacity needs to be postulated (Emery and Trist 1973).

Emery and Trist (1973) go as far as to say that system behaviour in the placid, randomised environment does not involve choice. Hence, such environment would necessitate a *state-maintaining system* (Ackoff 1971). However, even a modest planning horizon and storage capacity is adaptive to the system in such environment (Emery and Trist 1973). Appropriate learning behaviour in the placid, randomised environment is conditioning rather than trial-and-error. Consequently, to survive in these environments, higher-order systems must degrade their learning accordingly, yet they will also strive to create more order in the randomness (ibid.).

Emery and Trist (1973) consider this type of environment as an extreme theoretical limit. They recognise it as relevant for "some secondary aspect" of an organisation and as likely to occur in environments designed to maximise prediction and control of human behaviour, for example, the blank, unvarying environments of psychological conditioning experiments.

6.3.2 Placid, Clustered Environment

In the *placid, clustered environments* (Emery and Trist 1965), goals and noxiants are not randomly distributed, but occur together in certain ways. The probability of an organisation's survival is thus critically dependent on its position in the environment (Emery and Trist 1973). To reach these "optimal locations", clustering of resources and development of competences, subordinate to the strategic objective, are required. Organisations tend to grow in size and become hierarchical, with a tendency towards centralised control and coordination (Emery and Trist 1965).

The need arises to distinguish strategy from tactics. Survival in the placid, clustered environment requires a threshold mechanism to evoke reaction only to the more general aspects of the environment rather than dealing tactically with each environmental variance as it occurs (Emery and Trist 1973).

An organisation must be at least goal-directed to adapt this type of environment (Emery and Trist 1973): the course of action is determined more by the goal of the system than by the immediately present goals and noxiants. A *goal-seeking system*, according to Ackoff (1971), has a choice of behaviour: it does not react deterministically but can respond differently to particular events in an unchanging environment until a particular outcome is attained (Emery and Trist 1973). Survival of the system is contingent on its knowledge of its environment.

6.3.3 Disturbed-Reactive Environment

The *disturbed-reactive environment* (Emery and Trist 1965) is like a placid, clustered environment in which more than one organisation of the same kind is postulated. This co-presence has fundamental implications on the environmental field: what each organisation knows about the environment can also be known by another, which is also known by this other (Emery and Trist 1973).

This type of environment gives rise to actions aimed at invoking tactics of other organisations so that one may further its goals. The organisation must therefore be able to choose between a number of possible tactical options (Emery and Trist 1973). Such a *purposeful system* (Ackoff 1971) exhibits will: it can change its goals as well as select ends and means. The capacity or power to move at this will in the face of competitive challenge becomes a more defining objective than that of finding the optimal location (Emery and Trist 1973).

The disturbed-reactive environment is still a relatively stable ground. The competing organisations can be considered as an ultrastable unit (cf. Ashby 1960).

6.3.4 Turbulent Field

In the *turbulent field* (Emery and Trist 1965), the dynamic properties arise not only from the interactions of the organisations but also from the field itself—the "ground" is in motion. The complexity exceeds individual organisations' capacities for prediction and control; they cannot adapt to the turbulent environment through their direct interactions but must rely on commonly held values as the control mechanism in the field (ibid.).

Emery and Trist (1973) identify four trends that together contribute to the emergence of dynamic field forces:

- Organisations becoming so large that their actions induce autochthonous processes in the environment
- The emergence of active field forces due to the increasing interdependence between the economic and the other facets of the society
- The increasing rate of change and deepening interdependence between organisations and their environment due to the increasing reliance upon scientific research and development
- The radical increase in the speed and ease of communication and travel

6.4 Types of Change Interventions

Three types of enterprise change interventions are frequently distinguished in literature. These types go with different names, but labels such as restructuring, reengineering, and rethinking (Keidel 1994) capture the essence and are commonly used.

6.4.1 Restructuring

In *restructuring* (Hamel and Prahalad 1994; Keidel 1994) type of interventions, strategic design actions are mostly focused on the number of nodes (size) and links (density), for example, downsizing or expansion in the resource base (Dijksterhuis et al. 1999), number of organisational units, and number of organisational levels (Keidel 1994).

Hamel and Prahalad (1994) point out that change interventions of this type is often "denominator management", aimed at reducing the denominator component of return on investment: investment, net assets, capital employed, or headcount. Whereas growing the net income would require insight into new growth opportunities, changing customer needs, required new competencies, and so on, cutting the denominator "*doesn't need much more than a red pencil*" (Hamel and Prahalad 1994, p. 9). They liken downsizing to "corporate anorexia" that can make an organisation thinner, but not necessarily healthier.

6.4.2 Reengineering

Reengineering (Hammer and Champy 1993; Hamel and Prahalad 1994; Keidel 1994) the organisation pertains to changing the position of nodes or links within the organisation (Dijksterhuis et al. 1999), for example, through process innovation, redesign of business processes, or redeployment of resources.

Reengineering is about *radical redesign of business processes* to achieve dramatic performance improvements (Hammer and Champy 1993). It tends to be tactical, rather than strategic, focusing on operational processes with a relatively near-term improvement time frame (Keidel 1994). According to Hamel and Prahalad (1994), it offers at least the hope of getting better, not just smaller. However, the real goal of reengineering is often reduced costs rather than higher customer satisfaction. Also, reengineering measures tend to be about catching up with competition rather than "competing for the future".

6.4.3 Rethinking

Rethinking (Keidel 1994), as well as *reinventing* industries and regenerating strategies (Hamel and Prahalad 1994), addresses organisational identity, purpose, and capabilities (Keidel 1994). Strategic design actions are about changing the content of nodes and links (Dijksterhuis et al. 1999). Such changes pertain to properties such as individual and collective mindsets, norms and beliefs, and organisational culture.

According to Keidel (1994), organisational design mirrors the mental models of people, that is, the organisational cognition. The leverage of rethinking lies in cognitive change, not behavioural; and in distinctive organisational capabilities, not in resources or processes. While "thinking about thinking" is difficult, the potential of rethinking is significant. It is rarely pursued for immediate or even mid-term ends (ibid.).

6.5 Three Information Technology Realms

In earlier work, we have postulated a tri-partite approach to enterprise architecture (Korhonen and Poutanen 2013) or, more broadly, three "IT Realms" (Korhonen and Hiekkanen 2013).

Technical realm has an operational focus and is geared to present-day value realisation. IT can be said to follow business; it is used to create resources, such as information assets or application and technology infrastructure. IT planning is a rational, deterministic, and economic process that aims at business–IT alignment, operational efficiency, and IT cost reduction. The focus of IT is on operational quality and reliability—producing predictable outcomes on a consistent basis. Variance is eliminated through cascaded goals, metrics, and internal controls. Human error is removed from the production process through established work practices, quality standards, and policies that regulate discretion.

This is the realm of technically oriented IT work: information systems design and development, enterprise integration, solution architecture work, and IT operations. It also addresses architectural work practices and quality standards, for example, architectural support of implementation projects, development guidelines, and change management practices.

Socio-technical realm plays an important role as the link between strategy and execution: the business strategy is translated to the design of the organisation so that the strategy may be executed utilising all the facets of the organisation, including IT. Knowledge about the internal operation and construction of the organisation is of essence in enabling organisational change (Hoogervorst 2009). IT has an enabling role of enhancing organisational competencies (cf. Peppard and Ward 2004), that is, abilities to utilise and mobilise organisation-specific resources to strategic ends.

This is the realm of business domains and their assigned business activities; business functions and business concepts that these business domains need to perform their assigned business activity; and high-level business processes that show how the business domains collaborate to achieve the organisational goals and strategies (Versteeg and Bouwman 2006).

In the *ecosystemic realm*, the organisation relates to its business ecosystem, industry, markets, and the larger society, co-evolving vis-à-vis its environment: its business ecosystem and the society at large. The perspective shifts from the relatively stable, closed, and controllable system of a self-sufficient enterprise to the relatively fluid, open, and transformational system-of-systems of networked, co-evolving, and co-specialised entities. The focal organisation is objectified from the outside, as a co-evolutionary constituent within the broader business ecosystem.

In the *ecosystemic realm*, IT enables strategic capability (cf. Peppard and Ward 2004); in other words, business follows IT.

6.6 Three Degrees of Enterprise Change

In the following, we operationalise the three degrees of enterprise change in terms of their scope, environmental complexity, type of intervention, nature of change, and the role of IT in change, as summarised in Table 6.4 and illustrated in Fig. 6.1. The three degrees of change are elaborated below.

Table 6.4 The three degrees of enterprise change

	First degree	Second degree	Third degree
Scope	Operational	Tactical	Strategic
Environmental texture	Static Clustered	Disturbed-reactive	Turbulent field
Type of intervention	Restructuring	Reengineering	Rethinking
Conceptualisation of change	Static	Dynamic	Complex
IT realms involved	Technical	Technical Socio-technical	Technical Socio-technical Ecosystemic
Focus of IT	Reliability Cost containment Efficiency	Validity Value creation Effectiveness	Resilience Value innovation Efficacy

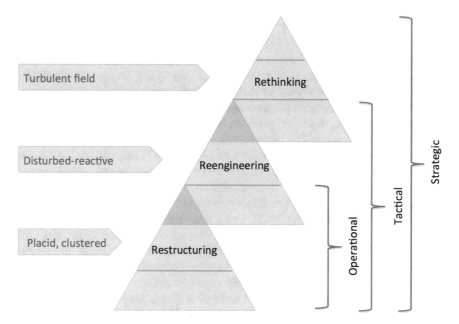

Fig. 6.1 The environmental complexity determines the type and scope of enterprise change

6.6.1 Scope of Change

Enterprise changes of the first degree take place within the operational scope of the added-value domain (Hoebeke 1994). In this scope, the actual day-to-day work of the change initiative takes place in change projects (Greefhorst and Proper 2011).

Enterprise changes of the second degree are of tactical scope. As any level of change requires consideration of all subordinate levels (Rouse 2005), this scope would embrace both the added-value domain and innovation domain (Hoebeke 1994). The overall enterprise change is executed through a portfolio of change programmes. The definition, overall planning and mutual synchronisation of these programmes are additional concerns within this scope (Greefhorst and Proper 2011).

Enterprise changes of the third degree are strategic in scope and span all three work system domains: added-value, innovation, and value systems (Hoebeke 1994). They embrace the tactical scope of change but further encompass the overall enterprise transformation at the strategic level: strategic direction, strategy formulation, and execution (Greefhorst and Proper 2011).

6.6.2 Environmental Contingency

Enterprise changes of the first degree appear to be requisite in environments, whose environmental texture (Emery and Trist 1965) is placid and clustered. Historically, this environment has been "man's accustomed social habitat" (Trist 1977). It represents the first departure from the theoretical limit for the organisation: placid, randomised environment, where the planning horizon is zero and the organisation's behaviour fully predictable. The organisation clusters resources to competences that allow systematic provision (Rowbottom and Billis 1987) to cater for the general need in the environment (cf. Emery and Trist 1973). Enterprise changes of the first degree pertain to resizing these resource clusters.

Enterprise changes of the second degree would address the disturbed-reactive environment (Emery and Trist 1965). The organisation must be able to choose between tactical options and to set and change its goal, that is, its strategic intent (cf. McMorland 2005). Changes of the second degree are about changing the way in which resources are used vis-à-vis these changing goals.

Enterprise changes of the third degree would be needed in the face of the turbulent field (Emery and Trist 1965). The organisation is subject to increasing entanglement with its environment at the institutional level (Parsons 1960) and must increasingly rely on value-based controls to maintain cohesion (Emery and Trist 1965). Accordingly, changes of the third degree go deep into shared values, norms, and beliefs that need to be changed to enable full-system transformation.

6.6.3 Type of Change Interventions

Removing the waste (Stratum I), improving the work processes (Stratum II), and changing the ways of producing and providing products and services (Stratum III) exemplify change interventions of the restructuring type (cf. Hamel and Prahalad 1994; Keidel 1994). They take place within a certain resource base that can be scaled up (e.g. increasing production capacity) or down (e.g. reducing headcount).

Restructuring is typically conceptualised as *static change* (Eoyang and Holladay 2013): the situation before is compared to that of after, but there is no consideration of movement between the two. This simplified view is applicable to changes that are short-term or limited in scope, when there are few complicating factors and control of the environment can be assumed. Same change can successfully be made in similar circumstances.

Change interventions of the second degree would be about reengineering (cf. Hamel and Prahalad 1994; Keidel 1994): reassembling resources to altogether new Stratum III work systems of production or service delivery in order to ensure comprehensive output that caters for a given territorial or organisational society (cf. Rowbottom and Billis 1987).

Reengineering could be characterised as *dynamic change* (Eoyang and Holladay 2013) that assumes a predictable, yet moving, endpoint, towards which multiple forces cause movement. The endpoint can be changed by manipulating those forces. This view of change is applicable to progressions or state-based changes with one-way causality, few influences, and clear boundaries.

Enterprise changes of the third degree would focus on whole-system enterprise transformation that calls for rethinking (cf. Hamel and Prahalad 1994; Keidel 1994) type of change interventions.

The respective view of change would be *dynamical change* (Eoyang and Holla-day 2013) that results from unknown forces acting unpredictably and whose path or outcomes cannot be predicted or controlled. Patterns emerge, but can only be discerned in retrospect. An example of this variety would be a cascading change, when the accumulated tensions and pressures are released in an unpredictable and un-controlled way. This view of change is applicable when boundaries are open, many factors influence events, and root causes are elusive.

6.6.4 The Role of Information Technology

The role of IT in enterprise change varies by the degree, ranging from operational support to a strategic driver. With each additional degree of enterprise change, a new IT realm would be activated and the emphasis in the previous realms shifted, accordingly. This proposition is illustrated in Table 6.5.

In enterprise changes of the first degree, IT investments usually pertain to one-off application or solution development and are based on expected IT cost reductions (cf. Ross 2003; Ross et al. 2006). With the focus on efficiency, cost contain-ment, and reliability, they are typically geared to restructuring type of changes: automating operational work and business processes in Technical Realm. The de-livered systems may fully fulfil the specified business needs, but with the lack of technology standards and enterprise-wide IT architecture, the proliferation of legacy systems and idiosyncratic point-to-point integrations renders the application land-scape inert, expensive, and risky in the face of change.

In enterprise changes of the second degree, IT plays a dual role of supply and de-mand. On the one hand, enterprise-wide IT architecture in Technical Realm provides efficiencies through technology standardisation and centralised shared infrastructure

Table 6.5 Focus of IT in different degrees of enterprise change

	First degree	Second degree	Third degree
Ecosystemic			Strategic IT capability and digital business models
Socio-technical		Enterprise architecture	Modular architecture
Technical	Development to require-ments	Technology standardisa-tion, shared infrastructure	Optimised core of digi-tised data and processes

(cf. Ross 2003; Ross et al. 2006). On the other hand, resources and IT investments are shifted from application and solution development to enterprise (business) architecture (cf. Korhonen and Molnar 2014), business process management, portfolio management, and the development of IT-enabled competences. With the focus on effectiveness, value creation, and validity, IT enables reengineering type of changes: IT is increasingly leveraged to *informate* (Zuboff 1985) knowledge work and appropriate business processes.

Enterprise changes of the third degree are driven by IT. The business model is digital and enabled by IT-enabled strategic capability. With the focus on efficacy, value innovation, and resilience, IT enables continuous reconfiguration of *unbundled* and *liquefied* (Normann 2001) resources, through which the organisation can shift its value proposition vis-à-vis its ecosystem (Vargo and Akaka 2009) in alignment with semi-coherent strategies. The core of data and processes is optimised and digitised in Technical Realm. It is difficult to make changes to that core, but building new products and services onto the core becomes easier and faster. Modular architecture (cf. Ross 2003; Ross et al. 2006) in Socio-Technical Realm enables strategic agility through reusable modules built upon the optimised core or by allowing locally customised modules to connect to core data and core processes. While not reducing the need for standardisation, the modular architecture allows for local customisation and provides a platform for innovation.

6.7 Conclusion

In this chapter, we proposed a typology of three degrees of enterprise change, while also discussing the nature and potential role of IT in these different degrees of enterprise change. Each successive degree of change is progressively wider in scope, more sophisticated in type, and absorbs an increasing amount of environmental complexity.

Chapter 7
Enterprise Transformation from a Social Perspective

Wolfgang A. Molnar

Abstract Modern enterprises continue to develop their profile into an even more complex assembly. Reasoned by increasing environmental turbulences and deliberate changes, researchers and practitioners need to acknowledge that addressing transformations of enterprises is a multiplex interplay between different factors. Identifying enterprises as social systems means that the system elements are social individuals and that the essence of an enterprise's operation lies in the capabilities and interaction between involved social actors. Insights from sociology literature may help to address transformations of enterprises adequately. Rooted in the sociology literature, a framework for the analysis of change is brought forward, involving: *origin*, *type*, *momentum* and *trajectory*. By enriching those dimensions with concepts from socio-technical literature, a powerful instrument is forged to analyse and address transformations of enterprises.

7.1 Introduction

Modern enterprises experience different trends due to increasing environmental turbulences and deliberate changes (Harmsen and Molnar 2013). One trend that enterprises experience is the bias to become more dynamic. Previously static enterprises need to adapt and partly reinvent their eco-system in an increasing pace, so that they can progress or at least maintain their status. The increased dynamics of enterprises may relate to projects or programmes that relate to development, marketing or other activities. Increased attention is drawn on agile methods, which may leverage the dy-

W.A. Molnar
Warwick Business School, Coventry, UK

ZF, Friedrichshafen, Germany
e-mail: wolfgangmolnar@gmail.com

© Springer International Publishing AG, part of Springer Nature 2017   71
H.A. Proper et al. (eds.), *Architectural Coordination of Enterprise Transformation*,
The Enterprise Engineering Series, https://doi.org/10.1007/978-3-319-69584-6_7

namic capabilities of enterprises. Another trend relates to the approaches enterprises may undertake. Traditional enterprises were able to solve many problems with rather generic solutions. However, modern enterprises require the capability to create situational solutions, such as "just-in-sequence" or "just-in-time" logistics. In addition, enterprises are in a permanent state of flux. Elements of an enterprise that were initially considered stable may become "transformational", due to several reasons, such as new regulations, technological change, and stakeholder influence.

The experiences of modern enterprises are not limited to the trends mentioned above, but these examples provide an idea of the growing environmental turbulences and intended changes. To handle this continuous motion, present-day successful enterprises have well-defined role models and priorities, while also enabling the processes to be agile enough. Hence, these enterprises may re-innovate themselves and do not rely on mechanistic and organic processes and structures (Weick and Quinn 1999). As a result, transforming enterprises is more than planned change, initiated by people on purpose or in response to environmental changes (Dunphy 1996)—it is a combination of deliberate and/or organic changes, as well as serendipity.

Previous research in the field of enterprise transformation hardly expanded on "nonlinear processes". Those nonlinear processes include organic and serendipitous changes, and we imply that proper understanding of organisational change must allow emergence and surprises. This means that the possibility of organisational change must be take into account, when having consequences beyond those initially imagined or planned (Greenwood and Hinings 1996). When agents perform planned activities or even routines, these activities may contain the seeds of change (Giddens 1984, pp. 1–5). Hence, even supposed to be stable structures of an organisation, such as routines, are changeable. Change is potentially always there, if only we are willing to see it (Feldman 2000).

Understanding enterprises as social systems with a purpose requires any study to take the social dimension into consideration. In doing so, we try to have a holistic perspective for generating space for a comprehensive study of transforming enterprises. Previously, attempts by the traditional, strong functionalistic literature failed to provide significant help. More recently, researchers called for more self-reflection within the field of enterprise transformation and more balanced discourse with respectively more advanced frameworks that help practitioners better achieve their goals (Molnar and Korhonen 2014). In doing so, insights into social aspects of transforming enterprises are scant, and practitioners only have a partial view on the engineering of socio-technical systems as conveyed by related literature (Molnar and Korhonen 2014). In order to have a holistic perspective for a more comprehensive study of transforming enterprises, we looked into the work of a contemporary sociologist Anthony Giddens. Giddens' ideas aid the study of changes and we think that his categorisation of various dimensions into a framework of change is a pertinent structuration-foundation for a new perspective of addressing transformations of enterprises.

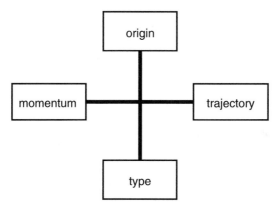

Fig. 7.1 Framework to analyse social change. Reprinted with permission from Giddens (1984). © 1984 Politi Press, Cambridge, United Kingdom; reprinted with permission

7.1.1 Structuration-Foundation

Giddens is recognised as a well-known sociologist and is known for his contributions in scientific studies of human society and its origins, development, change and organisations. Research domains, such as information system research, frequently cite his work as well (Jones and Karsten 2008). He categorised various dimensions of change in a framework, so that 'the assessment of the nature of specific forms of episode' may take place (Giddens 1984). This assessment is founded on four different dimensions: *origin*, *type*, *momentum* and *trajectory* (Fig. 7.1).

We think that those dimensions (origin, type, momentum and trajectory) are interwoven and cannot be separated in steering analysis of transformative processes of enterprises. In addition, the incorporation of various details of other literature leverages the structuration-foundation of pertinently assessing the nature Harmsen and Molnar (2013).

7.1.2 Origin

In understanding the origin of social change, various considerations are relevant. These considerations may be obtained from different perspectives, such as internal vs. external causes (Rouse and Baba 2006) or improvement vs. renewal (De Caluwé and Vermaak 2003). These perspectives only show a fraction of the potential bandwidth of change origins, but provide a first stand in applying the structuration-foundation. Moreover, the variety of different considerations provides an initial attempt to assemble the potential origins of changes that can be investigated when studying enterprise transformation. Therefore, we do not advocate for the conventional perspective of internal vs. external or any other perspective, because in differing settings, the analysis of varying factors may make sense. Consequently, there is no silver bullet for providing one unique origin factorisation that helps in all possible situations (Harmsen and Molnar 2013).

7.1.3 Type

The type of social change relates to how intensive and extensive change is. Giddens (1984) relates this to the profoundness of changes, which relates to the situation "before and after" the change. Those changes may involve formal and informal aspects of an organisation (De Caluwé and Vermaak 2003), pertaining to the structure of communication, power and sanctions. The formal organisation may involve its architecture, rules, roles, responsibilities, etc. The informal organisation consists of coalitions, psychological needs, power, informal leadership, moral, social codes, etc. Giddens (1984) emphasises the potential thresholds of changes that can hinder the morphosis between overall societal types. In the understanding of enterprise transformations, this relates to the potential hurdles that need to be taken (e.g. just enough formal structures, or just enough loyalty) when organisational change (should) happen. Hence, a critical threshold of characteristics of change needs to be met in order for profound organisational change to occur (Harmsen and Molnar 2013).

7.1.4 Momentum

Temporal aspects of organisational change are related to the dimension momentum. Macro-level changes understood as episodic changes involve periods of routines and periods of breaching of those routines. Giddens (1984) described his framework to analyse social change as a tool to assess the features of certain episodes. However, we believe the structuration-foundation for a new perspective of approaching transforming enterprises fits well with the analyses of non-episodic changes as well. Non-episodic changes (micro), the ongoing adjustment of practices so to speak, have a momentum of their own. This momentum is continuous and small changes may accumulate and result in essential transformations (Lanzara 1999). Therefore, the temporal characteristic of different momentums (macro and micro levels of analysis) is an important dimension in analysing social change (Harmsen and Molnar 2013).

7.1.5 Trajectory

Giddens (1984) details the dimension of trajectory only superficially by stating that it concerns the direction of change. Different directions of change may involve different ways change is achieved. De Caluwé and Vermaak (2003) describe different ways of change and label those with different colours, such as yellow, blue, red, green, white, silver and steel-print. Varying levels of rationality, intuition and social aspects may alter the direction of change and consequently influence this process. For example, blue colour symbolizes the pure rational approach and intuition is not considered to determine aspects of the change process. Yellow colour stands for an exchange of power politics that drives the change process. In distinguishing different directions of change, the various colours provide a fine-grained conceptualisation of potential trajectories of transformation.

7.2 Applying the Structuration-Foundation

The strength of structuration-foundation is its ability to accommodate the study of change. An appropriate understanding of transforming enterprises should not favour one method over the other. However, some choices for researchers and practitioners are necessary in approaching transforming enterprises with the structuration-foundation. These choices are important in getting a sophisticated elaboration of what is happening from a non-particularistic and integrated perspective. The various dimensions of origin, type, momentum and trajectory can have different considerations. For example, the origin of enterprise transformation can be derived from different positions, such as internal vs. external causes (Rouse and Baba 2006) or improvement vs. renewal (De Caluwé and Vermaak 2003). The position that has to be taken for the analysis of transformation origins remains to be answered by the users of the structuration-foundation. Therefore, a general advice cannot be given for researchers and practitioners, since this choice is dependent on different situational factors. Consequently, a case-by-case decision needs to be taken, so that a comprehensive analysis from a holistic point of view can be accomplished. Similar choices need to be made for the type, momentum and trajectory of transforming enterprises.

7.3 Conclusions

Giddens' work concerns the nature of social systems and does not involve considerations of technologies or the influence of technology on social life (Jones and Karsten 2008; Poole and DeSanctis 2003). However, Giddens' contributions (such as the framework to analyse social change that is presented in this chapter) are appealing to transforming enterprises, because of its focus on structures and on the processes by which those structures are used and modified over time. In addition, we elaborated on the structuration-foundation so that it may involve various elements of additional literature, such as De Caluwé and Vermaak (2003). Involvement of additional literature leverages users of the structuration-foundation to have a holistic perspective. Therefore, researchers and practitioners may understand transforming enterprises better.

Chapter 8
More than Engineering: The Role of Subcultures

Hella Faller

Abstract This chapter introduces the notion of organisational subculture to ACET. During an enterprise transformation, enterprise architects interact with many different stakeholder groups coming from different departments, having different roles, functions and mindsets. We argue that enterprise architects need to pay attention to the existing organisational subcultures to get the different stakeholders on board. In this chapter, we explain that cultural differences have an indirect impact on ACET and that communication is an important intermediary factor. We reflect on potential consequences of ignoring cultural differences in the context of ACET. Finally, we suggest developing a framework to analyse the role of cultural differences in ACET. To this end, we introduce four research questions.

8.1 Introduction

When coordinating enterprise transformations, enterprise architects have to interact with a variety of stakeholders. These stakeholders have different interests, expertise and concerns, which need to be considered when designing, implementing and communicating an EA (Op 't Land et al. 2008; van der Raadt et al. 2010). However, stakeholders also differ in terms of their way of working and their way of thinking, that is, their work-related *world view*.

The different world views existing in an organisation are referred to as organisational subcultures (Detert et al. 2000; Hofstede 1998; Schein 2004). Such subcultures can, for instance, differ in terms of their preferences regarding control, their

H. Faller
knk Business Software AG, Darmstadt, Germany
e-mail: hella.faller@gmail.com

© Springer International Publishing AG, part of Springer Nature 2017

H.A. Proper et al. (eds.), *Architectural Coordination of Enterprise Transformation*, The Enterprise Engineering Series, https://doi.org/10.1007/978-3-319-69584-6_8

motivation or their orientation towards co-workers (Detert et al. 2000; Hofstede et al. 2010). Literature on enterprise transformation acknowledges the importance of being aware of organisational subcultures and their impact on the transformation success (Detert et al. 2000; Rouse and Baba 2006). Yet, most enterprise architecture literature (e.g. Lankhorst 2012; Sowa and Zachman 1992; The Open Group 2011) is engineering oriented and, as such, does not account for the role of cultural differences. However, as cultural differences have an impact on the success of enterprise transformations, they are likely to also have an impact on the ACET.

In this chapter, we argue why cultural differences should be considered in the context of ACET (Sect. 8.3) and illustrate potential consequences of not taking into account cultural differences in ACET (Sect. 8.4). However, before addressing the relevance of organisational subcultures, we present our definition of organisational subculture (Sect. 8.2).

8.2 What is an Organisational Subculture?

Culture can be studied on different levels depending on the unit of analysis, for example, the national level (Hofstede 2001), organisational level (Detert et al. 2000; Hofstede et al. 2010; Schein 2004) or organisational-subgroup level (Detert et al. 2000; Hofstede 1998; Schein 2004). When considering stakeholder differences in EA-guided enterprise transformations, we study organisational subgroups. Thus, organisational subcultures are our unit of analysis.

Culture—as a generic term—has been defined in different ways by different authors. Schein (2004) defines culture as "*a pattern of shared basic assumptions that was learned by a group and it solved its problems of external adaption and internal integration, that has worked well enough to be considered valid and, therefore, to be taught to new members as the correct way to perceive, think, and feel in relation to those problems*".

To describe culture more precisely Schein (2004) compares it to an iceberg which has three levels: artefacts, espoused beliefs and values, and underlying assumptions (Fig. 8.1). The tip of the iceberg corresponds to a culture's *artefacts*, for example, language, technology, clothing or buildings. Furthermore, artefacts are easier to change than other parts of the culture. The middle part of the iceberg represents the culture's *espoused beliefs and values*. Those beliefs and values include strategies, philosophies and goals of a group and characterise what is perceived as right or wrong. Beliefs and values cannot be seen on the surface but need a bit of digging to discover them. Also, changing beliefs and values requires more effort and more time than changing artefacts. The lowest part of the iceberg symbolizes a culture's *underlying assumptions*. They are taken-for-granted perceptions or beliefs of the members of a culture. Assumptions are difficult to discover, similar to the bottom part of an iceberg, which is deep below sea level and has the largest circumference. Finally, assumptions are the most difficult to change part of the culture.

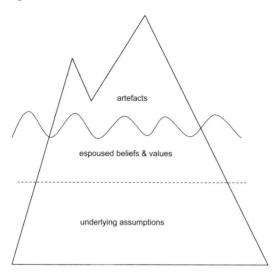

Fig. 8.1 The culture iceberg. © 2004 John Wiley & Sons, Inc.; reprinted with permission from Schein (2004)

The culture definitions of Schein (2004) and Hofstede et al. (2010) share that a culture is specific to a group. Hofstede et al. (2010) add the aspect of differentiating one culture from another one. In our own definition, we also consider that the adoption of a culture's values, etc., happens either consciously or unconsciously (Kraus et al. 2006). Thus, we define culture as *the sum of values, norms and attitudes, which are adopted consciously or unconsciously by the members of a group, and which distinguish the members of the group from those of another group*. In our research, we focus on organisational subgroups such as departments, hierarchy levels and functions.

8.3 Relevance of Organisational Subcultures in ACET

Traditional enterprise architecture approaches, such as the Zachman framework (Sowa and Zachman 1992), *The Open Group Architecture Framework* (TOGAF) (The Open Group 2011), CIMOSA (Computer Integrated Manufacturing Open System Architecture) (Kosanke 1995), ARIS (Architecture of Integrated Information Systems) (Scheer 2000) or TEAF (Treasury Enterprise Architecture Framework) (Department of the Treasury (United States of America) and Chief Information Officer Council 2000) are predominantly engineering oriented. They imply that change will be achieved by determining a clear result, that is, a to-be enterprise architecture, and by defining the steps to get to this result (Wagter et al. 2011).

These engineering-oriented frameworks largely ignore the influence of soft factors and especially organisational subculture. Yet, organisational subculture is considered an important factor of influence in enterprise transformation (Rouse and

Baba 2006). As a response, culture-oriented enterprise architecture approaches have emerged recently. GEA, for instance, focuses on the influence of enterprise coherence on the success of enterprise transformations (Wagter et al. 2011). GEA distinguishes several perspectives to govern a transformation, so as to improve the enterprise coherence (GEA 2011). One of these perspectives is organisational culture. In addition, Lange (2012) shows the importance of culture. He discusses enterprise architecture management culture, which is defined as the values and norms that are preferable when using EAM (Lange 2012). As one result of his study, which looks for factors that influence the success of enterprise architecture management, he concludes that cultural aspects have a direct impact on the use of enterprise architecture management and an indirect impact on the realisation of enterprise architecture management benefits. Thus, Wagter et al. (2011) as well as Lange (2012) strengthen the importance of cultural aspects in the context of enterprise architecture. However, they consider culture as just one of multiple factors. As a result, they do not go into detail regarding the question how organisational culture influences enterprise architecture.

In contrast, Steenbergen (2011) links specific cultural values to specific patterns of enterprise architecture techniques, for example, 'developing just enough architecture' or 'embedding enterprise architecture in the organisation'. She shows that the use of particular enterprise architecture techniques depends on three culture dimensions:

1. The degree of autonomy in an organisation
2. The attitude towards collaboration
3. An organisation's focus on either processes or results

For example, architects use different techniques to gain acceptance from division managers depending on the organisation's attitude towards collaboration. In collaborative organisations, architects would use the technique 'aligning the enterprise architecture format to the client perspective', while in less collaborative organisations they would use the technique 'making explicit the added value' (Steenbergen 2011). Aier (2014) analyses the role of organisational culture for the mechanisms of enterprise architecture principles,[1] namely, enterprise architecture principles grounding, enterprise architecture principles management, enterprise architecture principles guidance and enterprise architecture principles effectiveness, and their effects on enterprise architecture success. He concludes that organisational culture is a moderating factor for the relations between enterprise architecture principles mechanisms, their effects and enterprise architecture success. Based on his empirical study, Aier (2014) provides recommendations on how to best develop and introduce enterprise architecture principles in a given cultural environment (Aier 2014). Steenbergen (2011) and Aier (2014) focus on the influence of organisational culture on enterprise architecture. However, similarly to Wagter et al. (2011) and Lange

---

[1] Enterprise architecture principles are "*a restriction of design freedom for projects transforming enterprise architecture from an as-is state into a to-be state. An enterprise architecture principles should be based on corporate strategy. It does not include statements on particular business requirements but on the way these requirements are implemented*" (Aier 2014)

(2012), they focus on the organisational level of culture and do not study the impact of cultural diversity within an organisation.

Yet, in the field of enterprise transformation the importance of organisational sub-culture and of cultural differences is well acknowledged. Rouse and Baba (2006), for instance, state that next to the technical perspective, that is, the technical prob-lem that needs to be solved, enterprise transformations also comprise a behavioural perspective. The latter concerns *"the nature of human work groups and their inter-action with work processes; that is, how people are organised to accomplish work, how they interact with one another and with technology, and how they conceptu-alise work and understand the meaning of their actions"* (Rouse and Baba 2006). Following Niemietz et al. (2013), we interpret this perspective as a cultural perspec-tive where the nature of human work groups can be understood as organisational subcultures. The interaction with each other, the conceptualisation of the work and the understanding of the actions' meaning are related to the values and attitudes of a subgroup. Furthermore, a culture's norms concerning hierarchy and cooperation form the basis for the way people organise themselves (Niemietz et al. 2013).

Rouse and Baba (2006) consider organisations as socio-technical systems. Accordingly, they argue that during enterprise transformations an optimal solu-tion can only be reached when considering both the technical and the behavioural perspectives because they depend on each other. Likewise, van der Raadt et al. (2010) indicate that—next to technical EA means—the interaction between enter-prise architects and EA stakeholders is important for enterprise architecture to be effective. According to those authors, the main reason for enterprise architecture not being effective in practice, does not lie in the technical perspective—which seems to be handled well by practitioners—but in the behavioural perspective (van der Raadt et al. 2010). To account for the behavioural aspects of an enterprise transfor-mation, Rouse and Baba (2006) recommend that methodologies used in enterprise transformation should vary depending on the cultural context. Within ACET, this suggestion has the consequences that enterprise architects need to pay attention to the existing organisational subcultures when interacting with different enterprise ar-chitecture stakeholders (Fig. 8.2) to ensure to *"get them on board"*.

Figure 8.2 represents a simplification of stakeholder interactions taking place in ACET. As enterprise architects have the role of coordinators, they interact with the (key) stakeholder groups such as operations management or change manage-ment (van der Raadt et al. 2008). Furthermore, the different stakeholder groups communicate with each other. Note that the arrow between change management and project management exemplifies the interaction between stakeholder groups. (To avoid overcrowding, Fig. 8.2, we decided not to include more arrows for this type of interaction.) Finally, each stakeholder group comprises multiple individuals potentially belonging to different departments.

Cultural differences can exist between each of the represented groups, that is, on a departmental level or on a stakeholder-group level. The latter also includes the enterprise architects themselves who may be culturally different from (some of) the stakeholders they interact with. The cultural differences shown in Fig. 8.2 are likely to impact the effectiveness of ACET.

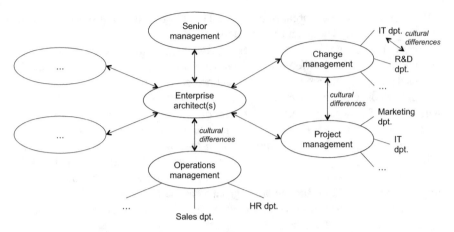

Fig. 8.2 Stakeholder diversity (© Springer-Verlag Berlin Heidelberg 2008; reprinted with permission from van der van der Raadt et al. 2008) and potential cultural differences in the context of enterprise architecture

8.4 Potential Consequences if Cultural Differences Are Ignored

Our earlier work (Niemietz et al. 2013) investigates the consequences of cultural differences for the work of enterprise architects in the context of enterprise transformations. The findings are based on semi-structured expert interviews with eleven senior enterprise architects and one management consultant familiar with enterprise architecture.

Our main findings are that (1) *cultural differences have an indirect impact on ACET* and (2) that *communication is an important intermediary factor* between cultural differences and the effectiveness of architects in enterprise transformations.

The findings of Niemietz et al. (2013) are summarised in Fig. 8.3. Specifically, Fig. 8.3 shows that cultural differences can cause the following communication defects: no shared frame of reference, inappropriate means of communication, inappropriate communication style, lack of communication and over-communication. Furthermore, Fig. 8.3 indicates how such defects may influence ACET. We now explain each of the links in further detail.

Subcultures can differ regarding the desired amount of communication (Niemietz et al. 2013). Here we find two communication defects: over-communication and lack of communication. Consider the scenario of an architect providing information during an enterprise transformation: when architects address a large number of subjects in a short period of time, they run the risk that some people perceive this as *over-communication*. As a result, the provided information may be treated as being irrelevant just because of the large amount of communication. Consequently, that group of people is likely not to commit to the transformation (Fig. 8.3).

However, the same amount of communication can be perfect for another group of people. Thus, if the architect adapts his entire communication to the first group of people, the second group will perceive this behaviour as a *lack of communication*.

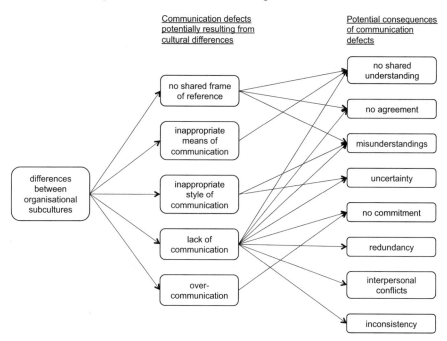

Fig. 8.3 Potential consequences of cultural differences and communication defects (adopted from Niemietz et al. 2013)

In the context of enterprise transformations, this is likely to lead to uncertainty in the group that prefers more communication (Fig. 8.3). This finding is also supported by literature on EA (Aier and Schelp 2010; Nakakawa et al. 2010a). The described scenario illustrates that different subcultures require a different amount of communication. Both too much and too little communication can have a negative impact on ACET. Therefore, enterprise architects need to be aware of such differences to be able to adapt the amount of communication to the respective preferences.

An illustrative scenario of cultural differences resulting in a lack of communication is shown in Fig. 8.4: a head of department of an enterprise receives a change request from an external customer. As the enterprise wants to use enterprise architecture to coordinate their enterprise transformations, the ideal procedure of handling such change requests is to first consult the architect to what extent the request fits the enterprise's architecture. However, in this particular scenario this procedure is not followed by the head of department due to cultural differences between the architect and the head of department (see upper part of Fig. 8.4). As the head of department wants to take his own decisions (autonomous decision-making), is short-term oriented and likes to work on his own (isolation), he does not consult the architect first. Instead, he directly accepts the change request. It results in the requested change conflicting with the enterprise's architecture. If the architect had been consulted, she would not have agreed to that project. Thus, in this scenario the cultural pro-

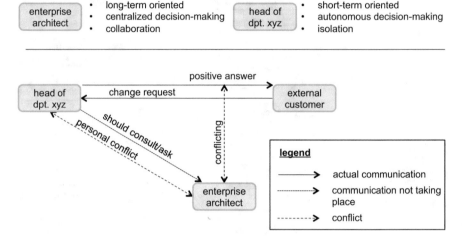

Fig. 8.4 Illustrative scenario of cultural differences decreasing the effectiveness of ACET

file of the head of department leads to behaviour that conflicts with the enterprise architecture.

A second potential conflict—this time on a personal level—may arise between the architect and the head of department: if the architect is not aware of the cultural differences between him and his colleague, he is likely to take his colleague's behaviour personally.

Another finding of Niemietz et al. (2013) is that the way of interpreting pictures and texts depends on a person's values and beliefs. Such differences in the *frames of reference* (Fig. 8.3) can be twofold: (1) two groups address different things using the same vocabulary, which leads to misunderstandings; (2) two groups address the same thing but use a different vocabulary and therefore do not understand each other. Both scenarios can cause disagreement among the stakeholders. The finding that cultural differences are a major challenge in achieving shared understanding is also emphasised in other contexts, such as software development (Nakakoji 1996). Given the important role of models in enterprise architecture having a shared frame of reference is particularly interesting in the context of ACET. However, if cultural differences are not taken into account, frames of reference are likely to differ among stakeholders without them being conscious about that. Also, subcultures differ in terms of their preferred *communication style* (Gilsdorf 1998; Niemietz et al. 2013). An example presented in Niemietz et al. (2013) refers to an architect who likes to build in small mistakes when communicating models. He discovers that similar minded people appreciate this communication style because they like to be challenged and can show that they notice the mistake. However, management's reaction to this style is completely different: this subculture does not interpret the mistake as an intended challenge but as a mistake as such, which triggers a feeling of uncertainty concerning the architect's expertise. As communication plays an important role in ACET, it is especially crucial that architects are aware of the different preferences regarding the communication style (Op 't Land et al. 2008; Steenbergen 2011). If such differences are not considered, architects are likely to encounter misunderstandings and uncertainty among the stakeholders (Fig. 8.3). As a consequence, architects risk that stakeholders will not involve them anymore.

Similar to the communication, style cultures can vary concerning their preferred *communication means* (Niemietz et al. 2013). For instance, some subcultures prefer face-to-face communication as their predominant communication means, whereas other subcultures prefer computer-based communication (Niemietz et al. 2013). Thus, the communication channel should be adapted to the audience at hand (Sledgianowski and Luftman 2005). Otherwise, a possible consequence is that important information is not perceived as such and therefore does not receive the required attention (see Fig. 8.3). This can result in a lack of shared understanding between two (or more) subcultures. To adapt the communication means to the audience, the respective persons need to be aware of the different preferences.

8.5 Conclusion

As discussed in this chapter, cultural differences are likely to have an indirect impact on the effectiveness of ACET. Particularly, cultural differences may influence communication. Figure 8.3 suggests different types of communication defects as consequences of not taking into account cultural differences. Such defects can result among others in uncertainty, a lack of shared understanding, redundancy or misunderstandings. To prevent or at least reduce those direct and indirect consequences architects need to be aware of organisational subcultures. To this end, we suggest developing a framework to analyse the role of cultural differences in ACET. Ideally, such a framework provides architects with potentially relevant cultural differences. In doing so, it helps architects to focus their attention. Furthermore, the framework should comprise a list of likely direct and indirect consequences of cultural differences. This could be an elaboration of the lists provided in Fig. 8.3. In addition, we consider it as important to study the links between cultural differences and the lists of consequences in more detail similar to the illustrative scenario presented in Fig. 8.4.

In summary, we suggest developing a framework that addresses the following questions:

Research Question 8.5.1 *What kind of cultural differences have a relevant impact on ACET?*

Research Question 8.5.2 *What are the direct consequences for ACET if cultural differences are not taken into account?*

Research Question 8.5.3 *What are the indirect consequences for ACET if cultural differences are not taken into account?*

Questions 8.5.1–8.5.3 aim at sensitising architects to organisational subcultures and at helping architects pay attention to relevant cultural aspects. Once architects are aware of the cultural differences relevant in the context of the respective enterprise transformation, they probably wish to take some action to reduce the negative impact on ACET. Therefore, another important question is:

Research Question 8.5.4 *How can architects intervene to prevent or reduce the direct consequences of cultural differences?*

Chapter 9
The Need for a Use Perspective on Architectural Coordination

Stefan Bischoff

Abstract This chapter highlights the importance of the use perspective for designing ACET. Based on a reflection of use-related information system literature and a review of the use-related enterprise architecture literature, the importance of the use perspective for the appropriate design of ACET is emphasised. Additionally, the importance of acceptance and use of ACET is identified as an important prerequisite for enterprise transformation support and benefit creation. From the users' perspective, ACET appears in the form of different artefacts (e.g. models, methods, and principles) that need to be specifically addressed by the management of ACET in order to ensure a use-centric design. Different groups of artefacts are identified that need to be embedded in the organisation differently following a use-centric perspective. Finally, the chapter proposes a research agenda that needs to be completed to design ACET from a use-centric perspective. The research agenda consists of four steps (understand user's behaviour, understand the acceptance of architectural coordination for supporting enterprise transformation, understand the continuous use of architectural coordination for supporting enterprise transformation, and design enterprise architecture/architectural coordination from a use-centric perspective) that are broken down into six research questions.

9.1 Introduction: The Importance of a Use Perspective on ACET

Enterprise architecture management has an image problem. As soon as employees hear the word enterprise architecture, *"eyes start to roll"* (Asfaw et al. 2009, p. 20 and further). This negative image has multiple causes. First, enterprise architecture management is perceived as restriction of design freedom because it allows

S. Bischoff
Institute of Information Management, University of St.Gallen, St. Gallen, Switzerland
e-mail: dv3_bischoff@web.de

© Springer International Publishing AG, part of Springer Nature 2017
H.A. Proper et al. (eds.), *Architectural Coordination of Enterprise Transformation*,
The Enterprise Engineering Series, https://doi.org/10.1007/978-3-319-69584-6_9

organisational change only within predefined boundaries (Dietz 2008; Hoogervorst 2009) and therefore limits employees' professional design freedom. Second, based on the tradition of enterprise architecture management and its origin from IT architecture (Schmidt and Buxmann 2011), it is mostly designed following a design-to-built (Marchand and Peppard 2008) approach. Architects design enterprise architecture artefacts (e.g. as-is and to-be models, methods, and principles) and offer the descriptive and prescriptive artefacts in the form of accessible information supply. Possible users (e.g. transformation managers) therefore are free to access the enterprise architecture artefacts or acquire the required information differently. As ACET aims at supporting enterprise transformation by providing appropriate enterprise architecture artefacts (i.e. architectural coordination), it should incorporate the use perspective and develop an understanding of how enterprise transformation managers use enterprise architecture artefacts and what influences their use behaviour. Consequently, the use perspective needs to be addressed during the design activities of ACET to ensure an effective and efficient final design.

In order to successfully address the transformation managers' needs and design ACET appropriately, the current approach of enterprise architecture design needs to be shifted from a design-to-built paradigm to a design-for-use paradigm (Marchand and Peppard 2008). In addition to shifting the design paradigm, architectural coordination managers need principles that help them to design their systems from a use-centric perspective (Marchand and Peppard 2008).

This chapter proceeds as follows: First, the importance of the use perspective for designing architectural coordination is highlighted from a general and an ET-specific point of view. Second, enterprise architecture artefacts are introduced as the interface between the architectural coordination functions and enterprise transformation managers. Third, an analysis of the state of the art of use-centric architectural coordination and enterprise architecture literature is presented, highlighting the lack of use-centric architectural coordination and enterprise architecture research. Fourth, a concept is presented that highlights the importance of distinguishing different classes of enterprise architecture artefacts from a use perspective, when it comes to designing enterprise architecture artefacts. Fifth, an agenda for researching ACET from a use-centric perspective is presented.

9.2 Importance of the Use of Architectural Coordination

The importance of the use of information systems, in general, has been widely discussed and researched in literature. Various studies highlight the importance of use for value creation of information system. Benbasat and Zmud (2003) state that "usage" is the direct prerequisite for information system impact and value creation.

From a practitioner point of view, value creation and therefore use is an important argument that helps managers to justify their budget for system development and operation. In times of rising cost pressures, the business-case-based justification of information system investments gains importance. Information systems should only be implemented and maintained if they contribute value to the organisation. Therefore, use behaviour needs to be one major target variable that managers need to influence to increase the value contribution of their systems and consequently keep their information systems and the unit they manage alive. High-value contribution helps to justify the existence and size of their unit, and to argue against cost and staff reductions that are initiated by senior management.

In scientific literature, use is traditionally researched from two perspectives. Initial use of an information system (i.e. acceptance) and ongoing (i.e. continuous, post-acceptance) use of an information system. Based on the theory of reasoned action (TRA) (Ajzen and Fishbein 1980; Fishbein and Ajzen 1975), Davis (1986) introduced the technology acceptance model (TAM) as one of the first theories related to the use of information systems (Davis 1986, 1989; Davis et al. 1989). This work and the related theory of planned behaviour (TPB) (Ajzen 1991) initiated a comprehensive research stream that intensively studies the users of information systems, their attitudes towards the information systems, and their acceptance (i.e. first-time use) behaviour. Subsequent models including TAM2 (Venkatesh and Davis 2000), TAM3 (Venkatesh and Bala 2008), the unified theory of acceptance and use of technology (UTAUT) (Venkatesh et al. 2003), and UTAUT2 (Venkatesh et al. 2012) enhance the level of explained variance of the dependent variable by adding additional constructs to the research models. While these theories focus on technology acceptance, another use-related research stream, which originated in the expectation confirmation theory (ECT) (Oliver 1977, 1980), investigates the continuous use intention (Bhattacherjee 2001; Bhattacherjee et al. 2008). Use-related research streams intensively study constructs like perceived usefulness, perceived ease of use, and behavioural use intentions of users towards different specific information systems (Hess et al. 2014).

The general models and theories aim at the use of information systems and mostly do not take the characteristics of specific types of information system into account. However, additional research is required to address specific questions and to rigorously research the use of ACET. Therefore, the use perspective needs to be sufficiently tailored to ACET in order to be helpful and applicable. Unless further specified, the understanding of use in the proposal at hand follows the view of Bhattacherjee (2001), who relies on the perspective of continuous use (i.e. continuity, ongoing, post-acceptance, and post-adoptive use) of an artefact.

Building upon the importance of use for impact creation and utility, the concept of value co-creation (Maglio and Spohrer 2008) applies to ACET. As with information systems in general, benefits of ACET are achieved in the users' specific use scenario and during the specific use process (Maglio and Spohrer 2008). In other words, the benefit creation of ACET is based on the individual transformation context of ACET users and the tasks that these users have to fulfil while applying ACET. The benefits are initially created on the level of the individual transformation and have an impact on the organisation in general.

Following the general acceptance- and use-related research streams, it becomes obvious that ACET managers need to aim at two goals from a use-centric perspective: First, they need to achieve the acceptance of architectural coordination for supporting enterprise transformation. Second, they need to apply measures to establish continuous ACET use behaviour during transformations to ensure an ongoing value creation through ACET.

9.3 ACET Artefacts from the Users' Perspective

From the users' perspective, architectural coordination can have different roles during an enterprise transformation:

1. It can appear as an information provider or supporter of different transformation activities (The Open Group 2011).
2. It is the restrictor of design freedom (Dietz 2008; Hoogervorst 2009; The Open Group 2011).

Thus, ACET appears in two different shapes, materialised in the form of artefacts, which support and impact enterprise transformation. Descriptive artefacts, in the form of as-is models, fulfil the information provider role and document the current state of an organisation's enterprise architecture. Prescriptive artefacts document the desired future state of the enterprise architecture, in the form of to-be models, and restrict enterprise transformation managers' freedom to act by defining standards and principles that need to be followed by any initiative (e.g. transformations) that has an effect on the enterprise architecture. Due to the fact that enterprise architecture artefacts are important interaction vehicles for ACET, architectural coordination managers need to pay special attention to the use-centric design of enterprise architecture artefacts for enterprise transformation support.

As a consequence, enterprise architecture artefacts not only need to be specifically designed in order to address the special needs of enterprise transformation from a content perspective but also need to be embedded in the overall organisation and enterprise architecture management landscape in the way that best addresses the requirements of enterprise transformation and enterprise transformation managers. The embedding of enterprise architecture artefacts in the organisation therefore needs to be aligned with the use preferences of enterprise transformation managers. Aspects that need to be considered include the way artefacts are accessed and the level of pressure that exists for using the artefact.

As discussed in more detail in Sect. 9.4, enterprise architecture is rarely considered as a means for supporting enterprise transformation. To address this issue and make sure that enterprise architecture artefacts are used in an enterprise transformation environment, architectural coordination preferences of enterprise transformation managers and their use behaviour concerning enterprise architecture artefacts need to be understood. Based on this understanding, the architectural coordination function as a whole (including the enterprise architecture artefacts and their embedment into the organisation) needs to be designed following the design-for-use paradigm. This makes sure that the architectural coordination function meets the requirements of potential users.

9.4 Relevant State of the Art of Use-Centricity in Literature

After the use perspective has been motivated from a practical perspective, a review of scientific literature is conducted to identify relevant concepts that help to design enterprise architecture artefacts and the organisational embedment of the architectural coordination function from a use-centric perspective.

In order to identify the most relevant publications, a literature search in the leading information systems and management science journals is conducted. The search is based on the *Senior Scholars' Basket of Journals* (Association for Information Systems 2011), the English language journals listed in the information systems and information management sub-ranking of the VHB Jourqual 2.1 ranking which are classified with a rating of 'A+', 'A', or 'B' (Verband der Hochschullehrer für Betriebswirtschaft 2011)[1] and a set of eight leading management journals (Barreto 2010).[2] All of these searches were limited to title and abstract.

For building the search term, synonyms of (continuous) use that are commonly used in scholarly literature are identified. Those are continuity, continuance (Bhattacherjee et al. 2008), ongoing use (Marchand and Peppard 2008), post-acceptance (Bhattacherjee 2001), post-adoptive use, and routinization (Cooper and Zmud 1990) of an artefact.

A first literature search with the term (using American English):

('architectural coordination' OR AC)

AND

(use OR usage OR continuity OR continuance OR post-acceptance OR routinization)

did not lead to any relevant results. Thus, the search term was extended. The more commonly used term for architectural coordination is enterprise architecture management. In order to include related literature in the analysis of the state of the art, the term: enterprise architecture and its abbreviation EA are also included in the search term for the literature search. The following search term (again, in American English) was therefore used:

('enterprise architecture' OR EA OR 'architectural coordination' OR AC)

AND

(use OR usage OR continuity OR continuance OR post-acceptance OR routinization)

This search resulted in 12 distinct results. Four publications were classified as relevant after an initial review of the titles and abstracts (Boh and Yellin 2007; Bradley et al. 2012; Peristeras and Tarabanis 2000; Ross and Beath 2006). The relevant

---

[1] Schrader and Hennig-Thurau (2009) present the method that is applied to create the VHB Jourqual rankings 2.x based on the predecessor ranking of Jourqual 2.1, which is Jourqual 2.

[2] The eight leading management journals according to Barreto (2010) are: Academy of Management Journal, Academy of Management Review, Administrative Science Quarterly, Journal of Management, Journal of Management Studies, Management Science, Organisation Science, and Strategic Management Journal.

literature is discussed below. Existing literature reviews addressing enterprise architecture management and the concept of architectural coordination are summarised and presented afterwards.

The research of Boh and Yellin (2007) focuses on the use of enterprise architecture standards. They identify measures that influence the use of different enterprise architecture standards and also hypothesise the effect of using defined standards. Their general research model hypothesises the effect of governance mechanisms on the use of enterprise architecture standards and contains four consequences of the use of enterprise architecture standards, namely reduced heterogeneity of physical IT infrastructure, reduced replication of IT infrastructure services, improved business application integration, and improved enterprise data integration. They empirically test and verify the impact of governance mechanisms on the use of enterprise architecture standards and therefore highlight the importance of well-defined and executed governance mechanisms on the use of one enterprise architecture artefact type (i.e. standards).

Bradley et al. (2012) as well as Ross and Beath (2006) base their research on the concept of enterprise architecture maturity and the related enterprise architecture maturity model that was published by Ross (2003). Bradley et al. (2012) explore the effect that enterprise architecture maturity has on the agility of an enterprise. They hypothesise this relationship using operational IT effectiveness and IT alignment as intermediary constructs and find the relation using the intermediary constructs to be significant based on a quantitative empirical approach. Ross and Beath (2006) focus on the effect that enterprise architecture maturity has on the selection of appropriate outsourcing strategies. They conclude with IT outsourcing strategies that are suitable for organisations that find themselves on different stages of enterprise architecture maturity.

Peristeras and Tarabanis (2000) address the aspect of enterprise architecture use in the setting of public administration. They incorporate the special characteristics of this setting into an enterprise architecture framework for public administration.

Additionally, relevant literature is identified in two domain specific academic outlets, the *Journal of Enterprise Architecture (JEA)* and the journal *Enterprise Modelling and Information Systems Architecture (EMISA)*. Google Scholar is used for searching these outlets with the term:

use OR usage OR continuity OR continuance OR 'post-acceptance' OR routinization

This search then resulted in 37 hits in JEA and one hit in EMISA from which seven (JEA) and zero (EMISA) are relevant.

The results can be assigned to one group which addresses application scenarios for EA (Bernard 2006; Greefhorst et al. 2013; Gryning et al. 2010; Niemann 2005) (also see below for a detailed analysis) and another group which discusses the value of enterprise architecture use (Cameron and McMillan 2013; Greefhorst et al. 2013; Niemann 2005; Rodrigues and Amaral 2010; Tamm et al. 2011a).

The rather small number of identified use-related papers in the area of enterprise architecture is also confirmed by published literature reviews. Extensive literature reviews highlight lacking use focus in the area of EA (Aier et al. 2008;

Mykhashchuk et al. 2011; Schönherr 2009; Simon et al. 2013). Existing enterprise architecture research specialises on creating a common understanding of the research stream itself (Aier et al. 2008; Schönherr 2009; Simon et al. 2013), the use scenarios and focus of enterprise architecture (e.g. layers between infrastructure and strategy (Winter and Fischer 2007) are addressed by enterprise architecture), EA's anchoring within the organisation (Aier et al. 2008), and details regarding enterprise architecture artefacts [i.e. representations of the as-is, and to-be architecture in the form of models as well as method fragments and principles for transferring an as-is into a to-be architecture (Schönherr 2009)].

To discover the application scenarios of enterprise architecture in practice, a second literature search is conducted using identical restrictions as above (journal list, limitation to title and abstract, database) and the following search term:

('enterprise architecture' OR EA OR 'architectural coordination' OR AC)
AND
(application OR apply OR utilization OR utilisation OR utilize OR utilise)

The search leads to seven unique results. After an initial review of titles and abstracts, three are relevant (Boh and Yellin 2007; Weiss 2010, 2012). Boh and Yellin (2007) discuss the support of compliance, programmes, as well as reduced heterogeneity of physical IT infrastructure, consolidation of IT infrastructure services, business application integration, and enterprise data integration as application scenarios for enterprise architecture. Weiss (2010) presents the enterprise architecture application scenarios based on one case and highlights the following scenarios: Facilitation of integration and standardisation, definition of major development direction and the reference architecture, government of processes and policies, supervision of project implementations, and identification of shared assets. Weiss (2012) lists the definition of technology and data standards and application integration as additional application scenarios.

Additionally, JEA and EMISA are searched using Google Scholar with the term:

application OR apply OR utilization OR utilisation OR utilize OR utilise

The search leads to 29 hits in JEA and one hit in EMISA from which five (JEA) and zero (EMISA) are relevant after a review of titles and abstract (Greefhorst et al. 2013; Gryning et al. 2010; Niemann 2005; Sidorova and Kappelman 2011; Winter et al. 2007). The applications scenarios that are discussed in the individual publications are listed in Table 9.1.

The review of the state-of-the-art literature reveals the missing use-focus in the existing architectural coordination and enterprise architecture body of knowledge despite the fact that a vast amount of application scenarios exists and is presented in literature (cf. Table 9.1). The only publication that was identified in top information systems and management journals is research by Boh and Yellin (2007) on the influence of governance mechanisms on the use of enterprise architecture standards and the benefits that the use of enterprise architecture standards has in organisations. The literature analysis is summarised in Fig. 9.1.

Table 9.1 Enterprise architecture application scenarios

ID	Application Scenario	Source
1	Compliance support	Boh and Yellin (2007), Greefhorst et al. (2013), Winter et al. (2007)
2	Programme support and project portfolio planning	Boh and Yellin (2007), Greefhorst et al. (2013), Weiss (2010), Winter et al. (2007)
3	Heterogeneity reduction of physical IT infrastructure	Boh and Yellin (2007)
4	Consolidation of IT infrastructure services	Boh and Yellin (2007)
5	Business application integration	Boh and Yellin (2007), Weiss (2012), Winter et al. (2007)
6	Enterprise data integration	Boh and Yellin (2007), Winter et al. (2007)
7	Integration and standardisation	Bernard (2006), Weiss (2010, 2012)
8	Definition of major development direction and the reference architecture	Greefhorst et al. (2013), Weiss (2010)
9	Government of processes and policies	Niemann (2005), Weiss (2010)
10	Identification of shared assets	Weiss (2010)
11	IT business alignment	Gryning et al. (2010), Sidorova and Kappelman (2011), Winter et al. (2007)
12	Business continuity planning	Winter et al. (2007)
13	Security management	Winter et al. (2007)
14	Technology risk management	Winter et al. (2007)
15	Project initialisation	Greefhorst et al. (2013), Winter et al. (2007)
16	Business process optimisation	Winter et al. (2007)
17	Quality management	Winter et al. (2007)
18	Post-merger integration	Winter et al. (2007)
19	Adoption of commercial off-the-shelf software	Winter et al. (2007)
20	Sourcing decisions	Greefhorst et al. (2013), Winter et al. (2007)
21	IT service management	Winter et al. (2007)
22	IT operations costs management	Winter et al. (2007)
23	IT consolidation	Winter et al. (2007)
24	Strategic, tactical, and operational decision support	Greefhorst et al. (2013)
25	System requirements determination	Greefhorst et al. (2013)
26	Knowledge transfer	Greefhorst et al. (2013)
27	Stimulation of discussion	Greefhorst et al. (2013)
28	Capability-based planning	Greefhorst et al. (2013)

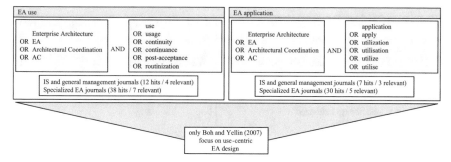

Fig. 9.1 Summary of enterprise architecture use and enterprise architecture application literature

The research agenda proposed in this chapter aims at addressing this research gap with a special focus on the use of the architectural coordination function and enterprise architecture artefacts for supporting enterprise transformation. In conclusion, the agenda advocates the use-centric design of ACET.

9.5 Managerial Implications for Architectural Artefacts

Enterprise architecture artefacts represent the interface between the architectural coordination function and the transformation manager. Therefore, the artefacts need to be designed from a use-centric perspective. Bischoff et al. (2014) find four different classes of enterprise architecture artefacts that can be distinguished from a use-centric perspective based on the use intensity in practice and their susceptibility for pressure to use the artefact. Bischoff et al. (2014) argue that artefacts need to be designed and managed differently depending on their characteristics in both dimensions. The resulting matrix is visualised in Fig. 9.2.

The quadrants can be interpreted as follows (Bischoff et al. 2014):

1. The enterprise architecture superstar class consists of enterprise architecture artefacts which show a beyond median use intensity and a below median impact of pressure on use intensity. Enterprise architecture superstars are used even in the absence of pressure (Bischoff et al. 2014).

2. The enterprise architecture shelf-warmer class consists of enterprise architecture artefacts that are used with below median intensity and show below median impact of pressure on use intensity. Enterprise architecture shelf-warmer artefacts are mainly enterprise architecture principles, for example, "*shared use of data*", "*consistent definitions*", and "*reusability*" (Bischoff et al. 2014).

3. The enterprise architecture annoyances class consists of artefacts that are used with a below median intensity and show an above median impact of pressure on use intensity. Even though pressure has an above median impact on use, it is not applied in practice in order to influence the use intensity. Consequently, artefacts

	I – EA superstars	EA pressure beneficiaries – IV
High use intensity	A.3 Process map A.4 Model of organizational structure A.5 Role catalog A.6 Map of applications A.8 Platform model A.9 Hardware landscape A.24 Ease of use A.26 Standardization	A.1 Product catalog A.2 Map of company goals A.15 Target application landscape A.17 Roadmap A.19 Business Continuity
Low use intensity	A.7 Data model A.21 Shared use of data A.22 Consistent definitions A.23 Being independent of technologies A.25 Reusability II – EA shelf-warmers	A.10 Business interaction matrix A.11 Application / data matrix A.12 Application / organization matrix A.13 Application / technology matrix A.14 Target process map A.16 Target hardware landscape A.18 Programs A.20 TCO analysis EA annoyances – III
	Low impact of pressure on use intensity	High impact of pressure on use intensity

Fig. 9.2 Four classes of enterprise architecture artefacts. © 2014 IEEE. Reprinted, with permission, from Bischoff et al. (2014)

associated with this quadrant do not have perceived value for the organisation and managers do not foster their use by applying pressure (Bischoff et al. 2014).

4. The enterprise architecture pressure beneficiaries class consists of artefacts that are used with an above median level of intensity and show an above median impact of pressure on use intensity. Consequently, either pressure is applied towards using the artefacts or the artefacts are used on a voluntary basis because their benefits are perceived by the users (Bischoff et al. 2014).

This previous study highlights the importance of situative and artefact-specific design and management of enterprise architecture artefacts that can also be used in different ways to support an enterprise transformation. To foster continuous use, artefacts need to be designed and managed depending on the class they belong to.

Thus, an initial step of research should (1) identify which artefacts are important for enterprise transformation and then (2) determine, based on the artefacts' classification, suitable design and management strategies.

9.6 Conclusion

In putting the users in the main focus of the ACET design goal, it is important to first understand their interaction with the architectural coordination function during an enterprise transformation. Therefore, the initial research step needs to create a profound understanding of enterprise transformation managers' use behaviour and their interaction with the architectural coordination functions. In order to obtain this understanding, the following two research questions need to be answered:

Research Question 9.6.1 *How are enterprise architecture artefacts used in practice to support enterprise transformation?*

Research Question 9.6.2 *How can enterprise architecture artefacts that are used in enterprise transformation be classified?*

Both research questions contribute to the research objective: *Understand how enterprise architecture artefacts are used during enterprise transformation.*

After the user interaction has been understood, further understanding needs to be established regarding the factors that influence enterprise transformation managers' initial and continuous use of ACET. As acceptance is the initial step of information system adoption and therefore a prerequisite for continuous use (Bhattacherjee et al. 2008; Cooper and Zmud 1990; Venkatesh et al. 2003), corresponding factors and cause–effect relations (Chmielewicz 1994) need to be identified first. Thus, the identification of factors that influence the *acceptance* of ACET represents part one of the second step of the research agenda. The identification of factors influencing the *continuous* use of ACET represents part two of the second step of the proposed research agenda. Consequently, the following research questions need to be answered in the second step:

Research Question 9.6.3 *Which factors influence the acceptance of enterprise architecture artefacts for supporting an enterprise transformation?*

Research Question 9.6.4 *Which factors influence the continuous use of enterprise architecture artefacts for supporting enterprise transformation?*

Both research questions contribute to the research objective: *Understand the use of architectural coordination for supporting enterprise transformation.*

After the influencing factors for ACET acceptance and continuous use are identified, the cause–effect relations need to be converted into means–ends relations (Chmielewicz 1994) that are represented by suitable design principles and management guidelines contributing to acceptance and continuous use of ACET (step three of the proposed research agenda). Consequently, the research questions are:

Research Question 9.6.5 *How do enterprise architecture artefacts need to be designed from a use-centric point of view to ensure their acceptance for enterprise transformation support?*

Research Question 9.6.6 *How do enterprise architecture artefacts need to be designed from a use-centric point of view to ensure their continuous use for enterprise transformation support?*

Both research questions contribute to the research objective: *Design ACET from a use-centric perspective.*

The answers to the previously presented research questions help to design ACET from a use-centric perspective. Another important task towards a comprehensive embedment of ACET is to completely anchor ACET within the organisation and institutionalise it (Weiss et al. 2013). This aspect is presented in Chap. 12 in more detail.

The use perspective is also central to enterprise architecture models. Models can become "*boundary objects*" and play a vital role in establishing shared understanding during an enterprise transformation, but only when they are designed from a use-centric perspective. Principles to that effect are provided in Chap. 19.

Chapter 10
Enterprise Coherence Governance: Involving the Right Stakeholders

Roel Wagter and Hend*erik* A. Proper

Abstract In this chapter, we argue that ACET requires the involvement of (at least) two complementary types of frameworks. From a Blue-print thinking perspective, a design framework is needed to structure the actual architectural design thinking. Existing frameworks such as Zachman, IAF, Dya and TOGAF are candidates for the role of the design framework. Which of these frameworks fits best a specific organisation depends on the type of organisation and the best fitting design philosophy. Next to a design framework, the Yellow-print thinking perspective suggests the use of an organisation-specific engagement framework that is concerned with the question of which groups of stakeholders to include in enterprise architecture decision-making during an enterprise transformation, and how to operationally engage them. This framework depends, more than a design framework, on the (strategic) priorities of the organisation, and the stakeholders involved in enterprise transformations. Moreover, depending on the scope and impact of an actual enterprise transformation, more situation-specific tuning of the engagement framework may be needed. The engagement framework suggested by the GEA method involves the (organisation-specific) enterprise coherence dashboards.

10.1 Introduction

Efforts to transform an enterprise, from its business processes to the underlying IT, often fail. In Op 't Land et al. (2008), the authors provide a summary of possible causes for failures of strategic initiatives: "*The road from strategy formulation to*

R. Wagter (✉)
Solventa B.V., 3439 ML Nieuwegein, The Netherlands
e-mail: roel.wagter@solventa.nl

H.A. Proper
Luxembourg Institute of Science and Technology, Esch-sur-Alzette, Luxembourg

© Springer International Publishing AG, part of Springer Nature 2017   99
H.A. Proper et al. (eds.), *Architectural Coordination of Enterprise Transformation*,
The Enterprise Engineering Series, https://doi.org/10.1007/978-3-319-69584-6_10

strategy execution, including the use of programmatic steering, is certainly not an easy one to travel. Research shows that less than 60% of the strategic objectives in organisations are reached". In addition, our own experiences with enterprise transformations in practice also indicate that existing methods and frameworks for enterprise architecture often fail to contribute to the success of such transformation projects.

As argued by Op 't Land et al. (2008) and Wagter (2009), architecture should offer senior management the means to obtain insight, and to make decisions about the direction of enterprise transformations. As such, it should act as a means to steer enterprise transformations, while in particular enable senior management to govern coherence. In 2006, these experiences and insights triggered the consultancy firm Ordina to initiate a multi-client research programme, resulting in the development of the GEA method (Wagter et al. 2007; Wagter 2009). As a prelude to the actual development of GEA, in line with design science (Hevner et al. 2004), a survey was conducted among the participating organisations to identify the requirements on GEA. This survey showed that these experiences were not limited to Ordina only, but was shared among a broad range of client organisations participating in the programme. The underlying issues were also considered grave enough for the participating client organisations to indeed co-invest, in terms of time and money, in the development of GEA.

This chapter and Chap. 18 are based on elements from the GEA method, in particular those pertaining to the involvement of the right stakeholders.

10.2 Beyond Engineering

Enterprise transformations typically touch upon various aspects of an enterprise, while the resulting changes are likely to have a profound and lasting impact (see Sect. 1.2). As a result, enterprise transformations involve many stakeholders with differing stakes and interests, who will try to influence the direction and/or speed of the transformation accordingly.

As suggested in general project/programme management approaches (Franckson and Verhoef 1999; PMI 2001; Axelos 2009), it is important to manage the interests and stakes of stakeholders explicitly. This particularly applies to situations where there is a large variety of stakeholders involved, such as enterprise transformations.

As also argued in Chap. 8, stakeholder communication in enterprise transformation requires more than an engineering approach. Several existing architecture approaches and frameworks, such as Zachman (Sowa and Zachman 1992), DYA (Wagter et al. 2005), Abcouwer (Abcouwer et al. 1997), Henderson and Venkatraman (Henderson and Venkatraman 1993), TOGAF (The Open Group 2009), IAF (van't Wout et al. 2010), and ArchiMate (Lankhorst 2012; Iacob et al. 2009), advocate a rather "engineering-oriented" style of communicating with senior management and stakeholders in general. The architecture frameworks underlying each of these approaches are very much driven by "engineering principles", and as such correspond to a Blue-print style of thinking about change (De Caluwé and Vermaak

2003). To act as a steering instrument for senior management, a Blue-print style of thinking, however, does not suffice. Stakeholder interests, formal and informal power structures within enterprises, and the associated processes of creating win-win situations and forming coalitions, should also be taken into consideration. In terms of De Caluwé (De Caluwé and Vermaak 2003), this is more the Yellow-print style of thinking about change.

In the remainder of this chapter, we will therefore start by exploring the underlying causes that drive the need to explicitly manage stakeholders during enterprise transformations in terms of *social complexity* and *fragmentation* (Sect. 10.3). We then continue by considering the impact of fragmentation on enterprise transformation, in particular its impact on *enterprises coherence* and the need to govern this coherence explicitly (Sect. 10.4). This then provides us the insight to formulate specific requirements towards approaches for ACET (Sect. 10.5).

10.3 Stakeholder Fragmentation in Enterprise Transformation

To explain how social complexity may seriously jeopardise the success of a project and/or programme, Conklin (2003b) has coined the term *fragmentation*:

> Fragmentation suggests a condition in which the people involved see themselves as more separate than united, and in which information and knowledge are chaotic and scattered. The fragmented pieces are, in essence, the perspectives, understandings, and intentions of the collaborators.

Conklin (2003b) also argues that stakeholder *fragmentation* is one of the key forces that threatens the success of projects and/or programmes (such as enterprise transformations). There is a clear danger that stakeholder variety, and the potential fragmentation it may cause, is not seen and/or acknowledged on time. As Conklin (2003b) states:

> Fragmentation can be hidden, as when stakeholders don't even realise that there are incompatible tacit assumptions about the problem, and each believes that his or her understandings are complete and shared by all.

Conklin (2003b) identifies two core factors that contribute towards fragmentation: *social complexity* and *wickedness*. Below we will discuss these factors in more detail.

As discussed in Sect. 1.2, local optimisation may have a detrimental effect on the ability of enterprise transformations to meet their goals. We argue that this tendency for "local optimisation" is actually a symptom of stakeholder fragmentation.

10.3.1 Social Complexity

Conklin (2003b) introduces the notion of social complexity as the number and diversity of stakeholders involved in a project. In terms of this definition, if the number of stakeholders and influencers of an enterprise transformation increases, and/or the diversity of their stakes increases, then the social complexity of the enterprise transformation is also said to increase.

Specific stakeholders might even harbour contradicting stakes and interests themselves. Such contradictions might for example involve short-term needs vs. long-term needs, and local (business unit) needs vs. global (enterprise-wide) needs. The actual prioritisation between such needs may depend on the role/perspective the stakeholder takes. Therefore, when "counting" the number of stakeholders it is actually better to think in terms of *stakeholder roles* rather than merely counting people.

Stakes and interests are not the only contributors to the *diversity* of the players involved in an enterprise transformation. As discussed in Chap. 8, cultural diversity is also a major factor influencing success and failure of transformations, as it largely determines the attitudes of stakeholders towards the way they regard the world, their position in negotiations, their attitude to changes, etc. This can be summarised by the pseudo formula:

$$social\ complexity = \#\ stakeholder\ roles \times diversity\ of\ stakes \times diversity\ of\ cultures$$

10.3.2 Wickedness

Another major factor contributing to stakeholder fragmentation is the inherent complexity of the "problem" that is to be "solved" by the project/programme. Large-scale transformations of enterprises tend to behave as *wicked problems* (Rittel and Webber 1973; Conklin 2003b). As discussed by Conklin (2003b) and Head and Alford (2015), *wicked problems* distinguish themselves from *tame problems* in that:

- A wicked problem is not understood until after the formulation of a possible solution.
- Solutions to wicked problems are not simply right or wrong. One might be better than the other, but there is no clear right or wrong.
- Wicked problems have no clear stopping rule, that is, it is not clear when the problem has been solved.
- Every wicked problem is essentially novel and unique.
- Every solution to a wicked problem is a "one shot" operation. Trying out a possible solution (if possible at all), will already alter the circumstance towards future attempts.
- Wicked problems have no clear given alternative solutions.

It should be noted here that *tame* problems are not necessarily *easy* problems. For example, Fermat's *Last Theorem* (no three positive integers a, b, and c can satisfy the equation $a^n + b^n = c^n$ for any integer value of n greater than two), is indeed a hard problem. At the same time, however, it is a highly tame problem.

Enterprise transformations are wicked by nature in the sense that more often than not, the precise requirements of a solution are not known clearly beforehand. It is also not clear what challenges may have to be overcome "along the way", while the circumstances/context under/in which the transformation takes place changes during the transformation.

As mentioned before, the factors of *wickedness* and *social complexity* actually amplify each other (Conklin 2003b). This can be summarised by the pseudo formula:

$$fragmentation = wickedness \times social\ complexity$$

10.4 The Need to Govern Enterprise Coherence

Enterprise architecture is generally positioned as a means to steer and coordinate enterprise transformations. As argued by Op 't Land et al. (2008) and Wagter (2009) for example, architecture should offer senior management the means to obtain insight in, and to make decisions about, the direction of enterprise transformations. As such, it should act as a means to steer the direction of enterprise transformations. At the same time, however, experience in practice shows (Wagter 2009) that enterprise architecture fails to deliver on its promise to steer the direction of a transformation, and essentially succumbs to the powers of stakeholder fragmentation.

10.4.1 Enterprise Coherence Governance

Wagter (2009) results from the multi-year and multi-party research project GEA. This programme was triggered by the observation that enterprise architecture fails to deliver on its promises. A survey (Wagter et al. 2007) held at the start of the GEA research programme showed that key triggers for the participants to participate in the programme were indeed:

- Many enterprise transformation efforts fail
- Failing to adopt a holistic approach to address key business issues frequently resulted in a unilateral approach from an IT-oriented perspective
- Existing architecture methods fall short in meeting their promises because:
    - They are set up from an IT perspective only
    - They hardly address the strategic level of the organisation
    - They are set up in terms of the Business/IT gap
    - Their underlying IT architectures applied on the enterprise-wide level are unjustly called EAs

The GEA programme took the following as its driving hypothesis (Wagter et al. 2013a; Wagter 2013):

> the overall performance of an enterprise is positively influenced by a proper coherence among the key aspects of the enterprise, including business processes, organisational culture, product portfolio, human resources, information systems, IT support, etc.

where *enterprise coherence* is defined as:

The extent to which all relevant aspects of an enterprise are connected, necessary to let the enterprise meet its desired results.

What is to be regarded as relevant aspects, as referred to in the above definition, is organisation-dependent. Moreover, the clarity (and resolve) with which an organisation has identified/prioritised these aspects is one of the parameters determining their ability/maturity to govern enterprise coherence. In Wagter et al. (2012d, pp. 28–52), we have discussed the concept of the (organisation-specific) coherence dashboard, which enables organisations to precisely express the relevant aspects that need to be connected.

As argued above, during enterprise transformations, *stakeholder fragmentation* is likely to have a negative impact on enterprise coherence, unless explicitly governed. A key first step in the aforementioned GEA programme was the development of an Enterprise Coherence-governance Assessment (ECA) (Wagter et al. 2011, 2012d) to obtain a clearer understanding of the challenges to enterprise coherence and its associated governance of coherence, as well as the impact of enterprise coherence governance on organisational performance. An assessment (Wagter et al. 2011) done among the participating organisations showed that more then 85% of the organisations involved in the first ECA studies lack explicit enterprise coherence governance as part of their traditional enterprise architecture approaches.

10.4.2 Beyond Blue-Print Thinking

The driving hypothesis of the above mentioned GEA programme was translated to the ambition to extend the means of enterprise architecture management with the ability to better govern enterprise coherence (Wagter 2013; Wagter et al. 2011, 2012a,b, 2013b). As a result, the main challenge facing the GEA programme (Wagter 2009, 2013) was to develop a strategy to better manage stakeholder fragmentation, and as a result better govern enterprise coherence.

To enable enterprise architecture management to better deal with (potential) stakeholder fragmentation, it was necessary to, as also argued in Chap. 8, look beyond a traditional "engineering style" of thinking. To more precisely define what is meant by "engineering style", we turn to the work of De Caluwé and Vermaak (2003), who have identified a number of core perspectives on change processes in organisations:

Yellow-print thinking—Bring the interests of the most important players together by means of a process of negotiation enabling consensus or a win-win solution.

Blue-print thinking—Formulate clear goals and results, then design rationally a systematic approach and then implement the approach according to plan.

Red-print thinking—Motivate and stimulate people to perform best they can, contracting and rewarding desired behaviour with the help of HRM-systems.

Green-print thinking—Create settings for learning by using interventions, allowing people to become more aware and more competent on their job.

White-print thinking—Understand what underlying patterns drive and block an organisation's evolution, focusing interventions to create space for people's energy.

When we used the term "engineering style", we, therefore, actually refer to a Blueprint style of thinking. As suggested by De Caluwé and Vermaak (2003), it is recommendable to also take the other (complementary) perspectives into consideration when changing/transforming (parts of) an enterprise

Traditional enterprise architecture approaches and frameworks, including, for example, the Zachman (Sowa and Zachman 1992) and IAF (van't Wout et al. 2010) frameworks, the ArchiMate language (Lankhorst 2012; Iacob et al. 2012), as well as the DYA (Wagter et al. 2005) and TOGAF (The Open Group 2011) architecture methods, essentially take a Blue-print perspective on change. Each of these approaches is based on an a priori fixed *design philosophy* in terms of which different perspectives are identified, usually going from *business* to IT (the so-called Business-to-IT stack). The identified perspectives, are solely based on a *prescriptive* design philosophy, following a pure rational line of reasoning (i.e. following Blue-print style of thinking), rather than on the actual stakes and interests of the key stakeholders in a specific organisations. The latter would require the inclusion of a more Yellow-print style of thinking.

When indeed including a Yellow-print style of thinking, it also becomes necessary to look beyond the traditional Business-to-IT stack focus of most existing enterprise architecture approaches and frameworks, which has also been identified by Proper and Lankhorst (2014) as one of the important trends in enterprise architecture. Case studies involving the use of GEA (e.g. Wagter et al. 2012b) indeed also support this view. We return to this issue in Sect. 10.5.

10.4.3 Engaging Stakeholders

Including a Yellow-print style of thinking in enterprise architecture practices would also suggest the integration of methods and techniques such as the Soft-Systems Methodology (Checkland 1981), Group Based Modelling (Vennix 1996), Collaboration Engineering (Briggs 2004; Briggs et al. 2006), IBIS (Conklin 2003a), and Dialogue Mapping (Conklin 2005) into an approach for ACET.

Early results on the use of such techniques to better involve stakeholders of enterprise transformations can be found in, for example, Nabukenya (2005, 2009), and Nabukenya et al. (2007, 2009) in terms of collaborative strategies to formulate policies/principles for Business-IT alignment, and in Nakakawa et al. (2011a, 2010b) and Nakakawa (2012) in terms of a collaborative approach for the formulation of enterprise architectures.

Some of these results have been operationalised in terms of, for example, GEA's enterprise coherence dashboard (Wagter et al. 2012a, 2013a) and the CAEDA approach (Nakakawa et al. 2013, 2011b; Nakakawa 2012).

10.5 Requirements for Enterprise Coherence Governance

As argued by Op 't Land et al. (2008) and Wagter (2009), architecture offers a means for management to obtain insight into the organisational structure, as well as to make decisions about the direction of enterprise transformations. As such, it should act as a means to steer enterprise transformations, while in particular enabling senior management to govern the enterprise's coherence. We regard enterprise architecture as the appropriate means to make enterprise coherence explicit, as well as controllable/manageable, or at least influenceable.

The GEA project (Wagter 2009) used four key sources to identify the requirements for enterprise coherence governance:

1. The involvement of stakeholders, and senior management in particular
2. Management control
3. Change management
4. General systems theory

Below we discuss these requirements in more detail. Requirements we would consider to be not only relevant to the GEA project, but to architectural coordination in general.

10.5.1 Stakeholder Involvement

Effective governance of enterprise coherence requires an active involvement of senior management. This, however, implies two important requirements:

Strategy driven—It is necessary to take the concerns, and associated strategic dialogues, of senior management as a starting point. In other words, the way in which architecture is integrated into the strategic dialogue should take the concerns, language, and style of communication of senior management as a starting point. When not doing so, it will be difficult to really involve senior management. Moreover, the strategic dialogues provide the starting point for steering enterprise transformations and to guard coherence.

Respecting social forces—The social forces within an enterprise, be they political, informal, or cultural in nature, should be a leading element in governing enterprise coherence. As discussed in the introduction, an important reason for using architecture to steer and coordinate enterprise transformations is the fact that those design decisions which, in principle, transcend the interests of a specific project can be guarded/enforced that way.

Doing so, however, also requires a strong commitment from senior management to these design decisions. Local business stakeholders, such as business unit managers, who have a direct interest in the outcome of a project, may want to lead projects in a different direction (more favourable to their own local/short-term interests) than would be desirable from an enterprise-wide perspective. Such divergent forces are also likely to lead to erosion of the desired enterprise coherence. This explains the need to reduce the space for own interpretation on lower management levels by substantiating the decisions, made on strategic level, with unambiguous arguments harmonising all concerns at stake.

As argued above, existing architecture approaches (Sowa and Zachman 1992; van't Wout et al. 2010; Lankhorst 2012; Iacob et al. 2012; Wagter et al. 2005; The Open Group 2011) operate from a Blue-print style of thinking. The above requirements clearly suggest the use of another style of thinking in terms of stakeholder interests, formal and informal power structures within enterprises, as well as the associated processes of creating win-win situations and forming coalitions. According to De Caluwé and Vermaak (2003), this would be more of a Yellow-print style of thinking about change. In the GEA programme, the latter line of thinking was taken as a starting point, by taking the perspective that the actual social forces and associated strategic dialogues within an enterprise should be taken as a starting point, rather than the frameworks of existing architecture approaches, suggesting the full makeability of an organisation.

The latter does not imply that the existing "Blue-print style frameworks" are not useful. On the contrary. An engineering perspective is much needed. At the same time, it needs to be embedded in a Yellow-print-oriented process. Architecture models produced from an engineering perspective potentially provide thorough underpinning of the views, sketches, and models used in the strategic dialogues with senior management. However, rather than structuring the models and views in terms of 'information architecture', 'application architecture', and 'infrastructure', they would have to be structured based on those domains that are meaningful within the strategic and political dialogue in an enterprise, for example, in terms of 'human resourcing', 'clients', 'regulators', 'culture', 'intellectual property', and 'suppliers'. Needless to say that this is also highly organisation-specific.

10.5.2 Management Control

One of the leading theories in the field of management control is "*Levers of Control*" by Simons (1994). Simons identifies the following levers of control:

1. Diagnostic control systems used to monitor and adjust operating performance
2. Belief systems that communicate core values such as mission statements, credos, and vision statements
3. Boundary systems that define the limits of freedom, such as codes of conduct and statements of ethics

Table 10.1 Enterprise coherence governance requirements from a management control perspective

Lever of control	Requirement
Diagnostic control systems	Goals have to be an element of enterprise coherence at the level of the purpose of an organisation and objectives an element of enterprise coherence at the design level of an organisation
Belief systems	The level of purpose of the organisation must be within the scope of enterprise architecture This requirement is associated with the previously mentioned requirement *scope*
Boundary systems	Boundaries must be made explicit since boundaries define relations between angles of an organisation and as such form a basic asset of enterprise coherence
Interactive control systems	The effect of intended strategic interventions on the enterprise coherence should be made clear interactively and beforehand

4. Interactive control systems that provide strategic feedback and vehicles to update and redirect strategy such as competitive analysis and market reports

These levers of control led us to the following insights. To give direction on a strategic level we have to distinguish between a *sustainable* purpose and a *changeable* shape of an organisation. The purpose is formulated on the level of purpose and the shape is described on the design level. Belief systems typically contribute to the level of purpose. This leads to the requirements for enterprise coherence governance, as shown in Table 10.1.

10.5.3 Change Management

A third foundation for requirements on enterprise coherence governance is based on the notion that organisations are a social technical combination of humans and supporting technology. Here we refer to the work of Balogun et al. (2003): "*Exploring Strategic Change*". The basic idea is that every choice made in a change process should be based on the context and the purpose of the change process. A study conducted by Reitsma et al. (2004) "*What is the best change approach*" has enhanced this basic idea with the statement that there is a link between the choice of approach and purpose of the change. Since this study concerns successful change processes (in various sectors), the conclusion has been drawn that it is sensible regarding change processes to consider on which organisational aspects the change is essentially focused and in line with this to choose an appropriate approach.

Based on these insights the requirements on enterprise coherence governance as formulated in Table 10.2 were derived.

Table 10.2 Enterprise coherence governance requirements from a change management perspective

Socio-technical combinations	Requirement
Choice made in a change process should be based on the context and the purpose	The scope of enterprise coherence governance should include both internal and external angles of the organisational transaction environment
	The purpose of a change process should be in line with the goals on the level of purpose and objectives on the design level
	The organisational aspects that are dominant in the solution for a business issue, determine the choice of approach
	Every change process should be argued by the application of the enterprise coherence governance before execution
Choice of an appropriate approach determines the success	The *solution direction and choice of approach* should be just one element of the decision
	Regarding the decision-making process, enterprise coherence governance should contribute to both the solution direction and choice of approach of a business issue
	Enterprise coherence governance should guide the realisation of the *solution direction and choice of approach* of a business issue
	An appropriate approach needs appropriate enterprise coherence products

10.5.4 General Systems Theory

The second theoretical foundation concerns the general systems (cybernetics) perspective, where an organisation is seen as a controllable open system (de Leeuw 1982). The control paradigm, as introduced by de Leeuw (1982) and de Leeuw and Volberda (1996) for example, identifies a set of conditions for effective control. Compliance with these conditions also implies a promise, namely to achieve an effective control situation. These conditions are (de Leeuw 1982; de Leeuw and Volberda 1996):

1. The controlling system must have a goal to guide it in governing the controlled system.
2. The controlling system must have a model of the controlled system.
3. The controlling system must have information about the controlled system, namely the state of the specified system parameters and subsequent acting environment variables.
4. The controlling system must have sufficient control variety.
5. The controlling system must have sufficient information processing capacity to transform information (3), using a model (2), taking into account the objectives (1) into effective control measures (4).

Based on these conditions for effective control the requirements for enterprise coherence governance as listed in Table 10.3 were derived.

Table 10.3 Enterprise coherence governance requirements from a general systems perspective

Conditions for effective control	Requirement
Specify a goal to the controlled system	Objectives have to be an element of enterprise coherence at the design level of an organisation
Have a model of the controlled system	The model of enterprise coherence must represent the dynamics of the design level of an organisation
Have actual information about the controlled system	The actual state of enterprise coherence must be represented on a permanent basis, including current state as well as future directions
Have sufficient control variety	Enterprise coherence governance must have sufficient levers to influence enterprise coherence on the design level, and support the interdependency with the level of purpose as well. The latter should include: forward and backward governance, event driven and cyclic governance, single and multi level governance (recursivity and projection)
Have sufficient information processing capacity	Restrict the complexity and information overload by differentiating enterprise coherence in several interdependent levels. Allocate sufficient resources to enterprise coherence governance, distinguished by processes, products, people, means, governance, methodology and all based on a clear vision

10.6 Conclusion

As also suggested by Proper (2014), we argue that ACET requires the involvement of (at least) two complementary types of frameworks. From a Blue-print thinking perspective, a *design framework* is needed to structure the actual architectural design thinking Proper and Op 't Land (2010). Existing frameworks such as Zachman (Sowa and Zachman 1992) and IAF (van't Wout et al. 2010), ArchiMate (Lankhorst 2012; Iacob et al. 2012), DYA (Wagter et al. 2005), or TOGAF (The Open Group 2011) are candidates for the role of the design framework. Which of these frameworks fits best to a specific organisation, depends on the type of organisation, and the best fitting design philosophy.

Next to a *design framework*, the Yellow-print thinking perspective suggests the use of an organisation-specific *engagement framework* that is concerned with the question of which groups of stakeholders to include in enterprise architecture decision-making during an enterprise transformation, and how to operationally engage them. This framework depends, more than a design framework, on the (strategic) priorities of the organisation, and the stakeholders involved in enterprise transformations. Moreover, depending on the scope and impact of an actual enterprise transformation, more situation-specific tuning of the engagement framework may be needed.

The engagement framework suggested by the GEA method involves the (organisation specific) *enterprise coherence dashboards* (Wagter et al. 2011, 2012d) as will also be discussed in Chap. 18.

Chapter 11
Information Requirements for Enterprise Transformation

Nils Labusch

Abstract In this chapter, we aim at analysing information requirements and providing an analysis of related dimensions. Thus, an overview of research in the field is provided and dimensions are derived. Furthermore, the management mechanisms related to information processing in terms of the organisational information processing theory during enterprise transformations are described. This leads to an examination of where and how enterprise architecture management could occur in the information processing in organisations.

11.1 Introduction

Transformation managers are concerned with many challenges (Labusch and Winter 2013; Uhl and Gollenia 2012; Ward and Uhl 2012) that are oftentimes induced by the complexity of the transformation task (Purchase et al. 2011), the uncertainty involved (Huy 1999), and the high amount of decisions that need to be taken during the course of the enterprise transformation (McGinnis 2007). In order to deal with these challenges, enterprise transformation managers need to be provided with different inputs of which they need to be aware. One of those inputs is information. An appropriate information provision enables dealing with complexity and uncertainty by purposefully providing information to take necessary decisions.

According to Laudon and Laudon (2006, p. 14), *information* is "*data that have been shaped into a form that is meaningful and useful to human beings.*" In contrast, *data* "*are streams of raw facts representing events occurring in organisations or the*

N. Labusch
Institute of Information Management, University of St.Gallen, St. Gallen, Switzerland
e-mail: nils.labusch@gmail.com

© Springer International Publishing AG, part of Springer Nature 2017
H.A. Proper et al. (eds.), *Architectural Coordination of Enterprise Transformation*,
The Enterprise Engineering Series, https://doi.org/10.1007/978-3-319-69584-6_11

physical environment before they have been organised and arranged into a form that people can effectively understand and use" (Laudon and Laudon 2006, p. 14). Thus, when referring to information in this chapter, the understanding is not limited to technical aspects of information processing. A *requirement* is defined by the IEEE (1990, p. 62) as "*(1) A condition or capability needed by a user to solve a problem or achieve an objective. (2) A condition or capability that must be met or possessed by a system or system component to satisfy a contract, standard, specification, or other formally imposed documents. (3) A documented representation of a condition or capability as in (1) or (2).*" In consequence, an *information requirement* describes information that is needed by a user to achieve an objective. The most substantial objective in terms of ACET is to take meaningful decisions that enable the success of the enterprise transformation.

Managerial information provision can face serious problems. Fredenberger et al. (1997) mention examples like piecemeal information formats, faulty presentations, information irrelevant to problems, or non-timely information provisioning.

Processing information and providing an overview of organisational dependencies is one of the major tasks of EAM (Boh and Yellin 2007; Strano and Rehmani 2007). For this reason, the information perspective is valuable in terms of the ACET research. The role of the enterprise architect is considered "*one of making order out of chaos by taking the overwhelming amount of information available and presenting it in a manner that enables effective decision-making*" (Strano and Rehmani 2007, p. 392). Solid foundations have emerged about information processing mechanisms in organisations, most considerably the organisational information processing theory (OIPT) (Clark et al. 2006; Galbraith 1974; Premkumar et al. 2005; Tushman and Nadler 1978).

This chapter proceeds as follows: In the second part, an overview of the related state of the art is provided. Dimensions of enterprise-transformation-relevant information are introduced in the third part. Part four emphasises the information processing in the organisation. Part five asks how enterprise architecture management can contribute to information processing and thus provides a foundation for the following parts.

11.2 State of the Art

When an enterprise is being transformed, a large number of decisions need to be taken (McGinnis 2007). To take these decisions, manifold information has to be collected, consolidated and processed (Fry et al. 2005; Singh et al. 2011). A major success factor during an enterprise transformation is being aware of the importance of information requirements. A McKinsey study with more than 2000 participants (Roy and Kitching 2013) finds that having information about the progress of an enterprise transformation accounts for a four times higher likelihood of success. Kilmann (1995) recognises a dysfunctional information provision, for example, by purposefully withholding information, as a major hinderer of transformation. He considers the willingness to exchange information as a prerequisite to conduct successful enterprise transformations. McAdam (2003) identifies sharing and exchanging information as an important part in the human resources management during an enterprise transformation. Rouse and Baba (2006, p. 69) state that decision-making processes in enterprise transformations "*can be substantially improved by making them evidence based or data driven, thereby enhancing the quality and timeliness of resource allocation decisions*".

Information requirements have been a topic in information systems research for a long time, especially in the context of executive or management information systems. For this purpose, frameworks exist that strive after helping to determine the appropriate information requirements (Byrd et al. 1992; Gordon and Miller 1976; Gorry and Scott Morton 1971; Yadav 1985). The claimed goal in this research stream is "*determining correct and complete information requirements*" (Byrd et al. 1992, p. 118). Early analysis of requirements is considered to be a success factor for IT implementation by many top-level managers (Byrd et al. 1992). However, determining such requirements is described as a difficult challenge since managers have not much time to articulate their information requirements (Watson and Frolick 1993).

Nevertheless, the mentioned frameworks provide rather abstract guidance. In addition, they focus mainly on financial aspects of managerial tasks and on supporting the daily business instead of enterprise transformation. Fredenberger et al. (1997) provide a framework that is more specifically designed for the purpose of enterprise transformation. Its focus is on the analysis of information requirements that intermediary managers (thus, managers that are responsible to turn around a company being in a crisis) pose. According to the authors, dealing with crisis management differs from regular management: partners are less benevolent (due to the financial losses incurred), and time is scarce. Therefore, different planning and control processes are needed. The framework of Fredenberger et al. (1997) still puts a focus on financial information requirements and identifies, among others, information about financials, expenses, costs, personnel, market working capital, and assets as important.

Summarised, the existing frameworks and related literature on information requirements provide a rather finance-oriented perspective and seldom focus explicitly on enterprise transformations. Information about strategy, structure, systems, people, and culture especially needs to be processed and available to lever the transformation process (By 2007). Thus, information requirements should be identified while keeping this purpose in mind. In the following part, dimensions of information requirements in enterprise transformations are discussed.

11.3 Dimensions of Information Requirements

Information requirements can be posed in different dimensions during an enterprise transformation. A clarification is necessary to understand how the term "information" should be interpreted in the ACET context. Rough guidance for this discussion is drawn from socio-technical systems theory (Bostrom and Heinen 1977) that distinguishes people, tasks, technology and structure as important constructs of a socio-technical system (like the organisation that is affected from the enterprise transformation).

11.3.1 People: Consumers of Information

During the course of an enterprise transformation, a lot of stakeholders require information. In general terms, those who are leading the enterprise transformation and those who are affected can be distinguished (Stiles et al. 2012).

Concerning the latter, traditional change management strongly emphasises appropriate change communication (Kotter 1995). Establishing communication plans and stories is part of almost all change frameworks (e.g. Keller and Price 2011; Uhl and Gollenia 2012). The information that stakeholders may need differs depending on their position (Prosci 2014): Employees first need to be informed about the reasons of the change, direct consequences for themselves, the change process and later on about the details. Supervisors and middle-managers, in addition, need to be informed about roles during the enterprise transformation. For senior management, the information has to be more aggregated. For example, details about the enterprise transformation are only relevant on an aggregate level instead of very detailed process or procedure-related information. Aside from the internal stakeholders, customers and other external parties need information to adapt their processes and behaviour (Davidson 1993).

The stakeholders that are, apart from the senior management, in charge of the enterprise transformation could be subsumed as enterprise transformation management. Stakeholders of this group deal with managing the enterprise transformation (Stiles et al. 2012). This group needs a holistic overview and is responsible for managing the information provision to other groups. If information does not exist, the enterprise transformation needs to collect, consolidate and generate it. While in large enterprises this role might exist strictly separated from others (like portfolio management, project management, business engineering), in medium to small enterprises, such a strict distinction does not usually exist. Thus, in practice, the role of the enterprise transformation manager is often not directly mentioned—a search on LinkedIn in July 2014 revealed a total of 8.314 transformation managers but almost five million project managers on the platform. Thus, our understanding of the enterprise transformation manager (or the enterprise transformation management team) includes people that have the best overview of the enterprise transformation. It heavily depends on the specific enterprise transformation, who the best person is that should be addressed and who has information requirements that come closest to the information requirements of the role enterprise transformation. Addressing such managers and collecting their information requirements in practice is a challenging task due to the usually high workload that these experts have to perform (Watson and Frolick 1993).

11.3.2 Structure: Organisational Scope of Information

Enterprise-transformation-relevant information may be required concerning different organisational scopes, some of which are illustrated in Fig. 11.1.

Information concerning the environment of the organisation [also referred to as external information (Watson and Frolick 1993)] may include regulatory standards, customer-related information, etc. Such information may traditionally be received by trade journals, contacts in industry, customers, etc. (Watson and Frolick 1993). Information concerning the organisation may include lots of pieces that are related to the current state. Some examples are the current organisational units, processes, the culture, enterprise transformation history, etc. Such information is oftentimes collected by conducting meetings (Watson and Frolick 1993). On the enterprise transformation level, a multitude of relevant information may be collected, such as planned changes, projects, etc. Information about groups may focus on different departments, teams and other sub-groups of the organisation that are affected by an enterprise transformation (Gersick 1991). Information about stakeholders is comparably hard to gather, but enterprise transformation still needs to cover this perspective up to a certain degree.

11.3.3 Task: Purpose of Information

Information is required for different tasks during enterprise transformations. Abraham et al. (2013c) consider enterprises as systems in which several feedback loops run in parallel. Based on Åström and Murray (2008), they consider management as a cyclic feedback loop that involves transforming an enterprise. Based on this perspective, the organisation can be described by observable variables. Information about these variables flows to the responsible organisational actors. During the enterprise transformation, a subset of the observable variables, the controllable variables of the enterprise, are changed. This means, information about the necessary changes is provided as feedback to the organisation. In the described case, the information

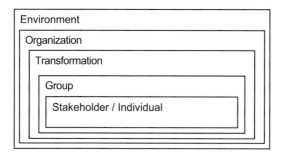

Fig. 11.1 Organisational scopes of information

has a steering function. It is not used to form a decision but it already represents the final decision (see Yadav (1985) for an explication of the decision process).

The information could already be relevant during an earlier stage in the decision process—when the decision is not yet taken but information is required to thoroughly take the decision and consider different scenarios. Here information conducts rather an informing task. The information could be further differentiated into those that directly have an effect on how to take the decision (e.g. a standard that needs to be applied) and those that only support the decision process (e.g. the number of affected employees).

11.3.4 Technology: Detail of Information

Information can be required in different levels of detail. The technology dimension is related to this degree of detail that the information is comprised of. Available information could be very detailed, for example, down to single technical attributes. In terms of the ACET project, it seems to be appropriate to rather consider a wide and, thus, less detailed perspective on enterprise transformation. Information is rather addressed on a high degree of abstraction containing less detail. This abstract information needs to be broken down to the level of a specific enterprise transformation or specific systems that are supposed to be developed.

11.4 Information Processing During Enterprise Transformation

After explicating possible dimensions of information requirements, special attention is needed on explicating how information is shared and value is created. The enterprise transformation manager needs to understand how information is processed in the enterprise during the enterprise transformation and he or she needs to know which of these information is relevant for the management tasks.

The well-established organisational information processing theory (OIPT) (Galbraith 1974, 1977) stresses three important issues: an organisation's information processing need, its information processing capability, and the fit between both. The OIPT applies to large organisations that are comprised of many specialist groups and resources who provide the output. These groups perform group-interdependent subtasks. However, the task performers are not able to communicate with all other dependent tasks performers in the organisation. Thus, mechanisms need to be established that allow for a coordination of the different groups and handling uncertainty. Some basic mechanisms are prevalent in almost every organisation: (1) Coordination by rules or programmes, suitable for routine tasks that occur in a very predictable manner and can be precisely described; (2) hierarchy, suitable for higher levels of uncertainty; and (3) coordination by targets and goals, suitable for very high levels of uncertainty.

The described mechanisms become problematic when uncertainty increases and too many exceptions occur (e.g. during transformations). Rules, for example, are only efficient if situations are foreseen and already documented. Hierarchy may become overloaded when too many exceptions occur (since supervisors are overloaded with decision workload). Coordination by goals and sub-goals only works well when these are properly defined.

When transformation occurs, uncertainty increases and so does the amount of information that needs to be processed (Galbraith 1974). How far information needs to be processed depends on the individual corporate environment and organisational structure. Tushman and Nadler (1978) differentiate the tasks that need to be conducted by different properties: subunit task characteristics (are the tasks predictable?), subunit task environment (is the environment often changing?), interunit task interdependence (how dependent is the subunit from others?). They further argue that organismic (and thus more self-organising) structures can better cope with an increased information processing need than mechanistic ones. However, this comes at the costs of less control and potentially slower response time.

No matter how well the organisation is able to deal with a certain level of information processing need, if an enterprise transformation occurs, the current configuration of processing need and capability needs to be adjusted. The theory provides mechanisms that help to reduce the processing need and to increase processing capability. The first mechanism to reduce the processing need is the *creation of slack resources*. This may include increasing budgets to decrease the interdependence of business units. The result would be a planned redundancy. The second proposed mechanism is the *creation of self-contained tasks* (e.g. change organisation from resource-based to output-based by organising the hierarchy by products instead of functions).

When the information processing need cannot be lowered and no longer handled by the existing structures, the capability of the organisation to deal with the new circumstances needs to be increased. For this purpose, two mechanisms are proposed by the theory. First, the organisation could conduct investments in *vertical information systems*. This means, to introduce systems that allow transferring decision relevant information faster to decision-makers that are positioned higher in the hierarchy. Such systems can be IT systems but also organisational roles like assistants or support departments. The mechanism works especially well with information that is easy to quantify and formalise. The second introduced mechanism is the *creation of lateral relationships* (establishing joint decisions by establishing teams, task forces or direct contacts that range across the lines of authority but do not escalate necessary decisions within the hierarchy). The mechanism attempts to avoid overloading of the hierarchy by increasing the information processing capability on lower levels. This mechanism is especially realised in matrix organisations that have different lines of authority.

To decide which mechanisms to apply, detailed information about the current information processing and the anticipated information processing need are necessary. This means that not only the sheer mass of information is important, but also information that reduces equivocality (Daft and Lengel 1986) (i.e. reducing the amount of different interpretations). Managers need to apply their experience to interpret the information cues or discuss them to achieve a common understanding of the situation (Daft and Lengel 1986).

11.5 Information Provision in the Context of ACET

In this chapter, the potentials of enterprise architecture management to support the described information provision during enterprise transformation are elaborated. Not every kind of information is suitable to be provided by enterprise architecture management. Figure 11.2 provides a first draft on how information requirements that are supported by enterprise architecture management might be limited.

Basically, information that is provided by enterprise architecture management arrives, in some sort, for all stakeholders in the end. However, in the first place, the enterprise transformation management seems to be the primary consumer during a transformation. Since the steering mandate is oftentimes given to the enterprise transformation management, information in most cases serves the purpose of being informative rather than directly steering. The scope of enterprise architecture management is on the organisation and the transformation initiative rather than on the environment or individual stakeholders or groups. Information may be provided with different amounts of details, depending on the topic area. For example, information about IT systems might be provided in a very detailed way, while information about business goals is less available.

Information provision is not a simple task. Information is not just handed over at a certain point of time from the supplier to the consumer. Instead, the information supplier (in this case, enterprise architecture management), is involved during many process steps of information processing. Corner et al. (1994) as well as Clark et al. (2006) distinguish different steps that information processing is comprised of. While the first authors describe a strategic context and distinguish encoding, storage/retrieval, decision, action and outcome, the latter suggest information generation, dissemination and interpretation. Thus, information processing is not

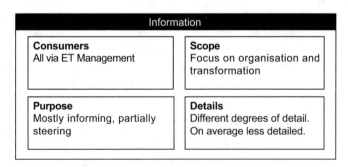

Fig. 11.2 Information characteristics

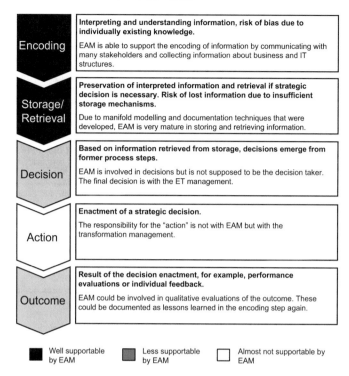

Well supportable by EAM   Less supportable by EAM   Almost not supportable by EAM

Fig. 11.3 Information processing steps and enterprise architecture management support (based on Corner et al. 1994)

one single activity, but a complex process that needs different supportive means. Figure 11.3 discusses how information processing is conducted and where enterprise architecture management could be involved.

Enterprise architecture management can be used to overcome the information processing issues to support some of the mechanisms that OIPT proposes. When referring to the reduction of information processing need, the *creation of slack resources* cannot be supported by enterprise architecture management—here the strategy is simply "*add more resources*". The *creation of self-contained tasks*, however, provides more opportunities for enterprise architecture management. The goal is reshaping the tasks in the enterprise during the enterprise transformation. Such a restructuration would require deep and fundamental knowledge about the organisation itself. Here enterprise architecture management seems to be able to provide input. The core of the discipline is the knowledge about fundamental structures of the organisation—business or IT structures. The third proposed mechanism is *managing the environment*. The mechanism refers to influencing media or politics to achieve the organisation's goal to reduce information processing. Here enterprise architecture management seems to be unable to provide valuable support. For a summary, see Table 11.1.

Table 11.1 Enterprise architecture management support of enterprise transformations: reduction of the information processing need

Mechanism	Enterprise architecture management support
Creation of slack resources	Mechanism in general seems not to be efficient and rather to be an emergency solution. Thus, not suitable for enterprise architecture management support
Creation of self-contained tasks	Mechanism is not trivial to establish since a lot of knowledge about corporate structures and conducted tasks is necessary. Since is able to provide plenty of information about the corporate structures (e.g. applications, processes, goals), the mechanism has the potential to be supported by enterprise architecture management
Management of the environment	Rather influenced by public relations or lobbying, not the domain of enterprise architecture management

Table 11.2 Enterprise architecture management support of enterprise transformations: increase of the information processing capability

Information	Enterprise architecture management support
Investment in vertical information systems	Enterprise architecture management collects information and quickly provides information to top management. In addition, enterprise architecture management could provide information that is necessary to introduce IT that also aims at providing top management information
Creation of lateral relationships	For this mechanism, a business-oriented enterprise architecture management would be necessary. Based on capability or process documentations, enterprise architecture management could help to determine how teams should be staffed and guide their coordination without intervention by higher levels of the hierarchy

On the other side, to increase the information processing capability, the organisation could invest in *vertical information systems*. To support this mechanism, an enterprise architecture management would be required that collects information and provides them to the management. Enabling other stakeholders in the organisation to take their own informed decisions would not be in focus. Enterprise architecture management could also be involved by providing foundations for IT systems that enable the faster information transfer.

The second introduced mechanism is the *creation of lateral relationships*. To support the introduction of the second mechanism, enterprise architecture management would need to enable not only the top-management to take decisions but also line managers or even lower-level employees. Such a source of information for everybody could be used as foundation for the necessary coordination (Abraham et al. 2012a). For a summary, see Table 11.2.

11.6 Conclusion

In this chapter, information requirements as a concept were analysed and the organisational information processing theory was introduced. Further, this chapter examined where and how enterprise architecture management could occur in the information processing in organisations. On the one hand, the analysis provides understanding about the challenges and mechanisms that occur during a transformation from an information perspective. On the other hand, the analysis raises further questions about the role that enterprise architecture management plays or might be able to play.

In general, determining the information requirements is a difficult task. Lohman et al. (2003) identify different pitfalls in this endeavour: data availability and quality do not meet requirements, requested and provided information are unrelated, information needs are poorly assessed, and information is used in a non-performance increasing manner. To address some of these problems, a reference model for information requirements is developed in Chap. 20. Such models lower efforts since they are reusable and contain best-practices (Fettke and Loos 2007).

In addition, the analysis reveals three major areas where enterprise architecture management could be able to provide enterprise transformation support from an information perspective. First, enterprise architecture management is involved in the general information processing that an organisation conducts all the time (and not just during enterprise transformations) in addition to other departments and disciplines. Especially concerning information encoding and storage/retrieval, enterprise architecture management seems to be able to provide value. Second, in terms of lowering the information processing need that occurs during a transformation, enterprise architecture management can be involved in designing better-suited tasks. For this purpose, information about processes, projects and relations between stakeholders need to be provided by a business-oriented enterprise architecture management. Third, when the information processing need cannot be lowered any longer, enterprise architecture management is able to provide value to both proposed mechanisms that increase the information processing capability of the organisation.

However, while the theoretical analysis shows the value of enterprise architecture management for the management of enterprise transformations in general, concrete guidance for practitioners or scientists cannot be derived at the current state. The theoretical lens instead raises questions: Which information can enterprise architecture management exactly provide? Which information do enterprise transformation managers in specific types of enterprise transformations exactly need? Is the same information always needed, or is different information requested in the different types of transformation? What can architects do in addition to the currently known enterprise architecture management approaches to further extend the value of EAM? This book is going to provide answers and thoughts in the following parts.

Chapter 12
Institutionalisation of ACET: Needs and Foundations

Simon Weiss

Abstract In this chapter, we elaborate on the critical need to anchor, that is, institutionalise, architectural coordination in organisations in order to make ACET effective and be able to capture value from it. We do so by first explaining the problem, namely to bring ACET into more effective operation among stakeholders. We then review several theoretical lenses that may contribute to a solution of the problem, concluding that institutional theory is a powerful perspective to inspect in detail. The chapter then explains institutional theory foundations and applies them to the ACET context. We close with a roadmap of research questions culminating in a prescriptive, design-oriented solution for institutionalising ACET in organisations.

12.1 Introduction

Various ACET-specific problem areas and solution approaches are discussed in this book. This is done under the notion that the ACET *toolset* is particularly fuelled by contributions from enterprise architecture management and enterprise transformation. On the enterprise architecture management side, we can find well-developed artefacts such as meta-models for representing current and future states of an EA (Aier and Gleichauf 2010; Iacob et al. 2012; Winter and Fischer 2006), principles for governing its design and evolution (Aier 2014; Greefhorst and Proper 2011), frameworks for overarching reference (IFIP-IFAC Task Force on Architectures for Enterprise Integration 2003; The Open Group 2011), good practices (Ross and Beath 2006), and software tools to support architects' work (Matthes et al. 2008). On the enterprise transformation side, we find reference of why and how transformations happen and how they are addressed (Rouse 2005; Rouse and Baba 2006),

S. Weiss
Institute of Information Management, University of St.Gallen, St. Gallen, Switzerland
e-mail: simon.weiss@hsgalumni.ch

© Springer International Publishing AG, part of Springer Nature 2017
H.A. Proper et al. (eds.), *Architectural Coordination of Enterprise Transformation*,
The Enterprise Engineering Series, https://doi.org/10.1007/978-3-319-69584-6_12

a classification and decomposition of transformations for a situational transformation approach (Baumöl 2005, 2006), as well as guidelines of how to execute single transformations with the aid of existing methods such as value management, business process management and programme management (Uhl and Gollenia 2012). This chapter discusses the challenge of bringing architectural coordination, and in this sense the foregoing toolset, into more effective operation by means of institutionalising it among ACET stakeholders.

Architectural coordination represents a critical and difficult part of EAM, as it denotes the task of coordinating and mediating architectural concerns among different groups and individuals in an organisation. *Architectural* refers to the broad and aggregate perspective into the business-to-IT stack (Winter and Fischer 2006) as encompassed by enterprise architecture management, whereas *coordination* refers to "*the process of managing dependencies among activities*" by the means of formal and informal coordination mechanisms (Malone and Crowston 1994; Williams and Karahanna 2013). The critical issue is that despite the aforementioned achievements, it remains challenging for practitioners to effectively anchor, that is, institutionalise, architectural coordination in an organisation (cf. Tamm et al. 2011b). However, coordination of architectural changes due to concurrently executed projects and programmes across organisational functions and/or levels is necessary to compose these activities into larger purposeful wholes (Holt 1988). These coordinated larger purposeful wholes, for example, enterprise transformations, are in general to achieve overarching goals, to leverage synergies and to make the transformation or enterprise architecture itself more effective and efficient. Architectural coordination addresses these coordination challenges from an architectural view. ACET applies architectural coordination to the scenario of supporting enterprise transformation. The problem exploration of this chapter focuses on architectural coordination, asking what can be done to diffuse and entrench it in an organisation so as to make AC (Enterprise Transformation) more effective.

Indeed, several schools recently identified entrenching a cross-departmental function like enterprise architecture management in an organisation as a difficult albeit critical task. Ross and Quaadgras (2012, p. 1) for example, found that "*business value accrues through management practices that propagate architectural thinking throughout the enterprise*". This means that architectural coordination practices need to be actively promoted and diffused in order to deliver their full potential. In a similar vein, several highly renowned enterprise architecture and enterprise transformation scholars agree upon the growing value of enterprise architecture for enterprise transformation and emphasise the necessity and challenge of adopting architectural thinking (Winter 2014) as a form of fostering AC integrated into an organisation (Gardner et al. 2012). Relating to the institutionalisation of another cross-departmental function, business process management (BPM), vom Brocke et al. (2012) likewise emphasise the necessity of governance structures, that is, defined roles, agreed upon terminology, chosen methodology and tools, being "*actually lived by all employees*". In order to achieve this, respective structures "*need to be perceived as useful and easy to apply*" (vom Brocke et al. 2012).

vom Brocke et al. conclude their motivation for dealing with means for institutionalising BPM by attesting that most BPM initiatives fail because of a lack of adoption.

With respect to architectural coordination, we see similar patterns and challenges. A definition of the architectural coordination toolset is hardly sufficient. In order to make ACET effective, it is necessary to institutionalise architectural coordination in the organisation. The difficulty and criticality of institutionalising architectural coordination has several reasons. One reason might be found in the fact that architectural coordination partially aims at utilising potential synergies in an organisation by *restricting the design freedom* of affected stakeholders (Dietz 2008; Hoogervorst 2009). Yet, reasonable arguments exist to do so, that is, to pursue a global optimisation (e.g. reducing functional redundancies on the overall application landscape) based on a coordinated enterprise-wide perspective instead of several only local optima found in the individual goals of projects or organisational units, etc. However, affected stakeholders are often reluctant to follow architectural norms and values, to take part in the coordination effort and to eventually also give up some autonomy. As adequate stakeholder participation is critical for architectural coordination, respective stakeholders (1) need to be convinced of architectural coordination practices, (2) understand the necessity for coordination and (3) must be willing to take part in architectural coordination. If they do not, much of the aforementioned toolset may not realise its expected benefits.

Besides architectural coordination's inherently abstract and design-restricting nature, the challenge of institutionalising architectural coordination may also be explained by the observation that so far enterprise architecture management was much more concerned with technical issues addressing business and IT matters. Only few works take a more dedicated organisation or people perspective (e.g. Aier 2014; Ross and Beath 2006; Ross and Quaadgras 2012). As noted however, for architectural coordination to be effective, it is crucial that many stakeholders take part in and comply with it. This problem area is also acknowledged by other scholars. Asfaw et al. (2009, p. 20), for example, attest that "*Enterprise architecture has an image problem*" and Winter and Aier (2011, p. 320) note that "*only very few organisations consistently apply and manage enterprise architecture principles*" and that principle enforcement difficulties may be related to the way the principles are defined and justified.

In conclusion, this chapter's problem perspective deals with the challenges of making regulations, norms and values pertaining to architectural coordination stick in the organisation so as to give them "*a rule-like status in social thought and action*" (Meyer and Rowan 1977). To discuss this challenge, we first portray different potential theoretical perspectives on the issue (Sect. 12.2), prior to discussing concepts from institutional theory as our choice for underpinning this problem perspective in Sect. 12.3. The chapter concludes by deriving relevant research questions from the problem perspective discussion.

12.2 Theoretical Perspectives on the Effective Anchoring of ACET

When going beyond solely technical issues and incorporating socio-economic aspects into the area of interest, one faces tremendously increased problem complexity. In this sense, we are confronted with an even more wicked problem space than ACET techniques alone already deal with. In contrast to tame problems, *"wicked problems"* are those where at maximum the definition of the problem is clear, but the solution is not (Head and Alford 2015). This is due to the fact that wicked problems are complex and comprise an economic as well as a social component where different values and perceptions encounter each other. Furthermore, they are unique in each problem situation (Conklin 2005; Head and Alford 2015). Thus, (generally) solving a wicked problem is hardly possible. Rather, generating an understanding of the problem and its possible solutions is at the core of tackling these kinds of problems (Conklin et al. 2007).

In our case, we ask for alternative theories and concepts that may inform us on how to bring architectural coordination into more effective operation among stakeholders. To that end, wide bodies of knowledge in sociology, political science, psychology and organisational sciences with many potential possibilities for grounding and informing this issue exist. This chapter restricts itself to providing a brief review of prominent theories used in information systems research that offer insights and perspectives for building an understanding of the wicked problem of institutionalising architectural coordination.

As part of ACET-related enterprise architecture research, several approaches were adopted to underpin and inform this rather practice-driven discipline with theoretical foundations. Abraham and Aier (2012), for example, look at ACET challenges from a *game theory* perspective. Generally speaking, *"game theory concerns the behaviour of decision-makers whose decisions affect each other"* (Aumann 2008). Abraham and Aier translate three games from game theory into organisational coordination situations and analyse how enterprise architecture management may help in these situations and how enterprise architecture management should be designed, accordingly. Abraham and Aier conclude that an application of game theory helps theorising and classifying a certain set of ACET situations. Their perspective is related to the problem of institutionalising architectural coordination in the sense that game theory can provide input as to how stakeholders may behave and decide when their goals are conflicting with architectural coordination purposes. On the other hand though, implications derived from game theory are generally limited by the theory's strong assumptions such as rationality of players and information asymmetry.

Another approach to make enterprise architecture artefacts more effective was taken by understanding the role of culture (Aier 2013, 2014). Aier (2013, p. 1) proposes to *"take* organisational culture *as a highly aggregated construct describing the context of enterprise architecture management initiatives for building situational–or for that matter culture sensitive enterprise architecture management methods–into account*" as he finds that the success of enterprise architecture management in general (2013) and of enterprise architecture principles in particular (2014) are moderated by an organisation's or business unit's culture. In general, the analysis of organisational culture deals with the way humans behave as part of an organisation and what meanings they attach to certain actions and values. To that end, Schein (2010) distinguishes three levels of culture ranging from artefacts (visible organisational structures and processes, but hard to decipher), to espoused values (espoused justifications such as strategies, goals and philosophies), to basic underlying assumptions (the ultimate source of values and action in terms of unconscious, taken-for-granted beliefs, perceptions, thoughts and feelings). In most cultural information system studies, culture is analysed on the intermediate values level and incorporated as mediating or contextual variable. However, despite its importance (Rouse and Baba 2006), it is generally agreed that organisational culture is both difficult to capture and to design. Still, Keller and Price (2011) found that organisations with an open and transparent, but also operationally disciplined, culture perform better. These characteristics can be seen as both arguments and enablers for institutionalising architectural coordination: On the one hand, architectural coordination fosters project and architectural transparency, and it calls for operational discipline to the better end of architectural coordination. On the other hand, if an organisation already exhibits these cultural characteristics, it may be more receptive to architectural coordination in the first place.

A popular theory that aims at understanding and predicting how new ideas and technology spread through social groups is the diffusion of innovations theory (Rogers 2003). Diffusion of innovations combines the concepts of adoption and diffusion. Adoption takes place at the individual level where people may adopt or reject an innovation, whereas diffusion describes the aggregate percentage of individuals that adopted an innovation as well as the respective process thereof. Similar to other large theories, diffusion of innovations represents an umbrella for many concepts such as diffusion models, diffusion processes, adopter categories, and key elements and antecedents that influence an innovation's diffusion success. However, diffusion of innovations also makes several assumptions and comprises comparably simple theoretical models as pointed out and criticised by Lyytinen and Damsgaard (2001). They note that diffusion of innovations is well-suited to explain individual adopters' behaviours with respect to a static technological artefact, but that diffusion of innovations lacks constructs and explanations for complex and networked innovations. To that end, they propose to take further concepts into account such as political or institutional models as well as theories of team behaviour. Nielsen et al. (2014) make a similar point in their recent work by pointing out that diffusion of innovations regards innovations often as fixed or immutable and ready-to-wear artefacts that are reproduced and transmitted without subsequent modification. To account for the more complex, socio-economic processes of diffusion, Nielsen et al. (2014), in their analysis of mobile IT use within Danish home care, build upon concepts from institutional theory instead. Indeed, concepts from institutional theory mirror the problem of institutionalising architectural coordination inside organisations well. In the next chapter, we will therefore provide a more detailed view into this perspective.[1]

Outside ACET-related research, Aladwani (2001) for instance, in an attempt to overcome workers' resistances to implementation of enterprise resource planning (ERP) systems, suggests to adapt *marketing* concepts and strategies. Concurrently grounded in *change management* practices, he proposes a model of successful ERP adoption. By employing change management as foundation, his approach is similar to ours, as change management can be regarded as the practical counterpart to the aforementioned theories. Change management is particularly related to diffusion of innovations in organisations and deals with mechanisms to change attitudes, habits and values of individuals or teams, usually as part of transformation projects (Greenhalgh et al. 2004).

Thus, on the one hand, change management practices may provide guidance on how to introduce architectural coordination. The other way round though, Espinoza (2007) argues, enterprise architecture is also able to encourage change. The aforementioned concepts for embedding new practices in organisations originated largely from organisational sciences. Besides them, the unified theory of acceptance and use of technology (UTAUT) (Venkatesh et al. 2003) as well as the DeLone and McLean (2003) information system success model have received a lot of attention in information systems research. In part, these models conceptualise constructs that are relevant for and can be adapted to our issue of making a coordination/management approach stick in organisations (cf. Weiss and Winter 2012). Accordingly, respective constructs and their measurement items may contribute to the understanding of our problem. However, in their nature, both models are rather technology-oriented and try to predict the initial usage intention of comparably immutable information system. In contrast to this, we are concerned with a mutable coordination/management approach to be long-term entrenched in organisations. We therefore intend to build upon foundations from organisation and/or social sciences with a closer focus on entrenchment and social dynamics.

In conclusion, all aforementioned concepts and theories have in common that they aim at making information system artefacts more effective by considering their surrounding socio-economic context. This indicates that AC-related information systems research is progressing by incorporating dimensions other than the better understood technical ones. However, what is missing is an elaborate conceptualisation that (a) pinpoints critical elements relevant for entrenching architectural coordination and bringing it into more effective operation, (b) takes social processes and idiosyncrasies into account, and (c) is based on solid theoretical grounds. This chapter and its respective problem perspective intend to narrow that gap. Following the general review of the playing field above, the next chapter will therefore review in depth the theory that shares its name with our challenge of institutionalising architectural coordination. We choose concepts from institutional theory as the informing foundation for our perspective, because institutionalisation "*is concerned*

---

[1] A thorough comparison of *diffusion* and *institutionalisation* is provided by Colyvas and Jonsson (2011).

with stickiness, or how things become permanent" as opposed to, for example, diffusion, which *"is concerned with spreading, or how things flow"* (Colyvas and Jonsson 2011, p. 30). As motivated, we are interested in clues that go beyond an initial straw fire of adoption, but make architectural coordination stick and, ideally, self-reproducing in organisations. These considerations represent a core focus of institutional theory (Colyvas and Jonsson 2011).

12.3 An Institutional Theory Perspective on ACET

Parts of this chapter have been adopted from Weiss et al. (2013).

12.3.1 Institutional Theory Foundations

Institutional theory deals with questions of how and why institutions get adopted, refused and changed over space and time. Institutional theory is contributed to by a wide field of research analysing institutional effects and processes following various research methods in the disciplines of economics, political science, sociology and organisational studies on varying levels ranging from world-system and societal level to organisational sub-system and individual level [for an overview, see for instance, Hall and Taylor (1996) and Scott (2013)]. In our case, we build upon the new institutionalism in organisational analysis that developed from the foundational works of Meyer and Rowan (1977), DiMaggio and Powell (1983) and Zucker (1977). In this chapter we review the basic concepts from this stream prior to discussing our adoption of this theoretical lens at the micro, that is, intra-organisational, level.

According to Jepperson (1991, p. 145), an *institution "represents a social order or pattern that has attained a certain state or property"*, which Meyer and Rowan (1977, p. 341), in other words, refer to as *"a rulelike status in social thought and action"*. Institutionalisation *"denotes the process of such attainment"* (Jepperson 1991, p. 145). Institutions coordinate interactions, distribute tasks and roles, and define relationships among the actors (Walgenbach and Meyer 2008). As such, institutions provide stability and meaning to social life (Scott 2013), and they enable ordered thought, expectations and behaviour. But, they may also hinder critical reflection and the detection of more efficient ways of organising (Zucker 1987). Consequently, institutions influence division of labour, specialisation and productivity, and determine how efficient commercial activity may take place. The configuration and efficacy of institutions are therefore decisive factors for hampering or facilitating economic performance, prosperity and social development (Zucker 1987).

Classic examples of institutions are traffic rules, the handshake, systematic bookkeeping, contracting and human resource management departments. These examples represent institutions that are commonplace today and that have attained a rulelike status and a high degree of resilience. However, what actually makes these examples in to institutions? Four criteria can be derived from literature concerning the formation or existence of an institution and the applicability of institutional concepts, respectively.

- First, the practice in question should not be a "*fad*", but something that exists a prolonged period of time and reaches entrenchment as opposed to initial adoption only (Zeitz et al. 1999).
- Second, institutionalisation takes place on both the macro and micro levels (Davis and Greve 1997; Walgenbach and Meyer 2008). Both levels are interlinked and forces fuelling an institutionalisation come from multiple levels (Currie 2009; Zeitz et al. 1999). Respective institutionalising practices and structures manifest both across and within organisations (Colyvas and Jonsson 2011).
- Third, institutional theory originates from and presumes a social context with boundedly rational actors (humans) (Greenwood et al. 2008, 2011). An institution is shaped and enacted through social systems.
- Fourth, institutionalisation is bound to legitimacy (Suchman 1995) in terms of norms, values and beliefs. Based thereon, institutionalised practices may eventually become self-sustaining. This is important for not equating institutionalisation with formal authorisation or faddish innovations (Colyvas and Jonsson 2011).

Notably, none of these four criteria dealt with the degree of diffusion of a practice. Diffusion and institutionalisation may mutually support each other, but they should not be conflated. As Colyvas and Jonsson (2011, p. 29) point out in their matrix comparing diffusion and institutionalisation, practices exist that are "*ubiquitous but not accepted*" (diffusion: yes; institutionalisation: no), and practices exist that are "*accepted, but not prevalent*" (diffusion: no; institutionalisation: yes).

Institutions can be analysed through what Scott (2013) termed the *three pillars of institutions*. The most prominent—the *regulative pillar*—underscores how institutions constrain and regularise behaviour through coercive mechanisms and regulative rules. The *normative pillar*, focusing on social obligation and binding expectations, calls attention to norms and values, which prescribe and evaluate how and to which valued ends things should be done. Finally, the *cultural-cognitive pillar* stresses underlying, taken for granted, shared conceptions and beliefs embraced by the mechanism of mimicries, that is, imitation. The presence of a certain pillar/diffusion mechanism may vary strongly between institutions, though. Considering the handshake as a form of mutual agreement, the regulative mechanisms are essentially not present. Traffic rules in turn are usually imposed through mechanisms of all three pillars.

The decisive underlying proposition of institutional theory is that organisations are deeply embedded in social and cultural contexts as part of which organisational structures and management practices are influenced by institutional demands. According to this, the institutional view can be summed up as follows: (1) An institution exerts pressures on actors to comply with the institution's demands (DiMaggio and Powell 1983). (2) Actors' compliance to institutional pressures is primarily motivated by an attainment of legitimacy and consequent survival in the institutional environment (Meyer and Rowan 1977). (3) Actors do not act solely rationally and autonomously—they are inherently influenced and constrained by their institutional environment (Scott and Meyer 1991).

Concerning the level of analysis, the so-called macro level (focusing on the sectoral, field or global level) has been the primary level of institutional analysis so far: The aforementioned "actors" in this case are organisations or groups of organisations that adapt to expectations and demands of the institutional environment, that is, demands from outside the organisational boundaries. However, this view has also been criticised: Some argue that people were situated in an *"iron cage"* (DiMaggio and Powell 1983), others that the behaviour of organisations and individuals in organisations appear as *"oversocialized"* (Powell 1991). As a consequence, Oliver (1991), for example, has drawn attention to the fact that organisations may indeed respond differently, that is, more actively and interest-driven, to institutional pressures aside from compliance. Furthermore, Zucker spearheaded research at the micro level (Powell and Colyvas 2008), where the organisation may be regarded as institution and individuals or groups of individuals inside the organisation as responding actors (cf. Zucker 1991). As a matter of fact, this micro level has been paid increased attention to recently. In their profound review, Greenwood et al. (2008) see this level as one direction for future research, stating that other levels of analysis aside from the organisational field or environment level *"have been rarely considered. For example, few studies treat the organisation as the level of analysis [ldots] or examine how the organisation might be treated as an institutional context for understanding* intra*organisational behaviour."* The ACET perspective adopts this micro level of analysis. In doing so, our research connects to the recent work by Pache and Santos (2013), who, on a micro level and likewise building upon work by Oliver (1991), conceptualise how individuals in organisations respond to competing institutional logics.

In an information systems context, institutional theory has been considered in many facets. The interplay between IT and organisational research (e.g. Orlikowski and Barley 2001), the influence of institutional pressures on information system adoption (e.g. King et al. 1994; Teo et al. 2003), the interaction between IT and institutions (e.g. Soh and Sia 2004), institutionalisation and de-institutionalisation processes of IT (e.g. Baptista 2009), or a more general argumentation that and how theories from other disciplines can and should be used to contribute to information systems research (e.g. Boudreau and Robey 1996; Markus and Robey 1988) are a few prominent examples. However, the vast majority of studies are rather generic and take place at the inter-organisational level of analysis, as is shown in the model review by Mignerat and Rivard (2009). Similar to Greenwood et al. (2008), they conclude that there is room for an institutional perspective to be applied to the level of organisational sub-systems such as groups, departments and processes (Mignerat and Rivard 2009). Out of the 53 papers reviewed by Mignerat and Rivard, we analysed all papers that were attributed to the micro level of analysis, that is, where either the entity from which pressures arise and/or the entity on which pressures are exerted are located at an intra-organisational level. We identified 11 papers where management, employees, groups or individuals were in the focus of studies at the organisation or individual level of analysis. From these studies, we found six studies to be informative to the present problem perspective in a wider sense. Most notably, top (but also local) management championship and commitment were found to be strong influencing factors for an institutionalisation of IT or of information system concepts such as knowledge platforms (Purvis et al. 2001), web technologies (Chatterjee et al. 2002), IT use in general (Lewis et al. 2003), or information system security concerns (Hu et al. 2007). In these studies, management is considered an institution exerting in particular normative pressures on organisational actors. To that end, the management provides significance and legitimisation to the respective system and its use within an organisation. Furthermore, an "*organising vision*" has been found to be substantial for institutionalising an innovation (Swanson and Ramiller 1997). An organising vision is a focal community idea for the application of an information system innovation in organisations. It facilitates interpretation and legitimisation of an innovation as well as mobilisation of resources and actors for its realisation (Swanson and Ramiller 1997). Lastly, Phang et al. (2008) point at several measures that fostered organisational learning of an enterprise-wide e-government information system. For example, managers may consider to first equip employees with required IT knowledge, and to then align their performance appraisal and training with corporate goals (Phang et al. 2008). In conclusion of this review, we see several factors that we envisage to be also relevant for an institutionalisation of architectural coordination. However, none of the aforementioned studies dealt with enterprise architecture management specifically. Furthermore, we would like to look beyond the well-researched effect of top management support and create a broader picture of antecedents for architectural coordination's institutionalisation.

12.3.2 Application of Institutional Theory Concepts to ACET

During the past 10 years that we have been actively involved in what could best be described as action design research projects (Sein et al. 2011) in the area of enterprise architecture management and enterprise transformation, it became obvious that, despite methodological achievements, EAM's line of thought is challenging to institutionalise. We conclude that the enterprise architecture management approach does not only have to be methodically sound, but, in order to become effective across large parts of an organisation, it also needs to respect an organisation's system of social norms and values that structure interactions. We argue that the latter issues are particularly important for architectural coordination for several reasons: First, while being an increasingly important function to manage proliferation and dependencies of information systems, architectural coordination as well as related enterprise architecture management approaches are still rather young corporate functions compared to marketing, production or controlling, for example. Consequently, the awareness of architectural requirements, the necessity for a coordinated approach to enterprise architecting, transformation and standardised procedures are still lacking widely (Gardner et al. 2012). Second, architectural coordination is not only a technical issue, but to a large extent also a social and political one, because (1) architectural coordination is about coordinating changes/transformations across levels and departments in an organisation, which, after all, is about coordinating and arbitrating between people. (2) Architectural coordination is concerned with overarching transparency, dependency-analyses, planning, etc., for transformation and decision support, which is oftentimes depreciated by certain stakeholders who, for instance, have no interest in transparency. (3) Finally, architectural coordination affects and pressures a high number of heterogeneous stakeholders (Dijkman et al. 2004; Kurpjuweit and Winter 2007). Third and last, institutionalising architectural coordination practices is essential as it is the nature of architectural coordination to coordinate different, possibly heterogeneous, stakeholder groups that need to accept and follow architectural coordination guidelines and values in order to realise expected business benefits (Ross and Quaadgras 2012).

With a view to adopting institutional theory concepts to our specific enterprise architecture management/architectural coordination problem area and to the less common analysis level (micro/intra-organisational level), we will briefly discuss the theory's general applicability.[2] Concerning the four characteristics of institutions discussed before, we argue that they hold true for our problem.

- First, enterprise architecture management is no fad, but a diffusing practice to manage complex business-IT relationships (Gardner et al. 2012).
- In this respect, second, enterprise architecture management is driven by accounts on both micro and macro levels. From a rather macro perspective, enterprise architecture management is a growing concern due to general trends such as a proliferation of information systems in society and business, regulatory requirements (e.g. banking and energy provider reporting regulations), competition and pressure for efficiency (leading to the need for, e.g., complexity management, synergies and agility in information systems) and societal demands (e.g. expectation of proper information systems management; personal data security concerns). More specifically, enterprise architecture management manifests by a growing amount of research in this area (Mykhashchuk et al. 2011; Simon et al. 2013), professional enterprise architecture organisations (e.g. CAEAP, IFEAD, The Open Group), governmental enterprise architecture initiatives [e.g. FEAF, DoDAF, Clinger-Cohen Act (OCIO 1996)], as well as large amount of enterprise architecture tools and consulting services offered by industry. At the micro level, enterprise architecture management then actually take place in organisations, where respective practices and tools are implemented. Driving individuals and groups on this level usually are enterprise architects and management.
- Third, enterprise architecture management has a strong social component as mentioned earlier. Although this aspect has been less dealt with in research so far, it is acknowledged that stakeholder attitude towards and acceptance of enterprise architecture management is critical for its success. Also, stakeholders oftentimes have resistances to adopt enterprise architecture management practices, even though it would be rational to do so. As each socio-organisational

---

[2] Here, we look at enterprise architecture management as architectural coordination's superordinate management practice, as it is the more common term in literature and practice.

context is different, every organisation theorises and translates enterprise architecture management differently, which is typical for institutionalisation processes (Nielsen et al. 2014).

- Fourth, despite lacking legitimisation within individual organisations, enterprise architecture management generally represents a legal and legitimate practice that has shown to yield organisational benefits.

Concerning extant literature, there is so far only a limited amount of research on enterprise architecture management/architectural coordination taking an institutional perspective. Hjort-Madsen's work stands out by investigating how enterprise architecture implementation (Hjort-Madsen 2006) and adoption (Hjort-Madsen 2007) is dependent upon and shaped by institutional forces, noting that this issue is underrepresented in enterprise architecture research so far. He shows that interoperability and information systems planning, which can be facilitated through enterprise architecture management, are not only technical issues, but that economic, political and contextual factors are just as important. Focussing on public sector research, he identifies three types of enterprise architecture planning adopters (accepters, improvers, transformers) (Hjort-Madsen 2007). The adopter types illustrate that a certain level of compliance to national enterprise architecture planning requirements does not necessarily lead to sincere administrative reform. The latter is only achieved if forces from both micro and macro level promote transformation. Iyamu (2009, p. 221), similar to our perspective, focus on the intra-organisational level of EAM's institutionalisation, noting that *the design and development of enterprise architecture has proven to be easier than its institutionalisation*. Based on two case studies, he presents six internal barriers to the institutionalisation of enterprise architecture management and relates them to four elements of the enterprise architecture management development and implementation process. However, while the identified barriers are informative to management, his overall propositions remain to be rigourously evaluated.

We intend to complement and advance this limited institutional perspective on enterprise architecture management. In doing so, we focus on the micro (intra-organisational) level, build upon solid foundations from institutional theory and intend to empirically test relevant factors for architectural coordination's institutionalisation. Concerning the use of institutional concepts, our perspective is particularly inspired by the institutional framework of Oliver (1991), as it mirrors the mechanisms of our problem. On a generic level, she developed a typology of strategic responses to institutional pressures and presents institutional factors that affect the occurrence of certain response strategies. When setting up architectural coordination, one may principally observe the same mechanisms: Affected stakeholders have different reactions towards the architectural coordination approach—while some may follow immediately and dedicatedly, others will perceive it as constraining (Dietz 2008) and unnecessary, and therefore try to defy and manipulate respective endeavours. Considering these similar mechanisms, we see applying institutional and in particular Oliver's concepts to our architectural coordination context at the intra-organisational level as a promising, informing perspective (see Pache and Santos (2013) for a related approach). In doing so, we regard architectural coordination as pre-institutionalised, as in practice it often is. At the pre-institutionalised stage, new structures *"appear in response to existing problems"* (Mignerat and Rivard 2009). They provoke change, but are still far from being taken for granted. According to Mignerat and Rivard's model, they undergo, prospectively, the theorisation and diffusion phases at this stage [for a deeper elaboration and alternative terminology see Tolbert and Zucker (1996)].

In conclusion, the here-portrayed problem of institutionalising architectural coordination is complex, but important. It is important, because the ACET toolset will stay behind its potential, or even diminish again, if architectural coordination is not respected and sustainably embedded in an organisation, that is, institutionalised in terms of, at least, the regulative and normative pillar. Eventually though, architectural coordination should become part of an organisation's culture and identity to be fully institutionalised. As illustrated, institutional theory provides a reasonable conceptual lens for this issue as well as models and factors that may help us understand and tackle this *"wicked problem"*. We adopt an institutional theory perspective as its line of thought lies at the core of our problem, namely to derive factors and design principles that support giving architectural coordination a *"rulelike status"* and make it *"structure social interactions"* in an organisation with respect to architectural (and transformational) concerns. In this chapter, we therefore reviewed specific architectural coordination challenges that appear addressable from an institutional theory perspective. The institutional perspective helps us to (a) contribute to an explanation for the observable challenges of embedding architectural coordination in an organisation, and (b) provide reference on how to approach these challenges.

12.4 Conclusion

Reflecting the previous arguments, this chapter has answered the question of what constitutes the problem of institutionalising architectural coordination. It has furthermore set forth what institutional theory can contribute to inform the solution to the problem. Based on these conceptual foundations, we can define the following forward-looking research questions geared towards a solution for the problem:

Research Question 12.4.1 *What are the antecedents for institutionalising architectural coordination?*

Research Question 12.4.2 *How does the institutionalisation of architectural coordination contribute to enterprise architecture management's benefit realisation?*

Research Question 12.4.3 *What are the carriers of architectural coordination's institutionalisation (inside and outside the focal organisation)?*

Research Question 12.4.4 *Which design principles should be obeyed to foster an institutionalisation of architectural coordination?*

Answering these research questions should bring us a considerable step forward on how to foster an institutionalisation of architectural coordination in organisations. Research Question 12.4.1, Research Question 12.4.2 and Research Question 12.4.3 are primarily of explanatory nature. As part of this, they deal with building cause–effect relationships that elaborate the problem further and indicate which causes have to be dealt with for a successful solution. For example, answering Research Question 12.4.1 would provide determinant factors (antecedents) fostering architectural coordination's institutionalisation. Answering Research Question 12.4.2 would verify that the antecedents and architectural coordination's institutionalisation are worthwhile in terms of a contribution to organisational benefits attributable to enterprise architecture management. Answering Research Question 12.4.3 would shed light on who and what drives (legitimises) architectural coordination, and what contradicts it. A possible starting point for structuring such an analysis may be the "*institutional pillars and carriers*" framework from Scott (2013, p. 96). Drawing on the explanatory insights, the final question is more design-oriented and should consequently lead to practical means–ends relations. The expected contribution is to provide practical guidance in the form of design principles (Gregor and Hevner 2013; Gregor et al. 2013) for enterprise architects and management. However, such design efforts raise the question as to the extent to which institutions are actually designable. Drawing on the *agent-based* view (Scott 2008) of institutionalism, we hold the opinion that architectural coordination's institutionalisation is not ultimately designable (as, e.g. in a crafting, technical sense), but influenceable, as institutionalisation is also "*a product of the political efforts of actors to accomplish their ends and that the success of an institutionalisation project and the form that the resulting institution takes depend on the relative power of the actors who support, oppose, or otherwise strive to influence it*" (DiMaggio 1988, p. 13). On the other hand, we acknowledge that institutionalisation is also something that evolves slowly "*from the collective sense-making and problem-solving behaviour of actors confronting similar, problematic situations*", which represents the *naturalistic* view into institutional construction (Scott 2008, p. 222).

Chapter 13
The Need for Model Engineering

Sybren de Kinderen

Abstract In this chapter, we argue for a component-based approach for the construction of (visual) conceptual models, so that these models are tailored to the context-specific characteristics of a particular enterprise transformation. We offset this component-based approach against (a) "one-size-fits-all" languages, such as the enterprise architecture modelling language ArchiMate, (b) federated languages, whereby languages are related by defining (semi-)formal model transformations, and (c) domain-specific language design.

13.1 Introduction

Conceptual models emerge as instruments for the architectural coordination of transformations. Instead of merely expressing software concerns (such as coding support), conceptual modelling increasingly focuses on enterprise concerns, such as modelling the as-is/to-be state of an enterprise (Lankhorst 2012; Stirna and Persson 2012), knowledge sharing (Stirna and Persson 2012), ensuring acceptance of business decisions (Stirna and Persson 2012), or analysing cost structures (Lankhorst 2012) and more. Note that when we use the term 'model' in this chapter, we use it to refer to a conceptual model: "*a purposely abstracted and unambiguous conception of a domain*" (Falkenberg et al. 1998; Proper et al. 2005), which, through

S. de Kinderen
University of Duisburg-Essen, Universitätsstr. 9, 45141 Essen, Germany
e-mail: sybren.dekinderen@uni-due.de

© Springer International Publishing AG, part of Springer Nature 2017
H.A. Proper et al. (eds.), *Architectural Coordination of Enterprise Transformation*,
The Enterprise Engineering Series, https://doi.org/10.1007/978-3-319-69584-6_13

visualisation, fosters communication amongst a group of stakeholders. Thus, for this chapter, we use a more specific interpretation of the term 'model' compared to the 'ACET model' (refer to Sect. 16.1 for a definition of the ACET model).

ArchiMate is an Open Group standard language for modelling an enterprise architecture (Lankhorst 2012; Iacob et al. 2012). It emphasises a holistic perspective on an enterprise, showing how products and services are realised by business processes, and how in turn these business processes are supported by IT applications and physical IT infrastructure. Furthermore, the recent motivational extension of ArchiMate allows for relating cross-organisational concerns to stakeholder requirements and motivations. Figure 13.1 shows an example ArchiMate model for the insurance industry, with a particular emphasis on relating different enterprise perspectives. For example, Fig. 13.1 shows how the business processes *"eligibility check"* and *"underwrite insurance"* are supported by the IT application *"Risk assessment application"* (via the IT application service *"Risk assessment service"*). Thus, as far as modelling languages go, ArchiMate forms a useful point of departure for supporting architectural coordination.

13.2 Limits to One-Size-Fits-All Languages

Yet ArchiMate is not a "catch all" solution for the model-based support of architectural coordination. Predominantly, ArchiMate currently lacks expressiveness for modelling domain-specific issues, such as linking an architectural design to its economic rationale (van Buuren et al. 2005; de Kinderen et al. 2012a), a cross-enterprise, model-based, analysis of security concerns (Feltus et al. 2012), expressing essential business model concerns (Meertens et al. 2012), and more. Depending on the nature of the transformation at hand, we may therefore lack expressiveness on context-specific transformation concerns.

As a response, several proposals for extending the ArchiMate meta-model with domain-specific concerns have been made (van Buuren et al. 2005; Feltus et al. 2012; Meertens et al. 2012). Each viewed in their own right, these proposals form reasonable ArchiMate extensions—akin to the motivation extension of ArchiMate.

However, to merely keep extending the ArchiMate language with domain-specific concepts will in the longer run likely lead to "modelling spaghetti" (cf. de Kinderen et al. 2012a). This in turn likely results in a violation of conceptual parsimony, one of the key ArchiMate design principles that points out a need for an economical design of conceptual modelling languages (Lankhorst et al. 2010, p. 8). This issue generally holds for integrated languages such the Unified Modelling Language (OMG 2003).

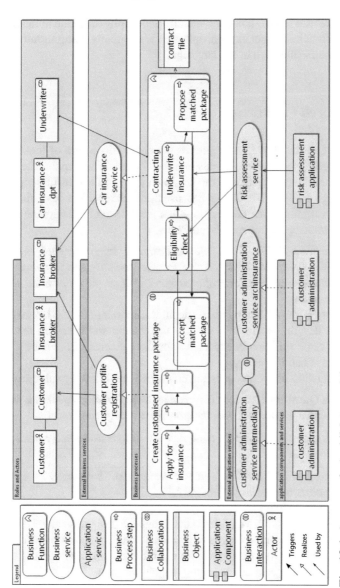

Fig. 13.1 An example ArchiMate model

As long as one uses a "one-language-fits-all" philosophy then, due to the continuing extension with domain-specific concepts, one is inevitably going to run into issues with the economical design of the language.

13.3 Research Questions

As a response to the above, we argue for the economic design of transformation-specific modelling languages. To this end we formulate two main research questions: one from the perspective of the language user, and one from the perspective of the language designer. We do this because these stakeholders have differing concerns, and so different research questions that are relevant for designing a language dealing with transformation-specific concerns.

Research Question 13.3.1 *How can we design a language such that it is on the one hand sufficiently expressive for the domain-specific concerns of the architecture-driven transformation at hand, and on the other hand sufficiently economic in use?*

For end users of our language, we deem it important that the language is economic in design, so that it is easy to understand and use. Yet, the language should also be sufficiently expressive for the concerns of the enterprise transformation at hand.

We can actually break this question down into the following sub-questions:

Research Question 13.3.1.1 *How can we design a language that is sufficiently expressive for domain-specific enterprise transformation concerns?*

Research Question 13.3.1.2 *How can we design a language such that it is economic in use?*

Research Question 13.3.2 *How can we design new languages by mixing and matching parts of existing languages?*

For language developers, economy of design pertains to the plug-and-play of existing languages. Here the idea is that language designers can take inspiration from existing languages, thus saving time and reusing good ideas. For example: to reuse the actor-role distinction from ArchiMate, or the notion of economic reciprocity from the value modelling language e³value.

13.4 Candidate Existing Approaches

Various existing approaches exist that can provide "ingredients" for addressing our research questions. Below, we discuss three types of approaches, involving (1) language federation, (2) situational method engineering, and (3) domain-specific language design. For each, we describe how the approaches can be useful for answering our research questions, and where they fall short.

13.4.1 Expressing Architectural Concerns by Language Federation

Language federation is one candidate for constructing languages that express domain-specific transformation concerns. With language federation, one selects the languages needed to express various transformation concerns. Subsequently, one links these languages based on their underlying meta-models. This "linking" ranges from lightweight, textual meta-model correspondences (Pijpers et al. 2012) to formal, computer-supported transformations (de Kinderen et al. 2012a; Derzsi et al. 2008).

First and foremost, such language federation is useful because one can capitalise on complementary languages. Take for example the federated approach proposed by de Kinderen et al. (2012a), whereby the value modelling language e^3value is transformed into ArchiMate via the transaction modelling language DEMO.

Transformation Case: Bridging e^3Value to ArchiMate via DEMO

e^3value has been proposed as a suitable candidate for adding an economic rationale to enterprise architectures expressed in ArchiMate (van Buuren et al. 2005; Lankhorst et al. 2010). On the one hand, ArchiMate complements e^3value by specifying the business processes and information systems necessary to realise a value constellation. In addition, ArchiMate interrelates business processes and IT systems, thus allowing for systematically propagating a change happening on a business process level to an IT systems level and vice versa. On the other hand, e^3value complements ArchiMate in terms of providing an economic rationale, for example in terms of profitability calculations, for an enterprise architecture modelled in ArchiMate (whereby an enterprise architecture largely constitutes business processes, and how these are supported by IT systems).

However, to transform between e^3value and ArchiMate models, we should mitigate the different levels of abstraction naturally expressed by these languages. Here, the different levels of abstraction pertain to, on the one hand, the economic transactions stemming from e^3value and, on the other hand, the information systems and business processes stemming from ArchiMate. In particular, we miss formal guidance for creating process models, in ArchiMate, that realise the economic transactions from e^3value.

To deal with the difference in abstraction level between e^3value and ArchiMate, we use DEMO transaction patterns as a bridge between the respective languages. In model transformation terms (Czarnecki and Helsen 2006; Levendovszky et al. 2002), DEMO acts as a transformation engine between e^3value and ArchiMate. It specifies the transformation rules necessary to bridge between an e^3value model and an ArchiMate process model. DEMO can act as such a transformation engine through its process-based patterns that describe the social interactions, as business process steps, necessary to realise economic transactions.

Figure 13.2 depicts the proposed e^3value-DEMO-ArchiMate transformation. The top layer depicts the transformation of the e^3value and ArchiMate meta-models

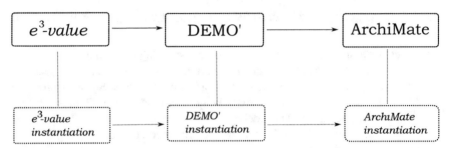

Fig. 13.2 Transforming e^3value into ArchiMate via DEMO. © Springer-Verlag Berlin Heidelberg 2010; reprinted with permission from de Kinderen (2012a)

via the DEMO meta-model. Meanwhile, the bottom layer depicts that instantiated e^3value and ArchiMate meta-models require an instantiation of the DEMO meta-model as well. In particular, we require an instantiation of the DEMO transaction pattern to help us in translating economic transactions into business processes.

From the e^3value-DEMO-ArchiMate example transformation, we can clearly observe that putting languages together can provide an added expressiveness of transformation concerns. In addition, federated approaches allow for maintaining a coherence across models. This means that—through well-defined transformation—changes in one model can be propagated through other models. Maintaining such model coherence is particularly relevant given that we deal with enterprise architectures, which by their very nature deal with issues that cut across different concerns. These different concerns, in turn, are naturally expressed by different languages.

Returning to our research questions, we thus find that federated approaches provide useful features: (1) they allow us to precisely select those languages that we need, which provides a good first step towards economic language use (Research Question 13.3.1.1), and (2) we can rely on complementarity between existing languages, which provides a good first step towards economic language design (Research Question 13.3.1.2). However, to the best of our knowledge, transformation approaches focus on expressing the actual transformation between two models in terms of syntactic and semantic correspondences. As a result, the pragmatics of transformations are largely ignored, leaving open "*why*" questions pertaining to model transformation. As such current transformation approaches leave open at least the following two important "*pragmatic*" questions: (1) for any set of languages A_1, $A_2 \ldots A_n$: for what purposes do we need to define a transformation between A_1, $A_2 \ldots A_n$? And, (2) given the purpose, between what particular subset of concepts from languages A_1, $A_2 \ldots A_n$, do we transform?

13.4.2 Situational Method Engineering

Situational method engineering is concerned with providing structured, formal support for the development of situation-specific methods out of smaller method pieces (Henderson-Sellers and Ralyté 2010). The situation-dependent componential approach implicit in situational method engineering, combined with the fact that languages are also a part of SME (Henderson-Sellers and Ralyté 2010), thus makes it also interesting to also briefly reflect on the suitability of situational method engineering for our research purposes.

As we point out in de Kinderen and Proper (2013), in situational method engineering, some early work exists on goal-oriented selection of method fragments (Chiniforooshan Esfahani et al. 2010; Ågerfalk and Fitzgerald 2006; Rossi et al. 2004). For example, Chiniforooshan Esfahani et al. (2010) use the goal modelling technique i* to characterise the capabilities of method fragments. Subsequently, he links these capabilities to the overall goal that one wants to achieve by employing a set of method fragments. However, taking a goal-oriented perspective on Situational Method Engineering is under-researched. This is also pointed out by Henderson-Sellers and Ralyté (2010, p. 465), who in a recent state-of-the-art point out that it is a notable research challenge to (semi-automatically) move from stakeholder requirements to a suitable set of method fragments. This suggests that the situational method engineeringliterature is immature when it comes to the economic design of languages (see Research Question 13.3.1.1 and Research Question 13.3.1.2).

In addition, the situational method engineering body of knowledge focuses on methods in general. As a result, situational method engineering literature forgoes concerns specific to language construction, such as relationship types and various ways to merge concepts. For our purposes, however, such language-specific concerns are vital.

13.4.3 Domain-Specific Language Design

Concentrating on languages specifically, domain-specific languages play an important role in the software engineering domain. Domain-specific languages refer to task- or purpose-specific languages, expressing exactly those concepts needed for modelling the domain at hand (Mernik et al. 2005). This is opposed to General Purpose Languages, such as C++ or Java. By employing domain-specific languages, software engineers gain an increase in domain expressiveness, and claim an increase in ease of use (Mernik et al. 2005).

Note that a domain-specific language can be used to express anything (e.g. a domain-specific language can also be a programming language), but that we are of course interested in visual domain-specific languages, that is, domain-specific languages that can act as communication vehicles to coordinate enterprise transformations. To design domain-specific languages, software engineers typically employ feature diagrams (Mernik et al. 2005; van Deursen et al. 2000). In feature diagrams, one designs a domain-specific language by specifying an abstract feature (e.g. 'browsing') into more detailed ones (e.g. 'get' or 'post' features for 'browsing') until one derives specific language concepts. Logical operators ((X)OR, AND) are used for feature specification.

Feature diagrams are interesting for us in the sense that they allow for purposeful design (in line with Research Question 13.3.1.1). Moreover, by definition they propose a set of concepts exactly in line with the modelling need at hand (in line with the economic language design proposed in Research Question 13.3.1.2).

However, in feature diagrams everything is a "feature", tailored to software concerns. In contrast, we are interested in designing a language to support an enterprise transformation, in particular in fostering communication amongst actors participating in the transformation. Thus, we deal with concerns of intentional humans. These concerns are different from pure software concerns expressed as "features", as we have to deal with differences in actor's background, interests and expertise, conflicting/complementing interests, and more.

Furthermore, feature diagrams design a language from scratch, while, in line with Research Question 13.3.2, we are interested in capitalising on the reuse of existing languages.

13.5 Our Approach: Component-Based Language Composition

Now we introduce the basic ideas behind our approach, called e^3RoME, for creating a language that is both fit for the purposes of the transformation at hand, and that is economic in design. As stated, we elaborate these basic ideas further in Chap. 21.

In line with situational method engineering (discussed in Sect. 13.4), a key idea of e^3RoME is to treat languages as building blocks that one (intelligently) mixes-and-matches to create a modelling language that fits precisely with the transformation-specific purposes at hand. In brief, we do this by (1) expressing language elements in terms of the value they provide. For example, for ArchiMate a value is "*link business process and IT perspectives*" and (2) linking this value to the purposes of the transformation under consideration. For example, a more abstract purpose that can be achieved by ArchiMate is "*Model the to-be state of the enterprise*".

Note that, with our approach, we aim at creating a domain-specific language rather than on creating a coherent federated set of languages. We focus on domain-specific languages as they allow for a gain in domain-expressiveness (Mernik et al. 2005; van Deursen et al. 2000), and makes the language easy to use. After all, a domain-specific language fits exactly with the communication purposes of the transformation at hand.

13.6 Conclusion

In this chapter, we defined the need for a language engineering approach that is on the one hand sufficiently expressive for the purposes of the transformation at hand, and on the other hand sufficiently economic in design. We showed that one-size-fits-all languages, prominently ArchiMate, are not fit for creating transformation-specific languages since their extensions with transformation-specific concerns lead to "modelling spaghetti": cluttered models that are difficult to design and interpret. Furthermore, we discussed how model transformation approaches, approaches from situational method engineering, and feature diagrams provide us with interesting ideas, but that each area lacks an integrated framework that is fit for achieving our research purposes.

Chapter 14
Steering Transformations with Architecture Principles

Diana Marosin and Sepideh Ghanavati

Abstract This chapter introduces an overview on the formulation of architecture principles, guidelines for a semi-formal definition and rules for modelling the architecture principles. We give insights on analysis and impact evaluation of aforementioned principles on the design of architecture models and on the implementation of enterprise architecture.

14.1 Introduction

According to Rouse (2005), enterprise transformation concerns fundamental change that alters an enterprise's relationship with one or more key constituencies (e.g. stakeholders, other organisations, governments, and internal departments) in a substantial way. Transformation can involve new value propositions in terms of products and services and define new ways of how these are delivered and supported. Also, a transformation process has to describe how the enterprise is organised to provide these offerings. Given the large scale of a transformation, organisations need to divide and align the new offerings into smaller pieces, typically in terms of programmes and projects.

Experience in corporate practice shows that, in a top-down sense, transformations follow business and IT strategies, while in a bottom-up sense, they follow the projects and programmes driven by business units. This raises the need for a coordination mechanism between these elements, to safeguard that they all contribute

D. Marosin (✉)
SopraSteria, Leudelange, Luxembourg
e-mail: marosin.diana@gmail.com

S. Ghanavati
Department of Computer Science at Texas Tech University, Lubbock, TX, USA

© Springer International Publishing AG, part of Springer Nature 2017   147
H.A. Proper et al. (eds.), *Architectural Coordination of Enterprise Transformation*,
The Enterprise Engineering Series, https://doi.org/10.1007/978-3-319-69584-6_14

towards the strategic direction of the organisation and support the transformation process as a consistent whole.

Keeping the projects and programmes in line with the general strategic views is addressed by formulation and usage of *(enterprise) architecture principles*.

Architecture principles are defined in different ways. They may be defined as "*a family of guidelines (. . .) for design*" (Hoogervorst 2004) or "*general rules and guidelines, intended to be enduring and seldom amended, that inform and support the way an organisation fulfills its mission*" (The Open Group 2011), or "*how the design of an enterprise will meet the essential requirements*" (Greefhorst and Proper 2011). In each case, they are destined to play an important role when talking about transformation and rationalisation of design decisions taken in the context of an enterprise transformation.

In our work, we adopt the view of Greefhorst and Proper (2011), and consider architecture principles as declarative statements, used to "*build a bridge from the strategy to the more specific designs*", with the role to "*normatively restrict the design freedom*". In order to achieve their purpose, principles have to be refined and made specific for each organisational context they are applied to. This refinement results in so-called *design instructions*. Design instructions usually contain concepts used in the actual construction of the enterprise (e.g. value exchange, transactions, services, contracts, processes) and use a representation language [e.g. UML (OMG 2007), ArchiMate (Iacob et al. 2012), BPMN (OMG 2011), DEMO (Dietz 2015)].

In Fig. 14.1, we position architecture principles and architecture instructions in report with the strategy and vision of the organisation, new programmes and projects, as well as exterior factors. The grey blocks represent elements that belong to the organisation, such as the organisation's vision and goals, the strategy, the architecture principles, the architecture instructions, the existing projects and new project's propositions, together with the governing business rules and data objects.

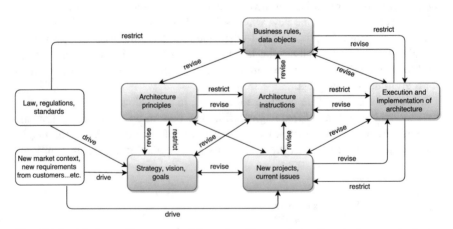

Fig. 14.1 Positioning architecture principles and architecture instructions in the context of enterprise transformation

The white blocks represent the exterior factors, such as laws, regulations, standards, together with the changing market and requirements from customers.

The logical flow from strategy to concrete enterprise architecture design is represented by a chain of restrictive relationships. Covering the top-down layers of the enterprise, from the strategy to the implementation, each step introduces a new level of abstraction and limitations in the design space.

In practice, it is confirmed that given *good reasons*, architecture principles can be violated or revised, and not all architectural decisions are taken based on the formulated architecture principles (Greefhorst and Proper 2011; Marosin et al. 2014; Marosin and Ghanavati 2015; Marosin et al. 2016). In addition, new projects could be accepted even if they violate the principles. Our hypothesis is that a chain of revision can be triggered anywhere in between the constitutive blocks of an architecture and does not have to follow a bottom-up refinement structure.

In Fig. 14.1, the exterior influences, such as current laws, regulations or standards, alongside new market situations and demands from customers are also represented, because the regulatory world constrains tremendously the mission and the means by which an organisation tries to achieve its strategic goals. Also, the strategy and goals of the organisation are in a constant state of change and adaptability to the new market conditions and the demanding requirements that come from the stakeholders. However, for the purpose of this chapter, we do not delve too deeply in to the analysis of these concerns.

The current scope of our research space is limited to checking and keeping consistency between architecture principles and architecture instructions and their revision/restriction relationships, as represented in Fig. 14.1. To that end, we propose a method to support management and evaluation of using architecture principles in the context of an enterprise transformation. Our research questions with respect to ACET are:

Research Question 14.1.1 *How to support creation and formalisation of operational architecture principles?*

Research Question 14.1.2 *How to represent architecture principles in a semiformal language?*

> **Research Question 14.1.2.1** *What are the needed language constructs?*

> **Research Question 14.1.2.2** *What are the modelling constraints?*

By answering these research questions, we set grounds for providing analysis and methods to check the consistency between architecture principles and the enterprise architecture (e.g. consistency and traceability from architecture principles to design decision when new projects are introduced).

14.2 Challenges in Using and Evaluating Architecture Principles

Even if reduced in scope, the endeavour to answer our research question (see Sect. 14.1) raises a number of challenges that we summarise and explain (non-exhaustively) below as follows:

1. *The structural definition of architecture principles.* In general, the definition, usage, management and enforcement of architecture principles in organisations is poorly understood (cf. Winter and Aier 2011). Moreover, frameworks like TOGAF (The Open Group 2011) provide guidelines for a so-called good set of principles and a structure, but in practice each organisation defines its own set of principles. However, a more detailed architecture principle definition is still not necessarily a better definition.
   To overcome this challenge, Sect. 22.2 will provide a minimal structure to ensure a consistent and operational definition for architecture principles.

2. *Ambiguity introduced by the natural language formulation and scattered information.* It is not uncommon to find modalities such as *should* without further clarifications about the pre- and post-conditions in the definition of architecture principles. In addition, ambiguities about the object to which the principle refers to can be seen. Consider an architecture principle such as "*We should use different channels to communicate with customers*". This short formulation raises questions such as *on which channels, how many channels* or *when to communicate*.
   Discussions with the concerned stakeholders should be carried on to be able to clarify the intention of such statements and the rationales behind this formulation, and all missing information should be presented in the textual representation of the architecture principles.

3. *Lack of traceability between architecture principles and their underlying rational.* Architecture frameworks advise to capture and document the rationale of introducing architecture principles in the organisation. However, this is not always the case and sometimes a clear mapping from the strategy and goals to the refined architecture principles is missing. This practice is contrary to the intended purpose of defining and using architecture principles in the first place, which is "supporting the organisation to fulfill its missions and goals."

4. *Inability to measure the impact and implementation of architecture principles.* Winter and Aier (2011) identify that "*the difficulties regarding the enforcement of enterprise architecture principles seem to be related to the inability to measure enterprise architecture principle's implementation*". Additionally, "*low values for the involvement of relevant stakeholders and for low regular usefulness checks also contribute to the low extend and low usage of enterprise architecture principles from a business perspective*".
   In Sect. 22.3, we discuss guidelines on how to make architecture principles more operational. Furthermore, in Sect. 22.5 we discuss the evaluation of the impact of architecture principles on design decisions.

5. *Lack of methodology to refine architecture principles in architecture (design) instructions.* Before considering measurements and evaluation of implementation, consistency checks or enforcement strategies, organisations should consider defining architecture principles in such a way that they are *implementable*. In our work, we position architecture instructions as a refinement of architecture principles (see Fig. 14.1). However, in many cases in practice there is no refinement methodology and this step is based on experience and interpretation of the situation at hand. Our hypothesis is that in the textual representation of the principle, there should be added references on how this refinement is made. In Sect. 22.2, we also provide guidelines for a semi-formal representation of architecture principles as support to overcome this challenge.

6. *Formalism and tool-support.* Difficulties regarding the enforcement and measurements of principles were pointed out before in the work published by Winter and Aier (2011). There were different efforts made in formalising the architecture principles in such a way that they become specific enough to provide the desired limitation in the design space. Efforts in this direction were made by Chorus et al. (2007) and van Bommel et al. (2007). Op 't Land and Proper (2007) discuss the expected impact of principles on the architecture, define rules for formulating the principles in a *SMART* way and give real-world examples.

   However, this work does not provide a formal language to represent the principles, but it recognises the need for one, alongside with the *"mechanisms to indeed enforce principles and guide designers in their design activities"*. To that end, in Sect. 22.1, we refer to an open source Eclipse-based plugin for representing our models.

14.3 Conclusion

In this chapter, we reflected on the need for more explicit support for the creation and formulation of architecture principles, such that they are implementable and operational. We motivated this in Sect. 14.2, by presenting non-excursively the challenges practitioners and enterprises face when using architecture principles. In Chap. 22, we provide more operational guidelines, as well as a semi-formal framework to represent architecture principles in a semi-formal language, providing answers to Research Question 14.1.1 and Research Question 14.1.2.

Chapter 15
The Need for Explicit Decision-Making Strategies

Georgios Plataniotis

Abstract In this chapter, we discuss the need to support ACET with information on the rationalisation of design decisions. By doing so, enterprise architects can have an enhanced comprehensibility of the existing, as-is, architecture which helps them to better coordinate the enterprise transformation towards the future, to-be, enterprise architecture design.

We start by briefly describing the important steps of an enterprise transformation, some possible problems that arise due to the lack of design rationalisation and then we discuss how existing design rationale techniques can be extended to support the capturing of design rationales for enterprise architecture.

15.1 Introduction

Modern enterprises have to cope with different challenges such as new business models and incorporation of new technologies. These challenges require organisations to be flexible and adaptable to this constantly changing environment. To ensure that enterprises have the required transformation capabilities (Government of the United States of America 2002), senior management has to make informed decisions on the design of the core organisational structure, as well as the IT that will support this structure (Lankhorst 2012). Furthermore, modern enterprises have to conform to different types of requirements. For example, legal requirements impose transparency in their operations, etc. (Ghanavati et al. 2009). Situations like these, underline the need for a mechanism that will assist senior management and stakeholders with enterprise transformations.

G. Plataniotis
e-Government Center for Social Security (IDIKA), Likourgou 10, 105 51 Athens, Greece
e-mail: georgeplataniotis@gmail.com

© Springer International Publishing AG, part of Springer Nature 2017   153
H.A. Proper et al. (eds.), *Architectural Coordination of Enterprise Transformation*,
The Enterprise Engineering Series, https://doi.org/10.1007/978-3-319-69584-6_15

A well-established perspective for the management of enterprise transformations, used both in academia and industry, is the domain of enterprise engineering (Harmsen et al. 2009). Enterprise engineering involves the use of an engineering-based approach for the design of enterprises. Enterprise engineering activities can be categorised in three main steps (Harmsen et al. 2009):

Assess—The identification (diagnosis) of the problem/status that the transformation has to solve in the enterprise. This assessment provides the motivations as well as the requirements for the transformation.

Aim—The identification of how the transformation will solve the problem. In other words the design of the appropriate to-be enterprise design (selection of treatment).

Act—The implementation of the designed enterprise transformation, analogous to the application of the treatment.

The execution of assess, aim, act steps follows the paradigm of PDCA cycle and should be highly iterative. The more the iterations that are executed, the better is the improvement of the transformation outcomes and the closer enterprise gets to the transformation goal (Moen and Norman 2006).

Enterprise architecture has been positioned as a steering instrument (Op 't Land et al. 2008; Hoogervorst 2004), supporting the steering needs of stakeholders during the assess, aim and act processes. A variety of domain-specific languages for the modelling of has been created, such as the ArchiMate (Iacob et al. 2012) standard. Enterprise architecture modelling languages provide a holistic overview and they help enterprise architects to realise the dependencies between business and IT. Furthermore, stakeholders from these domains can understand how their work influences other domains in the enterprise. For example, how a new software application influences an existing business process in the enterprise.

An important aspect during an enterprise transformation is, as stated before, the analysis of the problem/status of the enterprise. Enterprise architecture modelling languages provide this information by representing enterprise architecture designs. However, the design rationale of the enterprise architecture design, which actually provides justification for the design, is not captured by these languages. Design issues, alternatives and decisions behind the resulting models are often left implicit. Although we should be careful with the analogy, experience from the field of software architecture shows that leaving design rationales implicit leads to "*Architectural Knowledge vaporisation*" (cf. Jansen and Bosch 2005).

Amongst others, such lack of transparency regarding design decisions can cause design integrity issues when architects want to maintain or change the current design (Tang et al. 2007). This means that due to a lacking insight of the rationale, new designs are constructed in an ad hoc manner, without taking into consideration constraints implied by past design decisions.

Also, according to a survey for software architecture design rationale (Tang et al. 2006), a large majority of architects (85.1%) admitted the importance of design rationalisation in order to justify designs. Another interesting finding of this survey was that architects declared that after some time they frequently forget their own decisions. Moreover, anecdotal evidence from six exploratory interviews conducted with senior enterprise architects suggests that architects are often external consultants. This, of course, potentially increases the architectural knowledge gap of the enterprise architecture. The successor architect tries to understand and analyse the architecture by searching through architectural designs and unstructured requirements documentation. Based on these evidences, we conducted a survey amongst 35 enterprise architecture practitioners (Plataniotis et al. 2013b). The results indicated the usefulness of capturing rationalisation information and in parallel the lack of frameworks that are capable of capturing such an information in a structured way.

The usefulness of capturing design rationales in enterprise architecture is also acknowledged by a case study, which we conducted in a Luxembourgish Research and Technology Organisation (LuxRTO) (Plataniotis et al. 2014b). The involved stakeholders indicated that such a design rationale approach would raise their awareness of past problematic situations in the architecture, while also protecting them from repeating the same mistakes again.

Analogous to medicine, capturing and maintaining design rationales has parallels with keeping the medical history of a patient. Regardless of the doctor's critical ability, the medical history can provide valuable information which facilitates the diagnosis and in turn the treatment of a patient. Medical history is much more valuable than diagnostic tests and examinations. We argue that enterprise architecture models should be complemented with design rationale information. By doing so, architects would be able to make a better assessment of the as-is situation and in turn coordinate better future enterprise transformations.

15.2 Design Rationale

In this section, based on design rationale literature (Dutoit et al. 2006; Burge and Mistrik 2008), we briefly present what design rationale is, its basic characteristics, and how it can help us address the aforementioned issues. This introduction will help readers understand why design rationale matters and focus on the domain-specific challenges of enterprise architecture.

15.2.1 What is Design Rationale?

Design rationale management is concerned with strategies to make the underlying decision-making and rationale of designs (Lee and Lai 1991) explicit. In the 1970s, design rationale was explored in different domains, such as political debates and civil engineering. Since 1980, the software engineering community has incorporated design rationale, leading to the development of several approaches. However, capturing rationalisation in the domain of enterprise architecture, which is a relatively new domain compared to software engineering is still unexplored. Enterprise architecture introduces more challenges than software architecture, since artefacts from different domains of the enterprise, such as software, business processes, etc., should be aligned efficiently.

Design rationale provides the underlying justification knowledge behind designs and it can be captured and/or used during the design process. Designers can use this information during the analysis of existing designs/architectures to better understand the existing (as-is) design/architecture. Additionally, by using this information they are able to better explain past decisions to newcomers and therefore facilitate design communication and teaching process.

15.2.2 Design Rationale Fundamentals

Concepts that are fundamental to design rationale are:

- A *design process* (MacLean et al. 1991) comprising the activity of selecting an appropriate design for an artefact. A *design* (MacLean et al. 1991) is the description of an artefact that is detailed enough to be used for the implementation of that artefact. A design is *appropriate* when it describes an artefact that satisfies the given requirements and at the same time does not introduce unanticipated consequences by means of side/after effects. There are two types of artefacts: physical artefacts, such as buildings, IT infrastructure, and cognitive artefacts, such as software applications. Enterprise architecture deals with both types of artefacts since IT infrastructure, software and business processes are described in enterprise architecture designs.
- A *designer* is anyone that participates in the design process. The term *participates* varies per design rationale approach. Even users or clients can be considered as designers.
- The *design rationale* itself, then provides the underlying reasoning which determines the design of the artefact. Design rationale not only discusses the properties of artefacts but also other reasons which influence the design of an artefact. Furthermore, design rationale approaches can also discuss the reasons behind the selection of specific requirements since requirements are also part of the design. Last but not least, the feedback received after the execution of design decisions can also be part of design rationale.

15.2.3 Types of Design Rationale Approaches

The research field of design rationale is continuously expanding and a large number of design rationale approaches have been introduced. It is very important to understand how these approaches are differentiated. This insight will help us to determine the specific objectives for the domain of enterprise architecture. Below, we discuss different factors of categorising design rationale approaches and we reveal the main trends. Furthermore, we highlight the main issues in each category and facilitate their comparison.

There are three main ways to characterise design rationale approaches: (1) by looking how the design rationale is *represented* and *processed*, (2) by identifying if the design rationale approach *describes* or *prescribes* the design, and (3) by examining the *intuitiveness* of the design rationale approach in the design process.

15.2.3.1 Representation and Processing of Design Rationale

In the majority of the approaches, the design rationale information is divided into *chunks* which have specific properties and relationships. These chunks are usually represented by means of a conceptual, fixed or semi-formal schema which describes their properties and relationships. Another approach is linking these chunks to specific properties of a design artefact. With this way we achieve traceability from the actual design to the design rationale information.

There are three main processes that should be considered during the implementation of a rationale management system:

Design rationale capturing—This process describes the elicitation of the architectural knowledge from designers and its capturing. Design rationale can be captured with different ways. It can be done by the designer or by a professional who is specialised in design rationale documentation. Another way is to extract this information from records of communication among stakeholders of the project. Yet another way is by capturing design rationale during the use of a design support system.

Design rationale formalisation—This process describes the formalisation of the architectural knowledge into a appropriate design rationale representation. The formalisation shall facilitate the different uses of design rationale, such as design teaching, communication etc.

Using design rationale—This process describes the provision of design rationale in a way that is useful to interested stakeholders.

Rationale management systems should provide concrete process implementations. For example, an important distinction is whether the design rationale processes will be carried out during the design process (a priori) or after (a posteriori). Another distinction is if these processes are combined or they are executed separately. In the past years, most of the design rationale approaches described the capturing and formalisation process in a single process. However, in recent years, the approaches presented were either focusing on capturing or formalisation of design rationale information. For instance, the formalisation can be done by the same people who produce the rationale or by specialised personnel in rationale formalisation. Another way is that a specialised software system is responsible for the formalisation of informally stated rationale. Finally, concrete implementations should be provided regarding the access to design rationale information. Possible approaches are the use of hyperdocuments which summarise the rationale, information retrieval techniques for the identification of relevant information and knowledge-based techniques that inform user for possible design rationale information.

15.2.3.2 Descriptive or Prescriptive Design Rationale

Descriptive approaches are designed to capture the thinking process of designers without intervening in this process. Their main focus is on organising the design rationale after the design decisions have been made. They are mostly used for design teaching and maintenance activities. Therefore, the nature of these approaches is to provide a *descriptive* model of the decision-making process of designers.

Prescriptive approaches focus on intervening in the activities of designers. Though this intervention they aim to improve the decision-making process and reasoning of designers and in turn make the design more concrete and persistent. In parallel, prescriptive approaches can be also used to capture and organise the reasoning behind design decisions and play as well the role of descriptive approaches. Therefore, descriptive and prescriptive approaches are not necessarily mutually exclusive.

15.2.3.3 Intrusiveness of Design Rationale

Another parameter of differentiation among design rationale approaches is their intrusiveness in the design process. It can be evaluated by how much the approach intrudes in the actual design process or by the way it intrudes. For example, an approach can be highly intrusive during the capture of the design rationale and less intrusive during the retrieval of this information or the other way round. Possible ways to measure the intuitiveness can be the effort needed for using the approach or the level of restriction of the design freedom.

The more-intrusive approaches intervene in the design process by guiding the way that design rationale is captured by the designers. These type of approaches use standardised schemas which guide the designer on his design activities, on the elements of information that are captured and the way that these elements are interrelated.

The less-intrusive approaches aim to provide a more loose way of intervention in the design process. The less-intrusive concept for design rationale appeared due to concerns about the capturing effort of design rationale approaches. More specifically, the research community perceived intrusiveness as an obstacle for the adoption of design rationale mechanisms from practitioners.

15.2.4 Design Rationale Approaches and Related Work

Below, we position the need for design rationale against existing requirements engineering approaches and the motivation extension of the ArchiMate language. We argue that this is an important comparison since these approaches provide also a certain degree of rationalisation, but as we will see, from a different point of view. We briefly discuss what is the added value of design rationale especially for the domain of enterprise architecture.

Goal-oriented requirements engineering approaches (Horkoff and Yu 2013; Liaskos et al. 2011; Elahi and Yu 2012) propose mechanisms for decision analysis and prioritisation of requirements. However, requirements engineering approaches deal with the problem-space of an architecture. Despite the fact that some concepts from goal-oriented modelling can be used to describe design rationales, goal-oriented concepts are more generic. For one, a goal can denote a high-level, strategic goal (e.g. "*make more profit*") pertaining to the problem-space. However, a goal can also denote very specific, attribute-level, criteria pertaining to the solution-space, such as the criterion "*have good usability*" for a software application.

Differently, in the words of Burge and Brown (2000), design rationale approaches focus on the "solution-space". The solution-space comes after the translation of high-level goals into more specific ones (which Burge and Brown (2000) refer to as the requirements space), and before the specific design (the design-space). Figure 15.1 provides the positioning of design rationale with regard to requirements engineering space and design/solution-space.

Furthermore, since its second version, the ArchiMate language has had a motivation extension. The motivation extension is used to model the reasons behind architectural changes, but lacks concepts common to existing rationalisation approaches. For example, it does not capture design alternatives, the used decision-making strategy or unanticipated consequences of decisions.

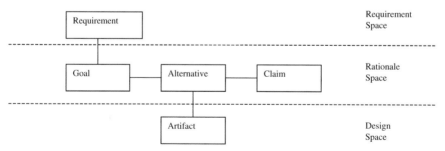

Fig. 15.1 Design rationale positioning

15.3 Design Rationale and Enterprise Architecture

As already discussed, design rationale is a well-established domain and a plethora of approaches have been developed in the area of Software Architecture, etc. However, the domain of enterprise architecture still remains unexplored. In a survey (Plataniotis et al. 2013b) that was conducted among 65 enterprise architecture practitioners, it was indicated that they rarely document their design decisions in a standardised way. Instead of a standardised method, they capture rationale information by using word processors and other unstructured methodologies. Possibly, this lack of a standardised way of documenting and using rationale information in enterprise architecture discourages practitioners from capturing this information.

As a first step on the identification of the design rationale challenges for the domain of enterprise architecture, we explored enterprise architecture literature (Lankhorst 2012; Greefhorst and Proper 2011; van't Wout et al. 2010) and we identified some key points regarding design rationale and capturing of design decisions in enterprise architecture. The following list summarises our findings:

- An enterprise architecture should not only capture the relationships between business and technology, but also the environmental changes and the process of the architectural change.
  A good architecture should also discuss these issues by means of the architectural decisions and their relationships with business goals. The way that architectural decisions are related is also important for describing the impact of these decisions on different aspects of the organisation. By doing so, stakeholders are able to, for example, identify which improvements can a specific IT system bring in relation to the cost of acquiring that system.
- The architects should also be able to externalise the underlying decision-making and their actions while they are modelling. By doing so, they will be more aware of what they are doing and think in a more explicit and rational way.
- Lankhorst (2012) refers to specific *document modelling actions* that would be useful during an enterprise transformation. It is explicitly mentioned that recording of rationales related to traceability, accountability, etc., as well as the documentation and revisiting of rejected alternatives are important actions.
- The complexity of the enterprise architecture domain imposes the need to create modelling languages that describe the architecture with different ways or viewpoints. ArchiMate (Iacob et al. 2012) is a representative example of this philosophy.
  In enterprise architecture literature (Lankhorst 2012), we can find a classification in three main classes of enterprise architecture viewpoints, respectively for: designing, decision-making and informing. Viewpoints for designing assist architects and designers with their design process. Viewpoints for decision-making assist stakeholders by providing them better insights regarding traceability of their design decisions, rationale and support their decision-making process by means of decision-making techniques. Finally, information viewpoints provide the means to inform stakeholders about the enterpriser architecture, enhance their understanding and improve their commitment.

- A common situation in various IT projects is that designers have too much design freedom during the planning of to-be architectures. This freedom results in lengthy design processes. Enterprise architecture principles (Greefhorst and Proper 2011) play a significant role there, by reducing the design freedom and in turn the complexity of decision-making processes.
- Currently, enterprise architecture modelling languages such as ArchiMate can relate the various entities of enterprise architecture with specific motivational elements. By doing so, it would be feasible to assess in more detail how concrete enterprise architecture decisions contribute to the realisation of specific organisational goals.

15.4 Objectives of a Rationale Management System

A rationale management system for enterprise architecture should be capable to address the aforementioned issues. However, the thorough capturing of rationalisation information even for simpler designs than enterprise architecture is a very labourious and costly procedure. The socio-technical nature of the domain of enterprise architecture increases the capturing effort even further. Designers of such systems have to select which parts of information are the most critical to be captured by the system. Moreover, the designers of rationale management systems have to make decisions between formality or informality of the captured information and the way that this information should be captured. This potentially introduces an even higher diversity of interactions that should be captured.

By having already speculated on the need for rationale management systems in enterprise architecture, and some of the key issues involved, we now consider a case study (Plataniotis et al. 2014c) in a LuxRTO, where we identified main objectives and challenges for the development of a rationale management for enterprise architecture. These findings can also be used to adapt existing design rationale approaches of other domains towards the domain of enterprise architecture.

Challenge 1—One of the main goals of enterprise architecture is the provision of reasoning of design decisions. However, the capturing of reasoning during an enterprise architecture design process is challenging due to the fact that the design decisions have to satisfy the requirements of stakeholders from different domains (Business, IT). As we previously saw in our case study, different factors influence their decision-making, which in turn affect the quality of design decisions. Situations such as time stress, budget restrictions or the conformance with organisational principles are common in enterprise architecture and change the way in which stakeholders make design decisions. The objective for rationale management in the context of enterprise architecture is to capture this reasoning process. In doing so, stakeholders which analyse enterprise architecture designs will be capable to better understand why specific decisions were made and under which decision-making—context.

Challenge 2—Another important aspect of design rationale approaches is the alignment between business and IT. This means that the IT artefacts should support effectively the realisation of new business processes. As we saw, during an enterprise transformation several design decisions are made, both on the business and IT side. These design decisions rarely exist in isolation. Rather, design decisions are often cross-cutting and intertwined. A rationale management system for enterprise architecture should be able to capture the different types of relationships among design decisions. For example, design decisions made on business levels can infer design decisions in IT level of the organisation and vice-versa. On the other hand-design decisions can be interrelated with a specific enterprise architecture artefact or domain of the enterprise. A regulation management system should be able to distinguish between these different relationships of design decisions. In this way, it would better express the traceability and dependencies of design decisions in enterprise architecture.

Challenge 3—Another important objective is the traceability between an enterprise architecture and the underlying design decisions. More specifically, during the analysis of the enterprise design, stakeholders should be able to identify which design decisions constitute specific enterprise architecture artefacts and how the design decisions of these artefacts are related with other design decisions in the architecture. For example, we can start tracing from the addition of the new application interface of the financial application and we can check which decisions are related with this artefact.

Challenge 4—Sometimes, design decisions can have unanticipated consequences in the artefact itself or in different artefacts in the enterprise architecture. As an example, consider the design decision based on a spreadsheet template that had negative consequences in the use of a budget forecast business process. A rationale management system should also keep track of these incidents and how they were addressed by means of newer decisions. By doing so, enterprise architects who want to analyse and have a holistic view of the architecture can identify existing vulnerabilities in the enterprise which can be prevented by remaking the same design decision in future architectural transformations.

Challenge 5—Design decisions are quite often based on assumptions. Having a more explicit representation of architectural decisions, and their underlying assumptions, enables traceability. For example, in terms of formal reasoning towards *what-if* analysis if given assumptions change.

15.5 Conclusion

To conclude this chapter, we define a set of concrete research questions. We argue that these research questions can address the above-mentioned objectives and in turn the challenges for a rationale management system for enterprise architecture.

Research Question 15.5.1 *Which are the essential concepts that rationalise design decisions in enterprise architecture?*

There is a plethora of approaches for the rationalisation of different domains (civil, software architecture). These approaches have introduced different sets of domain-specific concepts. By answering this research question, we aim to identify which concepts from existing frameworks can be used for the domain of enterprise architecture and what is actually missing to provide a holistic overview of design rationale in enterprise architecture. The identification of these concepts will provide a taxonomy of rationalisation information for enterprise architecture and in turn the basis for the development of a design theory for the same purpose. The challenge, from a design theory point of view, is the identification of possible relationships among these concepts which in turn will enhance the utility of the design theory.

Research Question 15.5.2 *How do we make the underlying decision-making process that was executed during the enterprise architecture design explicit?*
As also stated, the decision-making environment in enterprise architecture is challenging due to the implication of different stakeholders from different domains and due to factors that affect the decision-making process. We argue that the capturing and representation of this underlying information can assist stakeholders during the inspection of the as-is architecture to analyse the evaluation process for specific decisions and recognise which factors actually influenced this decision-making process. By doing so, they can consult for their future evaluations by following/avoiding good/bad evaluations from past decision-making processes.

Research Question 15.5.3 *How do we capture and represent different decision relationships in enterprise architecture?*
The confrontation of this research question will provide a holistic overview and traceability of the enterprise architecture. The domain of enterprise architecture introduces several challenges since decisions from a specific domain (IT) can be related with decisions of the same or another domain (Business). The same applies also for the outcomes of enterprise architecture decisions since the application of a specific decision may introduce problematic situations in different domains of the enterprise. To cope with this research question we will investigate existing design rationale approaches from different domains and we will identify the specificities imposed by the domain of enterprise architecture.

Research Question 15.5.4 *How to use explicit representations of design rational as a base for reasoning?*
The long-term research goal is to explore the possibility of explicitly linking architecture-level design decisions with their underlying assumptions. The aim of doing so is to make the rationalisation of these decisions explicit and traceable, so that one can formally reason about them in terms of a logic-based framework. This will enable explicit reasoning about the connections between the enterprise's architecture, the associated design decisions, and their underlying assumptions. Formalising the elements in an architectural decision model has been shown to be useful for the structuring of knowledge, and the measuring of the quality of existing decisions.

In Part III, the above research questions will be addressed in terms of two possible elements of an ACET design theory. In particular, a framework to represent the rationale underlying architectural decisions (Chap. 23) and a logic-based framework to reason about these decisions (Chap. 24).

Part III
Harvesting Components of an ACET Design Theory

Where the previous two parts explored the challenges facing ACET from a practical and a theoretical perspective, respectively, this part will discuss a collection of components for a possible design theory for ACET. As mentioned in Sect. 1.5, these design components have been "harvested" from the work of the individual researchers in the programme. Instead of an integrated method, this collection of components constitutes method fragments that can be arranged in different ways depending on the perspective taken and, most of all, on the actual enterprise architecture management approach, the enterprise transformation type, and the transformation's context. Collectively, these components aim to address the challenges identified in Part I from an empirical perspective and Part II from a more theoretical and/or literature perspective.

- In Chap. 16, the key ACET concepts will be discussed that underpin the other components explained in the ensuing chapters.
- Chapter 17 provides a reference framework, more specifically a catalogue of capabilities needed for doing ACET. As such, it also provides guidance on which elements/artefacts of enterprise architecture can be used to support which aspects of enterprise transformation.
  The framework as a whole provides a structure for the solution components that addresses the challenges presented in Part II.
- In Chap. 18, we zoom in on the engagement of stakeholders in decision making during ACET. A framework for stakeholder involvement is presented that specifically aims to manage the coherence between different key perspectives of an enterprise. The framework specifically aims to meet the challenges identified in Chap. 10.
- To convey information, and to improve shared understanding among communities of practice during enterprise transformation, one of the major communication devices are models. Chapter 19 provides concrete guidelines to use models as communication devices, particularly by regarding them as boundary objects. These guidelines provide partial answers to the challenges identified in Chaps. 9 and 10.
- During an enterprise transformation, many stakeholders with extensive and diverse information requirements need to be coordinated. These requirements need to be fulfilled by enterprise transformation managers. Providing decision-relevant information for an enterprise transformation is important. Chapter 20 provides a reference model for the information requirements for ACET.
  The presented reference model aims to meet the challenges discussed in Chaps. 9 and 11.
- Given the importance of models for ACET, it is also important to take care in selecting and engineering modelling languages. Chapter 21, therefore, introduces a design artefact for value-based componential language engineering. In doing so, Chap. 21 aims to meet the challenges identified in Chap. 13.
- Architecture principles provide a normative means to direct and coordinate enterprise transformation. Chapter 22 provides an overview on the formulation of architecture principles, while also providing guidelines for a semiformal

definition of principles. As such, Chap. 22 aims to provide answers to the challenges discussed in Chap. 14.

- Chapter 23 defines a framework to capture architecture design decisions. This framework allows for a contextualisation of the decision-making process of a single decision and a comparison of decision outcomes to the original decision-making process.
  The resulting framework aims to meet some of the challenges identified in Chap. 15.
- In Chap. 24, a logic-based framework is presented that enables formal reasoning of the design decisions captured using the framework presented in Chap. 23. This will enable consistency checks of the underlying rationales and advanced impact/what-if analysis when confronted with changes.
  The resulting logic-based framework aims to address some of the challenges identified in Chap. 15.
- Not all ACET problems are equal, and ACET solutions therefore need to be configured to address the specifics of the respective ACET problem. While many additional contingencies might also be relevant, the most important differences of ACET problem situations result from the enterprise architecture management approach and transformation type. Chapter 25 identifies strategies for situation adaption of ACET.
  Chapter 25 also aims to address some of the challenges identified in Chap. 12.

Chapter 16
ACET Constructs

Sybren de Kinderen

Abstract In this chapter, we discuss the key ACET concepts that underpin the other components as discussed in the ensuing chapters.

16.1 General ACET Constructs

16.1.1 Enterprise Transformation

We define an enterprise transformation as a fundamental, purposeful change to one or more key constituencies of the extended enterprise. Here, *constituencies* include products/services, channels, partner constellation, or otherwise. Furthermore, *purposeful* change refers to an intended, engineered, change—as opposed to an emerging/evolutionary change that happens organically and in an unplanned manner. Meanwhile, a transformation is *fundamental* in the sense that it disrupts the everyday operations of the enterprise (Rouse 2005). In addition, an enterprise transformation is typically:

- Related to the long-term objectives of an enterprise
- Of a cross-functional/departmental/organisational nature, that is, having an enterprise-wide instead of a purely local impact

S. de Kinderen
University of Duisburg-Essen, Universitätsstr. 9, 45141 Essen, Germany
e-mail: sybren.dekinderen@uni-due.de

© Springer International Publishing AG, part of Springer Nature 2017   169
H.A. Proper et al. (eds.), *Architectural Coordination of Enterprise Transformation*,
The Enterprise Engineering Series, https://doi.org/10.1007/978-3-319-69584-6_16

16.1.2 Architecture

We adopt the ISO/IEC 42010:2007 definition of architecture: "*The fundamental organisation of a system, embodied in its components, their relationships to each other and the environment, and the principles governing its design and evolution*" (IEEE 2000).

16.1.3 Enterprise Architecture

As implied by its name, we define *enterprise architecture* as the architecture of the enterprise. However, an enterprise is typically a sociotechnical system, in that it consists of a collection of actors that have a common goal (The Open Group 2011). Therefore, in addition to the predominantly technical ISO definition, we stress that an enterprise architecture has a strong social dimension. Particularly, for *enterprise* architecture it is vital that the aforementioned *fundamental organisation of a system* is based on actor consensus, so that it is embodied in/intertwined with (everyday) enterprise operations.

16.1.4 Enterprise Architecture Management

As implied by name, *enterprise architecture management* (EAM) entails the management of Enterprise Architecture (EA). EAM encompasses both (1) how to describe and envision representations of a diverse set of artefacts and their dependencies, but also (2) how to reach consensus among stakeholders about the current status and the desired future state of the enterprise.

16.1.5 Coordination

Coordination can be defined as "*the process of managing dependencies among activities*" (Malone and Crowston 1994, p. 87) with the goal to achieve larger, purposeful wholes (Holt 1988). Accordingly, coordination deals with three major themes: first, the interdependence of tasks; second, the relation to outcome achievement; and third, the concept of process.

Coordination may also be seen as a state or condition, "*but that state can be maintained only to the extent that the environment is stable, participation is continuous, work tasks and activities are stable, products and services do not change, and the means of coordination are maintained*" (Williams and Karahanna 2013).

In line with the aforementioned definition, we focus on coordination as a process.

16.1.6 Method Fragment/Method Chunk

A method fragment can be considered as an atomic part of a method (Henderson-Sellers and Ralyté 2010), whereby Henderson-Sellers and Ralyté (2010) define a method (admittedly somewhat circularly) as . . . *an approach to perform a software/ systems development project*. Based upon a synthesis on key method fragment characteristics by Cossentino et al. (2008), a method fragment can be considered to consist of the following main parts: the actor(s) involved, the fragment activity (what the fragment does), the fragment guidelines (how to perform the fragment's activities), and the fragment result.

16.1.7 Model

A model is a purposeful abstraction of reality. In addition, in line with Bjeković et al. (2014), we consider that models manifest themselves as artefacts that are acknowledged by at least one observer to represent some aspect of importance. This excludes mental models/conceptions from our definition of a model, which reside in the mind only.

16.1.8 Stakeholder

According to the well-established management model of the University of St. Gallen, stakeholders can be understood as (translated from German) *"organised or unorganised groups of people, organisations and institutions, that are affected by entrepreneurial value creation, and sometimes also by (environmental) damage creation"* (Rüegg-Stürm 2004).

16.2 Key Constructs for ACET Method Fragments

16.2.1 Value

Traditionally, economics and marketing literature distinguish between value-in-use and value-in-exchange (Ramsay 2005). With value-in-use, one considers how a product/service is actually valuable to the customer, in terms of utility (a product/service is a means to an end), aesthetics (a product/service has a perceived beauty), or otherwise; in monetary terms, one expresses value-in-use is as the maximum willingness to pay. With value-in-exchange, one considers the exchange of a product/service to the customer without its actual use; in monetary terms, one expresses value-in-exchange in terms of the price that the customer actually has to pay for a product/service.

We interpret value in line with the notion of value-in-use. This is consistent with Vargo et al. (2008), who consider that value is largely cocreated between customer and supplier when a product/service is actually used, rather than that value exist as an inherent part of the product/service prior to its use (the latter being expressed as part of the value-in-exchange perspective).

16.2.2 Organisational Subculture

We define organisational subculture as the sum of values, norms, and attitudes, which are adopted consciously or unconsciously by the members of an organisational subgroup (e.g. department, hierarchy level, function), and which distinguish the members of that subgroup from those of another subgroup (Schein 2004; Hofstede et al. 2010; Kraus et al. 2006).

16.2.3 Decision

We define decision as the choice made between alternative courses of action in a situation of uncertainty. Before we concentrate on the final choice between alternatives, we have to consider the whole decision-making activity as a whole. Therefore the decision-making process is described as a series of steps, starting with information output and analysis and culminating in resolution, namely, a selection from several available alternatives (Eilon 1969).

16.2.4 Architecture Principles

In line with Greefhorst and Proper (2011), we consider architecture principles as normative statements that restrict design freedom and that are used to "…*fill the gap between high-level strategic intents and concrete designs*" (Greefhorst and Proper 2011, p. 28).

16.2.5 Information Systems Model

An information systems model provides the static and dynamic aspects of an information system in terms of conceptual models (focusing on the business problem and not on technical aspects), design models (describing larger technical building blocks), and implementation models (closely related to software programming) (Ahlemann 2009).

An information model is an information systems model that focuses on information objects.

16.2.6 Reference Model

Compared to models that are used in a single context for a certain purpose, reference models are meant to be more generic (Luiten et al. 1993). Such a model is considered to be a conceptual framework that can be used as a starting point for (more specific) information systems design and development (Fettke and Loos 2007).

16.2.7 Community of Practice

'Community of practice' is a term to describe a group of people that (1) share a joint area of concern (e.g. share the same tasks in an organisation or are interested in the same topics), (2) regularly interact within a set of community-specific norms and relations, and (3) possess a shared repertoire of resources such as languages, methods, tools, stories, or other communal artefacts (Wenger 2000).

16.2.8 Boundary Object

Boundary objects are abstract or physical artefacts that support knowledge sharing and coordination among different communities of practice by providing common ground.

16.2.9 Institution

An institution *represents a social order or pattern that has attained a certain state or property* (Jepperson 1991). Said differently, an institution is a practice with *a rule-like status in social thought and action* (Meyer and Rowan 1977). Institutional practices may diffuse through coercive, normative, and mimetic mechanisms (DiMaggio and Powell 1983).

16.2.10 Institutionalisation

Institutionalisation can be defined as the process of establishing a practice as a norm, such that it gets a rule-like status in social thought and action (Meyer and Rowan 1977).

Chapter 17
Transformation Intelligence Capability Catalogue

Ralf Abraham, Simon Weiss, Nils Labusch, Stephan Aier, and Robert Winter

Abstract In this chapter we present a reference framework, more specifically a catalogue of capabilities, needed for doing ACET. As such, it also provides guidance on which elements/artefacts of enterprise architecture can be used to support which aspects of enterprise transformation. For architects, it shows where their services might generate value, if requested. For transformation managers, it provides a "*capability catalogue*", describing for which parts of enterprise transformation they may seek advice from the enterprise architects. The framework as a whole provides a structure for the solution components that addresses the challenges as presented in Part II, and it comprises of the perspectives of strategy, value and risk, design, implementation, and change. The capabilities of all the perspectives together support transformation management, which is concerned with the management tasks at the overall transformation level, and with the architectural coordination function, which forms an umbrella function of integrating the individual perspectives into a consistent whole.

The transformation intelligence capability catalogue provides a framework for the solution components that address the challenges presented in Part II. The underlying assumption of ACET and of the framework is that large enterprise transformations often involve several or all organisational units of an enterprise and that these organisational units operate primarily based on their local goals, information, resources, etc. An architectural coordination approach thus needs to integrate these

R. Abraham • S. Weiss • N. Labusch • S. Aier (✉) • R. Winter
Institute of Information Management, University of St.Gallen, St. Gallen, Switzerland
e-mail: ralf.abraham@unisg.ch; stephan.aier@unisg.ch

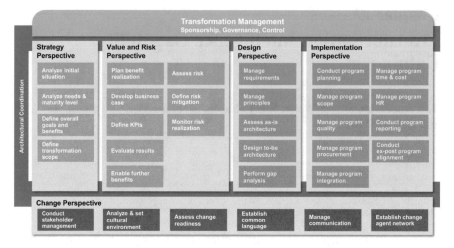

Fig. 17.1 Transformation intelligence capability catalogue

local perspectives to an enterprise-wide perspective in order to support an enterprise transformation adequately. Enterprise architects and the function of enterprise architecture management aiming at providing such enterprise-wide perspectives may therefore provide major parts of the architectural coordination to an enterprise transformation.

The transformation intelligence capability catalogue shows which parts of an enterprise transformation may benefit from architectural coordination, and it shows where architectural coordination, and therefore the discipline of enterprise architecture management, may be involved. For architects, it shows where their services might generate value, if requested. For transformation managers, it provides a "*capability catalogue*", describing for which parts of enterprise transformation they may seek advice from the enterprise architects. At this point, it is important to emphasise that neither can enterprise architecture support every aspect of enterprise transformation nor does enterprise transformation require every artefact of enterprise architecture. Instead, the transformation intelligence capability catalogue provides guidance which artefacts of enterprise architecture can use to support which aspects of enterprise transformation. The framework (see Fig. 17.1) is not intended to be applied uniformly towards any organisation; rather, since different organisations perform enterprise architecture in different ways (e.g. have different maturity levels of enterprise architecture) and face very specific contingencies in their transformation projects (e.g. size of the company, organisational culture, maturity towards change), the framework should be used by a specific organisation to indicate which of their enterprise architecture artefacts can support which aspects of their concrete enterprise transformation. Figure 17.1 depicts the transformation intelligence capability catalogue.

17.1 Role of the Capability Catalogue for ACET

The transformation intelligence capability catalogue depicts the connections between enterprise architecture management and enterprise transformation. It provides an integrated view of different yet complimentary perspectives in the course of an enterprise transformation. The transformation intelligence capability catalogue shows how disciplines as different as change management, programme management, value management, or enterprise architecture management all contribute to the common cause of enterprise transformation. By looking at these disciplines holistically from an architectural coordination perspective, the transformation intelligence capability catalogue is able to provide insight into enterprise transformation that would be missed if each of the perspectives was considered individually. The transformation intelligence capability catalogue is thus neither a transformation catalogue nor an enterprise architecture management catalogue. It is a catalogue that aims to support enterprise transformation by orchestrating different perspectives from an architectural vantage point.

Methodically, the transformation intelligence capability catalogue has been built over four design iterations (Labusch et al. 2013) following a collaborative design science research process (Otto and Österle 2012). The initial version has been derived from a review of literature on related disciplines such as strategic management, programme management, or change management. This initial version has then been refined and reflected jointly with a group of 11 experts from seven organisations (primarily in the insurance and utilities industries). The experts had leading positions in enterprise architecture management in their respective organisations, and each expert had several years of enterprise architecture management and industry experience.

The catalogue consists of the following perspectives: strategy, value and risk, design, implementation, and change. These perspectives support transformation management, which is concerned with the management tasks at the overall transformation level, and the architectural coordination function, which forms an umbrella function of integrating the individual perspectives into a consistent whole. It is important to note that these perspectives do not represent a phase or process model. Although, some of the perspectives may be more important than others in different stages of an enterprise transformation, the general assumption is that all of the perspectives are relevant throughout an enterprise transformation. For example, the value and risk perspective is not only relevant when planning an enterprise transformation and its respective value proposition. It will also be important during the actual implementation of an enterprise transformation for making sure that planned benefits are actually realised. And it may be important after the implementation of an enterprise transformation for evaluating the actual (sustainable) occurrence of the planned and implemented benefits, and for planning for achieving additional benefits after the enterprise transformation. These latter benefits may be discussed after the enterprise transformation because this potential was just unknown when starting the enterprise transformation.

Each of these perspectives comprise a set of capabilities (depicted as rectangular boxes in Fig. 17.1). It is important to note that these capabilities are described on an abstract level. In other words transformation intelligence capability catalogue does not prescribe how exactly to implement each of these capabilities. In fact, for most of these capabilities, academic literature as well as corporate practice provides a plethora of method fragments and techniques, many of them well-known in the organisations facing an enterprise transformation. It is therefore not reasonable to invent yet another set of method fragments and techniques. However, in the course of developing ACET we found that some of the capabilities and their respective method fragments and techniques would benefit from the particular ACET perspective. These are the method fragments that we focus in Part III.

17.2 Method Fragments of the Capabilities Catalogue

In the following, we introduce each of the six perspectives of the transformation intelligence capability catalogue. For those perspectives that are covered by an ACET method fragment, we will briefly introduce that fragment. For the other perspectives, we will point to alternative approaches that may be consulted when performing tasks related to that perspective. Figure 17.2 provides an overview of the mapping.

1. The strategy perspective is concerned with defining the overall transformation strategy and monitoring its implementation. In this perspective, the overall scope of the enterprise transformation has to be defined. The scoping has to be done based on the identified needs, but at the same time on the current maturity

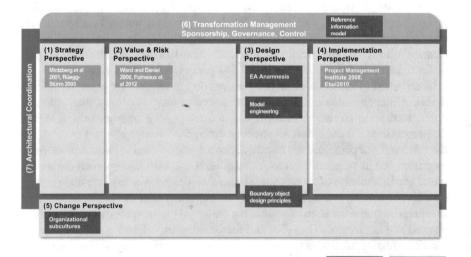

Fig. 17.2 Mapping of ACET method fragments to the corporate intelligence catalogue

level. Enterprise transformation is always a path-dependent activity, that is, possible transformation goals and scopes are to a certain degree predetermined by the initial situation, as well as the organisational maturity level towards transformation. This is the main reason why some organisations find it easier to change than others, independent of external circumstances.

Coverage within ACET: The strategy perspective is not covered directly by an ACET method fragment. We advise readers to consult strategic management literature, for example, Mintzberg et al. (2001) and Rüegg-Stürm (2005).

2. The value and risk perspective is primarily a quantitative perspective, as it aims to balance between cost, risk, and benefits. On the value side, strategic goals are broken down into smaller work packages, and business cases are defined for these. A particularly important task in this perspective is the definition of suitable KPIs. KPIs should follow the SMART scheme and be specific, measurable, actionable, realistic, and timely. A meaningful evaluation of benefits requires measurable, specific benefits that can be measured within the time frame of the enterprise transformation (timeliness). Likewise, KPIs should be actionable and realistic, otherwise they may even cause communication defects (Niemietz et al. 2013). For example, when transformation management provides unrealistic targets that are not actionable within the transformation strategy (e.g. establishing a KPI that measures absolute quality within a transformation project that aims primarily at cost cutting), employees might lose trust in the transformation management, or the sincerity and seriousness of the enterprise transformation. On the risk side, risks need to be identified and assessed. Assessment of risk is typically done in two dimensions: likelihood of risk occurrence and severity of impact of the undesirable event. Depending on the specific nature of the risk, mitigation measures for one or two of the dimensions can be defined. Consider the risk of a database failure: The likelihood of occurrence can be lowered by providing redundant power supply, strong security to guard against unauthorised access, etc. Additionally, assuming that the risk has materialised (the event has taken place; the database has failed), the severity of the impact can be lowered by providing a backup, or even a full replication on a second system, so that one can switch from the main system to the replica system without users even noticing. In other events, particularly when the consequences of the risk would be disastrous, mitigation measures can only aim at reducing the likelihood of occurrence. This is a characteristic trait of high-reliability organisations like nuclear power plants or air traffic service providers: the severity of the impact cannot be mitigated, so all risk management activities have to focus on lowering the likelihood of occurrence. Consider civil aviation: in the event of a crash, the (potentially fatal) consequences of that event cannot be mitigated, so elaborate schemes are in place to prevent such events from even happening (note: this is different in military aviation—here, parachutes can be issued).

Coverage within ACET: The value and risk perspective is not covered directly by an ACET method fragment. This perspective is central to disciplines like corporate controlling. Tested techniques exist within for both value management and risk management, for example, value dependency networks (Ward and Daniel 2006) or risk matrices (Furneaux et al. 2012).

3. The design perspective is primarily concerned with depicting the future enterprise state and facilitating the transition towards it. A central purpose of this perspective is providing design guidance by limiting the number of possible design alternatives. This is essentially a restriction of design freedom or design stress. A central capability in this perspective is the establishment and maintenance of architectural principles. These principles serve to document basic decisions and goals that shall be applied enterprise-wide to all programmes (e.g. preference for a certain programming language in software development projects or a preference of buying third-party application over own development initiatives). Moreover, requirement analyses, models depicting a desired future state, and gap analyses between the as-is and the envisioned to-be state are parts of this perspective.

   Coverage within ACET: This perspective is central to ACET. Several method fragments provide actual design guidance for enterprise architecture models, making them fit for use in enterprise transformation situations. The EA Anamnesis Approach (Chapter 23) enhances existing enterprise architecture models with design rationale information. For example, decision alternatives, criteria, and decision-making strategies may be captured in the model and may help understand why certain design decisions were taken. The Guidelines for Architecture Models as Boundary Objects (Chapter 19) give guidance on how the acceptance of models as boundary objects may be increased: models adhering to these design principles are more likely to be adopted as boundary objects, and can thus make a contribution towards establishing common ground among diverse communities of practice (e.g. fostering a shared understanding on transformation goals and plans between business and IT communities). The Model Bundling (Chapter 21) allows for the construction of domain-specific modelling languages and thus supports the generation of as-is and to-be models that have a high fit to a specific enterprise (e.g. by incorporating industry-specific concepts).

4. The implementation perspective covers the transition between the as-is and the to-be state of the enterprise. Central activities in this perspective are concerned with project and programme management. Especially the alignment between different programmes is essential for implementing a desired transformation plan in a consistent manner. Underscoring the importance of alignment, this perspective contains a dedicated activity for ex-post alignment.

   Coverage within ACET: The implementation perspective is not covered directly by an ACET method fragment. A rich body of literature exists on programme and project management (Axelos 2009; PMI 2008). This perspective has strong connections with the design perspective, as models of to-be states are important inputs for programme scoping, and gap analyses and principles are vital instruments in ensuring (or restoring ex-post) alignment.

5. In the change perspective, we focus on the people aspect of enterprise transformation. Conceptualising and implementing a communication strategy towards all relevant stakeholders is a vital part of enterprise transformation, yet one that

is often overlooked. However, many enterprise transformations fail due to a one-sided focus on technological issues, while giving too little attention to people management. Central capabilities in this perspective include stakeholder management, establishment of communication plans, and the analysis of the cultural environment the enterprise transformation is situated in.

Coverage within ACET: The change perspective is addressed by the Guidelines for Architecture Models as Boundary Objects (Chapter 19). It is concerned with designing enterprise architecture models in pursuit of shared understanding.

6. The transformation management perspective is concerned with managing, sponsoring, and governing the enterprise transformation. A steering board approves required funds and provides final decisions for issues that cannot be solved within one of the other perspectives (e.g. escalating conflicting goals between programmes that cannot be resolved within the design or implementation perspectives).

   Coverage within ACET: The transformation management perspective is addressed by the ACET Information Requirements Reference Model (Chapter 20). This method fragment provides a model detailing which information transformation managers typically request in enterprise transformation situations. The information objects contained in this model will touch most of the other perspectives as well, yet the focus on the user group of transformation managers and the integrated view this model provides are the rationale for associating this method fragment with this perspective.

7. Architectural coordination, finally, is ACET. By providing a high-level perspective on the enterprise, enterprise architecture management can perform an important information supply and coordination function in enterprise transformation. This is a distinct coordination function from, for example, corporate controlling, which provides a high-level quantitative perspective (i.e. focusing on financials). Architectural coordination contains both quantitative information (e.g. complexity metrics of process or software landscapes) and qualitative/structural information (e.g. detailed impact analyses at programme level).

Chapter 18
Coherence Management Dashboard for ACET

Roel Wagter and Hend*erik* A. Proper

Abstract In this chapter we discuss an elaborated theory about how to make explicit enterprise coherence. An important trigger to develop this new theory was that too many projects failed. This concerned even projects developed under architecture. Also our practical experiences showed that existing architecture methods too often did not result into the promised contributions to the creation of successful project results. The theory is a part of the research programme GEA. After an inventory of triggers and a translation of these triggers into a set of requirements, this innovation programme took for developing this theory the following hypothesis as a starting point: "*a positive correlation exists in organisations between the level of coherence and the level of performance*". Based on these triggers, requirements, and hypothesis, the GEA innovation programme developed a theory by which the enterprise coherence can be made explicit and the enterprise coherence can be governed. In this chapter this way of governing will be explained.

18.1 Introduction

This chapter is primarily based on results from the project developing the *general enterprise architecting* (GEA) method (Wagter 2009), in particular the enterprise coherence framework parts as discussed in more detail in Wagter et al. (2013a, 2012a). The development of the GEA method was based on several case studies (see, e.g., Wagter et al. 2012b, 2013b, 2012c) with the client organisations participating in the

R. Wagter (✉)
Solventa B.V., 3439 ML Nieuwegein, The Netherlands
e-mail: roel.wagter@solventa.nl

H.A. Proper
Luxembourg Institute of Science and Technology, Esch-sur-Alzette, Luxembourg

programme, using a combination of design science (Hevner et al. 2004) as the overall rhythm and case study research (Yin 2009) to leverage the findings from the case studies. In its current form (Wagter 2009), the GEA method comprises of three core ingredients (Wagter 2009).

Next to the Enterprise Coherence Assessment (ECA) that allows organizations to assess their ability to govern coherence during enterprise transformation, it involves an enterprise coherence framework and a (situational) enterprise coherence governance approach. The latter includes the identification of specific deliverables/results to be produced and the processes needed to produce these deliverables/results, as well as an articulation of the responsibilities and competences of the people involved. The enterprise coherence framework, which will be summarised below (and discussed in more detail in Chap. 18), enables enterprises to set up their own management dashboard in terms of the enterprise coherence that can be governed/improved during enterprise transformations.

The enterprise coherence framework part of GEA specifically aims to meet the challenges as identified in Chap. 10 and is therefore the focus of this chapter. It, enables enterprises to set up their own *management dashboard* in terms of which enterprise coherence can be governed/improved during enterprise transformations. This, enterprise specific, dashboard enables senior management to govern the coherence between key aspects of an enterprise during transformations.

In line with approaches such as Dialogue Mapping (Conklin 2005), SEAM (Wegmann 2003), and the Soft Systems Methodology (Checkland 1981), the enterprise coherence framework method (Wagter 2009) suggests to take the different stakeholder groups as a starting point, that is, better accommodating the actual interests of different groups of stakeholders, while creating room for the needed strategic dialogue and negotiations. GEA goes beyond these existing approaches by defining an organisation-specific *management dashboard* for ACET, in terms of what GEA calls an *enterprise coherence dashboard* (Wagter et al. 2011, 2012d).

This section, which is based on Wagter et al. (2013a, 2012a), is structured as follows. The central element in defining an enterprise specific *management dashboard* for enterprise transformations is the enterprise coherence framework, which will be introduced in Sect. 18.2.

18.2 The Enterprise Coherence Framework

The enterprise coherence framework (Wagter et al. 2012a) defines a series of coherence elements and coherence relationships, which together define the playing field for an enterprise's coherence. For a more comprehensive description of the enterprise coherence framework, we refer to our earlier work as reported in Wagter et al. (2012a).

By making the definition of these elements explicit in a specific enterprise, a coherence management dashboard results in terms of which one can gain insight in the "state of coherence" while also being able to assess the impact of potential/ongoing

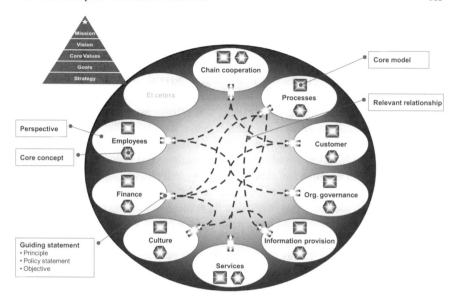

Fig. 18.1 GEA coherence elements

transformations. This then enables a deliberate governance of enterprise coherence during, or even driving, transformations.

In general terms, the enterprise coherence framework consists of a set of so-called *coherence elements* and *coherence relationships* between them. The overall level of cohesion within an actual enterprise is really determined by the explicitness of the coherence elements, and quality/consistency of the coherence relationships, in this enterprise. This also allows enterprises to govern their cohesion, in particular by guarding the coherence relationships. While this may sound abstract, the discussion of the coherence elements and their relationships is provided in the remainder of this chapter.

The enterprise coherence framework distinguishes three areas of coherence: coherence at the level of organisational purpose, coherence at the design level of the organisation, and coherence between these levels. Figure 18.1 provides a summary of the enterprise coherence framework. The different elements of the enterprise coherence framework will be elaborated below.

18.2.1 Coherence at the Strategic Level

At the level of organisational purpose, we essentially adapt the "*Strategic Development Process Model*" as proposed by Kaplan et al. (2008), the "*Strategy Formulation*" approach by Thenmozhi (2009), and the notion of endless pursuit of a company's mission from "*Building Your Company's Vision*" by Collins and Porras

(1996). Based on these theories, we distinguish five key coherence elements: *Mission*, *Vision*, *Core Values*, *Goals*, and *Strategy*:

Mission—The mission is a brief, typically one sentence, statement that defines the fundamental purpose of the organisation (Kaplan et al. 2008) that is "*enduringly pursued but never fulfilled*" (Collins and Porras 1996). It should include what the organisation provides to its clients and inform executives and employees about the overall goal they have come together to pursue (Kaplan et al. 2008).

Vision—The vision is a concise statement that operationalises the mission in terms of the mid-to long-term goals of the organisation. The vision should be external and market oriented and should express—preferably in aspirational terms—how the organisation wants to be perceived by the world (Kaplan et al. 2008). Senge (1990) indicates that in a vision there must be a creative tension between the present and the enticing imagination of the future and has to show enough ambition, which can be translated into goals and strategies.

Core values—The core values of an organisation prescribe its desired behaviour, character, and culture (Kaplan et al. 2008). We consider core values as guiding statements at the highest level of sense giving in an organisation. Together with the mission, the core values are therefore regarded as most invariant.

Goals—The vision operationalised in terms of concrete goals. These goals acts as success factors in judging the feasibility of strategies. The goals, as success factors, define the desired outcome (short-term goals) from successful strategy execution (Kaplan et al. 2008).

Strategy—A strategy of an organisation forms a comprehensive master plan stating how the organisation will pursue its mission. It should also maximise the competitive advantages and minimise competitive disadvantages (Thenmozhi 2009).

These coherence elements lead to the organisational purpose triangle as depicted in Fig. 18.2.

Fig. 18.2 The organisational purpose triangle

The coherence at this level can be derived, and made explicit, by the organisation's definitions of the coherence elements and establishing/assessing the consistency and quality of the relationships between the elements:

- The strategies should arguably lead to the achievement of the set goals, while not violating the core values.
- The goals should be in line with the vision of the organisation, and ultimately its mission, while being consistent with its core values.
- The core values should at least be consistent with the organisation's mission.

To indeed be able to establish/assess the consistency and quality of these coherence relationships, it is of great importance that an organisation's definitions of the elements are indeed available, and are explicit enough. They do constitute the fundamental drivers that shape the enterprise coherence at the design level of the organisation. In practice, the elements at the organisational purpose level are often documented in rather broad and informal terms, also increasing the risk of a low level of enterprise coherence at the design level.

To bring these coherence elements at the strategic elements to life, a few examples are provided in Table 18.1.

18.2.2 Coherence at the Design Level

At the design level, the organisation's strategy is translated into the blueprints of the operational organisation, involving among others. its business processes, financial flows, logistic flows, human resources, information systems, housing, machines, IT, etc. To achieve enterprise coherence, the coherence at the design level needs to be governed as well. Decision-makers need indicators and controls to indeed govern the coherence at this level.

The design level complements the level of purpose, by zooming in on more design-oriented concepts. A distinction between coherence at the level of organisational purpose and coherence at the level of design is consistent with the "*Structure follows strategy*" principle from Chandler (1969). The coherence elements at the design level are:

Perspective—An angle from which one wishes to govern/steer/influence enterprise transformations. The set of perspectives used in a specific enterprise depend very much on its formal and informal power structures, both internally and externally. Typical examples include culture, customer, products/services, business processes, information provision, finance, value chain, corporate governance, etc.

Core concept—A concept, within a perspective, that plays a key role in governing the organisation from that perspective. Examples of core concepts within the perspective Finance are, for instance, 'Financing' and 'Budgeting'.

Table 18.1 Examples of coherence elements on the level of purpose of an organisation

Cohesive elements	Statements
Mission	• To make people happy (Walt Disney) • To experience the joy of advancing and applying technology for the benefit of the public (Sony) • To bring inspiration and innovation to every athlete in the world (Nike) • To help leading corporations and governments be more successful (McKinsey)
Vision	Walt Disney: • Creativity + Innovation = Profits • One of the world's leading producers and providers of entertainment and information Sony: • We anticipate in the changing relationship between content, technology and the consumer by our four pillars: e-Entertainment, Digital Cinema, High-er Definition and PlayStation Nike: • Sustainable Business and Innovation is an integral part of how we can use the power of our brand, the energy and passion of our people, and the scale of our business to create meaningful change • The opportunity is greater than ever for sustainability principles and practices to deliver business returns and become a driver of growth, to build deeper consumer and community connections and to create positive social and environmental impact in the world
Core values	• Creativity, dreams, imagination, consistency, detail, preservation of the magic (Walt Disney) • Being a pioneer, authentic, doing the impossible, individual ability and creativity (Sony)
Goals	• To build a radically new kind of amusement park, known as Disneyland (in 1950s, Walt Disney) • Become the company most known for changing the worldwide poor-quality image of Japanese products (1950s, Sony)
Strategy	• Continued diversification consistent with Walt Disney's early actions • The company's increased focus on Sustainable Business and Innovation (SB&I) will be more seamlessly integrated across Nike's business strategies • Nike utilises innovation to produce top quality athletic footwear and apparel

Guiding statement—An internally agreed and published statement, which directs desirable behaviour. They only have to express a desire and/or give direction. Guiding statements may therefore cover policy statements, normative principles (Greefhorst et al. 2013), and objectives.

Core model—a high-level view of a perspective, based on, and in line with, the guiding statements of the corresponding perspective.

Relevant relationship—a description of the connection between two guiding statements of different perspectives.

The presence of a well-documented enterprise mission, vision, core values, goals, and strategy are preconditions to be able to determine the content of the coherence elements on the design level of the organisation, and they are the essential resources for this determination. See Fig. 18.1.

With the coherence elements at the design level in place, we now have an integrated framework of coherence elements that shape an organisation on both the level of purpose and the design level. In Chap. 4, we actually already provided an example of how the coherence management dashboard can be used as a steering mechanism in order to formulate answers to major business issues and how this way of working strengthens the enterprise coherence. In doing so, the dashboard allows an organisation to involve the right stakeholders (see Chap. 10).

In Fig. 18.3, a visualisation is provided on how occurrences of the coherence elements on the design level of an organisation are derived from the level of purpose. The metaphor shows the transition from an unstructured set of control information on the level of purpose into a structured coherent set of content, differentiated into the coherence elements on the design level.

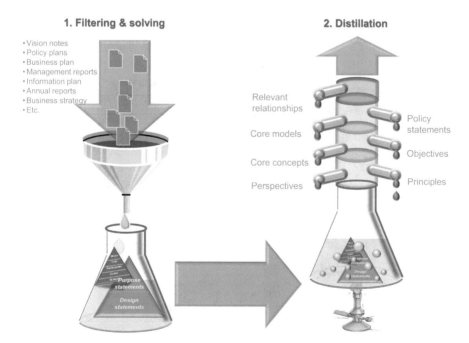

Fig. 18.3 Metaphor for the derivation of coherence elements on the design level

18.2.3 Coherence Between the Levels

Besides horizontal coherence on one level of contemplation, we also distinguish vertical coherence between two adjacent levels of coherence. To realise the strategic fit, as proposed in the *"Strategic Alignment Model"* of Henderson and Venkatraman (1993), we correlate the cohesive elements defined on the purpose level with the cohesive elements defined on the design level. This has been illustrated in Fig. 18.4.

The fundamental, transcendent, nature of the mission of a company gives a high-level understanding of the core activities to excel in, and the desired behaviour. Therefore the enterprise's mission harbours information on relevant perspectives and principles. The guiding statements should therefore also be motivated in terms of the mission. As soon as guiding statements are allocated to different perspectives, enterprise coherence is made explicit by coupling them by means of relevant relationships.

In its vision, an organisation elaborates on its envisioned position in the future. Vision statements indicate new candidate perspectives and/or new core concepts. They may also underpin and/or confirm the role of the already identified perspectives and core concepts. Furthermore the envisioned position of the organisation in the future is translated into principles and policy statements. Core values diffuse to the design level by way of principles. These values may also indicate major and minor focus areas to govern, respectively, the perspectives and core concepts. Objectives on the design level, defined as a more concrete formulation of an organisation's goal, are derived from the goals on the purpose level. Also goals may indicate major or minor focus areas to govern. Finally the strategy, seen as the strategic execution

Intensity of coupling		Core factors on design level						
Strong	++							
Weak	+			Guiding statemts				
		Perspectives	Core concepts	Principles	Objectives	Policy statements	Core models	Relevant relationships
Core factors on the level of meaning	Mission	++		++				++
	Vision	++	+	++		++		++
	Core values	+	+	++				++
	Goals	+	+		++			++
	Strategy	++	++	++	++	++		++

Fig. 18.4 Correlation between the cohesive elements on two interrelated levels of coherence

path to achieve the enterprise's goals, supplies the content to major focus areas, the perspectives; minor focus areas, core concepts; and directional information, guiding statements.

18.3 Coherence Management Dashboard

The enterprise coherence framework enables enterprises to set up their own dashboard to manage enterprise transformation, which then enables senior management to govern the coherence between key aspects of an enterprise during transformations. In Sect. 4.4 we already saw an example of such a management dashboard.

By making the definition of the coherence elements explicit in a specific enterprise, a (coherence) management dashboard results in terms of which one can gain insight in the "state of coherence", while also being able to assess the impact of potential/ongoing transformations. This then enables a deliberate governance of enterprise coherence during/driving transformations.

As mentioned before, the set of perspectives used by a specific enterprise on its coherence management dashboard is highly organisation specific. This set is not likely to correspond to the cells of well-known design frameworks such as Zachman (Zachman 1987) or TOGAF's content framework (The Open Group 2009). Such frameworks, however, can indeed play an important role in the development of the core models within the different perspectives. Based on their respective underlying "design philosophy", these more design/engineering-oriented frameworks provide a way (1) to ensure completeness and consistency from an engineering point of view, (2) to enforce/invite a specific line of reasoning on the design/construction of the enterprise, and (3) to classify/structure the different core models.

18.4 Case studies

The enterprise coherence framework, the enterprise coherence framework, together with the rest of the GEA method, involved several case studies (see, e.g., Wagter et al. 2012b, 2013b, 2012c) with the client organisations participating in the research.

Chapter 19
Guidelines for Architecture Models as Boundary Objects

Ralf Abraham

Abstract In this chapter, we derive design principles for architectural models, so that they support communication across different communities of practice by acting as *boundary objects*. Specifically, we derive design principles for overcoming a semantic knowledge boundary, a boundary that exists when different communities of practice fail to arrive at a shared understanding.

The boundary object properties associated with overcoming semantic knowledge boundaries are visualisation, modularity, abstraction/concreteness, and stability. For the visualisation property, we derive design principles from an experimental setup; for the latter three, we consult extant literature.

For the visualisation property, building cognitively efficient models is identified as an important contributor. For the modularity property, providing all information in one place and relying on user-based contextualisation is found beneficial. To balance between abstraction and concreteness, establishing navigation capabilities among different layers of abstraction is considered helpful. Finally, for the stability property, retaining a stable structure and a controlled versioning/release process is found beneficial.

19.1 Introduction

The diversity of the affected organisational entities (e.g. business units, divisions) in an enterprise transformation is mirrored by the diversity of the affected stakeholder groups: an enterprise transformation is typically a collaborative endeavour of diverse stakeholder groups such as enterprise architects, project/programme/portfolio

R. Abraham
Institute of Information Management, University of St. Gallen, Switzerland
e-mail: ralf.abraham@unisg.ch

© Springer International Publishing AG, part of Springer Nature 2017   193
H.A. Proper et al. (eds.), *Architectural Coordination of Enterprise Transformation*,
The Enterprise Engineering Series, https://doi.org/10.1007/978-3-319-69584-6_19

managers, or managers of the affected business units. Stakeholder groups that experience regular interactions and share similar working methods can be regarded as communities of practice. *"Community of practice"* is a term coined by Wenger (2000) to describe a group of people that (1) share a joint area of concern (e.g. share the same tasks in an organisation or are interested in the same topics), (2) regularly interact within a set of community-specific norms and relations, and (3) possess a shared repertoire of resources such as languages, methods, tools, stories, or other communal artefacts. A group of stakeholders who experience regular interaction and share similar working methods can be regarded as communities of practice.

Differences among the communities of practice involved in an enterprise transformation may be caused by multiple reasons: political interests, past experiences, or cultural differences as discussed in Chap. 8. Differences in organisational subcultures can lead to both positive and negative consequences: while diversity can be a valuable asset on the one hand, leading to out-of-the-box thinking and innovation, diversity may on the other hand also lead to communication defects.

When communication defects among communities of practice occur, shared understanding on transformation goals and each other's plans and objectives may be lost, or may not even exist in the first place. The need for collaboration among diverse communities of practice is well recognised in literature (Carlile 2004; Karsten et al. 2001; Nicolini et al. 2012), and shared understanding is regarded as a key success factor for successful enterprise transformation (Bisel and Barge 2010; Elving 2005; Ford and Ford 1995; Stensaker et al. 2008). Oftentimes, enterprise transformations fail (Kotter 1996; Sarker and Lee 1999), with one particular reason for failure being a lack of shared understanding (Okhuysen and Bechky 2009). We adopt a definition of shared understanding as the *"degree of cognitive overlap and commonality in beliefs, expectations, and perceptions about a given target"* (Cohen and Gibson 2003, p. 8).

To convey information, and to improve shared understanding among communities of practice during enterprise transformation, one of the major communication devices are models. Multiple views on an enterprise can be covered with the appropriate models (e.g. business process models or software models). To match the diversity of communities of practice in enterprise transformation, enterprise architecture models appear promising: enterprise architecture models address dependencies across partial views of an enterprise (e.g. business, technology) and are at a higher level of abstraction than models concerned with partial views. Enterprise architecture models are of interest to many diverse stakeholder groups because of the holistic overview they provide (Tamm et al. 2011a,b; van der Raadt et al. 2010).

Differences in knowledge, goals, and values among communities of practice can be conceptualised as knowledge boundaries. In this chapter, we focus on knowledge translation, that is, overcoming boundaries of interpretation. Carlile (2004) distinguishes three types of knowledge boundaries between communities of practice that become increasingly complex to cross: syntactic, semantic, and pragmatic knowledge boundaries. Only after a way has been found to establish shared understanding at these boundaries, knowledge can be transferred, translated, or transformed among the involved communities of practice.

A syntactic boundary exists due to different vocabulary between communities of practice. To create shared understanding at a syntactic knowledge boundary, a common lexicon must be developed (Carlile 2004; Kotlarsky et al. 2012).

A semantic boundary exists when communities of practice attribute different meanings to concepts, and have different interpretations of concepts (Carlile 2004; Hawkins and Rezazade 2012). To create shared understanding at a semantic knowledge boundary, common meanings must be developed by translating and negotiating among the different meanings of the involved communities (i.e. by identifying and resolving differences).

Finally, a pragmatic knowledge boundary exists when communities of practice have different interests which affect their ability and willingness to share knowledge. To create shared understanding at a pragmatic knowledge boundary, common interests among the communities of practice must be developed. When developing common interests, communities accept the possibility of altering their cognitive frames and having their knowledge structures transformed (Carlile 2002). In other words, they move towards each other in negotiating a compromise.

Boundary objects are a potential means to cross the aforementioned knowledge boundaries if they possess a syntactic, semantic, or pragmatic capacity (Rosenkranz et al. 2014). In this chapter, we focus on semantic knowledge boundaries, and those boundary object properties that enable a semantic capacity. In doing so, we aim to provide (partial) answers to the challenges as identified in Chaps. 9 and 10.

At a semantic knowledge boundary, both the architect and the enterprise architecture model play an important role in establishing shared understanding. Therefore, we decide to first invest in building a capacity for this particular knowledge boundary. We do not address syntactic knowledge boundaries, as these are likely covered by existing enterprise architecture models already (Rosenkranz et al. 2014; Valorinta 2011). Moreover, a syntactic capacity may be insufficient to create shared understanding in an enterprise transformation scenario, where the diversity among communities of practice is exceptionally large, and the encountered knowledge boundaries may be more complex than a syntactic knowledge boundary. We also do not address pragmatic knowledge boundaries, where the focus strongly shifts away from objects to the role of architects (Abraham 2013; Levina and Vaast 2005; Rosenkranz et al. 2014). Communities of practice need to find common interests to develop common solutions at such a knowledge boundary (e.g. agree on transformation goals or a concrete implementation strategy).

19.2 Boundary Objects

Boundary objects are abstract or physical artefacts that support knowledge sharing and coordination among different communities of practice by providing common ground. We follow the definition of Winter and Butler (2011): "*By identifying 'lowest common denominators', critical points of agreement, or shared surface referents, boundary objects provide a sufficient platform for cooperative action – but they do so without requiring the individuals involved to abandon the distinctive perspectives, positions, and practices of their 'base' social world.*" This definition highlights two central aspects of boundary objects: interpretive flexibility and retaining a community's identity.

Interpretive flexibility—Boundary objects provide common ground among communities of practice. When they are used for a shared purpose of multiple communities of practice, boundary objects provide a common point of reference and are thus *"weakly structured in common use"* (Star and Griesemer 1989). However, each of the communities involved uses the boundary object on a more detailed level for its specific purposes, therefore making the object *"strongly structured in individual site use"* (Star and Griesemer 1989). Put differently, boundary objects are artefacts carrying de-contextualised information: only within the communities involved does the information contained in a boundary object receive context (Hawkins and Rezazade 2012; Landry et al. 2009).

Retaining identity—While providing lowest common denominators, a shared point of reference, boundary objects do not aim to level the differences between the involved communities (i.e. to replace any other objects or practices the communities work with). Instead, they acknowledge each community's individual identity and allow it to preserve the practices of its social world.

Examples of boundary objects include physical objects such as prototypes (Carlile 2004), intangible objects like shared IT applications (Pawlowski and Robey 2004), maps and models (Star and Griesemer 1989), and abstract conceptualisations such as standardised forms and repositories (Carlile 2004; Star and Griesemer 1989).

19.2.1 Boundary Object Properties

In our previous work, we have taken a boundary object perspective on enterprise architecture models (Abraham 2013) and proposed a set of properties for overcoming various knowledge boundaries (Abraham et al. 2013b). These properties are described as follows. For a detailed description, see Abraham (2013):

Modularity—enables communities to attend to specific areas of a boundary object independently from each other, such as attending to individual portions of an ERP system.

Abstraction—serves the interests of all involved communities by providing a common reference point on a high level of abstraction. Local contingencies are eliminated from high-level views to highlight the commonalities.

Concreteness—addresses specific problems relevant to specific communities. Communities are able to specify their concerns and express their knowledge related to the problem at hand. Thus, interpretive flexibility is provided.

Shared syntax—provides a common schema of information elements, so that local use of information objects is uniform across communities.

Malleability—entails that boundary objects are jointly transformable to support the detection of dependencies and the negotiation of solutions.

Visualisation—entails that boundary objects do not rely on verbal definitions, but possess a graphical or physical representation (e.g. a drawing or a prototype).

Annotation—enriches boundary objects with additional information by individual communities in order to provide context for local use.

Versioning—traces changes to boundary objects, along with their rationale. Additional context is provided by reconstructing the chronological evolution of the boundary object.

Accessibility—includes informing interested communities about the boundary object using appropriate communication channels and other measures aimed at helping communities to use the boundary object, such as trainings. As a result, the boundary object is easier to access for the involved communities.

Up-to-dateness—includes timely communication of changes to the involved communities as well as responsibilities and processes for updating the boundary object.

Stability—implies that the structure and underlying information objects of a boundary object remain stable over time. Despite different local uses and annotations, boundary objects provide a stable reference frame: while changes at the periphery are possible, the core of the boundary object remains stable and recognisable.

Participation—means that relevant communities should be involved in the creation and maintenance of the boundary object, and that users should also include top management.

Based on a series of expert interviews (Abraham et al. 2013b), we consider the following properties to enable syntactic, semantic, and pragmatic capacities in boundary objects:

Syntactic knowledge boundaries—accessibility and shared syntax

Semantic capacity—visualisation, modularity, abstraction/concreteness, and stability

Pragmatic capacity—participation and up-to-dateness

Malleability, *annotation*, and *versioning* are not supported by our interview data. We will therefore focus on the boundary object properties of visualisation, modularity, abstraction/concreteness, and stability. These properties are essential for a semantic capacity.

19.2.2 Enterprise Architecture Models as Boundary Objects

Nicolini et al. (2012) argue for considering a broad range of object types when analysing communication among communities of practice. They present a framework of different object types that support collaboration among communities of practice: material infrastructures, boundary objects, epistemic objects, and activity objects.

Material infrastructures remain in the background and only become visible when they cease functioning. Examples of material infrastructure are communication systems (e.g. email, phone), or project documents. Activity and epistemic objects are central objects to the organisation's mission, for example, the products to be developed, or representations thereof. They motivate collaborative efforts (epistemic object) or stimulate negotiations (activity objects). The similarities between activity and epistemic objects become evident from the fact that the same instance is provided as an example for both object types in previous works [namely, a bioreactor (Nicolini et al. 2012) and an intellectual property database (Neyer and Maicher 2013)].

Boundary objects are positioned between material infrastructures and epistemic objects/activity objects. They provide interfaces between communities of practice, but they are the means to enable collaboration in the first place, rather than the ends of collaborative efforts. They are much more stable and defined than activity objects or epistemic objects, yet still malleable and interpretively flexible enough to not (yet) be considered material infrastructures. Different communities of practice can thus detect complementarities, differences, and dependencies between their own perspectives and the perspectives of others, and can incorporate others' perspectives into their own.

Out of the previously discussed objects in collaboration, we opt for conceptualising enterprise architecture as boundary objects. Enterprise architecture models are not ends in themselves, but they are rather used by organisations to derive future benefits, for example, supplying information to decision-makers, increasing business-IT alignment, or improving communication. Enterprise architecture models are not the ultimate output of an organisation, or the very reason for an organisation's existence—those would be the products or services the organisation eventually produces.

In enterprise transformation, the primary purpose of boundary objects is to provide a means for translation among different perspectives, not to motivate collaborative efforts in the first place. In ACET, therefore, enterprise architecture models are conceptualised as boundary objects, as they are a means of architecture for achieving the ends (coordination, and establishing shared understanding as an important facet of coordination) in a specific context (e.g. an enterprise transformation).

19.3 Semantic Boundary Object Capacities

Having motivated our choice of the boundary object lens to improve shared understanding in enterprise transformation, we now take a more detailed look into those properties that enable a semantic boundary object capacity: visualisation, modularity, abstraction/concreteness, and stability.

19.3.1 Visualisation

By improving the cognitive effectiveness, a boundary object can be made more accessible to different communities and easier to understand (Boland and Tenkasi 1995; Henderson 1991). To this end, a number of visualisation principles are provided (Moody 2009). Yet, these principles are general-purpose principles, applicable to any (conceptual) model. To assess the feasibility of the visualisation principles for our specific purpose—turning an enterprise architecture model into a boundary object—we performed an experiment.

19.3.2 Experimental Setup

We performed an experiment with the participants of an enterprise architecture seminar held in Finland in October 2013. This seminar was attended by 11 participants pursuing a PhD in information systems with a specific research interest in the enterprise architecture field. Some of the participants had prior industry experience. These participants serve as proxies for future enterprise architects. We presented them a fictitious, illustrative enterprise transformation scenario that described a merger between two telecommunication service providers. The communities of practice involved were the transformation management team on the one hand and the managers of the IT unit of one of the providers on the other hand. In the scenario, a capability map was envisioned to be helpful in identifying gaps or overlaps in the capability structure between the two individual service providers and the future merged enterprise. A capability map is an artefact type that aggregates software components into capabilities. Capabilities decouple business process activities from software components: business process activities do not access software components directly but indirectly via capabilities (Winter 2010). Figure 19.1 shows the initial capability map.

We specifically selected visualisation principles which improve the cognitive effectiveness for novices rather than for experts (Moody 2009, p. 772). The rationale behind this decision is that the principles shall be applied to create boundary objects for a heterogeneous set of communities of practice, rather than detailed models for a single expert community. The following visualisation principles have been selected from Moody (2009, p. 772): perceptual discriminability, semantic transparency, dual coding, and complexity management. The visualisation principle graphic economy—calling for a cognitively manageable number of graphic symbols—has not been selected, as only a very specific model has been investigated that did not contain an excessive number of different visual constructs.

After the visualisation principles had been explained, the participants applied them to the initial capability map. The stated objective of this exercise was to turn the capability map into a boundary object. The participants were given 20 min to perform this task (paper based rather than electronically). After the experiment, the participants assessed for each visualisation principle (1) whether they considered it

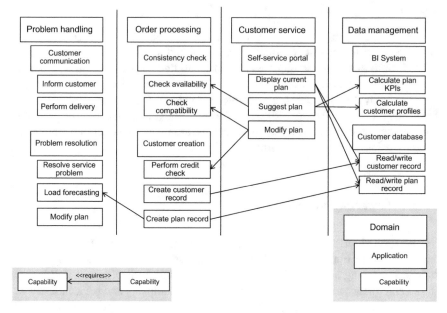

Fig. 19.1 Initial capability map

useful for constructing a boundary object and (2) whether they found it easy to use. Both questions were rated on five-point Likert scales, ranging from not at all useful/easy to use to very useful/easy to use. The visualisation principles are explained below. For each, the original model is depicted on the left-hand side, and the altered model (after application of the principle) is depicted on the right-hand side.

19.3.2.1 Perceptual Discriminability

The degree of perceptual discriminability indicates how easily and accurately different graphical symbols can be discriminated from one another. Variations in shape ("*primacy of shape*") or the use of colour as a second, redundant coding factor are examples of visualisation principles that can improve perceptual discriminability. Figure 19.2 gives an example.

19.3.2.2 Semantic Transparency

The degree of semantic transparency indicates how easily the meaning of a graphical symbol can be guessed from its appearance. Figure 19.3 gives an example where the fact that two capabilities belong to the same application is highlighted visually on the right-hand side.

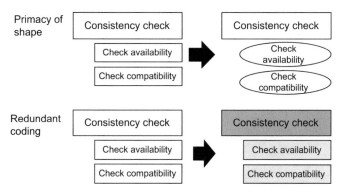

Fig. 19.2 Perceptual discriminability

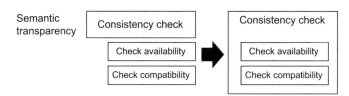

Fig. 19.3 Semantic transparency

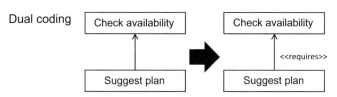

Fig. 19.4 Dual coding

19.3.2.3 Dual Coding

Dual coding refers to the representation of relationships both textually and graphically. Figure 19.4 presents an example.

19.3.2.4 Complexity Management

Complexity management refers to the use of techniques such as abstraction mechanisms to reduce the complexity of a representation. Figure 19.5 shows an example of a capability map broken down into several layers. Individual layers (L0, L1, L2) can be hidden from the users in order to reduce the overall complexity of the diagram.

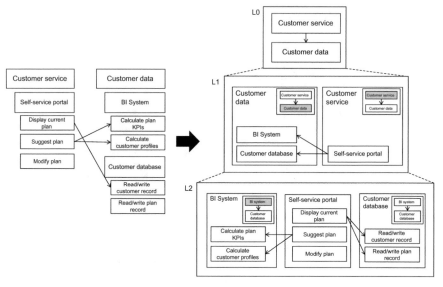

Fig. 19.5 Complexity management

19.3.2.5 Performance Attributes

This is a design rather than a visualisation principle, as it does not relate to the representation of the capability map but to its information content. Capabilities can be supplemented with performance attributes, indicating requirements towards the quality of service level (e.g. in terms of time, availability, or execution speed). Figure 19.6 gives an example.

19.3.3 Experimental Results

Figure 19.7 shows how the participants assessed perceived usefulness and perceived ease of use for each of the presented visualisation principles.

Complexity management appears to be the most useful visualisation principle, but also the most difficult to use. Semantic transparency, on the other hand, is considered both very useful and easy to use. Providing additional information on service quality also shows a favourable balance of usefulness and ease of use. On the other hand, visualisation principles such as perceptual discriminability (exemplified via primacy of shape and redundant coding) and dual coding are considered comparatively less useful for the purpose of creating a boundary object.

Overall, combining the visualisation principles of semantic transparency, complexity management, and the performance attributes principle (i.e. those principles with a perceived usefulness higher than 4.00) can be seen as the most promising candidates for creating cognitively efficient boundary objects.

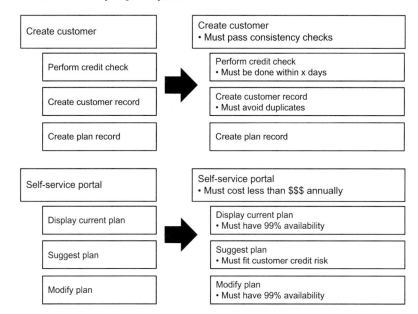

Fig. 19.6 Performance attributes

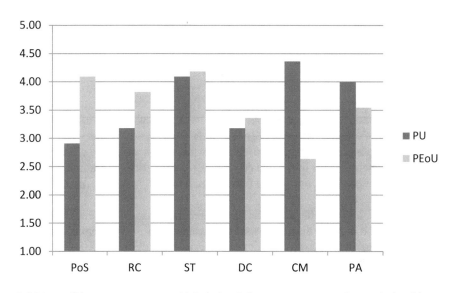

PoS: Primacy of Shape   RC: Redundant Coding   PU: Perceived Usefulness
ST: Semantic Transparency   DC: Dual Coding   PEoU: Perceived Ease of Use
CM: Complexity Management   PA: Performance Attributes

Fig. 19.7 Perceived usefulness and perceived ease of use per principle

Yet, the experimental results must be assessed with caution: a model does not become a boundary object at design time, but only during actual application. We asked designers of enterprise architecture models—in the specific case a capability map—whether applying a certain technique would increase the potential of the capability map to be adopted as a boundary object. Our respondents could therefore only assess a *"designated boundary object"*, which does not automatically become a *"boundary object-in-use"* (Levina and Vaast 2005). Moreover, as enterprise architects, all our respondents belonged to the same community of practice.

19.3.4 Modularity

When several communities of practice share a boundary object, a major design decision is when and by whom the information is filtered. Two extremes are possible: On the one hand, all communities of practice could look at the same model, which contains entirely unfiltered information. In this case, the users will have to contextualise and filter the available information themselves (user-based contextualisation). On the other hand, a viewpoint could be provided for each community of practice group, filtering the information that is considered relevant from the object designer's point of view. In this case, information filtering is already done at design time, when the viewpoints are constructed (designer-based contextualisation). An example for user-based contextualisation would be a global model at a high level of abstraction. Here, all communities of practice look at different parts of the overall model, but would be able to see other communities of practice's areas of concern at the periphery of their own core area. Abraham (2013) provides an example of a financial figures sheet at an insurance company, where the same sheet is used by both the business community to define objects such as contracts and premiums, and by the data warehouse community to identify which database tables to query for creating reports. An example for designer-based contextualisation would be a model with predefined viewpoints for individual communities of practice, so that one group of communities of practice does not see the information that is intended for other communities of practice.

In another example in the air traffic management domain, the findings of Landry et al. (2009) also indicate that user-based contextualisation enabled superior air traffic controller performance than designer-based contextualisation. Air traffic controllers explicitly preferred getting the whole picture and then doing the filtering themselves to receiving information from a predefined viewpoint. From these findings, Landry et al. (2009) propose the following design guidelines:

1. Provide a common picture for all collaborators.
2. Minimise the amount of information preprocessing by the designers. Leave information filtering to the user.
3. Provide continuous updates on changes to all collaborators (i.e. to all involved communities of practice).

Concerning the modularity property, we argue that user-based contextualisation is more appropriate for designing a boundary object than designer-based contextualisation. First, not all relevant communities of practice that may eventually use the boundary object are known a priori. Hence, one cannot predefine views that suit any potential user. Second, by showing what is happening at the periphery, communities of practice can more easily transfer knowledge between each other.

19.3.5 Abstraction/Concreteness

Models on different abstraction levels should be linked. Models on a high level of problem description aid in translating among different perspectives and generate common meanings. Models on a more detailed level are beneficial for establishing a common terminology by exposing community-specific vocabulary. The interlinking among different levels of problem description is also part of the complexity management visualisation principle.

In a study set in the domain of database modelling, Parsons (2003) reports on the differences between students' understanding of classification structures, depending on whether multiple local schemas or one global schema is provided. The findings partly confirm those of Landry et al. (2009), namely, that a global schema improves communication by relieving the subjects from manual integration effort (i.e. having to collect information from a variety of viewpoints). However, this is only the case when the information presented in the global schema is complementary to the information in local schemas (e.g. the fact that two synonyms "*client*" and "*account*" refer to the same entity can be more efficiently shown on a global schema). When there are conflicts between the global schema and the local schemas, the participants showed better problem understanding (hence better organisational communication) when presented with a number of local (i.e. community-specific) schemas than with a single global schema. Being able to rely on local representations helped subjects to identify and understand differences among their viewpoints. The authors conclude that a global schema should be constructed to leverage its effect on improving organisational communication when the viewpoints/classification/interests of two communities of practice are complimentary. However, local schemas should be preserved in order to be able to detect differences in interpretation (semantic boundary) and help the affected communities of practice resolve their conflicts (thereby crossing a pragmatic boundary).

Concerning the required balance between the properties of abstraction and concreteness, we argue for combining de-contextualised with contextualised models. When differences arise not only in interpretations but also in interests, organisational communication is improved by providing local schemas that can be consulted to resolve these conflicts: a high level of abstraction on the overall model is combined with low levels of abstraction on the linked detail models. This enables communities of practice to switch back and forth between global and local models (Pareto et al. 2010), combining the effectiveness of information retrieval in the global model with the conflict detection and resolution capability of the local model. In the case of enterprise architecture models for transformation, a global to-be model of the future state should be complemented by local models that depict to-be states of individual domains, like process architectures of organisational divisions. In case of disagreement, communities can then drill down from the global model to more specific views to detect and/or resolve differences.

19.3.6 Stability

Boundary objects need to have certain stability, a robust frame, to be considered trustworthy and legitimate sources of information. A boundary object that changes rapidly and, above all, unpredictably, tends to be ignored (Abraham 2013, p. 8). Another aspect the panellists stressed is stability: a constantly changing object fails to gain legitimacy and tends to be ignored. Yet, a boundary object must be kept up-to-date at the same time; otherwise, communities of practice might lose trust in a boundary object that provides outdated information (Abraham et al. 2013b, p. 35 f.). Release management processes (van der Hoek and Wolf 2003) can help to control the frequency of changes while regularly updating the contents, and thus balance between stability and up-to-dateness requirements. Change request towards a boundary object would then be collected, discussed, and evaluated (e.g. in an architectural board). Periodically, new versions would be released, ensuring that there is always an official version available.

19.3.7 Development of Boundary Object Design Principles

Although design principles have been mentioned by Gregor and Hevner (2013, p. 348) as "*knowledge contribution*" types and by Gregor (2006, p. 329) "*[p]rinciples of form and function*" as part of an information systems design theory, a precise definition of the term "*design principles*" has not yet emerged. We shall adopt the definition of van Aken (2004, p. 228) of a design principle as "*a chunk of general knowledge, linking an intervention or artefact with a desired outcome or performance in a certain field of application*". To describe our design principles, we will use the core meta model of Aier et al. (2011) for enterprise architecture design principles. Albeit our design object is different—boundary objects rather than enterprise architecture—we consider the meta model of Aier et al. (2011) as applicable for describing boundary object design principles as well. Similar to enterprise architecture design principles, we apply our design principles to achieve a desired outcome, we define an intended field of application, and we intend to create general knowledge, that is, design principles on a generic level that may be refined for application in

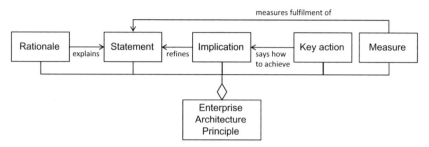

Fig. 19.8 Core meta model of enterprise architecture principle. © Aier et al. 2011, reprinted with permission from Aier et al. (2011)

a specific enterprise. While our design object is specific (an enterprise architecture model as a boundary object) rather than generic ("*grand design*", an entire enterprise architecture), our design principles also serve the core architectural purpose of restricting design freedom, or guiding design choices (Dietz and Hoogervorst 2008). The core meta model of an enterprise architecture design principle consists of the following components (see Fig. 19.8):

- The *rationale* provides the justification for applying the principle: why does applying this principle provide a benefit?
- The *statement* describes the objective of the principle: what should be done?
- The *implications* describe how the objective of the principle can be achieved: how can it be implemented?
- The *key actions* describe specific actions for implementing the principle.
- *Measures* say how the implementation success of the principle can be measured.

Except for key actions, all elements of this core meta model are on a generalised level: they apply to multiple enterprises. Key actions, on the other hand, must be taken in a specific enterprise: what does this mean for us, considering our unique context? For example, Aier (2014) argues that the organisational culture of an enterprise impacts the way principles should be applied. Since we intend to build generally applicable principles for designing boundary objects in enterprise transformation, we do not elaborate on key actions. Rather, these have to be derived with a specific enterprise and its context in mind.

Visualisation—Table 19.1 shows the design principle for the visualisation property.
Modularity—Table 19.2 shows the design principle for the modularity property.
Abstraction/concreteness—Table 19.3 shows the design principle for the abstraction/concreteness property.
Stability—Table 19.4 shows the design principle for the stability property.

Table 19.1 Visualisation design principle

Component	Explanation
Rationale	Cognitive efficiency is essential for understanding and accepting models
Statement	Design cognitively efficient enterprise architecture models to improve shared understanding in enterprise transformation
Implication	Apply the following design and visualisation principles that provide a desirable balance between perceived usefulness and perceived ease of use: • Semantic transparency • Complexity management • Performance attributes (design principle)
Key action	<To be defined per enterprise>
Measure	Less time is spent for finding information in the model (i.e. model content can be grasped faster) Less misunderstandings occur while reading the model

Table 19.2 Modularity design principle

Component	Explanation
Rationale	User-based contextualisation is more suitable for creating shared understanding than designer-based contextualisation
Statement	Provide all information in one view, so that users do the filtering themselves
Implication	Provide one common view of the model to all user groups • Group information relevant to one user group (e.g. in columns or spatially in a diagram) • Highlight parts of the overall model graphically, to help communities of practice locate their areas of concern • Provide users with the ability to discover information adjacent to their own area of concern
Key action	<To be defined per enterprise>
Measure	Existence of only one common view to capture the information previously stored in multiple views

Table 19.3 Abstraction/concreteness design principle

Component	Explanation
Rationale	Depending on the level of cooperation, respectively, the degree of conflict, one global or several local models are preferable
Statement	Provide users with the ability to navigate between different levels of problem description
Implication	Combine global, de-contextualised models with local, community-specific models • A global model is preferred when communities of practice have common meanings and common interests. Multiple local models are preferred when communities of practice need to develop common meanings or common interests • Explicate the links between models on different levels of abstraction
Key action	\<To be defined per enterprise\>
Measure	Users may conveniently navigate between different levels of abstraction

19.4 Discussion

We have analysed the properties of visualisation, modularity, abstraction/concreteness, and stability that are central for semantic capacity to designing boundary objects. From an experiment with PhD candidates in the field of enterprise architecture, we have identified two visualisation principles—semantic transparency and complexity management—that are, combined with the additional principle of performance attributes, especially relevant for boundary object construction in enterprise transformation.

For the modularity, abstraction/concreteness and stability properties, we have derived design principles from existing literature. We conclude that a boundary object should be contextualised by the users instead of by the designers, that different levels of abstraction should be interlinked to detect conflicting local interpretations, and that stability and up-to-dateness requirements should be balanced via a release management process.

Like with any research, the findings presented here must be interpreted cautiously. The sample in the experiment contained merely eleven participants who were potential creators, but only a subset of the end users of the proposed boundary object. The principles for modularity, abstraction/concreteness, and stability have been derived from experimental studies in literature that did not cover the specific

Table 19.4 Stability design principle

Component	Explanation
Rationale	A stable boundary object is able to gain legitimacy from communities of practice, while a boundary object that is perceived as too volatile tends to be ignored
Statement	Provide a boundary object whose structure remains stable and recognisable across communities of practice
Implication	Balance between the goals of stability on the one hand and providing timely updates on changes on the other hand • To minimise the frequency of changes and prevent ad hoc manipulation, define a change management process • Collect change requests, assess required changes, and release new versions periodically • Define a release management process, so that there is always one official version of the boundary object in circulation
Key action	\<To be defined per enterprise\>
Measure	Change and release management processes defined according to officially sanctioned standards Only one official version of the boundary object in circulation

phenomenon of enterprise transformation. Nevertheless, the four design principles provide actionable advice to enterprise architects, so that they can understand and subsequently enhance the capability of their tools (i.e. architectural models).

Chapter 20
The ACET Information Requirements Reference Model

Nils Labusch

Abstract In this chapter, we derive a reference model that provides a holistic perspective on enterprise transformations. The model includes two perspectives: On the one hand, information objects that enterprise architecture management can provide are included. On the other hand, information requirements that enterprise transformation managers posed during interviews are integrated with those discussed in literature. Both combined perspectives lead to a comprehensive overview of information requirements and objects that are relevant during enterprise transformations.

20.1 Introduction

During an enterprise transformation, many stakeholders with extensive and diverse information requirements need to be coordinated. These requirements need to be fulfilled by enterprise transformation managers. Providing decision-relevant information for an enterprise transformation is an important task (Galbraith 1974). In order to be able to fulfil this task, the enterprise transformation managers as much as the architects need to know what information is required for a successful enterprise transformation. While in Chap. 11 a discussion was provided how information processing is conducted and how enterprise architecture management could contribute to it in general, the question remains, what is the required information about? In order to answer this question, a literature survey and empirical studies were conducted. As a result, we were able to identify concrete information requirements that enterprise transformation managers have and at the same time information that architects can provide.

N. Labusch
Institute of Information Management, University of St.Gallen, St. Gallen, Switzerland
e-mail: nils.labusch@gmail.com

© Springer International Publishing AG, part of Springer Nature 2017   211
H.A. Proper et al. (eds.), *Architectural Coordination of Enterprise Transformation*,
The Enterprise Engineering Series, https://doi.org/10.1007/978-3-319-69584-6_20

Labusch (2015) summarises the topic of information requirements reference models as stated below. Commonly two understandings of the term *model* exist: Some consider models to be direct representations of reality, while others consider a model to be a construction by one or more modellers (Ahlemann 2009). For reference model design, usually the second perspective is taken (Ahlemann 2009). In this regard, models are considered to be a resulting artefact of conducted design research processes (Gregor and Hevner 2013; March and Smith 1995).

Models in information systems research describe processes (Becker et al. 2000), applications (Schaeffer et al. 1993), data (Inmon 2000), information requirements (Jaffe 1979), and many more aspects of an organisation. Models are core vehicles to analyse, design, and deploy IS (Becker et al. 1995; Fettke and Loos 2003). Ahlemann (2009) distinguishes models that focus on the business problem and not on technical aspects, models describing larger technical building blocks, and those models closely related to software programming.

The model that is discussed in this chapter contains information requirements of enterprise transformations. The presented reference model aims to meet the challenges as discussed in Chaps. 9 and 11.

Information requirements are one side of the coin, while fulfilling them by information supply is the other. The model type is strongly related to information models described in the IDEF0 method (NBS 1993) and is understood as a model that presents information needed in an organisation. However, since some confusion exists about the term "*information model*" (e.g. Becker and Delfmann 2007) also use it for process models), in the book at hand the term *information requirements model* is used.

Compared to models that are used in a single context for a certain purpose, *reference models* are meant to be more generic (Luiten et al. 1993). Examples of these models are the ISO OSI layer model (Zimmermann 1980), the Supply-Chain Operations Reference model (SCC 2009), or reference models for project management (Ahlemann 2009). While Thomas (2005) considers reference models as being used "*for supporting the construction of other models*", Fettke and Loos (2007) consider them to be conceptual frameworks that can be used as a draft for information systems design and development. Reference models aim at serving different purposes: accelerating design of information systems, reducing costs, helping to communicate innovation and best practices, reducing the risk of failure (Ahlemann 2009), or transferring domain knowledge in companies (Becker et al. 2010).

20.2 Research Approach

To analyse the information requirements during enterprise transformations, we conducted a literature survey (Labusch and Winter 2013) and an empirical qualitative study (Labusch et al. 2014a). This section provides a brief description of the research approach, the details can be found in the respective papers. The following description is based on the above-cited papers.

In the literature survey, the guidance given by Webster and Watson (2002) is applied to avoid reinvestigation of existing knowledge and thus increase rigour and relevance of the research (vom Brocke et al. 2009). In line with Elliot (2011), search terms are handled strictly since a huge body of literature from academic and non-academic sources is available in the topic area. Hence, the search is concentrated on top journals of information systems, management, and organisational science based on the Jourqual ranking (Schrader and Hennig-Thurau 2009) and the AIS basket of eight in order to include the mature and established knowledge. Further, a database search in the major management databases is conducted (Web of Knowledge, Springerlink, Ebsco) to include more recent or practice-based sources. In addition, specific journals and conferences (e.g. *Journal of Enterprise Transformation* or the PRET conference proceedings) are added to the survey. Articles in the journals are identified based on the title keyword "*transformation*" and in the databases based on the title search term:

(organisational OR strategic OR business OR enterprise OR corporate OR large-scale) AND transformation AND management

We interviewed eight transformation managers and ten enterprise architects. Two researchers independently coded the experts' responses. Potential contributions of enterprise architecture management and the needs of enterprise transformation management were added to different lists that for the purpose of developing the information model were merged later on. The results were triangulated with findings from the enterprise transformation management and enterprise architecture management literature. We have included this step to ensure that the enterprise transformation as much as the enterprise architecture management codes are consistent with a common understanding of both disciplines. The codes were grouped based on their semantic similarity. This grouping was again conducted by two independent researchers and consolidated in the first iteration.

The results are consolidated in the reference model. We provided the identified information requirements to practitioners in one organisation in order to evaluate if they were comprehensible and if major aspects were missing.

20.3 ACET Information Requirements Reference Model

The ACET information requirements reference model, as shown in Fig. 20.1, is comprised of eleven requirement areas that contain the different information requirements. Below, we briefly describe the requirements and summarise the design decisions taken during the development process. These decisions are based on literature and the empirical findings gathered during the interviews with domain experts.

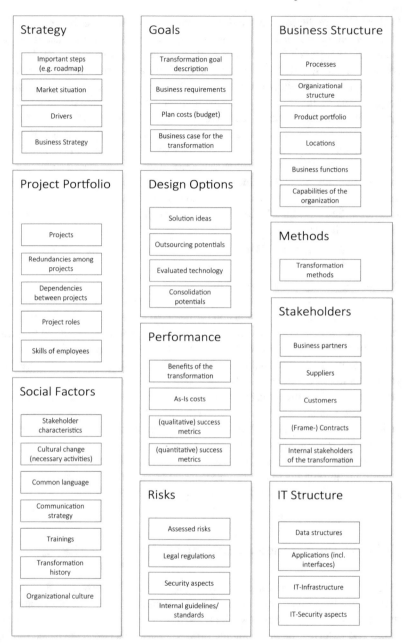

Fig. 20.1 ACET information requirements reference model

20.3.1 Strategy

Strategy is seen as an important part of enterprise transformations (Uhl and Gollenia 2012). The area addresses the strategy of the enterprise transformation itself. *Important steps* are described in a rather rough manner to provide guidance for all involved stakeholders. This can, for example, be done with the help of a transformation road map that is maintained by enterprise architects (Tamm et al. 2011a). Information about the *market situation* is necessary to safeguard the transformation and align the overall corporate strategy. This especially includes trends and developments in the market environment (Uhl and Gollenia 2012). The *triggers and drivers* of the enterprise transformation are also important information objects (Baumöl 2008). These can be regulatory aspects, necessary changes of the business model due to increased market pressure, etc. Knowledge about the *business strategy* is also required. The strategy of the concrete transformation needs to support the business strategy and thus needs to be aligned in terms of its goals.

20.3.2 Goals

To highlight the importance of defining and aligning the goals of the enterprise transformation (Jenkins 1977; Ward and Uhl 2012), they were included in an own area of information requirements. First, the transformation *goals* need to be described. For this purpose, a process is necessary that includes relevant stakeholders (Ward and Daniel 2006). In consequence, the *business requirements* need to be collected (Singh et al. 2011). Different techniques exist to identify these requirements (e.g. workshops or interviews with top-level executives). A specific perspective on the transformation goals is the budget, thus the *planned costs*. Staying with the prospected budget is considered to be a goal of every enterprise transformation. Therefore, this requirement is considered in the goal area of information requirements. Finally, a *business case* describes the goals in a very detailed way and is central information during the cause of the enterprise transformation.

20.3.3 Business Structure

Managers that are involved in the enterprise transformation need information about the business structure. This is related especially to the as-is structure which is supposed to be transformed. Only when managers are aware of this structure, resistances and other issues can be foreseen early enough to react. In today's organisations, information about *processes* is a vital part of this (vom Brocke et al. 2012). They can come along in various forms, including process chain diagrams or activity documentations. Closely related is the *organisational structure*. Maintaining the information (e.g. in terms of an organisational diagram) is a task that is usually conducted in the organisation. Having this information at hand is vital in order to create awareness about the affected stakeholders. Information about the *product portfolio* is also part of the business structure. Products also refers to services that are part of the value creation. The information is necessary to create awareness about relations of products. If, for example, one product should be replaced because its market value decreased heavily, it is vital to know if other products and services depend on it. In addition, knowledge about the different *locations* of the transformation is necessary. Many problems can be solved easier whenever responsible managers are in place and can directly communicate the essentials of the enterprise transformation (Abraham et al. 2013b). Furthermore, it might be necessary to distinguish different regulations and laws that locations are affected by. When the enterprise transformation is in a later stage, *business functions* are a relevant object of focus. Business functions are activities that are carried out by the organisational units of a company. They refine the business processes and contain different tasks. The last requirement in this area is *capabilities* of the organisation. Usually capabilities are a combined set of the above-illustrated elements. For example, an organisation can have the capability to support its customers—this capability is achieved by a combination of processes, business functions, IT systems, and employee skills.

20.3.4 Project Portfolio

The fourth relevant area is the project portfolio. Information requirements are mostly imposed by methods like PMBok (PMI 2008). The first important requirement is information about *projects* as such. An overview of the existing project portfolio is necessary to classify and prioritise the transformation activities. Information about *redundancies of projects* is relevant in order to reduce the efforts and thus the costs of the enterprise transformation. However, this information is difficult to gather and the architectural support included in ACET can provide significant value. Related to this requirement is information about the *dependencies of projects*. The information is relevant to prioritise needs and allocate resources. The information about project *roles* contains the various roles in the project to manage the transformation appropriately. This includes a clear assignment of persons to projects in order to make them feel responsible for the result delivery. The last information requirement in this area addresses *skills* of employees. This information is important for different reasons. First, people need to be allocated to projects or other tasks in the enterprise transformation management team. Second, if skills necessary for the enterprise transformation are missing, training needs to be conducted or personnel with the required skills needs to be hired.

20.3.5 Design Options

The information area of design options is strongly related to architectural foundations of ACET and highlights the plan-driven perspective. Information *about solution ideas* covers plans and ideas about possible solutions that need to be implemented to achieve the before investigated goals. The plural form is chosen to make clear that at this point, various scenarios are developed, which are weighed against each other by the responsible managers. *Outsourcing potentials* explicitly address outsourcing scenarios and contain information about possible process or system outsourcing activities. Evaluated technology addresses information about technology and its possible contribution for the enterprise transformation. For example, big data technology could be assessed concerning its use potential, or social media could be introduced for the communication of the enterprise transformation. *Consolidation potentials* contain information about possible amalgamations (not only technical in nature but also capability areas, departments, etc.).

20.3.6 Methods

Information about *transformation methods* addresses the availability of documentation on how to conduct enterprise transformations. This information is crucial for the success of enterprise transformations since methods and frameworks are able to increase the enterprise transformation success (Lahrmann et al. 2012). Many pitfalls during an enterprise transformation are already documented and could be avoided by applying established methods. That is why the decision was taken to add methods as an explicit information requirement to the model.

20.3.7 Social Factors

Traditionally, social factors are ranked very important whenever enterprise transformations are conducted (Kotter 1995). However, in reality, oftentimes managers lack the relevant information concerning these factors. *Stakeholder characteristics* need to be known in order to determine how to address the different stakeholders (Prosci 2014). It is very difficult to openly store this information—many successful enterprise transformation managers write down their most important stakeholders and their characteristics in secret documents they store at home. However, somehow a stakeholder analysis should be done. Necessary *activities for cultural change* are related to this former information requirement. This requirement contains the discussed and necessary steps for the specific organisation to conduct a cultural change (if planned so in the enterprise transformation strategy). A *common language* is another requirement concerning the social factors. As already discussed in Chap. 19, a common language, for example, in terms of boundary objects, needs to be considered in order to avoid misunderstandings and unnecessary delays (Abraham et al. 2013b; Cross et al. 2000). The *communication strategy* is based on the above-mentioned stakeholder characteristics and provides guidance on whom to address concerning what aspect of the enterprise transformation (Prosci 2014). Information about *trainings* (e.g. availability and necessity for certain roles) is related to the available skills in the organisation and contributes to the enterprise transformation by empowering employees and managers to conduct the enterprise transformation. Information about the transformation history contains lessons learnt and good practices. This information is very important since it directly relates to the specific organisation where the enterprise transformation takes place. Thus, generic guidelines can be evaluated against historical experiences. Information about the *organisational culture* is the last information requirement in this area. It can make a huge difference, if an enterprise transformation is conducted in a very formal organisation (e.g. a bank) or in a start-up culture (Breu 2001). The results of culture assessments should be available as an information item.

20.3.8 Performance

Information requirements concerning performance are mostly related to topics of management and benefit accounting. Having information about the *benefits* of the enterprise transformation available is considered as important (Ward et al. 2012). Especially because benefits can contradict each other, it is necessary to have an overview and possibly information about contradicting benefits that need to be harmonised. *As-is costs* are information about all current costs that occurred in connection with the enterprise transformation. Especially deviations with the planned costs are of interest because huge cost overruns can occur in ETs (Flyvbjerg and Budzier 2012). Information concerning *qualitative success measures* can be collected through interviews with key stakeholders. These are necessary to identify issues that are usually not codified in quantitative or monetary measures. *Quantitative measures* are required, too. Examples are customer satisfaction measures or lead times.

20.3.9 Stakeholders

The requirement area stakeholder addresses information requirements concerning the stakeholders that are involved in or affected by the enterprise transformation (Prosci 2014). This involves *business partners* (all partners who are neither customers nor suppliers, such as joint venture partners). Moreover, it involves *suppliers* and *customers* since these might need to change processes on their side or parameters of their products and services. For this reason, information about *contracts* is part of this area. Such information is required to identify contracts that cannot be easily terminated and need negotiation efforts (Baumöl 2008). In addition, it allows identifying frame contracts that could be used in order to avoid purchasing a service twice during the enterprise transformation. Furthermore, the *internal stakeholders* of the enterprise transformation are part of the requirements area. Knowing who is affected in order to connect this information with processes or social factor is necessary during the enterprise transformation.

20.3.10 Risks

Enterprise transformation managers require information about risks. In consequence, the *assessed risks* are part of this information area. Assessed risks can be the result of a risk assessment (Vellani 2007). In addition, a thorough documentation of *legal regulations* is necessary. In some cases such regulations are even the driver of the enterprise transformation. Information about security aspects (concerning different matters like IT, business, or investments) have to be considered in addition. Furthermore *internal guidelines and standards* need to be known (Cross et al. 1997). During the enterprise transformation, they may have to be changed.

20.3.11 IT Structure

Information about the IT structure is required in most transformations since almost all of them involve changes in the IT. First, this is related to the *data structures*. Whenever major processes, products, or services are changed, this also affects the stored data. Enterprise transformation managers need to know how their changes affect the data. They also need to know which *applications* and interfaces between these applications are affected because these are usually critical for the operations of the company. This is also the case for the IT *infrastructure*—managers need to know if new planned applications, for example, can still be run on the old hardware. In this regard also *security aspects* need to be considered.

20.4 Discussion

The reference model described above provides a holistic perspective on enterprise transformations. The perspective is twofold: On the one hand, information objects that enterprise architecture management can provide are included. On the other hand, information requirements that enterprise transformation managers posed during interviews are integrated with those discussed in literature.

Subsequently, two important questions occur. First, how mature is the specific organisation's enterprise architecture management department with regard to the information supply capabilities of enterprise architecture management in general?

Whereas enterprise architecture management in general is able to provide a wide range of information, a specific enterprise architecture management department may only be able to supply some information, depending on different context factors (e.g. the department's maturity, available skill sets, or the organisational anchoring of that department). For example, enterprise architecture management in a specific organisation might only be responsible for reporting on interdependencies among applications. While this is an important task during the enterprise transformation, such an enterprise architecture management is not necessarily able to provide information about business strategy. This, of course, can be changed and based on the model provided in this chapter, enterprise architecture management departments can analyse which information they might want to provide in the future to become more relevant during enterprise transformations.

The second important question is whether the consolidated information requirements are really needed in the concrete enterprise transformation in the specific organisation. This question is not trivial, since information requirements heavily depend on the type of enterprise transformation and the concrete environment. In order to simplify the adaptation to specific situations, the introduced model shall be made adaptable in a second step. For this purpose, different types of enterprise transformation are identified in Chap. 25 that allow for an easier adaptation. In addition, knowledge about the different types of enterprise transformation simplifies the communication of the reference model when dealing with enterprise transformation management.

Chapter 21
Model Bundling: Componential Language Engineering

Sybren de Kinderen

Abstract This chapter introduces a design artefact for value-based componential language engineering, as a response to the research questions defined in Chap. 13. The design artefact consists of two parts: (a) two formal ontologies, representing the stakeholder perspective/language-centric perspective, respectively. These two ontologies can be used to specify catalogues of language fragments, emphasising how these are valuable to stakeholders. (b) A procedural model, inspired by situational method engineering, for creating model bundles from the fragments in the catalogues. We illustrate the artefact with an experiment on combining the modelling languages e^3value, DEMO, and ArchiMate.

21.1 Introduction

In Chap. 13 we argued for a language engineering approach that caters to an *economic* design of conceptual modelling languages. For language users we reasoned that a language should be designed in line with the purposes of the modelling exercise at hand. As such, the language should contain exactly the amount of concepts needed for that purpose: no more (which would clutter the model) and no less (which would result in a decrease of language expressiveness). For language designers, we reasoned that economy of design refers to the reuse of existing modelling languages, so as to avoid having to design a language from scratch. We also showed how the current state of the art (on the design of domain-specific languages, situational method engineering, and model transformation) provides useful elements

S. de Kinderen
University of Duisburg-Essen, Universitätsstr. 9, 45141 Essen, Germany
e-mail: sybren.dekinderen@uni-due.de

© Springer International Publishing AG, part of Springer Nature 2017
H.A. Proper et al. (eds.), *Architectural Coordination of Enterprise Transformation*,
The Enterprise Engineering Series, https://doi.org/10.1007/978-3-319-69584-6_21

for an approach towards economic language design, and where these elements fall short.

In this chapter, we introduce a design theory for the economic design of modelling languages. Section 21.2 introduces the notion of model bundling. Section 21.3 introduces a language merging experiment, which will be used to illustrate the two major constituencies of our design theory: the two model bundling ontologies (Sect. 21.4) and the ontologies for language engineering (Sect. 21.5). Section 21.6 concludes with a discussion and directions for further research.

21.2 Model Bundling

We now introduce e^3RoME for model bundling, our design artefact for value-based language engineering. First we introduce the key ideas behind the main design artefact and briefly characterise this artefact in terms of its chief constituencies: the required input, activities, the involved roles, and its output. Thereafter, we discuss how our language engineering artefact is derived from a value-based selection mechanism for service bundling.

21.2.1 The e^3RoME Model Bundling Artefact

The e^3RoME design artefact can be characterised as follows:

- Inputs: (1) Purposes/modelling needs and (2) catalogue of model fragments and their capabilities. These inputs will be explained in further detail in Sects. 21.4.1 and 21.4.2, respectively.
- Roles: modelling stakeholders. This concerns both the modellers themselves and the stakeholders (in-)directly benefiting from the modelling. For example, inspired by Stirna and Persson (2012), one can identify the following roles for collaborative enterprise modelling: a *modelling expert*, a stakeholder with significant expertise in modelling languages; a *model facilitator*, a stakeholder facilitating the group dynamics while modelling; a *modelling sponsor*, the stakeholder that invests resources into the modelling effort; and the *end user*, who uses the (indirect) results of the modelling effort.
- Activities: (1) At "design time": Create a catalogue of model fragments, whereby each fragment is characterised by its capabilities. Furthermore, create a catalogue of modelling purpose/needs for the modelling stakeholders, in terms of a means-ends chain (explained in further detail in Sect. 21.4.1). This catalogue gradually specifies an abstract purpose/need into capabilities provided by fragments from the model catalogue. (2) At "run time": Find suitable combinations of language(s) (or language fragments) using modelling needs and model capability catalogues as input.

- Techniques: (1) Two formal ontologies for specifying languages from a value perspective (Sect. 21.4). (2) A procedure for value-based language engineering (Sect. 21.5).
- Results: combinations of modelling techniques, in line with modelling needs/ purposes.

21.2.2 Adapting a Value-Based Service Bundling Mechanism

A key idea is that for *model* bundling, we reuse a semiautomated, needs-driven, matchmaking mechanism for *service bundling*.

This service bundling method, coined e^3*service* by Razo-Zapata et al. (2012), de Kinderen (2010), and Akkermans et al. (2004), specifies, in a "smart" question answer game, a customer need into suitable service bundles.[1] For example: "*communicate with a family member abroad*" is satisfied by the service bundle:

$$\{\text{VoiP(Skype)}, \text{IP-access}\}$$

e^3*service* relies on multidisciplinary theory development. On the one hand, e^3*service* has business notions that allow for expressing commercial services and service needs. On the other hand, e^3*service* provides computational support, by means of software tools, for (semi)automated reasoning about service bundling.

For developing a model bundling artefact, it would be interesting to look at reusing (1) the value-based mechanism to translate customer needs into service bundles, (2) a decision-making method that balances the costs and benefits of such a bundle, and (3) the formal, software, tool support that exists for both.

Note that we should be careful with the shift from business-to-business to business-to-customer. e^3*service* was developed with end customers in mind, while we use e^3*RoME* in organisational context, that is, more business-to-business. This assumption can affect our basic matchmaking mechanism and, as such, will be addressed during our discussion on modelling stakeholders (Sect. 21.4.1).

21.3 Experiment: Integrating e^3*Value* and ArchiMate via DEMO

Now that we have introduced the basic idea behind e^3*RoME*, we discuss each of its elements in further detail: the formal ontologies that provide its key concepts (in Sect. 21.4) and a procedural model for using e^3*RoME* (in Sect. 21.5).

---

[1] Here bundling refers to the selling of a package of services at a single price (Guiltinan 1987; Stremersch and Tellis 2002).

We use a model bundling experiment from de Kinderen et al. (2012a) as a running example. In this model bundling experiment, we define a model transformation between the enterprise modelling techniques e^3value, DEMO, and ArchiMate. The key idea behind this transformation is to elaborate how a value network (expressed in e^3value) is realised in terms of supporting business processes and IT systems.

To model business processes and IT systems, we rely on the enterprise architecture modelling language ArchiMate. Furthermore, we rely on the modelling technique DEMO for assistance with process modelling. In particular, DEMO's transaction patterns provide us with guidelines on what specific business process steps should be considered to realise an economic transaction stemming from e^3value.

21.4 Two e^3RoME Ontologies

e^3RoME relies on formal ontologies to create a computer-supported method. Borst (1997, p. 11) defines an ontology as "*a formal specification of a shared conceptualisation*". This definition highlights two features of ontologies that are important to our research: (1) *a formal specification*, which we need since we aim for a semiformal, computer-supported, bundling method, and (2) *a shared conceptualisation*, which is important to ensure that the different stakeholders involved in the bundling use a common vocabulary, for example, with respect to what constitutes a model fragment.

Similar to $e^3service$, e^3RoME has two ontologies: one for expressing the stakeholder perspective and one for expressing the conceptual modelling languages as model fragments. The main reason for using two perspectives is that we can focus our effort on modelling those concerns that are of interest from a particular perspective (Finkelstein et al. 1992). For one, the value that particular stakeholders receive from applying a model fragment, and how this value helps them to satisfy a need, involves modelling different (namely, stakeholder-centred) concerns than those needed for modelling a library of specific model fragments. For now, we focus on the two $e^3service$ perspectives, but we are aware that more perspectives may also exist, for example, to express, independently of stakeholder concerns, that standardisation of a model can have value in terms of network effects.

As stated in the introduction, for illustration purposes, we replay an experiment on model integration and transformation of the conceptual modelling techniques e^3value, DEMO, and ArchiMate (see de Kinderen et al. 2012a,b). In particular, we formalise the pragmatic reasons behind integration and transformation of these techniques.

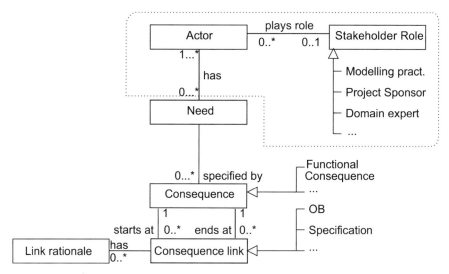

Fig. 21.1 The e^3*RoME* stakeholder perspective ontology (based on Razo-Zapata et al. (2011) and de Kinderen (2010))

21.4.1 The Stakeholder Perspective Ontology

The e^3*RoME* stakeholder perspective ontology, depicted in Fig. 21.1,[2] is grounded in the e^3*service* customer perspective ontology (see Razo-Zapata et al. (2011) and de Kinderen (2010, p. 106)). e^3*service*, in turn, is based on concepts from *established* needs analysis literature. Most notably, refer to Kotler (2000) for a discussion on needs, wants, and demands, and refer to Woodruff (1997), Gutman (1997), and Aschmoneit and Heitmann (2002) for a discussion on means-ends chaining.

Note that while e^3*service*, which constitutes the basis of our ontology, is aimed at analysing the needs of *end customers*, we see the application of its basic needs concepts in a business-to-business context as well: in logistics, where Mentzer et al. (1997) uses means-ends chaining to understand business needs of channel partners, and in the area of enterprise architecture, where van der Raadt et al. (2010) assess how enterprise architecture contributes to achieving the goals of individual (business) stakeholders. Furthermore, the notion of means-ends is central to the Business Motivation Model (BRG 2007), an OMG standard aimed at modelling both business and end-customer motivations.

In particular, in the above business-to-business references, means-ends chains are applied to link valuable attributes to more abstract stakeholder motivations.

---

[2] The border with the dotted line indicates additions to earlier work (Razo-Zapata et al. 2011; de Kinderen 2010, p. 106).

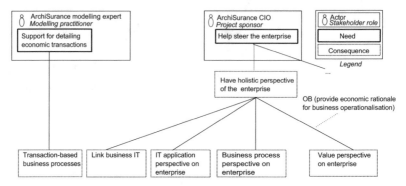

Fig. 21.2 An example stakeholder perspective catalogue

21.4.1.1 Actor

An actor is a physical entity occupying one or more stakeholder roles in an organisation. Since we concern ourselves with analysing the concerns of individual modelling stakeholders, actors are necessarily *human*.

Example: Figure 21.2 presents the stakeholder perspective catalogue for our running model transformation experiment. Here, we see that "*ArchiSurance CIO*" is an actor. Note: "*ArchiSurance*" is the company used as a running example in our model integration/transformation experiment.

21.4.1.2 Stakeholder Role

Stakeholder role is the role played by an actor in a conceptual modelling project. A role influences the responsibilities and required skills of an actors (Lankhorst 2012). In line with Stirna and Persson (2012), we distinguish between different modelling roles, including the "*Project sponsor*", who initiates the modelling project and is its main investor, and the "*modelling practitioner*", who actually creates the models (while assuming subroles of "*facilitator*" or "*tool expert*").

Example: "*ArchiSurance CIO*" has the role of a project sponsor.

As can be seen from our stakeholder perspective ontology, actors and stakeholders have been added as new concepts compared to e^3*service*. This was done to reflect that model engineering can involve multiple stakeholders having different, possibly conflicting, concerns (Ågerfalk and Fitzgerald 2006).

21.4.1.3 Need

A need represents a problem statement *independently* from a solution direction (see Kotler (2000)).

Example: "*Help steer the enterprise*" from the "*ArchiSurance CIO*".

21.4.1.4 Consequence

A consequence is anything that results—directly or indirectly—from using an object (Gutman 1997; Aschmoneit and Heitmann 2002). In our case, this object is a model fragment. Thus, a consequence is defined in a bottom-up manner: it results from applying a model fragment. We discuss how a consequence results from a model when introducing the model catalogue ontology (Sect. 21.4.2).

A need is typically *specified by* zero or more consequences. As such, the consequences—as results of a model fragment—show how a need is satisfied. *Example:* "*Have holistic perspective of the enterprise*" specifies the need to "*Help steer the enterprise*".

Eliciting consequences is done by asking the question: *What happens if we consume service X in which valuable property Y is contained?*.

A special kind of consequence, is a *functional consequence*, which represents the functional goal that can be achieved through the consumption of a model fragment. It represents the primary function that a customer is interested in. *Example:* The functional consequence "*Have holistic perspective of the enterprise*".

21.4.1.5 Consequence Link

A consequence link relates two consequences. For $e^3 RoME$, we have two types of relations:

- A consequence may have a *specification* link with one or more other consequences. Such consequence *laddering* (see Gutman (1997)) can be used to specify abstract consequences into more concrete consequences until a sufficiently detailed consequence is found for which solutions can be offered.
  Example: In our experiment, the consequence "*Have holistic perspective of the enterprise*" has a specification relation with the consequences "*Link business-IT*", "*Business process perspective on enterprise*", and "*IT application perspective on enterprise*". (See the customer perspective service catalogue in Fig. 21.2 for reference.)
- An optional bundling (OB in Fig. 21.1) relation between two consequences A and B indicates that consequence B can add value to consequence A, but that consequence B can also be acquired separately from A. Optional bundling is grounded in the marketing notion of demand interdependency (Guiltinan 1987). *Example:* The consequence "*Value perspective on enterprise*" can add value to the consequence "*Have holistic perspective on enterprise*".

21.4.1.6 Link Rationale

A link rationale shows *why* a relation between two consequences exists. *Example:* In our first experiment on integrating $e^3 value$ and ArchiMate (de Kinderen et al. 2012b), the optional bundling relation between the consequences "*Value perspective on enterprise*" and "*Have holistic perspective on enterprise*" has as a rationale "*provide economic rationale for business operationalisation*".

21.4.2 The Catalogue Perspective Ontology

In this chapter, we discuss the $e^3 RoME$ model catalogue ontology, which is grounded in $e^3 service$ supplier perspective ontology (see Razo-Zapata et al. (2011) and de Kinderen (2010, p. 111)).

We base our discussion on an ontology instantiation for our model integration experiment, presented in Fig. 21.3. In this catalogue, we see *model fragments*, such as "*Use DEMO transaction patterns*". *Value* is the main criterion to consider a part

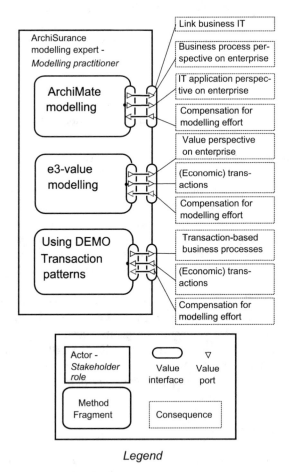

Fig. 21.3 A value-based catalogue of model fragments

of a model as a separate fragment. For example, "*Use DEMO transaction patterns*" is part of the larger DEMO method, which offers an extensive set of techniques and perspectives to model the essential aspects of an enterprise (Dietz 2006). Yet, DEMO transaction patterns provide value by themselves in the sense of offering strict guidance in translating economic transactions into business processes. Thus, "*Use DEMO transaction patterns*" is modelled as a separate fragment.

Similar to the e^3RoME stakeholder ontology, a model fragment is provided by an *actor* in a *stakeholder role*. For the model fragment "*Using DEMO transaction patterns*", an actor is "*ArchiSurance modelling expert*" in the role of "*Modelling practitioner*" (see Fig. 21.3).

In turn, a model fragment's value is conceptualised in terms of *consequences*, which are attached to model fragments via incoming and outgoing *value ports*. Outgoing value ports denote a consequence that is provided to the environment. For example, "*Using DEMO transaction patterns*" provides the consequence "*Transaction-based business processes*". On the other hand, incoming value ports are used to denote a consequence received from the environment, for example, "*Using DEMO transaction patterns*", requires "*Compensation for modelling effort*" and "*(Economic) transactions*".

Finally, the bundling of consequences is indicated by a *value interface*. A value interface (ovals in Fig. 21.3) groups value ports and denotes that either all consequences attached to the ports are to be exchanged or none at all. For example, for the fragment "*Using DEMO transaction patterns*", a value interface shows that the outgoing consequence "*Transaction-based business processes*" is compensated for by "*(Economic) transactions*" and "*Compensation for modelling effort*".

Note that in e^3RoME, as in $e^3service$, consequences can be attached to value interfaces as well, to indicate that the value of a fragment or bundle can be more than the sum of its parts. An example of this from our catalogue (Fig. 21.3) is provided by the fragment "*ArchiMate modelling*", which through its capability of modelling both business processes and IT applications also provides the added value of relating business processes and IT applications (which would not have been possible with two unbundled stand-alone techniques for modelling, respectively, business processes and IT applications).

It is important to emphasise that e^3RoME conceptualises repository fragments according to the consequences that they provide. This allows for matching between the stakeholder and model perspective catalogues.

21.5 Generating Model Bundles

We now show how to use the stakeholder and model repository ontologies to create model bundles, using the two catalogues instantiated for our experiment as input (see Figs. 21.2 and 21.3). Figure 21.4 provides a procedural model for e^3RoME.

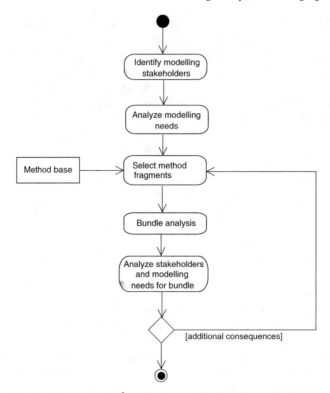

Fig. 21.4 Procedural model for the e^3RoME method. © 2010, S. de Kinderen; reprinted with permission from de Kinderen (2010)

21.5.1 Creating an Initial Model Bundle

In accordance with the e^3RoME procedural model, we start with *Identify modelling stakeholders*, using the typology from the e^3RoME ontology as input.

For our experiment, we initially identify one such stakeholder, a project sponsor, a role played by the ArchiSurance CIO.

Next we perform the step *Analyse modelling needs* of the found stakeholders, using the stakeholder perspective catalogue as input.

For our experiment, we find that the project sponsor selects the need "*Help steer the enterprise*" and find that this need is specified by, amongst others, the consequence "*Have holistic perspective on enterprise*". This consequence, in turn, is specified by—using the consequence specification link—the consequences "*Link business-IT*", "*Have holistic perspective on enterprise*", "*Business process perspective on enterprise*", and "*IT application perspective on enterprise*".

Thus we have so far elicited the consequence set:

{"*Have holistic perspective on enterprise*", "*IT application perspective on enterprise*",

"*Business process perspective on enterprise*", "*Link business-IT*" }

Subsequently, e^3RoME, similar to the $e^3service$ service bundling reasoning, considers consequences that have an *optional bundling* relation with the initially elicited consequences.

For our experiment, we thus find that the consequence "*Have holistic perspective on enterprise*" has an *optional bundling* relation with the consequence "*Value perspective on enterprise*", with the rationale to "*Provide economic rationale of business operationalisation*". Let us assume that, from the rationale, the project sponsor is also interested in receiving the consequence "*Value perspective on enterprise*". As such our initial set of consequences, as an outcome of the needs analysis step, is:

{ "*Have holistic perspective on enterprise*", "*IT application perspective on enterprise*",

"*Business process perspective on enterprise*", "*Value perspective on enterprise*",

"*Link business-IT*" }

Next, in the step *Select model fragments*, we use the value-based matchmaking mechanism from $e^3service$ to match the desired consequences to consequences-provided model fragments.

For our experiment, we provide a match with two fragments from our catalogue (Fig. 21.3): ArchiMate modelling and e^3value modelling.

Next, in the *Bundle analysis*, we have two subactivities: (1) to actually bundle the model fragments. This means that we do value-based matchmaking amongst the model fragments as well, besides showing how these individual fragments satisfy a need (as done in the step "*Select model fragments*"). We exemplify this bundling in more detail in Sect. 21.5.2, where we discuss the final bundle as depicted in Fig. 21.5. (2) To discover all bundle consequences (using concept of a value inter-

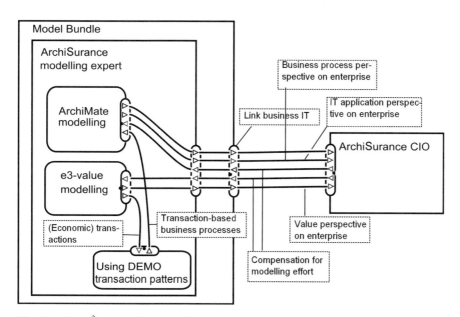

Fig. 21.5 The {e^3value, DEMO, ArchiMate} model bundle

face), and do a cost–benefit analysis with them using the scoring and ranking mechanism from $e^3service$. For example, for the model fragment "e^3value *modelling*", we find that to receive the consequence "*Value perspective on enterprise*", we have to provide "*Compensation for modelling effort*" (note that, as stated, we will not detail further the actual cost benefit analysis for this chapter).

For our experiment, we assume that the project sponsor indeed selects the initially created model bundle {ArchiMate modelling, e^3value modelling}.

21.5.2 Modifying a Model Bundle

For the created bundle, we perform the step *Analyse stakeholders and modelling needs for bundle*. This is a step that we introduced additionally to the $e^3service$ needs-driven bundling algorithm, to reflect that in situational method engineering the assembly of a model out of fragments may spin off the need for additional fragments (see, amongst others, Brinkkemper (1996, p. 277)). In our value-based approach, we analyse (1) whether new stakeholders are required for the bundle and (2) if the bundle raises new stakeholder concerns.

For our experiment, we find a second modelling stakeholder, "*modelling practitioner*". Being presented with the bundle, this stakeholder has the need to "*Support for detailing economic transactions*". As detailed in de Kinderen et al. (2012a), this need arises from the difference in abstraction level between economic transactions modelled in e^3value and the underlying detailed business processes and IT applications modelled in ArchiMate. Thus, we require structured support for translating between these techniques.

Using our stakeholder catalogue (Fig. 21.2), the "*Modelling practitioner*" finds that the need "*Support for detailing economic transactions*" is satisfied by the consequence "*Transaction-based business processes*" and decides to select it. As a result, we now have the updated set of consequences:

{ "*Transaction-based business process*", "*Have holistic perspective on enterprise*",

"*IT application perspective on enterprise*", "*Business process perspective on enterprise*",

"*Link business-IT*", "*Value perspective on enterprise*" }

Using these consequences as input, as can been seen in the procedural model (Fig. 21.4), we again perform the steps *Select model fragments* and *Bundle analysis*.

Using our value-based matchmaking mechanism for our experiment, we thus find the fragments "*ArchiMate modelling*", "e^3value *modelling*", and "*Using DEMO transaction patterns*".

Next, during *bundle analysis*, we again (1) bundle model fragments and (2) weigh costs/benefits.

For our experiment, we can see the resulting bundle in Fig. 21.5. Note here also what we mean by a bundle analysis of the model fragments themselves: namely, the value-based matchmaking algorithm, besides matching the consequences from the stakeholder catalogue to the consequences of the catalogue of fragments, also matches the valuable outcomes amongst fragments themselves. As such, we see that the fragment e^3*value* modelling produces as a valuable outcome "*(Economic) trans-actions*", which the model fragment "*Using DEMO transaction patterns*" trans-forms into "*Transaction-based business processes*", which in turn provides input to the fragment "*ArchiMate modelling*" [the specific bundling algorithm, related to the e^3*service* supplier ontology, is detailed in Akkermans et al. (2004)].

21.6 Discussion

This chapter has introduced e^3*RoME*, a design theory for value-based componential language engineering. We characterised e^3*RoME* in terms of its key constituencies, and illustrated it by means of a language engineering experiment on integrating the modelling languages e^3*value* and ArchiMate via DEMO.

We can now address the research questions posed in Chap. 13 as follows:

- Research Question 13.3.1.1: *How can we design a language that is sufficiently expressive for domain-specific enterprise transformation concerns?*
  e^3*RoME* introduces the notion of linking the value provided by different lan-guages to an overall transformation-specific modelling purpose.
- Research Question 13.3.1.2: *How can we design a language such that it is eco-nomic in use?*
  e^3*RoME* selects only those language components needed for the transformation at hand.
- Research Question 13.3.2: *How can we design new languages by mixing and matching parts of existing languages?*
  e^3*RoME* provides a mechanism for reusing parts of existing languages, inspired by an earlier approach developed for value-based service bundling.

Chapter 22
Principle-Based Goal-Oriented
Requirements Language

Diana Marosin and Sepideh Ghanavati

Abstract This chapter introduces an overview on the formulation of architecture principles, guidelines for a semiformal definition, and rules for modelling the architecture principles. As such, we aim to provide answers to the challenges as discussed in Chap. 14. In doing so, we give insights on analysis and impact evaluation of aforementioned architecture principles on the designed architecture models and on the implementation of enterprise architecture. Furthermore, we give directions for future research and summarise possible applications of our method, including managing architectural changes and making informed decisions.

22.1 Introduction

We recall that the underlying goal of this chapter is to check and manage the consistency or non-consistency between architecture principles and architecture instructions (cf. the research question in Sect. 14.1). In Sect. 14.2, we discussed a non-exhaustive list of challenges when evaluating the impact of architecture principles, for example, vagueness given by the natural language representation, lack of a common definition, and lack of tool support for representation and analysis.

Studying the current literature and observing the practices in enterprises, we notice that even if the architecture principles are company specific, they all seem to have common fields in their structure. In Sect. 22.2, we summarise multiple definitions and present a minimal structure to define architecture principles, such that

D. Marosin (✉)
SopraSteria, Leudelange, Luxembourg
e-mail: marosin.diana@gmail.com

S. Ghanavati
Department of Computer Science at Texas Tech University, Lubbock, TX, USA

© Springer International Publishing AG, part of Springer Nature 2017
H.A. Proper et al. (eds.), *Architectural Coordination of Enterprise Transformation*,
The Enterprise Engineering Series, https://doi.org/10.1007/978-3-319-69584-6_22

it results in a consistent set of useful, implementable, measurable, and enforceable architecture principles.

In order to overcome the challenges presented in Sect. 14.2, we propose a semi-formal framework, called *Principles-based goal-oriented requirements language.* Our framework uses a semiformal language, goal-oriented requirements language that enables us to better justify the architecture principles in relation with goals and vision of the organisation, to provide rationales for the decisions, and to run what-if analysis (e.g. see what happens if architecture principles support conflicting goals, if the set contains conflicting architecture principles, or if some architecture principles support the goals only partially). Goal-oriented requirements language is our language of choice because it is part of a standard [i.e. *user requirements notation* (URN) (Amyot et al. 2009)] and it includes a quantitative and qualitative evaluation mechanism and KPIs.

Moreover, goal-oriented requirements language can be extended with the help of *meta-data* and *URN links* concepts, such that the language becomes versatile and adaptable to different organisational contexts. This means that the same language and graphical notation could accommodate successfully any of the multiple definitions of architecture principles (see Sects. 14.1 and 22.2).

The tool support, jUCMNav (Amyot et al. 2012), which is an Eclipse-based plug-in, helps resolve the scalability issues of goal-oriented requirements language. However, in the rest of this chapter, we do not focus on the tool but on formalisation and representation. Instructions on how to use our framework and examples from a real case study can be found and downloaded online (van Zee 2016). The high-level building blocks of our framework are represented in Fig. 22.1.

The first goal-oriented requirements language model belongs to the organisation under discussion and contains its higher-level goals and strategies. This model contributes to the new projects and programmes and therefore contributes to the project's goal-oriented requirements language models. Each project has its own goals to achieve and has its own timely issues. Fulfilling project's goals implies that the goals of the enterprise are satisfied as well. Architecture principles contain two elements: the textual representation of the architecture principle, as defined by stakeholders and management board, and a semiformal representation in

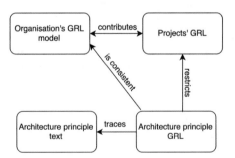

Fig. 22.1 Overview of principles-based goal-oriented requirements language framework. © 2014, D. Marosin; reprinted with permission from Marosin et al. (2014)

goal-oriented requirements language. The architecture principle is consistent with the organisation's goals and has the role to restrict the individual project's goals and tasks.

In the rest of this chapter, we explain how to formalise the set of architecture principles using goal-oriented requirements language, and we briefly discuss the analysis and evaluations that can be performed on a set of semiformalised architecture principles.

22.2 Guidelines for the Formulation of Architecture Principles

Lindström (2006) uses the characteristics of *"good requirements, originating from requirements engineering"* (e.g. IEEE Std 830-1998, Software Requirements Specification) to define the requirements for a good set of architecture principles. The authors distinguish between syntax (the form of the principle) and semantics (the meaning and content of the principles). The criteria for assessing the quality of architecture principles are as follows: verifiability, completeness, correctness, modifiability, unambiguity, consistency and stability. Similarly, the TOGAF standard (The Open Group 2011) lists five criteria that distinguish a set of good architecture principles: understandable, robust, complete, consistent and stable. Likewise, Op 't Land and Proper (2007) define two methodologies on how to create a SMART set of architecture principles (e.g. specific, measurable, achievable, realistic, time-related). Contrary to Lindström (2006), who leaves out the issue of prioritising the architecture principles, Op 't Land and Proper (2007) introduce this notion in their formulation and analysis. Based on the insights and requirements introduced by the aforementioned research, we define the following requirements for a set of architecture principles.

Understandable—Each principle should be sufficiently definitive and precise to be quickly grasped and understood by individuals and to support consistent decision-making in complex, potentially controversial situations. This definition is a result of combining the properties *Unambiguous*, *Robust* and *Specific*.

Complete—Every potentially important principle governing the management of the organisation is defined. We intentionally left out the reference to IT and technology as defined in TOGAF and created a more general requirement, applicable on all levels of an architecture. A possible sanity check for completeness is the list of questions defined by Op 't Land and Proper (2007), such as *"Are the stated principles relevant to the organisation?"*, *"Are all necessary principles defined?"*, etc.

Consistent—Principles should not be contradictory to the point where adhering to one principle would violate the goal of the other. Note that in practice there are recorded instances of conflicting architecture principles (Greefhorst and Proper 2011, pp. 128–133). In that case, multiple violations of one or another principle can result in a revision of the set of principles, until the set becomes consistent (Marosin et al. 2014).

Measurable—Both on the long term and short term, over the future architecture and project portfolio measurements are needed to assure that the organisation's goals are achieved and to check if the architecture principles are really followed and what is their impact on the organisation (Lindström 2006).

Stable—Principles should be enduring, yet able to accommodate changes. The organisation needs to establish a methodology for changing the set of principles which should be triggered when (a) a strategy or goals of the organisation change; (b) principles are conflicting; or (c) principles are constantly violated.

Based on the definitions and guidelines for formulating architecture principles in multiple literature sources and in practice, we define a set of minimum fields and information that architecture principles should contain, as follows:

Name—This field captures the essence of the architecture principle and should be easy to remember (Op 't Land et al. 2008; The Open Group 2011; Greefhorst et al. 2013).

Statement—This field is a clear, (presumably) unambiguous description of the principle (Op 't Land et al. 2008; The Open Group 2011; Greefhorst et al. 2013). The statement is in some sense a summary of the architecture principle itself, useful in human communication. However, it does not necessarily carry much semantics in a formal language.

Added value—This field states clearly what is aimed to be achieved when applying the architecture principle at hand (i.e. to which goals or softgoals of the organisation the architecture principle contributes to, either positively or negatively). Different researchers have named this field differently such as *Motivation* (Op 't Land et al. 2008; Wilkinson 2006) or *Rationale* (The Open Group 2011; Fischer et al. 2010). We identified this field in corporate practices also under the names *Future situation* and *Goal* (Marosin et al. 2014).

Impact and restrictions—This field defines the impact of the architecture principle on the design of another architecture principle or on the elements of the architecture, as well as the restrictions caused by enforcing the architecture principle at hand (Fischer et al. 2010). In practice, this field was also identified under the name *Constraints* (Marosin et al. 2014). It can also be called *Implications* (Op 't Land et al. 2008; Richardson et al. 1990; Lindström 2006).

Key actions—This field states what operational actions should be taken in order to follow the architecture principle at hand. In practice, this field is also called *Application* (Marosin et al. 2014), *Key Actions* (Fischer et al. 2010), *Assurance* (Op 't Land et al. 2008) or *Implications* (Hoogervorst 2004).

Preconditions—This field contains preconditions and requirements to be fulfilled before the principle can be applied. In practice, we found this field under the name *Implications*. Hoogervorst (2004) introduces the field *key actions for effectuating the architecture* to ensure that the principle can be followed.

Additional to the fields mentioned above, architecture principles may contain the following information in their definition:

Current situation—This field contains a description of the current situation with regard to the architecture principle at hand.

Future situation—This field contains a description of the supposed attainable situation, if the architecture principle at hand would be fully implemented and enforced in the organisation.

Architecture domain—This field states to which part of the architecture the principle is applied (e.g. business, infrastructure, organisation, etc.) (Hoogervorst 2004; Armour et al. 1999; Marosin et al. 2014).

22.3 Semiformal Representation of Architecture Principles

Goal-oriented requirements language which is based on the *i** language and the *use case maps* (UCM) notation is part of the URN standard. The URN standard is suitable to specify both functional and non-functional requirements for a proposed or an evolving system and analyse such requirements for correctness and completeness. Combing modelling goals and intentional concepts, quality attributes and scenario concepts, the standard enables reasoning about alternatives and proposes multiple algorithms for evaluation.

Goal-oriented requirements language describes business concerns, goals satisfactions and stakeholders' beliefs and dependencies. Goal-oriented requirements language intentional elements can be *Softgoals* ($\bigcirc$), *Goals* ($\bigcirc$), and *Tasks* ($\bigcirc$). Actors ($\bigcirc$) represent stakeholders of the system, the holders of intentions. *Softgoals*, represent what a stakeholder wants to achieve. Contrary to goals, softgoals do not have quantifiable measurements. *Goals*, however, are more precise, have quantifiable measurements and can be clearly achieved. *Tasks* represent solutions to (or operationalisations of) goals or softgoals. In order to be achieved or completed, softgoals, goals, and tasks may require *resources* ($\square$) to be available. *Beliefs* ($\bigcirc$) capture the rationales and justifications of goal-oriented requirements language intentional elements and their links.

Goal-oriented requirements language elements are connected by contribution, correlation, dependency and decomposition links. *Contribution* ($\rightarrow$) and *Correlation* ($\dashrightarrow$) links indicate desired impacts or describe side-effects of one intentional element on another intentional element. They can have a quantitative impact (integer value between -100 and 100) or a qualitative value, marked with the keywords: *make, help, some+, some-, hurt, break*. *Decomposition* ($+$) links allow an intentional element to be decomposed into sub-elements using AND, OR, XOR decomposition. *Dependency* ($\rightarrow\!\!\!-$) links model relationships between actors (one actor depending on another actor for something) and between other goal-oriented requirements language intentional elements.

The language can be extended and become domain specific by using *stereotypes* attached to the basic constructs of the language. Introducing stereotypes allows us to define a domain-specific notation for the architecture principles and introduce restrictions to assure the well-formedness of the models.

In Sect. 22.2, we summarised existing definitions for architecture principles as found in both the current academic literature and practice. We also presented existing guidelines and requirements for a good set of architecture principles, and we based our definition on these requirements. Following the aforementioned definitions, we introduce a new goal-oriented requirements language profile and annotate each constitutive element of an architecture principle with stereotypes, as presented in Table 22.1. We group all stereotypes related to architecture principles under the name *ST_Principle*. This semiformal representation and mapping enables us to leverage all analysis mechanisms and algorithms embedded in goal-oriented requirements language.

As an example, consider Table 22.2. There, we consider the textual representation of an architecture principle, as defined in *"Principles catalogue"* (Greefhorst et al. 2013, pp. 163–164). We map the natural language statements to goal-oriented requirements language intentional elements, creating the goal-oriented requirements language representation of the architecture principle, in Fig. 22.2.

Based on discussions and the guidelines provided above, the natural language description of the architecture principle is refined and stereotyped, such that it can

Table 22.1 Mapping architecture principles constructs to goal-oriented requirements language intentional elements

Enterprise architecture principle element	Stereotype value	Goal-oriented requirements language element
Name	≪Principle≫	Softgoal (◠)
Statement	–	Comment
Added value	≪AddedValue≫	Softgoal, Goal (◠)
Impact/restrictions	–	The value of goal-oriented requirements language links (e.g. quantitative impact (integer value between −100 and 100) or a qualitative value, marked with the keywords: *make, help, some+, some-, hurt, break*
Key actions	≪KeyAction≫	Task (◯)
Preconditions	≪Precondition≫	Softgoal, Goal, Task, Resource (▭)
Architecture domain	–	Actor (⬭)

Table 22.2 Natural language text representation of architecture principle: *Data is captured once* (© Springer-Verlag Berlin Heidelberg 2011; reprinted with permission from Greefhorst and Proper (2011))

Principle: Data is captured once

Type of information: data, application

Quality attributes: usability, efficiency

Rationale: It is inefficient and user-unfriendly to ask for the same data twice or more

Implications:

- Before acquiring data, it is first determined if the data is already available
- Data that is already available is pre-filled in forms
- Applications expose shared data for reuse by other applications

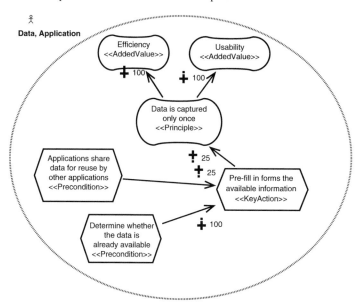

Fig. 22.2 Goal-oriented requirements language representation of architecture principle: *Data is captured once*

be further represented semiformally in goal-oriented requirements language. Each element of the textual definition has to be interpreted, simplified or enriched and then mapped to the goal-oriented requirements language stereotype.

For example, the type of information is mapped to the architecture domain. This element is represented as an *Actor* in *Principle-based goal-oriented requirements language framework*. The principle itself is represented as a softgoal and stereotype ≪Principle≫.

The (soft)goals that this architecture principle tackles, in our example, *usability* and *efficiency*, respectively, are mapped to softgoals in goal-oriented requirements language and are stereotyped as ≪AddedValue≫. The rationale of the principle could be represented as a belief, attached to the ≪Principle≫ intentional element.

The field *Implications* in the textual representation of the architecture principle contains mixed information. We interpret and identify the following elements.

The final representation of this architecture principle, using goal-oriented requirements language is presented in Fig. 22.2.

We interpreted and traced the natural language statements presented in Table 22.2 to goal-oriented requirements language (intentional) elements. However, when missing the organisational context in which this architecture principle is applied, as well as the discussions that lead to it, it is impossible to create a more detailed model. Therefore, this should be seen solely like an illustrative example on how to apply the method and stereotypes presented in Table 22.1. In Marosin et al. (2016), we evaluated this method together with enterprise architects from a *European Tax Administration*. The feasibility for such a method was confirmed for technology-related architecture principles, and the architects confirmed that based on discussions and professional experience, they could add qualitative/quantitative values to the goal-oriented requirements language links, as well as evaluate realistically the impact of the key actions on the realisation of architecture principles.

22.4 Constraints for Architecture Principle Representation

After identifying the constitutive elements of architecture principles, we constraint their representation in goal-oriented requirements language by defining specific *object constraint language* (OCL) rules for modelling. This assures well-formedness and correctness of the models.

The OCL is a declarative language for describing rules that apply to formal models. Due to its Eclipse OCL plug-in that support rule definitions, checking, and explanation, OCL can be integrated with jUCMNav. It is, therefore, possible to define and verify OCL rules for any goal-oriented requirements language model. We provide nine OCL rules for checking the well-formedness of the architecture principles[1]:

1. *An architecture principle must be modelled as a softgoal (PrincipleAsSoftGoal).* As stated before, the architecture principles are seen as "rules of conduct" and cannot be fully enforced. Since the architecture principles are defined on a high level of abstraction and are vague in nature, we preserve their scope and nature and enforce modelling any element that has the stereotype ≪Principle≫ as a softgoal intentional element.

2. *A key action must be modelled as a task (KeyActionAsTask).* By refining the architecture principles to the level of tasks, we ensure that architecture principles become operational.

3. *Architecture principles, added values, preconditions, and key actions cannot be modelled as beliefs (BeliefsNotStereoTyped).* This rule is required since beliefs in goal-oriented requirements language are different entities from the intentional elements (i.e. goals, softgoals, resources, and tasks). *Beliefs* capture the rationales and justifications of goal-oriented requirements language intentional elements and their links. However they are not considered in the evaluation (van Zee et al. 2015).

4. *Each architecture principle must have at least one contribution from a key action (KeyActionToPrinciple).* In order to implement the architecture principles, we consider it necessary to refine their definition until we reach the tasks' level. This means that it is necessary to clearly define the key actions for realising the architecture principle. Therefore, each intentional element that has the stereotype ≪Principle≫ must be refined to have at least one contribution from an intentional element with the stereotype ≪KeyAction≫.

---

[1] The implementation of the OCL rules is part of our *Principle-based goal-oriented requirements language* framework (van Zee 2016).

5. *If a precondition is introduced using a contribution link, the link must get the maximum value (ContributionFromPreconditionIsMax).* In goal-oriented requirements language, the evaluation algorithms depend on the values of the links. By giving the contribution the maximum value (e.g. 100 or *make*), we enforce that the precondition has at least high priority in the evaluation as the other intentional elements linked to the parent.

6. *If a precondition is introduced using a dependency link, the precondition must be modelled as a source (PreconditionAsSourceOfDependency).* In goal-oriented requirements language notation, the dependency links are modelled as follows: *target* —▶— *source*. We introduce this OCL rule in order to assure that preconditions are modelled correctly in a goal-oriented requirements language notation. A dependency link shows a relationship between a dependent intentional element which depends on a precondition's intentional element. At the time of the evaluation, the intentional element dependent on a precondition receives the minimum value between its own evaluation and the evaluation of the precondition.

7. *Each architecture principle must contribute to at least one (soft)goal (here stereotyped ≪AddedValue≫) of the organisation (PrincipleToGoal).* By introducing this rule, we assure that we do not introduce any architecture principle that has no real value for the goals of the organisation.

8. *Each (soft)goal (here stereotyped ≪AddedValue≫) of the organisation must have at least one contribution link from the set of architecture principles (GoalToPrinciple).* By introducing this rule, we assure that every goal of the organisation is also addressed by at least one architecture principle.

9. *The architecture principles should not propagate a "conflict" satisfaction value for added value (NoConflicts).* A set of two or more architecture principles must not have contradictory contribution links on the same goal. If this happens and the goal gets "conflict" satisfaction value, a warning is triggered and the set of architecture principles has to be revised in such a way that it is kept consistent.

As an example, consider the example we introduced before and its semiformal representation in goal-oriented requirements language, presented in Fig. 22.2. We check the semantic correctness of our model based on the previously defined OCL rules. In Fig. 22.3 we present the error log from jUCMNav. We can observe that the model is not following one of the OCL rules, because the precondition *Applications expose shared data for reuse by other applications* does not exercise a maximum contribution. Even so, the tool still allows running simulations and analysis. However this error points the architect or the modeller to a possible issue.

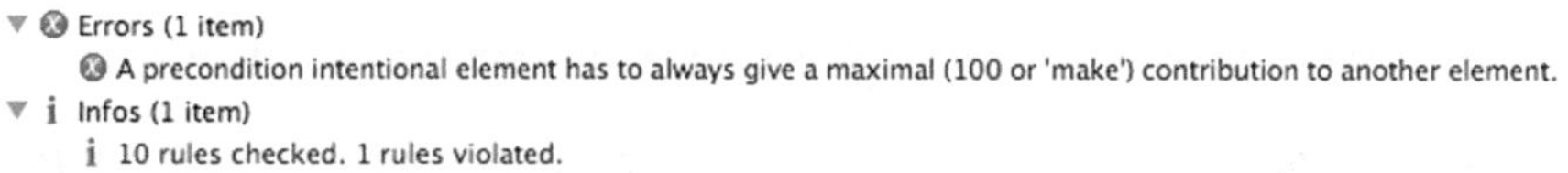

▼ ⊗ Errors (1 item)
    ⊗ A precondition intentional element has to always give a maximal (100 or 'make') contribution to another element.
▼ i Infos (1 item)
    i 10 rules checked. 1 rules violated.

Fig. 22.3 Log of semantic check errors for goal-oriented requirements language representation of architecture principle *Data is captured once*

22.5 Relevance and Consequences for ACET

In this chapter we present different kinds of analysis that are enabled by our semi-formal representation of the architecture principles. This represent directions for future research and play a pillar role in supporting decision-making when creating enterprise architecture, as well when guiding enterprise transformation.

22.5.1 Support for Formulation of Architecture Principles

We recall the challenges we identified in Sect. 14.3. Motivated by the observed importance of architecture principles and their guiding role in the transformation, in Sects. 22.2 and 22.3, we mainly focused on how to formalise and represent architecture principles in a goal-oriented modelling language. For this, we first presented requirements for good sets of principles, based on the current state of the art. Second, we introduced a *Principle-based goal-oriented requirements language* framework. The framework contains a new goal-oriented requirements language profile, created by adding stereotypes to the intentional elements. Furthermore, the correctness of the models is assured by defining nine OCL rules and running semantic checks on the resulted models.

In technology and engineering related problems, such formalism in goal-oriented requirements language is considered welcome and useful. The goal-oriented requirements language representations supports traceability between goals and strategy of the organisation and the layers of architecture, or it could be used to explain the rationales of principles to the involved stakeholders. Furthermore, the solution proposed seems feasible for the architects (Marosin et al. 2016), and the general opinion is that contribution links can be evaluated at design time.

22.5.2 Supporting Design Decisions Based on Architecture Principles

In Fig. 22.1, we introduce the constitutive elements of the *Principle-based goal-oriented requirements language* framework. Furthermore, we represent in Fig. 22.4 the relation between individual (design) decisions and new projects. In this layer, we propose introducing traceability links to the design decisions, integrating in our framework the work of Plataniotis et al. (2015a,b) and van Zee et al. (2014).

Likewise, in future work, we aim to capture the decisions taken based on the individual project's goals goal-oriented requirements language and the previous architecture principles goal-oriented requirements language and construct a knowledge-base system. The system should include past cases and suggest templates and solutions at runtime for developing the goal-oriented requirements language models.

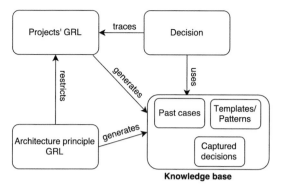

Fig. 22.4 Relation between architecture principles, design decisions, and the organisation's knowledge base. © 2014, D. Marosin; reprinted with permission from Marosin et al. 2014

22.5.3 Supporting Consistency Checks

The set of architecture principles itself needs a consistency mechanism in place (van Zee et al. 2016). There does not exist any formal mechanism to create a stable and consistent set of principle and to support changes in the set of principles. Such a mechanism should, first, trigger consistency checks on the models and revision of the current landscape when changes appear in the set of principles (e.g. addition, deletion, or modification of principles). Second, analysis of the current situation (e.g. current objectives or current environment of the organisation, as well as addition of new projects and programmes) should trigger changes in the set of principles. In order to realise the second type of revision, good traceability links between architecture principles and business processes are needed. This traceability is well supported by our framework (i.e. *Principle-based goal-oriented requirements language*) and by the existing modelling tools (e.g. jUCMNav).

22.5.4 Evaluate Consistency with Architecture Principles

We introduced in Sect. 22.1 the goal-oriented requirements language notation. It is possible, by means of a URN link, to connect goal-oriented requirements language intentional elements and UCM scenarios. This enables us to evaluate both the efficiency of using and introducing a specific architecture principle, as well as, to measure the (partial) compliance between the architecture principles and the implementation of architecture. For evaluating the consistency between different implementation of architecture elements and architecture principles, as well as the consistency between the intended scenarios and the architecture principles, we propose to leverage the URN links as implemented in the jUCMNav tool. To that end, in future work, we aim to define principles-related algorithms for the evaluation of the intentional elements.

As a proof of concept, we created a UCM scenario that simulates the use of an internet portal. From the user perspective, the following actions take place: (1) the user makes a request to receive a form; (2) the user receives the form; (3) if any data is pre-filled, the user verifies the correctness of the data; (4) if data is incorrect, the user corrects the data; and (5) the user submits the form. From the application perspective, when it receives a request from a user, the following actions take place: (1) It determines if the data is available. (2) If the data is available, it pre-fills a form. (3) It presents the form (empty or pre-filled) to the user.

We simulated the situation in which the application has the data available and presents it to the user. However, the data is incorrect and the user has to correct it before submitting the form. Based on the simulated path of the scenario, we update the satisfaction level of the goal-oriented requirements language intentional elements (see the goal-oriented requirements language model in Fig. 22.2).

In Fig. 22.5a, we present the initial situation, in which we cannot determine the satisfaction level of the two preconditions, *Determined whether the data is already available* ≪Precondition≫ and *Applications expose shared data for reuse by other applications* ≪Precondition≫, respectively. Therefore, the realisation of key action *Pre-fill in forms the available data* ≪KeyAction≫ is denied (quantitative evaluation −100).

Now, considering the first part of the UCM scenario, the fact that the architecture contains a building block with the responsibility to check the availability of data satisfies the precondition *Determined whether the data is already available*. This, in

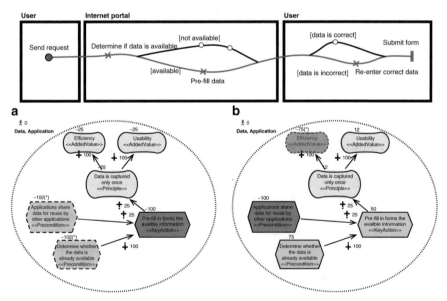

Fig. 22.5 Evaluation of goal-oriented requirements language intentional elements based on a UCM scenario

turn, propagates a satisfaction value for the key action *Pre-fill in forms the available data* ≪KeyAction≫, (weakly satisfied, quantitative evaluation +75), which propagates a weakly satisfied value for the architecture principle (quantitative evaluation +18). This situation is described in Fig. 22.5b.

However, the user had to correct its data. This affects the softgoal *Efficiency* ≪AddedValue≫; therefore, in Fig. 22.5b, this goal is denied (qualitative evaluation −100), even if the architecture principle was satisfied. This situation illustrates an inconsistency between the architectural implementation and the intended purpose of the architecture principle.

Note: For the scope of this illustrative example and for this chapter, we do not go in details regarding the evaluation algorithms available for goal-oriented requirements language intentional elements. This falls outside the scope of this work.

22.6 Discussion

In this chapter we presented a method to support creation and formulation of architecture principles, such that they are implementable and operational (cf. Research Question 14.1.1). We motivated our work in Sect. 14.3 by presenting non-excursively the challenges practitioners and enterprises face when using architecture principles. To support the practitioner's work, in Sect. 22.2, we provided guidelines and minimum requirements for defining the architecture principles.

In Sect. 22.1, we introduced a semiformal framework, called *Principle-based goal-oriented requirements language*. We presented the required language constructs to represent architecture principles in a semiformal language, here goal-oriented requirements language (cf. Research Question 14.1.2.1), and we introduced nine modelling constraints to assure the well-formedness of the models (cf. Research Question 14.1.2.2).

In Sect. 22.5 we include the relevance of our framework in an enterprise transformation context, therefore the relevance for the ACET method. We link our results to our future research agenda. By applying our framework for formalising architecture principles, we set grounds for the analysis of architecture principle's impact on the design decisions. Furthermore, we give insights on the possibility to define evaluation algorithms and methods of the consistency between architecture design and implementation and the defined architectural principles.

Chapter 23
The EA Anamnesis Approach

Georgios Plataniotis

Abstract In this chapter, we introduce our EA Anamnesis meta-model. With this metamodel we allow for (1) contextualising the decision-making process of a single decision in terms of cross-cutting/intertwining decision relationships and (2) a comparison of decision outcomes to the original decision-making process. The resulting framework aims to meet some of the challenges identified in Chap. 15.

23.1 Introduction

The EA Anamnesis metamodel allows for (1) contextualising the decision-making process of a single decision in terms of cross-cutting/intertwining decision relationships and (2) a comparison of decision outcomes to the original decision-making process. Figure 23.1 presents the EA Anamnesis metamodel. For comprehension purposes, the concepts of our metamodel will be introduced in three sections: decision properties (Sect. 23.2), decision-making process concepts (Sect. 23.3), and decision relationships (Sect. 23.4).

23.2 Decision Properties

Enterprise architecture decision—An enterprise architecture decision names the
   decision, either the made decision or the alternative decision (Proper and Op 't
   Land 2010). Regarding the distinction between made decision and alternative
   decision, see our later concept of a decision "state".

G. Plataniotis (✉)
e-Government Center for Social Security (IDIKA), Likourgou 10, 105 51 Athens, Greece
e-mail: georgeplataniotis@gmail.com

© Springer International Publishing AG, part of Springer Nature 2017   249
H.A. Proper et al. (eds.), *Architectural Coordination of Enterprise Transformation*,
The Enterprise Engineering Series, https://doi.org/10.1007/978-3-319-69584-6_23

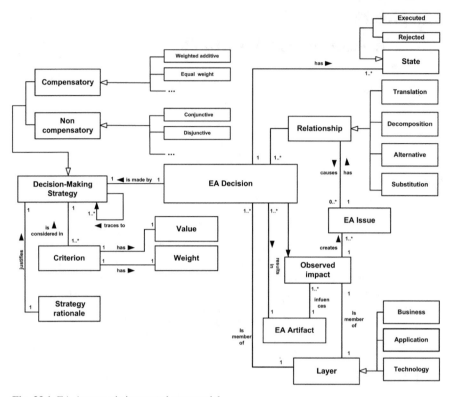

Fig. 23.1 EA Anamnesis integrated metamodel

Example: John makes the enterprise architecture decision "*Make customer profile registration via intermediary*".

Enterprise architecture issue—Similar to the concept of an issue from Tyree and Akerman (2005), an enterprise architecture issue represents the architecture design problem that enterprise architects have to address during the enterprise transformation process.

Example: The enterprise architecture issue "*Create an appropriate application service to support new business process*" resulting from the enterprise architecture decision "*Introduce a new business process for customer profile registration*".

Enterprise architecture artefact—An enterprise architecture artefact [similar to the concept of an architecture element (Tang et al. 2007)] is either the direct result produced from a set of executed enterprise architecture decisions or a representation of this result. For now, we use an enterprise architecture artefact to refer to architectural representations. Specifically, we use it as a bridging concept towards the enterprise architecture modelling language ArchiMate,

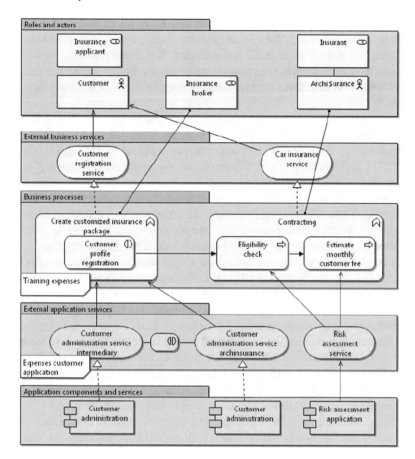

Fig. 23.2 ArchiSurance intermediary enterprise architecture model

whereby an enterprise architecture artefact allows us to link enterprise architecture decisions to concepts from ArchiMate.

Example: The enterprise architecture artefact "*Customer profile registration*" in the ArchiMate model in Fig. 23.2 is linked to, amongst others, the enterprise architecture decision "*Make customer profile registration via intermediary*".

Layer—In line with the ArchiMate language (Iacob et al. 2012), an enterprise is specified in three layers: *Business, Application, and Technology.* Using these three layers, we express an enterprise *holistically*, showing not only applications and physical IT infrastructure (expressed through the application and technology layers) but also how an enterprise's IT impacts/is impacted by an enterprise's products and services and its business strategy and processes.

Example: The enterprise architecture decision "*Make customer profile registration via intermediary*" is a part of the business layer of ArchiSurance.

State—An enterprise architecture decision can be in an executed or a rejected state (Kruchten et al. 2006). In an executed state, an enterprise architecture decision has already been made and executed. A rejected decision, on the other hand, is a decision that was considered as an alternative during the decision-making process but was rejected because another decision was more appropriate.

Example: John had to address enterprise architecture issue *"find an appropriate application to interface with the intermediary"*. *"Acquisition of COTS application B"* is the executed decision, whereas decisions *"COTS application A"*, *"COTS application C"*, and *"Upgrade existing application (inhouse)"* are the rejected (alternative) decisions.

Observed impact—The observed impact concept signifies an *unanticipated* consequence of an already made decision to an enterprise architecture artefact. This opposes to anticipated consequences, as indicated by relationships such as translation or decomposition. Observed impacts can be positive or negative.

In current everyday practice, architects model *anticipated* consequences using what-if scenarios (Lankhorst 2012). Unfortunately, not every possible impact of made enterprise architecture decisions can be predicted. This is especially true for enterprise architecture, where one considers impacts across the enterprise rather than in one specific (e.g. technical) part. The outcome of enterprise architecture decisions can be observed during an ex post analysis of the architecture (Proper and Op 't Land 2010). Some of the consequences of enterprise architecture decisions are revealed during the implementation phase, or during the maintenance of the existing architecture design. These unanticipated consequences are captured exactly by the concept of an observed impact.

For us the main usefulness of capturing observed impacts is that they can be used by architects to avoid decisions with negative consequences in future designs of the architecture.

Example: The enterprise architecture decision *"Acquisition of COTS application B"* has an observed impact *"Degraded user experience in the application use"*. This observed impact captures an unanticipated, ex post, side effect of acquiring COTS application B, due to unfamiliarity of users with the new user interface that COTS application B introduces.

23.3 Decision-Making Process Concepts

The decision-making process concepts of our metamodel focus on capturing (1) decision-making strategies that were used during the architecture design process for a specific enterprise architecture decision, (2) the rationale behind this specific decision strategy choice, and (3) available alternatives and criteria that were taken into account. Below we provide the description of these concepts.

Decision-making strategy—This concept captures the decision-making strategy used by the enterprise architect to evaluate the alternatives and make the actual enterprise architecture decision.

Depending on the decision-making context, the decision-maker uses different strategies to address the decision-making problem. In line with general theories on decision-making, our metamodel involves two main categories of decision-making strategies: compensatory and non-compensatory (Einhorn 1970; Payne 1976; Svenson 1979; Rothrock and Yin 2008). In our meta-model, we specify this as follows:

Compensatory strategy—This involves two alternatives:
- Weighted additive (WADD): In WADD strategies the criteria which evaluate the alternatives have different weights. The score of each alternative is computed by multiplying each criterion by its weight and then by taking the sum of these values. The alternative with the highest score is chosen by the decision-maker (Rothrock and Yin 2008).
- Equal weight: The score of each alternative is calculated by the same way as WADD strategies. The difference is that the criteria have the same weight (Rothrock and Yin 2008).

Non-compensatory strategy—This also involves two alternatives:
- Conjunctive: In conjunctive strategies, alternatives that fail to comply with a given threshold level of one or more criteria are immediately excluded from the decision-maker's choice set (Rothrock and Yin 2008).
- Disjunctive: In this strategy an alternative is selected if it complies with a minimum threshold level on at least one criterion, irrespective of its values on other criteria (Rothrock and Yin 2008).

In line with Einhorn (1970), Payne (1976), Svenson (1979), and Rothrock and Yin (2008), a hybrid decision strategy is also supported by our metamodel. The relationship "*trace to*" signifies the combination of two or more decision strategies during the decision-making process.

We should also mention that there is no restriction in the use of additional decision strategies. We include a set of common decision strategies, but we also denote in the metamodel that more decision strategies can be supported.

Example: John rejects "*acquisition of COTS application C*" because it exceeds the budget set beforehand by the top management. Thus, here John employed a conjunctive non-compensatory decision-making strategy.

Criterion—Criteria play an important role in our metamodel. Depending on the decision strategy that was used for the evaluation process, criteria can be compensatory or non-compensatory. For example, if a disjunctive strategy was used, the criteria that were used for the evaluation with this strategy are disjunctive. Furthermore, the concepts *value* and *weight* of criterion are included in our viewpoint. The value concept represents the value that the decision-maker assigns to this criterion during the evaluation process. The weight concept represents the importance of this criterion and is typically used in WADD strategies.

Example: After discarding *acquisition of COTS app C*, John considered three quality criteria in his evaluation, *usability*, *interoperability*, and *scalability*. *Interoperability* was considered as the most important, with a weight of 10.

Strategy rationale—In a decision-making process, the architect not only has to choose amongst some alternatives (actual decision-making process) but also has to select the decision strategy that satisfies his current evaluation needs. Actually, this concept represents the rationale for the decision strategy that was selected for the evaluation process. This is what is referred as model decision-making, decision-making about the decision process itself (Mintzberg et al. 1976).

As we discussed in Sect. 15.2.3, different factors affect the decision-making process and decision-makers should adjust their decision-making strategy accordingly. The concept of a strategy rationale enables a decision-maker to justify the reasons for his model decision.

Example: Time-stress provides the rationale behind the selection of a specific decision making strategy (metadecision), since it concerns decision-making about the decision-making process itself, independently of specific decision criteria such as usability.

23.4 Enterprise Architecture Decision Relationships

The role of relationship concepts is to make the different types of relationships between enterprise architecture decisions explicit. Based on ontologies for software architecture design decisions (Kruchten 2004; Kruchten et al. 2006), we define four types of relationships:

Translation relationship—Translation relationships illustrate relationships between decisions/enterprise architecture issues that belong to different layers/enterprise architecture artefacts. Architects translate the requirements that new enterprise architecture artefacts impose (enterprise architecture issue) to decisions that will support these requirements by means of another enterprise architecture artefact (Op 't Land and Proper 2007).

Example: The enterprise architecture decision *make customer profile registration via intermediary* translates to the issue *find an appropriate application service*. Subsequently, this issue translates to a second enterprise architecture decision *acquisition of COTS application B*.

Decomposition relationship—The Decomposition relationship is in line with *Comprises (Is Made of, Decomposes into)* of the ontology developed by Kruchten et al. (2006). Decomposition relationships signify how generic enterprise architecture decisions decompose into more detailed design decisions.

Example: The enterprise architecture decision *acquisition of COTS application B* has a decomposition relationship with enterprise architecture decision *Application interface type 1*. This is to indicate that choosing application B also implies the more detailed choice for a particular type of user interface.

Alternative relationship—This relationship type (Kruchten et al. 2006) illustrates the enterprise architecture decisions that were rejected (alternatives) in order to address a specific enterprise architecture issue.

Example: Rejected enterprise architecture decisions *COTS application A, COTS application C*, and *Upgrade existing application (inhouse)* have an alternative relationship with enterprise architecture issue *find an appropriate application to interface with the intermediary*. This signifies that these decisions were the alternatives for this issue.

Substitution relationship—A substitution relationship explicates how one enterprise architecture decision repairs the negative outcome of another enterprise architecture decision.

Example: The enterprise architecture decision *Acquisition of COTS application B* has a negative observed impact on the business process *Customer profile registration*. This is because it leads users to make mistakes, as we saw with the concept *observed impact*. As such, it is repaired by the enterprise architecture decision *Application interface 2*.

23.5 Discussion

In this chapter we introduced a metamodel for capturing enterprise architecture decision-making strategies, as well as interrelations between decisions. This metamodel integrates our decision-making process metamodel and decision relationships metamodel from earlier work. In so doing, the integrated meta-model allows for (1) contextualising the decision-making process of a single decision, in terms of (cross-cutting) relations with other relations, and (2) the comparison of a decision-making process with observed outcomes of a decision. This comparison of (ex ante) decision-making with (ex post) observed impact leads to better understanding of existing architectures. As such, it provides a first step towards learning from architecture decision-making.

Last but not least, one of our major challenges is to investigate the return of capturing effort for our approach. Our design rationale assists architects to better understand existing enterprise architecture designs, but the effort of capturing this information might be a dissuasive factor. To address this issue, our research will focus on ways to decrease the capturing effort. One way of doing this is by evaluating the actual practical usefulness of the concepts of the decision-making strategy viewpoint. For example, we capture the strategy rationale for selecting a decision-making strategy, but whether the effort for capturing this outweighs the received benefits remains to be seen.

Chapter 24
Formalising Enterprise Architecture Decision Models

Marc van Zee

Abstract In this chapter we introduce and validate a logic-based framework that serves as the underlying model for Chap. 23. The resulting logic-based framework aims to address some of the challenges identified in Chap. 15.

Our working hypothesis is that capturing of design knowledge in terms of a logic-based framework will enable consistency checks of the underlying rationales and advanced impact/what-if analysis when confronted with changes. We formalise a set of integrity constraints, which allow guidance of decision capturing during model creation and provide the means to perform consistency checks. We apply our formal framework to a practical case study from the insurance sector.

24.1 Introduction

Large and complex enterprises are a common occurrence in today's business environment. Such enterprises usually involve complex and interdependent business processes and IT systems. Enterprise architecture is used to model such enterprises in a holistic fashion by connecting their IT infrastructure and applications to the business processes they support. In turn this links them also to the products and services that are realised by those business processes (Op 't Land et al. 2008; Hoogervorst 2004). When creating an enterprise architecture, several design decisions have to be made. These decisions are to a large extent based on assumptions about the situation at hand. Such assumptions may relate to the goals the (individual) stakeholders have, strategic directions of the enterprise, architecture principles, requirements, and so on. In practice, enterprises are confronted with frequent changes and challenges to these assumptions.

M. van Zee
Google Research, Zurich, Switzerland
e-mail: marcvanzee@gmail.com

© Springer International Publishing AG, part of Springer Nature 2017
H.A. Proper et al. (eds.), *Architectural Coordination of Enterprise Transformation*,
The Enterprise Engineering Series, https://doi.org/10.1007/978-3-319-69584-6_24

257

Our long-term research goal is to explore the possibility of explicitly linking architecture-level design decisions with their underlying assumptions. The aim of doing so is to make the rationalisation of these decisions explicit and traceable, so that we can formally reason about them in terms of a logic-based framework. This will enable explicit reasoning about the connections between the enterprise's architecture, the associated design decisions, and their underlying assumptions. Formalising the elements in an architectural decision model has been shown to be useful for the structuring of knowledge, and the measuring of the quality of existing decisions (Zimmermann et al. 2009). Architects and designers who are not the original developers often have to control the quality of and maintain the enterprise architecture. These people need a good understanding of the architecture in order to work effectively. It is not typical in enterprise architecture for design rationales to be obtained from design specifications, because there is no systematic practice for capturing them. Even when some of these decisions are captured, they are not organised in such a way that they can be retrieved and tracked easily. Remedying this situation becomes critical and challenging when system requirements and operating environments continue to evolve (Tang et al. 2007). Having a framework to formally reason about decisions and their underlying assumptions also allows for decision types and dependency patterns to be defined, which helps to detect the incompleteness or inconsistency of a decision model. Finally, knowledge engineers working in other decision-capturing domains (i.e. not enterprise architecture) can reuse the model structure to organise their knowledge (Zimmermann et al. 2009).

In this chapter, we contribute to our long-term research goal by formalising a recently proposed framework for decision-making in enterprise architecture by Plataniotis et al. (2013a, 2014d) using set and graph theory concepts. The framework of Plataniotis et al. (2013a, 2014d) consists of a meta-model that serves as a basis for decision design graphs composed of enterprise architecture decisions, issues, observed impacts, and several types of dependency relations. We analyse the correspondence between the meta-model and the decision design graphs and propose a formal framework that captures the decision design graphs more precisely. Moreover, motivated by providing a better guidance on the use of the framework for *a priori* decision analysis and support, we extend the framework to cater for a more expressive notation of decision state, and we make precise several informally introduced concepts of Plataniotis et al. (2013a, 2014d) using integrity constraints. We apply our framework to a case study and show the benefits of our formal approach by demonstrating the possibility for a priori decision analysis through consistency checks on the integrity constraints.

The remainder of this chapter is structured as follows: In Sect. 24.2 we discuss the framework of Plataniotis et al. (2013a, 2014d). In Sect. 24.3 we use this discussion as a motivation to present our formal framework. In Sect. 24.4 we validate our framework for a priori decision analysis by applying it to our ArchiSurance use case. Finally, in Sect. 24.5 we position our work in state-of-the-art research.

24.2 Preliminaries

In this section, we briefly review the key components of the meta-model of Plataniotis et al. (2013a, 2014d), followed by a discussion. We use these observations as a basis for the formal framework that we will introduce in the next section.

24.2.1 Meta-model and Decision Design Graphs

Plataniotis et al. (2013a, 2014d) recently presented an approach for relating enterprise architecture decisions. Using a meta-model and a decision design graph, they explain how decisions from different enterprise domains (business, application, and technology) relate to each other. For example, how decisions taken on a business level affect IT decisions and vice versa. Their approach is inspired by well-known mechanisms for capturing architectural rationales in software architecture. The meta-model that was presented by Plataniotis et al. (2013a, 2014d) is depicted in Fig. 24.1. This meta-model serves as an underlying model for decision design graphs, of which an example is depicted in Fig. 24.2.

From now on, we will use the following naming convention: We will refer to the meta-model in Fig. 24.1 as the "meta-model", and the decision design graph in Fig. 24.2 as "decision graph". We will explain the details of the decision graph in more detail when presenting the case study, but in this chapter we will already use it to explain the main concepts of the framework, which consists of the following elements:

Enterprise architecture decision—represents a decision that has been made or rejected in order to resolve an issue. An enterprise architecture decision shows decisions that are captured in the context of an enterprise transformation (Proper and Op 't Land 2010). The decision graph contains a total of 13 decisions, from enterprise architecture decision D01 to enterprise architecture decision D13.

Enterprise architecture issue—represents an architectural design problem that enterprise architects have to address during the enterprise transformation process. In this way, they can be regarded as a motivation for the design decisions. The decision graph contains six issues, from enterprise architecture issue IS01 to enterprise architecture issue IS06.

Enterprise architecture artefact—serves as a bridging concept towards the enterprise architecture modelling language ArchiMate, whereby an enterprise architecture artefact links enterprise architecture decisions to ArchiMate concepts. For instance, enterprise architecture decision D01 in the decision graph is related to enterprise architecture artefact "*Customer profile registration Business processes*". Enterprise architecture issues are not related to artefacts.

Layer—is in line with the ArchiMate language (Iacob et al. 2012). An enterprise is specified in three layers: *Business*, *Application*, and *Technology*. Using these

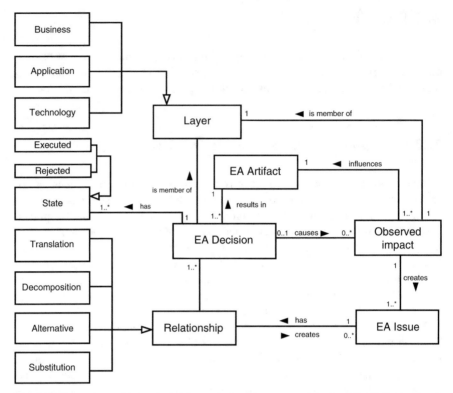

Fig. 24.1 Enterprise architecture decisions relationship meta-model. © 2013 IEEE. Reprinted, with permission, from Plataniotis et al. (2013a)

layers, an enterprise architect is able to model an enterprise *holistically*, showing not only applications and physical IT infrastructure (which are contained in the application and technology layers) but also how the IT impacts/is impacted by the products, services, and business strategy and processes. Enterprise architecture decisions are related to layers, for instance, in the decision graph enterprise architecture decision D01 is related to the Business Layer, while enterprise architecture decision D06 is related to the Application Layer.

State—represents the state of an enterprise architecture decision, which is either *Executed* or *Rejected*. In an executed state, an enterprise architecture decision has already been made and was accepted. A rejected decision, on the other hand, is a decision that was considered as an alternative during the decision-making process but was rejected because another decision was more appropriate. In the decision graph, the state of a decision is not explicitly represented, but it can be inferred from the relationships. A decision that has an *alternative* relation with an issue is rejected, while all other decisions are executed.

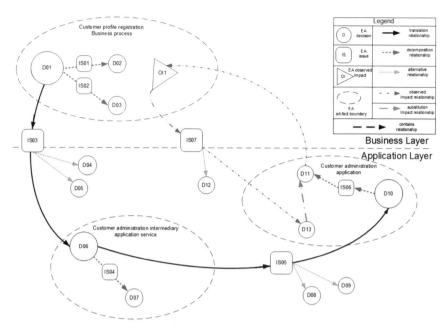

Fig. 24.2 Visualisation of enterprise architecture decisions relationships

Relationship—makes the different types of relationships between enterprise architecture decisions explicit. Based on ontologies for software architecture design
decisions, Plataniotis et al. (2013a, 2014d) define four relationships. The *Translation* relationship illustrates relationships between decisions and issues that
belong to different enterprise architecture artefacts. During the enterprise transformation process, architects translate the requirements that new enterprise architecture artefacts impose (enterprise architecture issues) to decisions that will
support these requirements by means of another enterprise architecture artefact. *Decomposition* relationships signify how generic enterprise architecture
decisions decompose into more detailed design decisions within an enterprise
architecture artefact. *Alternative* relationships illustrate the enterprise architecture decisions that were rejected (alternatives) in order to address a specific
enterprise architecture issue. *Substitution* relationships illustrates how one enterprise architecture decision replaces another enterprise architecture decision.
An enterprise architecture decision can be replaced when it creates a negative
observed impact in the enterprise architecture.
Observed impact—signifies an *unanticipated* positive/negative consequence of an
already made decision to an enterprise architecture artefact. This is opposed to
anticipated consequences, as indicated by the *Translation* and *Decomposition*
relationships. The main usefulness of capturing observed impacts is that they
can be used by architects to avoid decisions with negative consequences in future designs of the architecture (Plataniotis et al. 2013a).

For instance, in the decision graph decision D10 decomposes to decision D11 through issue IS06. D11 turns out to have a negative observed impact OI1, which is translated to a decision D13 through issue IS07 (alternative D12 for IS07 is rejected). D13 addresses the negative observed impact of D11 by substituting D11.

24.2.2 Reflection

The meta-model serves as the underlying formalism for the decision graph, but in this section, we motivate why this is not sufficient by discussing the differences between the meta-model and the decision graph. Several of these differences were also identified during the prototype implementation of the EA Anamnesis approach (Plataniotis et al. 2014a). We will take these remarks into account when formalising the decision graph in the next section.

According to the decision graph, the creation of a translation/decomposition relationship between two enterprise architecture decisions implies the creation of two separate relationships of the same type: one for the enterprise architecture decision to enterprise architecture issue and another one for the enterprise architecture issue to enterprise architecture decision. This creates information redundancy issues because this is not captured in the meta-model. The definition of at least one relationship of a specific type should imply that the other relationship should be of the same type. For example, in the decision graph enterprise architecture decision D01 is related with enterprise architecture issue IS03 through a translation relationship. Similarly, enterprise architecture issue IS03 is related with enterprise architecture decision D06 through a translation relationship. The definition of the relationship type between enterprise architecture issue IS03 and enterprise architecture decision D06 should imply the same relationship type between enterprise architecture decision D01 and enterprise architecture issue IS03, but this is currently not captured in the meta-model.

Furthermore, the meta-model provides two different types of states (executed and rejected) per enterprise architecture decision. Despite the fact that these two states adequately describe the state of an enterprise architecture decision during the a posteriori analysis, they don't provide enough expressivity in the a priori case. In the latter case, there is the need to express that an enterprise architecture decision is in an "open" state while enterprise architects examine the alternatives (Kruchten et al. 2006).

Whereas the meta-model provides the notion of "Observed impact", it does not explicitly distinguish between "positive observed impact" and "negative observed impact". For instance, in the decision graph enterprise architecture decision D11 has observed impact OI1, which creates an issue IS07. Thus, it seems that this observed impact is negative, but neither the meta-model or the graph are able to distinguish positive impacts from negative ones.

Finally, there are a number of assumptions on the design graph that have not been made explicit in the meta-model. Firstly, all issues in the graph have been resolved. Secondly, there is always a single decision that is executed in order to solve an issue, while the others are rejected. Finally, a decision that creates a negative observed impact is assumed to be replaced by a decision that addresses this impact. These three assumptions are not formalised, and we propose to do so using integrity constraints.

24.3 A Formal Model for Architectural Decision Modelling

In the previous section, we showed that the meta-model of Fig. 24.1 is not restrictive enough to characterise the decision design graph of Fig. 24.2 correctly. In order to resolve this issue and to obtain a consistent formalisation for the decision design graphs that allow for a priori decision modelling, we will introduce a formal model in this chapter.

24.3.1 Elementary Definitions for Architectural Decision Modelling

Basic concepts from set and graph theory are adequate to define the entities in the meta-model and the relations between them. We begin with representations for the meta-model elements *enterprise architecture decision*, *enterprise architecture issue*, and *observed impact*.

Definition 24.1 (Enterprise Architecture Issue). Let I be a set of enterprise architecture issues, where each issue $i \in I$ is a proposition representing the issue.

Rationale and example: An enterprise architecture decision issue (for short, issue) represents a single design concern. For now, we follow Plataniotis et al. (2013a, 2014d) and we do not add any attributes to the issues, but we recognise that this is certainly possible and a necessary extension. For instance, Zimmermann et al. (2009) attribute a total of 18 properties to issues that can be used to characterise them. Because such attributes do not have a specific purpose in our formal model, we leave them out for ease of exposition. The issues in the decision graph are $I = \{IS01, \ldots, IS07\}$.

Definition 24.2 (Enterprise Architecture Decision). Let D be a set of enterprise architecture decisions, where each decision $d \in D$ is a tuple (s, a, l) consisting respectively of:

- A state $s \in \{open, executed, rejected\}$
- An enterprise architecture artefact a
- A layer $l \in \{business, application, technology\}$

We also write s_d, a_d, and l_d to refer to the state, the artefact, and the layer of decision d, respectively.

Rationale and example: An enterprise architecture decision presents a possible solution to the design issue that is expressed by an enterprise architecture issue. The state s represents the current state of the decision. While Plataniotis et al. (2013a, 2014d) distinguish two different states of a decision (a decision is either "*executed*" or "*rejected*"), we extend this with an additional state "*open*". As we mentioned in the previous section, this is motivated by the fact that we aim to capture a priori decision analysis, which is different from the ex post approach of Plataniotis et al. (2013a, 2014d). The enterprise architecture artefact a of an enterprise architecture decision represents the enterprise architecture artefact to which this decision is related. Finally, the layer l is the layer on which the decision is made. Similar to enterprise architecture issues, we leave out additional attributes that do not have a specific purpose in our model. In the decision graph, decision D06 can be represented with (s, a, l), where $s = executed, a =$ "Customer administration intermediary application service", and $l = application$.

Definition 24.3 (Observed Impact). Let O be a set of observed impacts, where each observed impact $o = (v, a, l)$ consists of a value $v \in \{positive, negative\}$, an enterprise architecture artefact a, and a layer l. When $v = positive$, we say that o is a *positive observed impact*; when $o = negative$, we say that o is a *negative observed impact*. We also write v_o, a_o, and l_o to refer to the value, the artefact, and the layer of observed impact o, respectively.

Rationale and example: An observed impact is either positive or negative, where negative observed impacts create new issues. This formalisation allows for an explicit distinction between positive and negative observed impacts. In the decision graph, the only observed impact is OI1, which is negative, so we can formalise this as $OI1 = (v, a, l)$, where:

- $v = negative$
- $a =$ "Customer profile registration Business process"
- $l = business$

Definition 24.4 (Contains Relationship). Let $\prec_D \subseteq I \times D$ be a *contains* relationship between issues and decisions, $\prec_I \subseteq D \times I$ be a *contains* relationship between decisions and issues, $\prec_{O_{in}} \subseteq D \times O$ be a *contains* relationship between decisions and observed impact, $\prec_{O_{out}} \subseteq O \times I$ be a *contains* relationship between observed impact and issues, and $\prec_{DD} \subseteq D \times D$ be a *contains* relationship between decisions and decisions. We set the general *contains* relationship $\prec = \prec_D \cup \prec_I \cup \prec_{O_{in}} \cup \prec_{O_{out}} \cup \prec_{DD}$. If $(a \prec b)$, then we say that a contains b or that b is contained in a. We sometimes abbreviate $(a \prec b) \wedge (b \prec c)$ with $a \prec b \prec c$.

Rationale and example: The *contains* relationship is also used in Zimmermann et al. (2009) and allows us to define a single hierarchical structure, which serves as a table of content, allowing the user to locate issues and alternatives easily in the enterprise

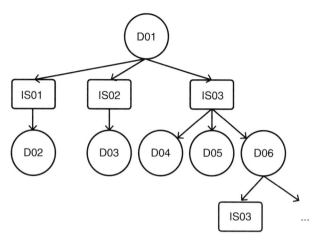

Fig. 24.3 The *contains* relationship ≺ for part of the decision graph

architectural knowledge and helping the knowledge engineer to avoid undesired redundancies. The *contains* relationship is the underlying dependency relation that we
use to build decision design graphs. We will use this relation to later define the four
types of *Relationship* entities that were introduced in the meta-model. These four relationships are relatively complex, so it helps to have a simple underlying representation of the decision hierarchy. Intuitively, the *contains* relationship can be obtained
by treating all arcs in the decision graph as of the same type. It contains, for instance,
the following relations: D01 ≺ IS01 ≺ D02, D01 ≺ IS02 ≺ D03, D01 ≺ IS03 ≺ D04
(see Fig. 24.3), but also D11 ≺ OI1 ≺ IS07 and IS07 ≺ D013 ≺ D11.

Definition 24.5 (Decision Design Graph). A *decision design graph* $\mathbb{D} = (D \cup I \cup O, \prec)$ consists of a set of decisions D, a set of issues I, a set of observed impacts O,
and a *contains* relationship ≺ that induces a graph containing issues, decisions, and
observed impacts of decisions.

Rationale and example: Modelling architectural decisions in itself is not new: Ran
and Kuusela also propose (but do not formalise) the notation of design decision
trees (Ran and Kuusela 1996). Zimmermann et al. (2009) propose a formalisation
that is comparable to ours, but our formalisation is specifically for enterprise architecture decision-making and uses decision graphs instead of trees.

24.3.2 Layered Decision Model and Logical Relations

The meta-model from Sect. 24.2 and the elementary definitions from SubSect. 24.3.1
allow knowledge engineers to capture decisions and organise the knowledge in a decision hierarchy. However, the resulting ordered architectural decision tree does not
yet support the vision of an active, managed decision model taking a guiding role
during architecture design. More relations between decisions, issues, and observed

impacts must be defined. In this chapter, we introduce the four relationships of Plataniotis et al. (2013a, 2014d) and formalise logical constraints by again applying concepts from graph theory.

Definition 24.6 (Translation Relationship). The *translation relationship* $R_T \subseteq D \times I \times D$ is a three-placed decision-issue-decision relationship $R_T(d_1, i, d_2)$, also denoted with

$$d_1 \xrightarrow{T(i)} d_2$$

that connects two decisions through an issue where these decisions are related to different enterprise architecture artefacts. Formally

$$\forall_{d_1, d_2 \in D, i \in I} : (d_1 \xrightarrow{T(i)} d_2) \Rightarrow (d_1 \prec i \prec d_2) \wedge (a_{d_1} \neq a_{d_2})$$

Rationale and example: Translation relationships indicate how a decision on one artefact translates to a decision on another artefact through an issue. Thus, having a translation relationship requires three entities: a decision, an issue, and another decision. For instance, the design graph contains the translation relationship

$$D01 \xrightarrow{T(IS03)} D06$$

This is a valid relationship, since we have $D01 \prec IS03 \prec D06$, and we also have $a_{D01} \neq a_{D06}$ because:

- $a_{D01} =$"Customer profile registration Business process"
- $a_{D06} =$"Customer administration intermediary application service"

Definition 24.7 (Decomposition Relationship). The *decomposition relationship* $R_D \subseteq D \times I \times D$ is a three-placed decision-issue-decision relationship $R_D(d_1, i, d_2)$, also denoted with

$$d_1 \xrightarrow{D(i)} d_2$$

that connects two decisions through an issue where these decisions are related to the same enterprise architecture artefacts. Formally

$$\forall_{d_1, d_2 \in D, i \in I} : (d_1 \xrightarrow{D(i)} d_2) \Rightarrow (d_1 \prec i \prec d_2) \wedge (a_{d_1} = a_{d_2})$$

Rationale and example: Decomposition relationships are similar to translation relationships, with the only difference that in decomposition relationships the two artefacts belonging to the decisions in the relation should be the same. For instance, the design graph contains the decomposition relationship

$$D01 \xrightarrow{T(IS01)} D02$$

which is valid because we have

- $D01 \prec IS01 \prec D02$
- $a_{D01} = a_{D02} =$"Customer profile registration Business process"

Definition 24.8 (Substitution Relationship). The *substitution relationship* $R_S \subseteq D \times D$ is a two-placed decision-decision relationship, also denoted with

$$d_1 \xrightarrow{S} d_2$$

that connects two decisions that are related to the same enterprise architecture artefacts. Formally

$$\forall_{d_1,d_2 \in D} : (d_1 \xrightarrow{S} d_2) \Rightarrow (d_1 \prec d_2) \wedge (a_{d_1} = a_{d_2})$$

Rationale and example: Substitution relationships are simpler than the previous two relationships in the sense that they contain only two elements. The decision graph contains only one substitution relationship:

$$D013 \xrightarrow{S} D11$$

Definition 24.9 (Alternative Relationship). The *alternative relationship* $R_A \subseteq I \times D$ is a two-placed issue-decision relationship, also denoted with

$$i \xrightarrow{A} d$$

that connects an issue with a rejected decision. Formally

$$\forall_{d \in D, i \in I} : (i \xrightarrow{A} d) \Rightarrow ((i \prec d) \wedge (s_d = rejected))$$

Rationale and example: The alternative relationship indicates decisions that have been rejected in the decision process. For instance, in the design graph we have

$$IS03 \xrightarrow{A} D04 \text{ and } IS03 \xrightarrow{A} D05$$

Definition 24.10 (Observed Impact Relationship). The *observed impact relationship* $R_O \subseteq D \times O \times I \times D$ is a four-placed decision-impact-issue-decision relationship, also denoted with

$$d_1 \xrightarrow{O(o,i)} d_2$$

which describes the effect of a negative observed impact on a decision, which is addressed by an issue and subsequently resolved by a decision. Formally

$$\forall_{d_1,d_2 \in D, i \in I, o \in O} : (d_1 \xrightarrow{O(o,i)} d_2) \Rightarrow (d_1 \prec o \prec i \prec d_2) \wedge (v_o = negative)$$

Rationale and example: The observed impact relation is the only relation in the design graph that has not been characterised by the meta-model. In the decision graph, enterprise architecture decision D11 causes a negative observed impact OI1, which is addressed by enterprise architecture issue IS07, which is subsequently resolved by enterprise architecture decision D13.

With these relations introduced, we will now define three logical constraints on enterprise architecture decision models. We stress that this list is by no means meant to be exhaustive. It represents a list of constraints that are suggested by the decision graph and from the discussion in Plataniotis et al. (2013a, 2014d). These constraints are used to check the decision graph for consistency. If the graph is not consistent, we are able to locate the inconsistency by determining what constraint is violated and for which element. This is useful input for the architect in the decision-making process.

Integrity constraint 1 *All issues should be resolved. For each issue, there should be a decision that is contained in this issue and that is executed:*

$$\forall_{i \in I} : \exists_{d \in D} : (i \prec d) \wedge (s_d = executed)$$

Rationale and example: An issue represents an architectural design problem that enterprise architects have to address during the enterprise transformation process. Having a consistency check for the status of the issue by verifying whether a decision has been executed to resolve it can assist the architect in detecting "*loose ends*". This is particularly useful in large and complex graphs with many interdependent nodes (Kleinmuntz and Schkade 1993).

Integrity constraint 2 *If a decision that is contained in an issue is executed, then all other decision that have a relation with that issue should be rejected:*

$$\forall_{i \in I} : \exists_{d \in D} : ((i \prec d) \wedge (s_d = executed)) \Rightarrow (\forall_{d' \in D} : (d \neq d') \Rightarrow (s_{d'} = rejected))$$

Rationale and example: This constraint describes a dependency between decisions that are contained in the same issue. The decision graph suggests that issues are solved by a single decision. This means that when a decision is executed that is contained in an issue, all other decision that are contained in this issue should be rejected. For instance, because decision D06 is executed, both decision D04 and D05 are rejected.

Integrity constraint 3 *If a decision contains a negative observed impact, then this decision should be replaced by a decision addressing the negative impact:*

$$\forall_{d \in D} : \exists_{o \in O} : ((d \prec o) \wedge (v_o = negative)) \Rightarrow \exists_{d' \in D, i \in I} : ((d \xrightarrow{O(o,i)} d') \wedge (d' \xrightarrow{R} d))$$

Rationale and example: The goal of having negative observed impacts is to be able to reconsider decisions that have caused this impact. This constraint addresses this idea by stating that negative observed impacts should result in the substitution of the decision that has caused the impact. For instance, decision D11 contains observed impact OI1. This constraint is satisfied for this impact because we have

$$D11 \xrightarrow{o(OI1, IS07)} D13 \text{ and } D13 \xrightarrow{S} D11$$

indicating that decision D13 substitutes decision D11.

24.4 Case Study: ArchiSurance

In this section we introduce the *ArchiSurance* case study that we will use to validate our logic-based framework for a priori decision analysis. We first introduce the case study, after which we apply it to our framework.

24.4.1 Introduction

This case is inspired by a paper on the economic functions of insurance intermediaries (Cummins and Doherty 2006) and is the running case used to illustrate the ArchiMate language specifications (Jonkers et al. 2012). *ArchiSurance* is the result of a recent merger of three previously independent insurance companies that now sells car insurances products using direct-to-customer sales model. The goal of the newly created company is to reduce its operation's and product's costs.

The merger has resulted in a number of integration and alignment challenges for the new company's business processes and information systems. These challenges appear in the *ArchiSurance* baseline business, application, data, and technology architecture.

Figure 24.4 presents the partial (Business and Application layers) ArchiSurance's direct-to-customer sales model, modelled with the enterprise architecture modelling language ArchiMate. Two business services support the sales model of ArchiSurance: *"Car insurance registration service"* and *"Car insurance service"*. ArchiMate helps us to understand the dependencies between different perspectives on an enterprise. For example, in Fig. 24.4 we see that the business service *"Car insurance registration service"* is realised by a business process *"Register customer profile"*. In turn, we also see that this business process is supported by the application service *"Customer administration service"*.

Although removing intermediaries in the supply chain leads to a decrease of operation costs, it also increases the risk of harmful risk profiles (Cummins and Doherty 2006). Such profiles lead insurance companies to calculate unsuitable premiums or, even worse, to wrongfully issue insurances to customers. As a response, ArchiSurance decides to use intermediaries to sell its insurance products. After all, compiling accurate risk profiles is part of the core business of an intermediary (Cummins and Doherty 2006). In our scenario, an external architect call *John* is hired by ArchiSurance to help guide the change to an intermediary sales model. John uses ArchiMate to capture the impacts that selling insurance via an intermediary has in terms of business processes, IT infrastructure, and more.

For illustration purposes we will focus on the translation of the new business process *"Customer profile registration"* to enterprise architecture artefacts in the application layer. The resulting ArchiMate model is depicted in Fig. 24.5. Here we see, for example, how a (new) business process *"Customer profile registration"*, owned by the insurance broker (ownership being indicated by a line between the broker and

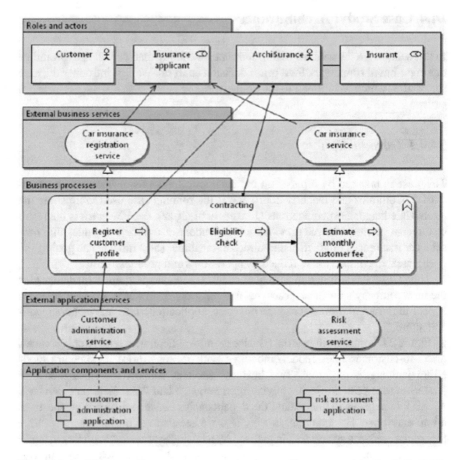

Fig. 24.4 ArchiSurance direct-to-customer enterprise architecture model © 2013 IEEE. Reprinted, with permission, from Plataniotis et al. (2013a)

the business process), is supported by the IT applications "*Customer administration service intermediary*" and "*Customer administration service ArchiSurance*".

24.4.2 Validation

In this chapter we demonstrate how the formal framework introduced in Sect. 24.3 supports a priori decision analysis of design graphs by consistency checks on the integrity constraints.

Our external architect John is in the process of transforming the ArchiMate model from Fig. 24.4 into Fig. 24.5. For the implementation of these enterprise architecture artefacts, a number of enterprise architecture decisions have to be made.

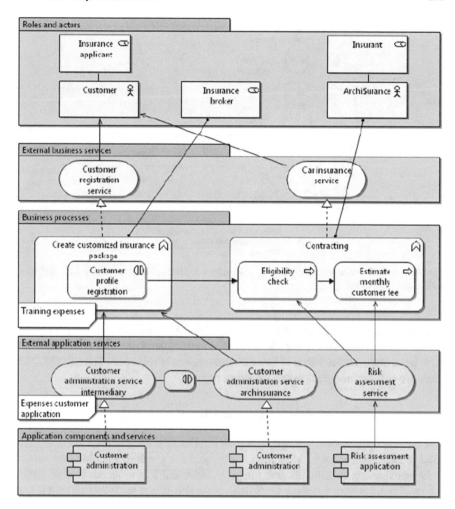

Fig. 24.5 ArchiSurance intermediary enterprise architecture model. © 2013 IEEE. Reprinted, with permission, from Plataniotis et al. (2013a)

John, in parallel with ArchiMate modelling language, uses our approach to capture the relationships of decisions and check the consistency of the decision graph.

John starts by adding the main decision "*Make customer profile registration via intermediary*" (D01) to the decision design graph. This decision belongs to the enterprise architecture artefact "*Customer profile registration Business process*". After the enterprise has decided to make this decision, three new issues arise, IS01, IS02, and IS03. Both IS01 and IS02 are addressed by making a decision that related to the same artefact. For IS03, which stands for "*Create an appropriate application service to support new business process*", there are three different decisions that can

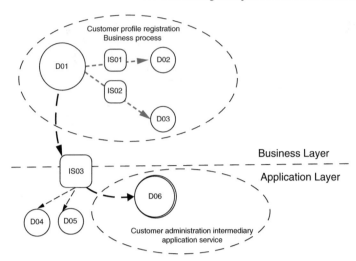

Fig. 24.6 ArchiSurance scenario: Integrity constraint 1 is violated as enterprise architecture issue IS03 is not resolved

be made in the Application Layer, namely, D04, D05, and D06 (see Fig. 24.6; the legend of the relations is in Fig. 24.2). At this moment, none of these three decision have been made, so the status of these three decisions is still open. Thus, in Fig. 24.6 there are two *Decomposition* relationships, namely,

$$D01 \xrightarrow{D(IS01)} D02 \text{ and } D01 \xrightarrow{D(IS02)} D03$$

and the other relations are simply *contains* relationship: $D01 \prec IS03, IS03 \prec D04$, $IS03 \prec D05, IS03 \prec D06$. After John has created the graph of Fig. 24.6, he checks it for consistency. It turns out that integrity constraint 1 is violated: Not all issues are resolved, because for issue IS03 there is no decision d such that $IS03 \prec d$ and $s_d = executed$. John can choose between these three decisions and selects decision D06, which stands for *"Introduce application service A"*, as the executed decision.

After having changed the status of decision D06 from *"open"* to *"executed"*, John checks the consistency of the graph again. This time, another inconsistency arises, namely, that integrity constraint 2 is violated. The reason for this is that since decision D06 is contained in issue IS03 (i.e. we have $IS03 \prec D06$) and D06 is executed (i.e. $s_{D06} = executed$), all other decisions that are contained in IS03 (i.e. decisions D04 and D05) should be rejected. Therefore, John decides to change the status of both these decisions from *"open"* to *"rejected"*. When John checks the graph for consistency now, he finds that the graph is consistent.

Decision D06 results in two new issues, of which *"Find an appropriate application to interface with the intermediary"* (IS05) is solved by *"Acquisition of COTS application B"* (D10), resulting in the enterprise architecture artefact *"Customer administration application"*. Decision D10 decomposes through issue IS06 in the decision *"Application interface type 1"* (D11).

Using the concept of an observed impact, John formalises that users of *"Customer administration application"* had difficulties using this new application interface. This is signified by the negative observed impact OI01 *"Degraded user experience in the application use"* (OI01). As such, enterprise architecture decision D11 *"Application interface 1"* has a negative observed impact on the business process *"Customer profile registration"*.

According to integrity constraint 3, a negative observed impact should be addressed by a decision replacing the original decision that causes the observed impact. Therefore, John translates the observed impact *"Degraded user experience in the application use"* via enterprise architecture issue IS07 *"have fitting application interface"* into *"replace of existing application interface with an interface similar to the old one"* (enterprise architecture decision D13), after having rejected the alternative decision *"Training of users on the new application"*. The last step John has to take is to replace enterprise architecture decision D11 *"Application interface type 1"* with enterprise architecture decision D13 *"Application interface type 2"*.

When the transformation has finished and all decisions have been made, John obtains the graph that is depicted in Fig. 24.2. This graph is consistent according to the integrity constraints.

24.5 Related Work

While most methods for decision modelling and analysis use visual notations from existing modelling methods like UML and the likes, their underpinnings still inherently benefit from mathematical formalisations. Communicating these formalisations to end-users alike does not require a steep level of training and can be easily communicated to them (Hall 1990), nor does the focus on a more rigorous specification of these mathematical underpinnings forsake using the other tools and notations that build and rely on them (Bowen and Hinchey 1995).

In the domain of software architecture, which is a subset of enterprise architecture, several design rationale approaches have been developed: *argumentation*-based approaches such as issue-based information system (IBIS) (Kunz and Rittel 1970), design rationale language (DRL) (Lee 1991), *template*-based approaches Tyree and Akerman (2005), and *model*-based approaches Jansen and Bosch (2005) and Tang et al. (2007). Most of them capture textually the architecture decisions, the rationales, the issues, and the implications. In addition, the model-based approach provides means to relate those decisions with the software artefacts and with other decisions.

About 20 years ago, Ran and Kuusela (1996) proposed a systematic approach to document, refine, organise, and reuse the architectural knowledge for software design in the form of a design decision trees that is a partial ordering on decisions put in the context of the problem requirements and the constraints imposed by earlier decisions. More recently, Tyree and Akerman (2005) recognised that architecture decision capturing plays a key role in what they call "demystifying architecture".

They stress that architecture decisions should have a permanent place in the software architecture development process. Moreover, it facilitates traceability from decisions back to requirements, and it provides agile documentation (which is crucial in an agile process where a team does not have the time to wait for the architect to completely develop and document the architecture).

Both Zimmermann et al. (2009) and Tang et al. (2007) recently proposed a comprehensive framework for decision capturing in software architecture. Zimmermann et al. (2009) also provide a formal framework, focusing mostly on the reusability of decision by distinguishing between alternatives and outcomes.

In the field of enterprise architecture, the literature is significantly more scarce. Even if software architecture is a subset of enterprise architecture, in this field different types of decisions exist, and they can have dependencies and relationship with artefacts and decisions from different layers of the architecture. Plataniotis et al.'s (2013a, 2014d) view complements model-based approaches for software architecture by providing more specialised attributes for enterprise architecture decisions as well as more specific dependency and relationship types between enterprise architecture decisions.

Finally, goal-oriented modelling frameworks [e.g. i* (iStar 2016), Tropos (Tropos 2016)] provide means to deal with the motivations of designs, being more expressive than the ArchiMate 2.0 (Iacob et al. 2012) motivation layer. Even so, their main focus is not to provide decision rationales.

24.6 Discussion

In this chapter we introduced a logic-based framework for capturing relationships between enterprise architecture decisions. This framework is based on recent work by Plataniotis et al. (2013a, 2014d). With this formalisation, we allow for capturing decision relationship dependencies and consistency checks on additional logical dependencies that we formalised using integrity constraints.

We demonstrated how these constraints can be used to check a decision graph for consistency. However, we did not yet present a framework that will actively search for solutions to inconsistencies and in this way support the architect in its decision-making process. To actually do this, a more elaborate representation of decision quality is needed, such that different decisions can be compared with each other. We see this as a promising direction for future work.

The integrity constraints that we have defined in this work are not meant to be a complete list. As we discussed above, each decision in the meta-model of Plataniotis et al. (2013a, 2014d) is either *Executed* or *Rejected*. Kruchten et al. (2006) argue that design decisions evolve in a manner that may be described by a state machine or a state chart. They distinguish between seven different states, which are *idea*, *tentative*, *decided*, *approved*, *rejected*, *challenged*, and *obsolete*. Having such an expressive representation of a decision allows for more complex constraints on the decision-making process. This is another promising direction for future work.

Finally, one of the biggest challenges in decision capturing is the problem of return of capturing effort. The fact that it takes architects much time to capture design-making strategies without having a direct benefit might be a discouraging factor. We believe that our approach simplifies the capturing effort by assisting the architect in its decision-making process. Part of our future research will focus on evaluating the actual practical usefulness of our approach.

Chapter 25
Situational Adaptations of ACET

Robert Winter and Nils Labusch

Abstract In this chapter we address the fact that not all ACET problems are equal, and ACET solutions therefore need to be configured to address the specifics of the respective ACET problem. We approach this configuration problem by means of situational method engineering. We find that the two most important differences of ACET problem situations result from the enterprise architecture management approach used and the respective type of the transformation. We therefore present classifications for enterprise architecture management and enterprise transformation and propose an appropriate ACET problem situation matrix. We finally demonstrate how ACET solutions are configured to a given problem situation.

25.1 Introduction

This chapter deals with the fact that not all ACET problems are equal, and ACET solutions therefore need to be configured to address the specifics of the respective ACET problem. In doing so, this chapter also aims to address some of the challenges identified in Chap. 12.

While many additional contingencies might be also relevant, the most important differences of ACET problem situations result from the enterprise architecture management approach used and the type of the transformation at hand. After summarising situational method engineering, and an explorative approach to identify

R. Winter (✉) • N. Labusch
Institute of Information Management, University of St.Gallen, St. Gallen, Switzerland
e-mail: robert.winter@unisg.ch

© Springer International Publishing AG, part of Springer Nature 2017   277
H.A. Proper et al. (eds.), *Architectural Coordination of Enterprise Transformation*,
The Enterprise Engineering Series, https://doi.org/10.1007/978-3-319-69584-6_25

problem situations, we present classifications for enterprise architecture management and enterprise transformation and propose an appropriate ACET problem situation matrix. We then show how, exemplarily from an information requirements
perspective, ACET solutions are configured to the respective problem situation at
hand.

25.2 Situational Method Engineering

Method engineering as a discipline initially only aimed at the systematic construction of methods that support the development of software artefacts (Brinkkemper
1996). As an approach, method engineering can, however, be applied to many other
domains that require complex solution engineering—such as the construction of information systems management methods. Situational method engineering enhances
the utility of method engineering by supporting not only the design of a generic
method but also a mechanism that composes method modules or configures a base
method so that the solution is systematically situated to the problem situation at
hand (Ralyté et al. 2008), that is, so that situation-specific context and situation-
specific design goals are considered. Specifically for management methods, Winter
(2012) proposed a situational approach. This approach involves the following steps:

1. Relevant design factors are inferred from observed management practices.
2. Solution patterns ("*archetypes*") are specified by clustering existing solutions
   with regard to the design factors identified in step 1.
3. Development paths are identified by relating as-is archetypes with to-be
   archetypes or by evaluating alternative archetypes with regard to certain design
   goals.
4. By comparing activity (or capability) components of the archetypes linked by
   development paths, differences can be systematically identified that constitute
   design patterns ("*project types*").
5. For the relevant design patterns, common activity (or capability) components
   are identified that constitute method modules.
6. Regarding the set of method modules identified in step 5, every relevant development can be represented as a certain composition. The overall set of composition rules constitutes the method's situational adaptation mechanism.

25.3 Classifying Enterprise Architecture Management
Approaches

While single architectural artefacts (like artefact maps or architectural guidelines)
are of a *model* instantiation nature, and situated architecture management approaches are of a *method* instantiation nature, enterprise architecture management

in its entirety can be understood as a situational management method. Hence situational method engineering can be applied in order to engineer a situational enterprise architecture management approach. In the following, we summarise how the management method situational method engineering approach presented above has been applied to enterprise architecture management, as reported by Winter (2012).

Step 1: An empirical data set of 119 companies describing their enterprise architecture management approach was tested against 54 potential enterprise architecture management design factors obtained from a literature survey. Thirty-eight factors proved to be significant and loaded on eight principal components: (1) IT operations support, (2) enterprise focus and management support, (3) enterprise architecture management governance, (4) IT strategy and IT governance support, (5) information supply, (6) integrative role of enterprise architecture management, (7) design impact, and (8) business strategy support.

Step 2: If these principal components are regarded as dimensions that span an eight-dimensional room where every company practice can be represented, agglomerative clustering allows identifying the three enterprise architecture management archetypes *"balanced, active enterprise architecture management"*, *"business-biased enterprise architecture management light"*, and *"IT focused, passive enterprise architecture management"* (Winter 2012).

Step 3: In this step, design goals have to be defined such that archetypes can be evaluated against those goals, and project types can be derived. For enterprise architecture management, an often observed goal vector integrates transparency, consistency, simplification, flexibility, and agility in the following form: enterprise architecture management should support IT/business alignment by having an impact on IT architecture as well as on business architecture (integrative role). As a consequence, enterprise architecture management results are used by business units as well as IT, and enterprise architecture management results are perceived to be useful for management. In order to create value, enterprise architecture stakeholders are involved, and enterprise architecture management is aligned with business objectives. IT/business alignment requires enterprise architects to have a broad network in the company and to integrate all relevant disciplines from business and IT. Based on such an enterprise architecture management design goal vector, both the *"IT-focused, passive enterprise architecture management"* archetype and the *"business-biased enterprise architecture management light"* archetype yield a comparatively low contribution. In contrast, the *"balanced, active enterprise architecture management"* archetype maximises the contribution. If the contribution of IT-focused, passive enterprise architecture management and business-biased enterprise architecture management light are not significantly different, four development paths are implied that need to be supported: (1) from no enterprise architecture management (minimum performance) to IT-focused, passive enterprise architecture management (medium performance), (2) from no enterprise architecture management (minimum performance) to business-biased enterprise architecture management light (medium performance), (3) from IT-focused, passive enterprise architecture management (medium performance) to balanced, active enterprise architecture management (maximum performance), and (4) from business-biased enterprise architecture management light (medium performance) to balanced, active enterprise architecture management (maximum performance). A direct path from no enterprise architecture management (minimum performance) to balanced, active enterprise architecture management (maximum performance) is not advised because too big steps ("leap frogging") across enterprise architecture management maturity stages is hard to observe—and might therefore be hard to achieve—in practice.

Step 4: Since each enterprise architecture management archetype is characterised by specific (average) values regarding the eight aggregate design factors (e.g. *"IT-focused, passive enterprise architecture management"* is characterised by high values of the design factor *"IT operations support"* and low values of the design factors *"enterprise-wide focus"*, *"integrative role"*, and *"design impact"*), every development can be characterised by a set of reductions or increases of these factors. For example, the development path *"From IT-focused, passive enterprise architecture management to balanced, active enterprise architecture management"* implies a reduction of IT operations support but an increase in enterprise-wide focus, integrative role, and design impact. For that transition, information supply, business support, and IT strategy and IT governance support are not relevant because their values do not differ significantly between the linked archetypes. The transition analysis can be detailed to the level of elementary activities (or capabilities). An example would be decreasing the realisation of *"Results of enterprise architecture management are used for coordination of IT development products"* and *"Results of enterprise architecture management are used for IT planning and infrastructure design"* and increasing the realisation of *"Business and IT departments actively seek advice from architects"*, *"Enterprise architecture stakeholders are actively involved in enterprise architecture management"*, and *"Architects have an extensive network within the company"*.

Step 5: After all dependency paths are analysed on a detailed level, standard modularisation techniques are applied in step 5 to derived method modules (see Fig. 25.1). The five modules *"IT operations support and IT strategy and IT governance support"*, *"Information supply and business strategy support"*, *"Enterprise-wide focus"*, *"Design impact and integrative role"*, and *"Enterprise architecture management governance"* have been identified.

Step 6: Each of the four development paths can be represented as a different composition of the five identified method modules: *"From No enterprise architecture management to IT-focused, passive enterprise architecture management"* is composed of the modules A and B, *"From No enterprise architecture management to business-biased enterprise architecture management light"* of the modules B and C, *"From IT focused, passive enterprise architecture management to Balanced, active enterprise architecture management"* of the modules C and D, and *"From Business-biased enterprise architecture management light to Balanced, active enterprise architecture management"* of the modules A and E. The composition of situated methods from reusable method modules is illustrated in Fig. 25.2.

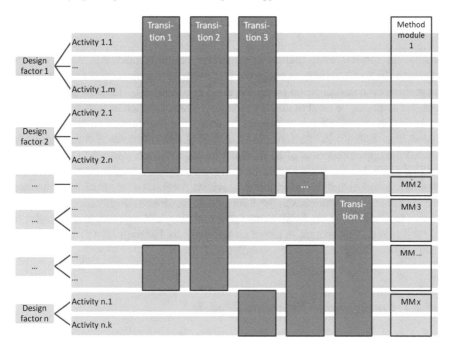

Fig. 25.1 Method modularisation based on transition activity sets. © IGI Global 2012; reprinted with permission from Winter (2012)

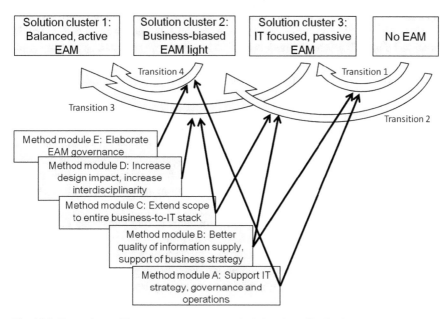

Fig. 25.2 Enterprise architecture management method situation. © IGI Global 2012; reprinted with permission from Winter (2012)

25.4 Classification of Transformation Types

While enterprise transformation management certainly possesses some method characteristics of a management approach, enterprise transformation as such—from an architectural coordination perspective—is represented by models. Such models can, for example, be used to illustrate the as-is states as much as the to-be states.

In the literature, various typologies for enterprise transformation have been proposed (e.g. Baumöl 2008; Safrudin et al. 2014). However, since we already discussed the appropriateness of an information requirements perspective concerning ACET, a suitable typology should be based on enterprise transformation information requirements and the information provision potential of enterprise architecture management. As a foundation, the information requirements reference model presented in Chap. 20 is used. We extend that model by adding configuration rules in the following. This section is based on the work by Labusch (2015) and Labusch et al. (2014b) but presents additional data and results.

25.4.1 Configurable Reference Models

In contrast to the enterprise architecture management example where an approach was reconstructed by configuring a (enterprise architecture management) method from reusable modules (method fragments), in this we situationally configure the (generic) information requirements reference model as discussed in Chap. 20.

Labusch (2015) summarises related research on reference models as follows. In order to be useful, reference models need to be adaptable and need to provide guidance on their adaption (Becker et al. 2007a). There are several mechanisms of reuse available that allow to adapt a reference model to the specific conditions of a situation: Becker et al. (2007b) differentiate analogy construction, specialisation, and configuration mechanisms. Analogy construction means to use parts of a model in situations that differ from those the original model was situated in. Specialisation is advisable when reference models have a high degree of abstraction that needs to be broken down (specialised) to a more specific situation. Configuration modifies components of the reference model based on predefined rules and requires that all variants are completely implied by the generic solution model and can be generated using a certain set of (configuration) rules.

In order to analyse the information requirements during enterprise transformations, we incorporate the work that is described in Chap. 20, where we consolidate information demands that occur in enterprise transformations into one single reference model. In the following subsection, we describe steps and results needed to configure this reference model for the information requirements of specific enterprise transformation types.

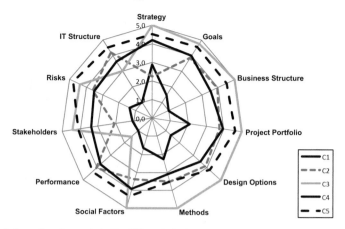

Fig. 25.3 Information demands in the different clusters

To understand the character of different types of enterprise transformations, we need to identify relevant contingency factors[1] and information requirements. Basically, these are differentiated into three groups: the environment of the enterprise transformation ("*the organisation*"), the enterprise transformation itself (goals, reasons, involved employees, etc.), and the actual information requirements of enterprise transformation managers.

To elaborate these elements, we designed a questionnaire that was then distributed to a total of 57 highly knowledgeable informants that are able to describe enterprise transformations as the unit of analysis. Respondents were, for example, enterprise transformation managers, CEOs, or programme managers. The informants were asked to rate the items based on a five-point Likert scale (Likert 1932). We were able to collect data from a variety of industries. We consider including multiple industries an advantage as we avoid industry-specific bias and thus increase the general applicability of the artefact.

We conducted a hierarchical cluster analysis (Ward's method, squared Euclidean distance) based on the information requirements illustrated in Chap. 20 (see the concrete information items in Fig. 25.3). To use as many cases as possible for the analysis, we handled missing values by replacing them with column (variable) means. If more than 10% of values were missing, we omitted the respective case. This procedure resulted in 38 enterprise transformations whose data were used for the cluster analysis.

---

[1] Earlier results and the method of the conducted study are also described in Labusch and Aier (2014), Labusch et al. (2014b), and Labusch (2015). The original contribution of this chapter is a more detailed embedding in the context of situational engineering and a discussion of the findings in the ACET context. In addition, more data was used for the analysis than in the previous studies.

We determined the number of configurations for our model based on the goal to provide meaningful guidance for the enterprise transformation support, but at the same time adhere to statistical criteria. For each split of the hierarchical clustering (based on the information requirements), we analysed which variables best describe the character of the enterprise transformation and if considerable differences could be observed.

As a result, a first separation into three clusters can be made to distinguish the size of the transformation (measured by the amount of employees affected). The second separation criterion is the primary trigger of the enterprise transformation (e.g. regulatory requirements, market demands). Further separations were not advised because values do no longer considerably differ in our dataset. Thus, we propose a five-cluster solution to enterprise transformation with regard to information requirements (see Fig. 25.3).

- Cluster C1 represents enterprise transformations that affect only hundreds of employees of an organisation that is transformed. The information requirements in these enterprise transformations are rather limited. With this comparably small number of affected people, the enterprise transformation seems to be conducted in a "*just do it*" manner with lean planning.
- Enterprise transformations in cluster C2 affect thousands of employees. They are mostly triggered by changes in the environment like, for example, new regulatory requirements. This is reflected in the low value of gathering strategy-related information—the necessity to transform is already given by external parties; thus strategy does not considerably matter in this case. The same holds for information about stakeholders. The company is forced to transform and in-depth information about stakeholder concerns is thus not required.
- Enterprise transformations in cluster C3 affect tens of thousands of employees and are triggered by changes in the power structure, for example, a new CEO or other leadership personnel. This is reflected in the information requirements: IT-related information is less relevant, and also performance is almost not considered being important. Instead, strategic information, goals, business structure, project portfolio, design options, methods, social factors, and stakeholders are strongly requested.
- Cluster C4 represents enterprise transformations that affect thousands of employees and are triggered by the need to change the offered products and services, combined with appropriate changes in IT and culture. Enterprise transformations in this cluster require information from all described areas. Due to their average size, they do not require the largest extent of information but rather average values.
- Enterprise transformations in cluster C5 affect tens of thousands of employees and are triggered by changes in the control and IT system of the company. We observe high information requirements in all areas.

25.4.2 Design of an Enterprise Transformation Information Model

We used the five identified clusters to provide guidance on which information is most important for which enterprise transformation type. We found the median to be an appropriate decision criterion due to its stability concerning outliers. When an information item was rated with at least the median value, it was included in the information model for the respective enterprise transformation type. Figure 25.4 below exemplarily illustrates the configuration of the reference model for clusters C3 and C4. 90

In concrete enterprise transformations, however, organisations need to further discuss and evaluate the model concerning their particular enterprise transformation instance. In addition, organisations need to determine which departments, disciplines, or information systems can provide which information. On the other hand, designers of, for example, information systems can use the model to analyse in which enterprise transformations their system could be applied and add value.

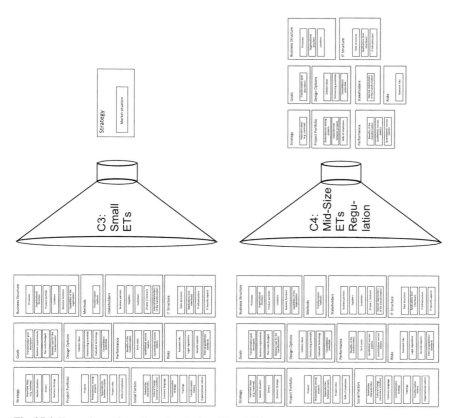

Fig. 25.4 Example configurations for clusters C3 and C4

25.5 Situations in ACET

With regard to method construction, architectural support of enterprise transformation is more complex than solely of enterprise architecture management or of enterprise transformations. As illustrated in Fig. 25.5, the support needs to consider the characteristics not only of the respective enterprise transformation type but also the characteristics of the respective enterprise architecture management type. The situational adaptation therefore needs to be designed in a two-dimensional way.

Figure 25.6 illustrates this two-dimensionality: On the one hand, enterprise architecture management types need to be distinguished as illustrated above. On the other hand, enterprise transformation types also need to be distinguished. In combination,

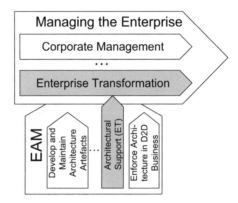

Fig. 25.5 Architectural support of enterprise transformation

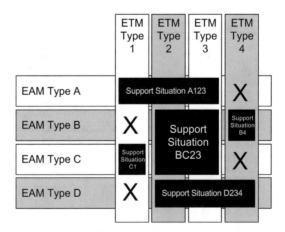

Fig. 25.6 Situativity of architectural support of enterprise transformation

ACET situations are then defined by the specific combination of an enterprise architecture management type (that defines the support) and an enterprise transformation type (that defines the demand).

Not every combination of enterprise architecture management types and enterprise transformation types needs to exist in the real world. In addition, some support types and some demand types could be similar enough to combine them into a single situation.

For constructing an appropriate situational method, the relevant support situations need to be identified empirically first. On that base, the in-depth analysis of respective demand and supply can be used to identify support modules and module configuration rules. For simplification purposes, we focus on only one enterprise architecture management type (generalised supply) and analyse how the five enterprise transformation types can be supported (see Fig. 25.7). This procedure can be easily adapted to any other enterprise architecture management type.

Enterprise transformations in cluster C1 can be supported by enterprise architecture management to a very limited degree. As only few people are involved, only information about the market situation can be provided by enterprise architecture management. However, since other disciplines are better suited to provide this kind of information, enterprise architecture management might simply not be the ideal discipline to support this kind of enterprise transformation.

Enterprise transformations in cluster C2 require, for example, information about processes and organisational structures that enterprise architecture management can provide. Furthermore, enterprise architecture management has some potential to contribute to the need of information about assessed risks and qualitative success metrics. Information about dependencies and redundancies among projects are also requested.

Enterprise transformations in cluster C3 can be well supported by enterprise architecture management since they require a large amount of information about strategy, goals, business structure, and the project portfolio. However, the core information that enterprise architecture management often provides (those directly or indirectly related to IT) are not strongly requested by enterprise transformations in cluster C3.

Cluster C4 can be partially supported by enterprise architecture management through providing information about strategic aspects and the project portfolio. IT-related information is not that much requested, and thus, enterprise architecture management needs to focus on business aspects to create added value here.

Enterprise transformations in cluster C5 require a huge amount of information directly or indirectly related to IT. Here also the "*traditional*" IT-related enterprise architecture management may take a central role and provide significant added value. In addition, information about the project portfolio is required that can also be provided by enterprise architecture management.

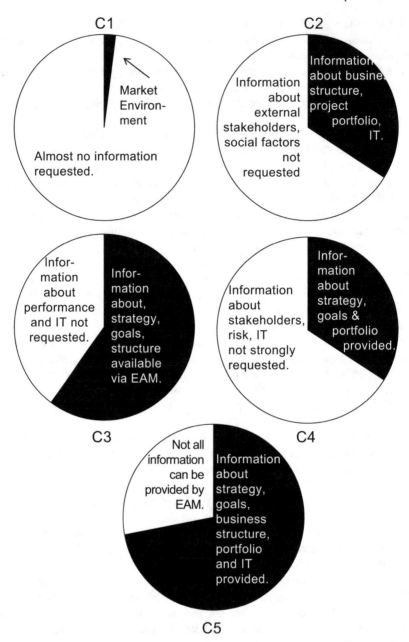

Fig. 25.7 Situativity of architectural support of enterprise transformation

25.6 Discussion

In this chapter we described the different mechanisms that are needed to configure ACET to meet the specific needs of a given context. We provided examples that underline why tailoring ACET is a complex task that needs to be conducted by considering different perspectives. We exemplified our considerations by focusing on the information perspective.

Configuration of ACET provides situation-specific support that increases the chance of ACET deliverables being considered as useful and appropriate by stakeholders. Thus, such a configuration can be seen as a precondition for the institutionalisation of ACET.

Part IV
Epilogue

Chapter 26
Conclusion and Reflections

Henderik A. Proper, Stephan Aier, and Robert Winter

Abstract In this chapter, we look back on the results presented in this book. As mentioned at the start of this book, the field of ACET is rather rich and diverse. As such, this book could only provide a humble beginning towards the creation of a more complete understanding of ACET and the development of an integrated set of instruments supporting ACET in practice. In this chapter, we therefore critically reflect on our experiences with the development of "large-scale" design artefact, such as an integrated method for ACET, as the research programme set out to do.

We will conclude with a list of suggestions for possible follow-up research in the domain of ACET. This list combines both the reflection on our experiences in the development of large-scale design theory and opportunities for further research on the level of the specific components as presented in this book.

26.1 Introduction

In this chapter, we will start (in Sect. 26.2) by briefly looking back on the results presented in this book. As mentioned at the start of this book, in Chap. 1, the field of ACET is rather rich and diverse. This is reflected in the results presented in this book, which originate from a broad research programme on ACET, involving four applied research projects. As such, this book could only provide a humble beginning towards the creation of a more complete understanding of ACET and the development of an integrated set of instruments supporting ACET in practice.

H.A. Proper (✉)
Luxembourg Institute of Science and Technology, Esch-sur-Alzette, Luxembourg
e-mail: e.proper@acm.org

S. Aier • R. Winter
Institute of Information Management, University of St. Gallen, St. Gallen, Switzerland

© Springer International Publishing AG, part of Springer Nature 2017
H.A. Proper et al. (eds.), *Architectural Coordination of Enterprise Transformation*,
The Enterprise Engineering Series, https://doi.org/10.1007/978-3-319-69584-6_26

As most of the research conducted in the context of the ACET research programme involved a design science approach (March and Smith 1995; Hevner et al. 2004; van Aken 2004; Peffers et al. 2007; Venable et al. 2012; Peffers et al. 2012; Gregor and Hevner 2013; Wieringa 2014; Venable et al. 2016), or at least covered some stages of design science, it is certainly relevant to reflect on the experiences gathered in the context of the ACET project. Even though this book only reports on an initial understanding of ACET and an initial set of components (of an integrated set) of instruments supporting ACET in practice, the ambitions at the start of the research programme were higher. It was, indeed, the ambition to develop an integrated design theory for ACET. This provides a good reason to, in Sect. 26.3, critically reflect on our experiences with the development of "large-scale" design artefact, such as an integrated method for ACET, as the research programme set out to do.

Finally, we conclude with a list of suggestions for possible follow-up research in the domain of ACET. This list combines both the reflection on our experiences in the development of large-scale design theory and opportunities for further research on the level of the specific components as presented in this book.

26.2 Summary of Results

In Part I, an analysis was provided of the current state of the ACET practice. This was used as an inspiration for a more detailed exploration of the challenges facing ACET from a more theoretical perspective. This, in particular, resulted in explorations of:

- The types of change and transformations that may occur (Chap. 6)
- Enterprise transformation from the perspective of social systems (Chap. 7)
- The role of subcultures in the coordination of transformations (Chap. 8)
- The role of a *use perspective* for architectural coordination (Chap. 9)
- The role of stakeholders and a strategy to better engage them (Chap. 10)
- The information requirements for doing ACET (Chap. 11)
- The sustainable organisational establishment of doing ACET (Chap. 12)
- The landscape of modelling languages for ACET (Chap. 13)
- The role of architecture principles (Chap. 14)
- The motivation and rationalisation of architectural decisions (Chap. 15)

In Part III, we discussed a collection of components for a possible design theory for ACET, which were "harvested" from the work of the individual researchers in the programme. Collectively, these components aimed to address the challenges as they had been identified in Part I from an empirical perspective, and Part II from a more theoretical and/or literature perspective. The harvested components included:

- Definitions of the key concepts underlying ACET (Chap. 16)
- A reference framework of services needed for doing ACET (Chap. 17)

- A strategy to engage stakeholders in decision-making during ACET (Chap. 18)
- Guidelines to use models as boundary objects (Chap. 19)
- A reference model for the information requirements for ACET (Chap. 20)
- An approach for component-based modelling language engineering (Chap. 21)
- Guidelines for the semiformal definition of architecture principles (Chap. 22)
- A framework to explicitly capture architecture design decisions (Chap. 23)
- A formal reasoning system for architecture design decisions (Chap. 24)
- Strategies for situation-specific adaption of ACET (Chap. 25)

26.3 Reflections on the Development of Large-Scale Methods

As stated before, the ambitions at the start of the ACET programme were to develop an integrated design theory for ACET. The ideal would have been to establish a validated topology of ACET components and provide support for integrating these components and concrete, situation-specific, configuration rules. As we will discuss below, this soon turned out to be too ambitious.

26.3.1 Change of Programme Strategy

Each of the different projects involved in the ACET programme conducted explorations of different aspects of the ACET problem space (see Part II). Soon, the heterogeneity and multifacetedness of these aspects showed that the development in integrated design theory for ACET would be too ambitious. A choice had to be made between the creation of a "superficial" overall method for ACET and a, for the moment, set of disconnected and partial, yet well founded, components towards a more comprehensive method for ACET. This resulted in a change of strategy, where the research efforts were compartmentalised, in the sense that each of the involved researchers focussed on a specific (set of related) aspects, with the aim to develop an initial explanatory theory covering the aspect (see Part II), and possibly a method component/fragment meeting the needs of covering that aspect (see Part III).

The work, as conducted by the individual researchers, can also be said to correspond to a set of focussed experiments towards the establishment of clearer requirements on an integrated ACET design theory. This can be seen as a strategy to deal with what van Aken and Nagel (2004) call the "fuzzy front end" of design-oriented research. In the case of ACET, the potential "fuzziness" is exacerbated by the fact that ACET would require the development of a large-scale method, to cover all work needed in the architectural coordination of enterprise transformations. In the remainder of this chapter, we aim to reflect on this in more depth.

26.3.2 A Method as a Design Theory

We see a method as capturing guiding/prescriptive knowledge on how to do/organise certain tasks. As such, it corresponds to a *reference model* that guides/directs the planning and/or execution of tasks in specific situations. This could, for example, be a reference model defining a flow of work or a set of rules/principles that should be upheld or defining a (modelling) language to be used.

When a method is further enriched with guidelines to tune the method towards situations at hand, one may refer to the method as a *situational* method. This corresponds to the notion of *artefact mutability* as defined by Gregor and Jones (2007), where in this case, the method is the artefact. Note: the guidelines for situational adaption can be seen as a "situational adaption method" and, as such, would be defined by its own reference model.

A method, as a reference model for action, should provide a clear identification of what its *claimed working* is, in terms of what would be achieved when indeed following the method, in a context that meets given preconditions. For example, (timely) availability of inputs needed inputs, situational factors such as the abilities of actors involved, etc. In terms of Gregor and Jones (2007), this *claim* leads to a number of *testable propositions*, which can also be said to correspond to the *theory* as brought forward by the method, in other words, the *design theory* of the method. As Wieringa (2014) puts it "*design science studies the interactions between an artefact and its context. We call theories about (artefact × context) design theories.*"

In the design/creation of a method, different styles of reasoning can be used. It may be derived *deductively* from other (design) theories. This deduction corresponds to the *justificatory knowledge* as discussed by Gregor and Jones (2007). The resulting method can/should then be validated in real-world situations. This can potentially also lead to refinements on the preconditions under which the method will produce its claimed effects.

A method can also be derived *inductively* from a broad corpus of real-world cases, by observing patterns and hypothesising over these. In this case, the *justificatory knowledge* would pertain to the empirical evidence found in the corpus of cases, and the observed patterns.

When there is only a limited number of cases available, one may resort to *abductive* reasoning, looking for patterns that at least match the available cases. Further evidence can then be sought by further validation on new cases and/or experiments.

For the development of a design artefact in general, and a method in particular, several other theories may be useful, providing more means to develop the *justificatory knowledge* underpinning the method's design theory. One may, for example, use and/or develop theories that capture propositions regarding the domain *in* and/or *on* which one aims to use the artefact/method.

26.3.3 Complexity and Uncertainty for the Use of Methods

The *Information Services Procurement Library* (ISPL) (Franckson and Verhoef 1999; Proper 2001) identifies different situational factors that should be taken into account when defining project plans, and risk mitigation strategies in particular. These situational factors are classified into four classes along two axes: *complexity* versus *uncertainty* and *target domain* versus *project domain*, where *target domain* refers to the domain in which the project/service is to make a change, while *project domain* refers to the project/service itself.

The effort of developing a method (such as ACET) also has to deal with a number of complexities and uncertainties, covering both the target domain of the method, that is, the domain in which it should have its (claimed) effect/result, and the method itself. This includes:

Target domain uncertainty—deals with uncertainties about properties that hold *in* the method's target domain, the specific aspects/parameters involved, the understanding of the actual class of problems that the method aims to contribute to, the stakeholders involved, their specific attitudes, etc.

Target domain complexity—involves the complexity of the (properties of the) method's target domain, complexity/heterogeneity of the specific aspects/ parameters involved, complexity and variety of the class of problems the method aims to contribute to, heterogeneity of the (stakes of the) stakeholders involved, etc.

Method domain uncertainty—deals with uncertainties about the precise working of specific concepts that can be used in the construction of the method, uncertainty about the validity of preconditions, etc.

Method domain complexity—pertains to the complexity of the method itself in terms of the complexity of its reference model, complexity of the guidelines towards situational adaptation and implementation, complexity of the definition of its preconditions, etc.

It is important to realise that when there is a large variety in the class of problems in which the method aims to "do its work", then the *law of requisite variety* (Ashby 1956) implies that the complexity of the method itself should be high enough to meet this variety, either in terms of a high complexity/variety of the reference model that defines the method or in terms of the guidelines defining its situational adaption. Note: this is separate from the *inherent* complexity of the "work" that the method aims to get done, which will also need to be reflected in the method itself.

26.3.4 Research Methodological Guidance

In the development of a method, different strategies can be used to deal with complexities and uncertainties. In the case of the ACET programme, the observed (Part I) uncertainty of the target domain, exacerbated by the complexity of the target domain, led to the conclusion that a series of *pre-studies* was needed into the different factors involved (Part II), as well as experiments with possible components of a method (Part III). This resulted in a reduction of the uncertainties, and an increased understanding of the complexities involved.

The strategy followed by the ACET programme can be seen as a strategy to deal with what van Aken and Nagel (2004) call the "fuzzy front end" of design-oriented research. In the case of ACET, the potential "fuzziness" of this front end is exacerbated by the fact that it would would require the development of a large-scale method to cover all work needed in the architectural coordination of enterprise transformations, that is, resulting in a high complexity on top of all the uncertainty.

Just as Franckson and Verhoef (1999) and Proper (2001) define strategies and heuristics on how to deal with complexity and/or uncertainty with regard to information-systems-related projects and services, one would need similar guidance for the development of methods. In methods for design theories, one would expect that the field of design science would provide such guidance. Regretfully, however, we did not find much guidance in the literature.

At the same time, one can certainly observe the existence of large-scale methods, such as TOGAF (The Open Group 2011), ISPL (Franckson and Verhoef 1999), ITIL (Axelos 2015), etc. These are, however, typically "best-practice"-based methods lacking rigorous validation, justificatory knowledge, and/or testable propositions.

Another way to deal with the uncertainties and complexities facing the development of a method is to enable early validations of method components, so as to obtain early feedback. In general, designed artefacts, such as methods, should be evaluated with regard to their ability to solve the addressed design problem (March and Smith 1995). Traditionally, the predominant approach in design science is that of evaluating artefacts once they have been designed ready for use (see, e.g., Hevner et al. (2004) and Peffers et al. (2007)). However, to enable feedback loops as early as possible, Venable et al. (2012) proposed the notion of *pre* and *post* artefact evaluation, where pre artefact evaluations involve evaluations of artefacts *before* they are built and post artefact evaluations are evaluations of artefacts *after* they have been built. That first differentiation of evaluation perspectives specifically targets the fact that feedback loops should be applied as early as possible, and not only after the design has been completed.

In a further differentiation, Venable et al. (2016) later distinguish naturalistic and artificial evaluations as well as formative and summative evaluations. This allows for the design of multistep evaluation strategies that provide many feedback opportunities, reflecting the changing character of the artefact as it matures in the design process. The distinction between evaluation characteristics reflects however more on the "how" of evaluation than the "what". As the artefact matures during the design process, different aspects of design knowledge dominate, which should be matched by corresponding evaluation episodes.

26.3.4.1 Multiple Levels of Detail in Method Design

An interesting contribution on the challenge of large-scale design artefact development is made by Daeuble et al. (2015). They provide a strategy for the (incremental) development of large-scale design artefacts that suggest to split a design artefact into smaller components based on a *segmentation framework*.

While being a potentially relevant way to deal with the *complexities* that faced the ACET programme, it would not have solved the *uncertainties* which the programme had to deal with. We would still have found ourselves at the fuzzy front end of design science. Nevertheless, towards follow-up research towards a more integrated ACET method, it could make sense to use a *segmentation framework* to structure further research efforts.

Based on our joint past experiences in the development of methods, we would suggest, for now, to consider the following levels of detail in such segmentation framework for methods:

Abstract structure—An overall perspective on roles, responsibilities, and tasks involved, types of deliverables to be produced, temporal dependencies between tasks, etc.

This would lead to one method component defining the overall "rhythm", with possible guidelines for situational adaptation, possibly in terms of general principles.

Concrete structure—A further operationalisation of the operational perspective in terms of concrete deliverables, and specific requirements on modelling languages to be used in producing these deliverables, approaches and techniques to be used, etc.

This is likely to lead to a set of alternative method components, whose relevance depends on the situational contexts, where each resulting component may have additional rules to tune things to a situation at hand.

Tools and techniques—A collection of (small-scale) methods, approaches, and techniques to support/direct the creation of the deliverables as identified in the (large-scale) method. For example, an approach for stakeholder management, modelling languages used to represent deliverables, collaborative decision-making, etc.

Reference material—Reference models, partial models/designs, design patterns, etc. that can be used as starting points, or guidelines, towards the creation of actual deliverables.

In terms of this suggested segmentation framework, the results, as discussed in this book, can be positioned as shown in Table 26.1. Note that we certainly do not claim that the elements listed in Table 26.1 are an integrated method for ACET.

Table 26.1 Mapping of results presented in this book

Abstract structure	Exploration	– Types of change and transformations that may occur (Chap. 6) – Enterprise transformation from the perspective of enterprises being social systems (Chap. 7) – The role of subcultures in the coordination of enterprise transformations (Chap. 8) – The role of a *use perspective* for ACET, in particular the *use* of the created architectural artefacts (Chap. 9) – The engagement of stakeholders during ACET (Chap. 10) – How a sustainable discipline of doing ACET can be established in an organisation (Chap. 12)
	Components	– Definitions of the key concepts underlying ACET (Chap. 16) – A reference framework of services needed for doing ACET (Chap. 17) – An overall strategy to engage stakeholders in decision-making during ACET (Chap. 18) – Guidelines to use models as communication devices (Chap. 19)
Concrete structure	Exploration	– The information requirements for doing ACET (Chap. 11) – The landscape of modelling languages for ACET (Chap. 13)
	Components	– Strategies for situation-specific adaption of ACET (Chap. 25)
Tools and techniques	Exploration	– The role of architecture principles (Chap. 14) – The motivation and rationalisation of architectural design decisions (Chap. 15)
	Components	– A reference model[a] for the information requirements for ACET (Chap. 20) – A method for value-based componental language engineering to express the models needed during ACET (Chap. 21) – Guidelines for the semiformal definition of architecture principles (Chap. 22) – A framework to explicitly capture architecture design decisions (Chap. 23) – A logic-based framework to formally reason on architectural design decisions (Chap. 24)

[a] This is a reference model at methodological level, and not at the level of a particular application/technology domain

26.4 Suggestions for Future Research

We conclude this chapter with a list of suggestions for possible follow-up research in the field of ACET, and the further development of design science research in general. This should only be considered as a source of inspiration. It is in no way intended as a formal research agenda. We certainly plan to follow up on some of these suggestions ourselves.

26.4.1 Sociocultural Context of ACET

The challenges regarding the social and cultural aspects as identified in Chaps. 6–8 have been met only partially by the components discussed in Chaps. 17–19. Many more challenges remain, for example, with regard to:

- A deeper understanding is needed of the nature of the social and cultural "forces" that may influence (initiate, strengthen, hamper, or derail) change in organisations, and possible "indicators" and "levers" to observe and mitigate these forces.
- Different strategies, contingent on the specific social and (sub)cultural contexts, need to be developed, to indeed achieve needed architectural coordination. This includes the elaboration of collaborative decision-making strategies and stakeholder management when dealing with social complexity.
- When using an explicit method for "doing" ACET, this method should, of course, be *institutionalised*. As such, this is also an organisational change, being exposed to the similar social and/or cultural forces as the actual architectural coordination an enterprise transformation has to deal with. How these forces influence the use and uptake of a method for ACET (and its elements/components) needs further investigation.

26.4.2 Enterprises Are in Motion

In line with Rouse (2005), this book considered enterprise transformation as being top-down initiated, premeditated, and fundamental change. There are, however, many more changes happening in organisations. These changes are also likely to (gradually) lead to an architectural impact and should, therefore, also be included in architectural coordination. Examples of such types of changes include:

1. *Organisational drift*, dealing with gradual misalignment between an enterprise's original intent (strategy, business model, operating model, etc.) and the actual operational activities (Mandis 2013)
2. *Self-organisation* as can be found in the context of self-steering teams (Prakken 2000; Achterbergh and Vriens 2009)
3. *Bricolage and emergence* that may, as argued by Ciborra (1992), provide enterprises with strategic advantages in terms of the bottom-up evolution of socio-technical systems that will lead to outcomes that are deeply rooted in an enterprise's organisational culture, and hence much more difficult to imitate by others

On might, therefore, even go as far as to say that enterprises are *in motion* (Proper 2014), where the word *motion* refers to "*an act, process, or instance of changing place*" (Meriam–Webster 2003). Sometimes this indeed involves a top-down and premeditated enterprise transformation, but there is more change happening in an enterprise than transformations.

This leads, amongst other, to the following challenges for architectural coordination:

- How does change in organisations occur, especially when we do not only consider top-down initiated, and premeditated, enterprise transformations? What are the needs for, and potential role of, architectural coordination in organisational change?
  As Magalhães and Proper (2017) argue, this also requires a stronger and deeper interaction between organisational sciences, management sciences, and enterprise engineering/architecture.
- Strategies are needed to "detect" bottom-up/emergent changes as they occur in organisation. Techniques such as process mining (van der Aalst 2011), software cartography (Sousa et al. 2011, 2009), and enterprise cartography (Sousa et al. 2011) are first examples of such techniques.

26.4.3 Enterprise Architecture Modelling

Chapter 13 explored some of the challenges in regard to models and modelling in the context of ACET. Models can capture crucial information regarding an enterprise's current architecture, its possible future architecture(s), and contextual information. In Chap. 11, the landscape of possibly relevant information was explored, while Chap. 9 explored the need for a use perspective on the deliverables (including models) produced in an ACET context. Taking this as input, Chap. 19 provided guidelines for the use of models as boundary objects, bridging different groups of stakeholders. Chapter 20 provided a reference framework for information requirements for ACET, thus providing a first insight into the broad landscape of information that can be captured by models. Finally, Chap. 21 provided a general approach to reason about the added value of models in relation to its planned use.
Remaining challenges include:

- Translation of the information requirements, as identified in Chap. 20, to an integrated landscape of modelling languages needed to capture the needed information.
  Standards such as ArchiMate (Iacob et al. 2012) do indeed provide a large coverage of this landscape. However, the continuous extension of the standard, and the plethora of suggested extensions and complementary modelling languages, indicates that more work is necessary (Bjeković et al. 2012).
  In addition, the advent of domain-specific modelling languages also indicates that a one-size-fits-all general-purpose language may not be the right/complete answer (Bjeković et al. 2012, 2014).
- Further elaboration of the guidelines to use models as boundary objects, in particular in relation towards different stakeholders and collaborative decision-making. This should also involve a clearer positioning of the role concepts of views and viewpoint from the IEEE (2011) standard.

26.4.4 Enterprise Architecture Principles

Chapter 14 explored the role of enterprise architecture principles in ACET, while Chap. 22 provided a strategy to better capture architecture principles in a semi-formal language, as well as providing potential evaluation strategies to assess the compliance to architecture principles.

Remaining challenges include:

- Further elaboration of the linkage between the concept of enterprise architecture principles and regulations, in particular where it concerns the formulation and capturing of motivations.
- Strategies to enable, in a not intrusive way, the formalisation (in semiformal languages) of architecture principles, as part of their formulation process.
- Improvement of hybrid (human and machine)-based assessment of the compliance of designs and/or actual implementations to architecture principles.
- Strategies to inspire/guide (architectural) design processes based on enterprise architecture principles. In other words, not just assessing if a "finished" design complies to a set of principles, but proactively aid/influence architects and designers during the actual design processes.

26.4.5 Architectural Decision-Making

In Chap. 15 we explored the need for, and context of, making architectural decisions more explicit. This referred both to the process of decision-making and the capturing of the actual decisions in terms of underlying motivations and trade-offs. Chapter 23 provided initial strategies to indeed make architecture design decisions more explicit, while Chap. 24 illustrated how formal logics can be used to reason over design decisions.

Some of the remaining challenges include:

- Integration into the collaborative decision-making processes as discussed in Chap. 18. It is such processes, where important (high-level) decisions are made, that provide input/context for more detailed design decisions later on.
- Integration with the formulation of architecture principles. The work reported in Chap. 23 focused on decisions regarding architectural designs in terms of, for example, ArchiMate (Iacob et al. 2012). However, the selection/formulation of enterprise architecture principles also involve a (design) decision with a rationale/motivation.

  It would thus be relevant to extend the work reported in Chap. 23 to make design decisions underlying architecture principles more explicit.
- Integration of enterprise architecture principles into architectural decision-making processes. This basically mirrors the point made above on the use of enterprise architecture principles to guide design processes.

- More research is needed on how to operationalise/leverage the design ratio-nales, in other words, further increasing the return of capturing effort. This work would extend the work reported in Chap. 24.
- More experimentation is needed on how to capture rationalisation of design decisions in a more natural way (reducing the capturing effort), in other words, as a natural result from the decision-making process, where the capturing effort directly benefits the progress and quality of the decision-making process rather than hampering it.

26.4.6 Integrated Method for ACET

As we mentioned before, the ambitions at the start of the ACET programme were to develop an integrated method for ACET. Such a design theory would have needed to involve a topology of ACET components and provide support for integrating these components and concrete situation-specific configuration rules.

As discussed in Sect. 26.3, this book brings together the results of what can be said to be "experiments" in the "fuzzy front end" of design science. The framework as discussed in Sect. 26.3.4.1 provides a suggested structure in the further develop-ment of large-scale methods, such as an integrated method for ACET.

The constructs identified in Chap. 16 provide a conceptual core of an ACET, while the framework as discussed in Chap. 17 provides a landscape map of the involved competences. An integrated method for ACET should provide guidance for the tasks of these competences, as far as they are related to architectural coordi-nation.

Further research could therefore involve the "populating", in terms of relevant method fragments, of the generic framework discussed in Sect. 26.3.4.1 for ACET, while using the framework presented in Chap. 17 as a domain-specific, that is, ACET-specific, landscape map.

26.5 Conclusion

This chapter provided a summary of the results presented in this book, as well as critical reflection regarding the development of large-scale design theories, as we intended within the ACET programme. We finished with the identification of a series of topics for further research.

References

Abcouwer, A., Maes, R., & Truijens, J. (1997). *Contouren van een generiek model voor informatiemanagement*. Primavera working paper, Universiteit van Amsterdam, Amsterdam, the Netherlands. In Dutch.

Abraham, R. (2013). Enterprise architecture artifacts as boundary objects - A framework of properties. In *ECIS 2013*, Paper 120. Last checked on July 15, 2016. http://aisel.aisnet.org/ecis2013_cr/120/

Abraham, R., & Aier, S. (2012). Architectural coordination of transformation: implications from game theory. In H. Rahman, A. Mesquita, I. Ramos, & B. Pernici (Eds.), *Knowledge and Technologies in Innovative Information Systems – Proceedings of the 7th Mediterranean Conference on Information Systems (MCIS 2012), Guimaraes, Portugal* (Vol. 129, pp. 82–96). Lecture Notes in Business Information Processing. Heidelberg, Germany: Springer. https://doi.org/10.1007/978-3-642-33244-9_6.

Abraham, R., Aier, S., & Labusch, N. (2012a). Enterprise architecture as a means for coordination – An empirical study on actual and potential practice. In H. Rahman, A. Mesquita, I. Ramos, & B. Pernici (Eds.), *Proceedings of the 7th Mediterranean Conference on Information Systems (MCIS 2012), Guimaraes, Portugal*. Last checked on July 15, 2016. http://aisel.aisnet.org/mcis2012/33/

Abraham, R., Aier, S., Labusch, N., & Winter, R. (2013a). Understanding coordination support of enterprise architecture management – Empirical analysis and implications for practice. In *Proceedings of the 19th Americas Conference on Information Systems (AMCIS 2013), Chicago, IL*. Last checked on February 15, 2017. http://aisel.aisnet.org/amcis2013/EnterpriseSystems/GeneralPresentations/13/

Abraham, R., Aier, S., & Winter, R. (2012b). Two speeds of EAM – A dynamic capabilities perspective. In S. Aier, M. Ekstedt, F. Matthes, E. Proper, J. L. Sanz (Eds.), *Trends in enterprise architecture research and practice driven research*

on enterprise transformation (pp. 111–128). Berlin: Springer. ISBN 978-3-642-34162-5.
https://doi.org/10.1007/978-3-642-34163-2

Abraham, R., Niemietz, H., de Kinderen, S., & Aier, S. (2013b). Can boundary objects mitigate communication defects in enterprise transformation? Findings from expert interviews. In R. Jung & M. Reichert (Eds.), *Enterprise modelling and information systems architectures (EMISA 2013)* (pp. 27–40). Bonn: Köllen. ISBN 978-3-88579-616-9.

Abraham, R., Tribolet, J., & Winter, R. (2013c). Transformation of multi-level systems – Theoretical grounding and consequences for enterprise architecture management. In H. A. Proper, D. Aveiro, & K. Gaaloul (Eds.), *Advances in Enterprise Engineering VII – Proceedings of the 3rd Enterprise Engineering Working Conference (EEWC 2013), Kirchberg, Luxembourg* (Vol. 146, pp. 73–87). Lecture Notes in Business Information Processing. Heidelberg, Germany: Springer. ISBN 978-3-642-38116-4.
https://doi.org/10.1007/978-3-642-38117-1_6

Achterbergh, J., & Vriens, D. (2009). *Organisations: Social systems conducting experiments.* Heidelberg, Germany: Springer. ISBN 978-3-642-00109-3.

Ackoff, R. L. (1971). Towards a system of system concepts. *Management Science, 17*(11), 661–671.

Ågerfalk, P. J., & Fitzgerald, B. (2006). Exploring the concept of method rationale: A conceptual tool. In K. Siau (Ed.), *Advanced topics in database research* (Vol. 5, p. 63). Hershey, PA: IGI Global. ISBN 978-1-591-40935-9.

Ahlemann, F. (2009). Towards a conceptual reference model for project management information systems. *International Journal of Project Management, 27*(1), 19–30.

Aier, S. (2013). Understanding the role of organizational culture for design and success of enterprise architecture management. In R. Alt & B. Franczyk (Eds.), *Proceedings of the 11th International Conference on Wirtschaftsinformatik (WI2013)* (pp. 879–894).

Aier, S. (2014). The role of organizational culture for grounding, management, guidance and effectiveness of enterprise architecture principles. *Information Systems and E-Business Management, 12*(1), 43–70. ISSN 1617-9846.
https://doi.org/10.1007/s10257-012-0206-8

Aier, S., Ekstedt, M., Matthes, F., Proper, H. A., & Sanz, J. (Eds.). (2012). *Proceedings of the 7th Workshop on Trends in Enterprise Architecture Research and Practice-Driven (TEAR 2012) and the 5th Working Conference on Practice-driven Research on Enterprise Transformation (PRET 2012). Held at the Open Group Conference, Barcelona, Spain* (Vol. 131). Lecture Notes in Business Information Processing. Heidelberg, Germany: Springer. ISBN 978-3-642-34162-5.
https://doi.org/10.1007/978-3-642-34163-2

Aier, S., Fischer, C., & Winter, R. (2011). Construction and evaluation of a meta-model for enterprise architecture design principles. In A. Bernstein & G. Schwabe (Eds.), *Proceedings of the 10th International Conference on Wirtschaftsinformatik (WI 2011), Zürich, Switzerland* (pp. 637–644).

Aier, S., & Gleichauf, B. (2010). Application of enterprise models for engineering enterprise transformation. *Enterprise Modelling and Information Systems Architectures (EMISA), 5*(1), 56–72.

Aier, S., Riege, C., & Winter, R. (2008). Unternehmensarchitektur – Literaturüberblick und Stand der Praxis. *Wirtschaftsinformatik, 50*(4), 292–304.

Aier, S., & Schelp, J. (2010). A reassessment of enterprise architecture implementation. In A. Dan, F. Gittler, & F. Toumani (Eds.), *Service-oriented computing* (Vol. 6275, pp. 35–47). Lecture Notes in Computer Science. Heidelberg, Germany: Springer. ISBN 978-3-642-16132-2.

Aier, S., & Weiss, S. (2012). An institutional framework for analyzing organizational responses to the establishment of architectural transformation. In *Proceedings of the 20th European Conference on Information Systems (ECIS 2012), Barcelona, Spain*, Paper 228.

Ajzen, I. (1991). The theory of planned behavior. *Organizational Behavior and Human Decision Processes, 50*(2), 179–211.

Ajzen, I., & Fishbein, M. (1980). *Understanding attitudes and predicting social behavior*. Englewood Cliffs, NJ: Prentice-Hall.

Akkermans, H., Baida, Z., Gordijn, J., Peiia, N., Altuna, A., & Laresgoiti, I. (2004). Value webs: Using ontologies to bundle real-world services. *Intelligent Systems, IEEE, 19*(4), 57–66.

Aladwani, A. M. (2001). Change management strategies for successful ERP implementation. *Business Process Management Journal, 7*(3), 266–275.

Alt, R., & Franczyk, B. (Eds.). (2013). *Proceedings of the 11th International Conference on Wirtschaftsinformatik (WI 2013), Leipzig, Germany*.

Amyot, D., Horkoff, J., Gross, D., & Mussbacher, G. (2009). A lightweight GRL profile for i* modeling. In *Workshop Proceedings of the Conference on Advances in Conceptual Modeling (ER 2009): CoMoL, ETheCoM, FP-UML, MOST-ONISW, QoIS, RIGiM, SeCoGIS, Gramado, Brazil* (Vol. 5833, pp. 254–264). Lecture Notes in Computer Science. Heidelberg, Germany: Springer. ISBN 978-3-642-04946-0.
https://doi.org/10.1007/978-3-642-04947-7_31

Amyot, D., Shamsaei, A., Kealey, J., Tremblay, E., Miga, A., Mussbacher, G., et al. (2012). Towards advanced goal model analysis with jUCMNav. In *Workshop Proceedings of the Conference on Advances in Conceptual Modeling (ER 2012): Florence, Italy: CMS, ECDM-NoCoDA, MoDIC, MORE-BI, RIGiM, SeCoGIS, WISM* (Vol. 7518, pp. 201–210). Lecture Notes in Computer Science. Heidelberg, Germany: Springer. ISBN 978-3-642-33998-1.
https://doi.org/10.1007/978-3-642-33999-8_25

Armour, F. J., Kaisler, S. H., & Liu, S. Y. (1999). A big-picture look at enterprise architectures. *IT Professional, 1*(1), 35–42. ISSN 1520-9202.
https://doi.org/10.1109/6294.774792

Aschmoneit, P., & Heitmann, M. (2002). Customer centred community application design: Introduction of the means-end chain framework for product design of community applications. *International Journal on Media Management, 4*(1), 13–20.

Asfaw, T., Bada, A., & Allario, F. (2009). Enablers and challenges in using enterprise architecture concepts to drive transformation: Perspectives from Private Organizations and Federal Government Agencies. *Journal of Enterprise Architecture, 5*(3), 18–28.

Ashby, W. R. (1956). *An introduction to cybernetics.* London, UK: Chapman & Hall. ISBN 0-412-05670-4.

Ashby, W. R. (1960). *Design for a brain: The origin of adaptive behavior.* Heidelberg, Germany: Springer.

Aspara, J., Lamberg, J.-A., Laukia, A., & Tikkanen, H. (2011). Strategic management of business model transformation: Lessons from Nokia. *Management Decision, 49*(4), 611–647.

Association for Information Systems. (2011). Senior Scholars' Basket of Journals.

Åström, K. J., & Murray, R. M. (2008). *Feedback systems: An introduction for scientists and engineers.* Princeton, NJ: Princeton University Press. ISBN 978-0691135762.

Aumann, R. J. (2008). Game theory. In S. N. Durlauf & L. E. Blume (Eds.), *The New Palgrave dictionary of economics.* Basingstoke, New York: Palgrave Macmillan.

Aveiro, D., Bjeković, M., Caetano, A., Fleischmann, A., Heuser, L., de Kinderen, S., et al. (Eds.). (2014). *Proceedings of the 16th IEEE Conference on Business Informatics (CBI 2014), Geneva, Switzerland* (Vol. 2). Los Alamitos, CA: IEEE Computer Society Press. ISBN 978-1-4799-5779-8.

Axelos. (2009). *Managing successful projects with PRINCE2.* London, UK: The Stationery Office. ISBN 978-0-113-31059-3.

Axelos. (2015). *ITIL foundation handbook.* London, UK: The Stationery Office. ISBN 978-0113314690.

Babüroğlu, O. (1988). The vortical environment: The fifth in the Emery-Trist levels of organizational environments. *Human Relations, 41*(3), 181–210.

Balogun, J., Hope Hailey, V., Johnson, G., & Scholes, K. (2003). *Exploring strategic change* (2nd ed.). Englewood Cliffs, NJ: Financial Times, Prentice Hall. ISBN 978-0-273-68327-8.

Baptista, J. J. (2009). Institutionalisation as a process of interplay between technology and its organisational context of use. *Journal of Information Technology, 24*(4), 305–319.

Barreto, I. (2010). Dynamic capabilities: A review of past research and an agenda for the future. *Journal of Management, 36*(1), 256–280.

Baumöl, U. (2005). Strategic agility through situational method construction. In R. Reichwald & A. S. Huff (Eds.), *Proceedings of the 5th European Academy of Management Annual Conference (EURAM 2005).*

Baumöl, U. (2006). Methodenkonstruktion für das Business-IT-Alignment. *Wirtschaftsinformatik, 48*(5), 314–322.

Baumöl, U. (2008). *Change management in organisationen: Situative methodenkonstruktion für flexible Veränderungsprozesse.* Wiesbaden, Germany: Gabler.

Becker, J., Beverungen, D. F., & Knackstedt, R. (2010). The challenge of conceptual modeling for product–service systems: Status-Quo and perspectives for reference models and modeling languages. *Information Systems and E-Business Management, 8*(1), 33–66.

Becker, J., & Delfmann, P. (2007). *Reference modeling – Efficient information systems design through reuse of information models.* Heidelberg, Germany: Physica-Verlag.

Becker, J., Delfmann, P., & Knackstedt, R. (2007a). Adaptive reference modeling: Integrating configurative and generic adaptation techniques for information models. In J. Becker & P. Delfmann (Eds.), *Reference modeling* (pp. 27–58). Heidelberg, Germany: Physica-Verlag.

Becker, J., Janiesch, C., & Pfeiffer, D. (2007b). Reuse mechanisms in situational method engineering. In J. Ralyté, S. Brinkkemper, & B. Henderson-Sellers (Eds.), *Proceedings of the IFIP WG8.1 Working Conference on Situational Method Engineering (ME 2007), Geneva, Switzerland* (Vol. 244, pp. 79–93). IFIP Advances in Information and Communication Technology. Heidelberg, Germany: Springer. ISBN 978-0-387-73946-5.

Becker, J., Rosemann, M., & Schütte, R. (1995). Grundsätze ordnungsmässiger Modellierung. *Wirtschaftsinformatik, 37*(5), 435–445.

Becker, J., Rosemann, M., & von Uthmann, C. (2000). Guidelines of business process modeling. In W. M. P. van der Aalst, J. Desel, & A. Oberweis (Eds.), *Business process management – Models, techniques, and empirical studies* (Vol. 1806, pp. 30–49). Lecture Notes in Computer Science. Heidelberg, Germany: Springer. ISBN 978-3-540-67454-2.

Benbasat, I., & Zmud, R. W. (2003). The identity crisis within the IS discipline – Defining and communicating the discipline's core properties. *MIS Quarterly, 27*(2), 183–194.

Bernard, S. (2006). Using enterprise architecture to integrate strategic, business, and technology planning. *Journal of Enterprise Architecture, 2*(4), 11–28.

Bhattacharya, P. J., Seddon, P. B., & Scheepers, R. (2010). Enabling strategic transformations with enterprise systems: Beyond operational efficiency. In *Proceedings of the 31st International Conference on Information Systems (ICIS 2010), St. Louis, MO*, Paper 55. Association for Information Systems. ISBN 978-0-615-41898-8. http://aisel.aisnet.org/icis2010_submissions/

Bhattacherjee, A. (2001). Understanding information systems continuance: An expectation-confirmation model. *MIS Quarterly, 25*(3), 351–370.

Bhattacherjee, A., Perols, J., & Sanford, C. (2008). Information technology continuance: A theoretic extension and empirical test. *Journal of Computer Information Systems, 49*(1), 17–26.

Bischoff, S., Aier, S., & Winter, R. (2014). Use IT or lose IT? The role of pressure for use and utility of enterprise architecture artifacts. In D. Aveiro et al. (Ed.), *Proceedings of the 16th IEEE Conference on Business Informatics (IEEE-CBI)* (pp. 133–140). ISBN 978-1-4799-5779-8. https://doi.org/10.1109/CBI.2014.56

Bisel, R. S., & Barge, J. K. (2010). Discursive positioning and planned change in organizations. *Human Relations, 64*(2), 257–283.

Bjeković, M., Proper, H. A., & Sottet, J.-S. (2012). Towards a coherent enterprise modelling landscape. In K. Sandkuhl, U. Seigerroth, & J. Stirna (Eds.), *Short Paper Proceedings of the 5th IFIP WG 8.1 Working Conference on the Practice of Enterprise Modeling, Rostock, Germany, November 7-8, 2012* (Vol. 933). CEUR-WS.org.
http://ceur-ws.org/Vol-933/pap3.pdf

Bjeković, M., Proper, H. A., & Sottet, J.-S. (2014). Embracing pragmatics. In E. Yu, G. Dobbie, M. Jarke, & S. Purao (Eds.), *Proceedings of the 33rd International Conference on Conceptual Modeling (ER 2014), Atlanta, GA* (Vol. 8824, pp. 431–444). Lecture Notes in Computer Science. Springer: Heidelberg, Germany. ISBN 978-3-319-12205-2.
https://doi.org/10.1007/978-3-319-12206-9

Boh, W. F., & Yellin, D. (2007). Using enterprise architecture standards in managing information technology. *Journal of Management Information Systems, 23*(3), 163–207.

Boland, R. J., & Tenkasi, R. V. (1995). Perspective making and perspective taking in communities of knowing. *Organization Science, 6*(4), 350–372.

Borst, W. N. (1997). *Construction of engineering ontologies for knowledge sharing and reuse*. PhD thesis, University of Twente, Enschede, the Netherlands.

Bostrom, R. P., & Heinen, S. (1977). MIS problems and failures - A socio-technical perspective. Part I - The causes. *MIS Quarterly, 1*(3), 17–32.

Boudreau, M.-C., & Robey, D. (1996). Coping with contradictions in business process re-engineering. *Information Technology & People, 9*(4), 40–57.

Bowen, J. P., & Hinchey, M. G. (1995). Seven more myths of formal methods. *IEEE Software, 12*(4), 34–41.

Bradley, R. V., Pratt, R. M. E., Byrd, T. A., Outlay, C. N., & Wynn, J. (2012). Enterprise architecture, IT effectiveness and the mediating role of IT alignment in US hospitals. *Informations Systems Journal, 22*, 97–127.

Breu, K. (2001). The role and relevance of management cultures in the organizational transformation process. *International Studies of Management and Organization, 31*(2), 28–47.

BRG. (2007). *The Business Motivation Model – Business Governance in a Volatile World*. Technical Report Release 1.3, The Business Rules Group.

Briggs, R. O. (2004). *On theory-driven design and deployment of collaboration systems* (Vol. 3198). Lecture Notes in Computer Science. Heidelberg, Germany: Springer. ISBN 3-540-23016-5.

Briggs, R. O., Kolfschoten, G. L., Vreede, G. J. d., & Dean, D. L. (2006). Defining Key Concepts for Collaboration Engineering. In R.-A. Guillermo & A. B. Ignacio (Eds.), *Proceedings of 12th Americas Conference on Information Systems (AMCIS 2006), Acapulco, México*.
http://aisel.aisnet.org/amcis2006/17/

Brinkkemper, S. (1996). Method engineering: Engineering of information systems development methods and tools. *Information and Software Technology, 38*(4), 275–280.

Burge, J., & Brown, D. C. (2000). Reasoning with design rationale. In *Artificial intelligence in design* (pp. 611–629). Heidelberg, Germany: Springer.

Burge, J. E., Carroll, J. M., McCall, R., & Mistrik, I. (2008). Rationale-based software engineering. In A. Dutoit, R. McCall, I. Mistrík, & B. Paech (Eds.), *Rationale-based software engineering*. Heidelberg, Germany: Springer. ISBN 978-3-540-30997-0.

By, R. T. (2007). Organisational change management: A critical review. *Journal of Change Management, 5*(4), 369–380.

Byrd, T. A., Cossick, K. L., & Zmud, R. W. (1992). A synthesis of research on requirements analysis and knowledge acquisition techniques. *MIS Quarterly, 16*(1), 117–138.

Cameron, B. H., & McMillan, E. (2013). Analyzing the current trends in enterprise architecture frameworks. *Journal of Enterprise Architecture, 9*(1), 60–71.

Carlile, P. R. (2002). A pragmatic view of knowledge and boundaries: Boundary objects in new product development. *Organization Science, 13*(4), 442–455.

Carlile, P. R. (2004). Transferring, translating, and transforming: An integrative framework for managing knowledge across boundaries. *Organization Science, 15*(5), 555–568.

Cashman, P. M., & Stroll, D. (1987). Achieving sustainable management of complexity: A new view of executive support. *Technology and People, 3*, 147–173.

Chan, Y. E. (2002). Why haven't we mastered alignment? The importance of the informal organization structure. *MIS Quarterly Executive, 1*(2), 97–112.

Chandler, A. D. (1969). *Strategy and structure, chapters in the history of the American Industrial Enterprise*. Cambridge, MA: The MIT Press. ISBN 0-262-53009-0.

CHAOS. (1999). *CHAOS: A Recipe for Success*. Technical Report, The Standish Group International, West Yarmouth, MA.

CHAOS. (2001). *Extreme CHAOS*. Technical Report, The Standish Group International, West Yarmouth, MA.

Chatterjee, D., Grewal, R., & Sambamurthy, V. (2002). Shaping up for E-commerce: Institutional enablers of the organizational assimilation of Web technologies. *MIS Quarterly, 26*(2), 65–89.

Checkland, P. (1981). *Systems thinking, systems practice*. New York, NY: Wiley. ISBN 0-471-27911-0.

Chiniforooshan Esfahani, H., Yu, E., & Cabot, J. (2010). Situational evaluation of method fragments: An evidence-based goal-oriented approach. In *Proceedings of the 22nd International Conference on Advanced Information Systems Engineering (CAiSE 2010), Hammamet, Tunisia* (pp. 424–438). Heidelberg, Germany: Springer. ISBN 978-3-642-13093-9. https://doi.org/10.1007/978-3-642-13094-6_33

Chmielewicz, K. (1994). *Forschungskonzeptionen der Wirtschaftswissenschaften* (3rd ed.). Stuttgart, Germany: Schaffer-PoeschelVerlag. In German. ISBN 978-3791091976.

Chorus, G. J. N. M., Janse, Y. H. C., Nellen, C. J. P., Hoppenbrouwers, S. J. B. A., & Proper, H. A. (2007). Formalizing architecture principles using object–role modelling. *Via Nova Architectura*. Last checked on July 15, 2016. http://tinyurl.com/hvaepms

Ciborra, C. U. (1992). From thinking to tinkering: The grassroots of strategic information systems. *The Information Society, 8,* 297–309.

Clark, B. H., Abela, A. V., & Ambler, T. (2006). An information processing model of marketing performance measurement. *The Journal of Marketing Theory and Practice, 14*(3), 191–208.

Cohen, S. G., & Gibson, C. B. (2003). In the beginning: Introduction and framework. In S. G. Cohen & C. B. Gibson (Eds.), *Virtual teams that work: Creating conditions for virtual team effectiveness* (pp. 1–14). San Francisco, CA: Jossey-Bass.

Collins, J., & Porras, J. (1996). Building your company's vision. *Harvard Business Review, 74*(5), 65–77.

Colyvas, J. A., & Jonsson, S. (2011). Ubiquity and legitimacy: Disentangling diffusion and institutionalization. *Sociological Theory, 29*(1), 27–53.

Conklin, J. (2003a). *The IBIS Manual: A short course in IBIS methodology.* Touchstone. Last checked on July 3, 2014. http://tinyurl.com/hcxk6j9

Conklin, J. (2003b). *Wicked Problems and Social Complexity.* Technical Report, CogNexus Institute, Edgewater, MD.

Conklin, J. (2005). *Dialogue mapping: Building shared understanding of wicked problems.* New York, NY: Wiley. ISBN 978-0-470-01768-5.

Conklin, J., Basadur, M., & VanPatter, G. K. (2007). Rethinking wicked problems – Unpacking paradigms, bridging universes. *NexD Journal, 10*(1).

Cooper, R. B., & Zmud, R. W. (1990). Information technology implementation research: A technological diffusion approach. *Management Science, 36*(2), 123–139.

Corner, P. D., Kinicki, A. J., & Keats, B. W. (1994). Integrating organizational and individual information processing perspectives on choice. *Organization Science, 5*(3), 294–308.

Cossentino, M., Gaglio, S., Henderson-Sellers, B., & Seidita, V. (2008). A Metamodelling-based Approach for Method Fragment Comparison. In T. A. Halpin, J. Krogstie, & H. A. Proper (Eds.), *Proceedings of the 13th Workshop on Exploring Modeling Methods for Systems Analysis and Design (EMMSAD 2008), Held in Conjunction with the 20th Conference on Advanced Information Systems Engineering (CAiSE 2008), Montpellier, France* (Vol. 337, pp. 419–432). CEUR-WS.org.

Cross, J., Earl, M. J., & Sampler, J. L. (1997). Transformation of the IT function at British Petroleum. *MIS Quarterly, 21*(4), 401–423.

Cross, R. L., Yan, A., & Louis, M. R. (2000). Boundary activities in 'boundaryless' organizations: A case study of a transformation to a team-based structure. *Human Relations, 53*(6), 841–868.

Cummins, J. D., & Doherty, N. A. (2006). The economics of insurance intermediaries. *Journal of Risk and Insurance, 73*(3), 359–396.

Currie, W. (2009). Contextualising the IT artefact: Towards a wider research agenda for IS using institutional theory. *Information Technology & People, 22*(1), 63–77.

Czarnecki, K., & Helsen, S. (2006). Feature-based survey of model transformation approaches. *IBM Systems Journal, 45*(3), 621–645.

Daeuble, G., Werner, M. 1., & Nuettgens, M. (2015). Artifact-centered planning and assessing of large design science research projects – A case study. In B. Donnellan, M. Helfert, J. Kenneally, D. VanderMeer, M. Rothenberger & R. Winter (Eds.) *Proceedings of the 10th International Conference on Design Science Research in Information Systems and Technology (DESRIST 2015), Dublin, Ireland* (pp. 343–357). Heidelberg, Germany: Springer. ISBN 978-3-319-18714-3.
https://doi.org/10.1007/978-3-319-18714-3_22

Daft, R. L., & Lengel, R. H. (1986). Organizational information requirements, media richness and structural design. *Management Science, 32*(5), 554–571.

Davidson, W. H. (1993). Beyond re-engineering: The three phases of business transformation. *IBM Systems Journal, 32*(1), 65–79.

Davis, F. D. (1986). *A technology acceptance model for empirically testing new end-user information systems: Theory and results.* PhD thesis, Sloan School of Management, Massachusetts Institute of Technology, Boston, MA.

Davis, F. D. (1989). Perceived usefulness, perceived ease of use, and user acceptance of information technology. *MIS Quarterly, 13*(3), 318–340.

Davis, F. D., Bagozzi, R. P., & Warshaw, P. (1989). User acceptance of computer technology: A comparison of two theoretical models. *Management Science, 35*(8), 982–1003.

Davis, G. F., & Greve, H. R. (1997). Corporate elite networks and governance changes in the 1980s. *American Journal of Sociology, 103*(1), 1–37.

De Caluwé, L., & Vermaak, H. (2003). *Learning to change: A guide for organization change agents.* London, UK: Sage Publications. ISBN 9-014-96158-7.

de Kinderen, S. (2010). *Needs-driven service bundling in a multi-supplier setting - the computational e^3 service approach.* PhD thesis, VU University, Amsterdam, the Netherlands.

de Kinderen, S., Gaaloul, K., & Proper, H. A. (2012a). Bridging value modelling to ArchiMate via transaction modelling. *Software & Systems Modeling,* 1–15. ISSN 1619-1366.
https://doi.org/10.1007/s10270-012-0299-z

de Kinderen, S., Gaaloul, K., & Proper, H. A. (2012b). Integrating value modelling into ArchiMate. In M. Snene (Ed.), *Proceedings of the 3rd International Conference on Exploring Services Science (IESS 2012), Geneva, Switzerland* (Vol. 103, pp. 125–139). Lecture Notes in Business Information Processing. Heidelberg, Germany: Springer. ISBN 978-3-642-28226-3.
https://doi.org/10.1007/978-3-642-28227-0_10

de Kinderen, S., Ma, Q., & Proper, H. A. (2014). Model bundling: Towards a value-based componential approach for language engineering. In *Proceedings of the 8th International Workshop on Value Modelling and Business Ontology (VMBO 2014), Berlin, Germany.*

de Kinderen, S., & Proper, H. A. (2013). e3-RoME: A value-based approach for method bundling. In S. Y. S. Shin & J. C. Maldonado (Eds.) *Proceedings of the 28th Annual ACM Symposium on Applied Computing (SAC 2013), Coimbra, Portuga* (pp. 1469–1471). ISBN 978-1-4503-1656-9. https://doi.org/10.1145/2480362.2480635

de Leeuw, A. C. J. (1982). *Organisaties: Management, analyse, Ontwikkeling en Verandering, een systeem visie.* Assen, the Netherlands: Van Gorcum. In Dutch. ISBN 9-023-22247-4.

de Leeuw, A. C. J., & Volberda, H. W. (1996). On the concept of flexibility: A dual control perspective. *Omega, International Journal of Management Science, 24*(2), 121–139.

DeLone, W. H., & McLean, E. R. (2003). The DeLone and McLean model of information systems success – A ten-year update. *Journal of Management Information Systems, 19*(4), 9–30.

Department of the Treasury (United States of America) and Chief Information Officer Council. (2000). Treasury Enterprise Architecture Framework: Version 1.0.

Derzsi, Z., Gordijn, J., & Kok, K. (2008). Multi-perspective assessment of scalability of IT-enabled networked constellations. In R. H. Sprague (Ed.), *Proceedings of the 41st Annual Hawaii International Conference on System Sciences (HICSS 2008)*, (p. 492). IEEE CS. Last checked on July 15, 2016 http://tinyurl.com/jronzpb

Detert, J. R., Schroeder, R. G., & Mauriel, J. J. (2000). A framework for linking culture and improvement initiatives in organizations. *Academy of Management Review, 25*(4), 850–863.

Dietz, J. L. G. (2006). *Enterprise ontology – Theory and methodology.* Heidelberg, Germany: Springer. ISBN 978-3-540-29169-5.

Dietz, J. L. G. (2008). *Architecture – Building strategy into design.* Netherlands Architecture Forum, Academic Service – SDU, The Hague, the Netherlands. ISBN 978-9-012-58086-1. Last checked on July 15, 2016. http://www.naf.nl

Dietz, J. L. G. (2015). *DEMOSL-3 DEMO Specification Language.* Technical Report, Enterprise Engineering Institute. http://tinyurl.com/j7a2kz7

Dietz, J. L. G., & Hoogervorst, J. A. P. (2008). Enterprise ontology in enterprise engineering. In *Proceedings of the 2008 ACM Symposium on Applied Computing* (pp. 572–579).

Dijkman, R. M., Quartel, D. A. C., Pires, L. F., & van Sinderen, M. J. (2004). A rigorous approach to relate enterprise and computational viewpoints. In *Proceedings of the 8th IEEE International Enterprise Distributed Object Computing Conference (EDOC 2004), Monterey, CA* (pp. 187–200). Los Alamitos, CA: IEEE Computer Society. https://doi.org/10.1109/EDOC.2004.1342515

Dijksterhuis, M. S., van den Bosch, F. A. J., & Volberda, H. W. (1999). Where do new organizational forms come from? Management logics as a source of coevolution. *Organization Science, 10*(5), 569–582.

DiMaggio, P. J. (1988). Interest and Agency in Institutional Theory. In L. G. Zucker (Ed.), *Institutional patterns and organizations: Culture and environment* (pp. 3–21). Cambridge, MA: Ballinger Publishing Company.

DiMaggio, P. J., & Powell, W. W. (1983). The iron cage revisited: Institutional isomorphism and collective rationality in organizational fields. *American Sociological Review, 48*(2), 147–160.

Dunphy, D. (1996). Organizational change in corporate settings. *Human Relations, 49*(5), 541–552.
https://doi.org/10.1177/001872679604900501

Dutoit, A. H., McCall, R., Mistrík, I., & Paech, B. (2006). Rationale management in software engineering: Concepts and techniques. In A. H. Dutoit, R. McCall, I. Mistrík, & B. Paech (Eds.), *Rationale management in software engineering* (pp. 1–48). Heidelberg, Germany: Springer. ISBN 978-3-540-30997-0.
https://doi.org/10.1007/978-3-540-30998-7_1

ECIS. (2013). *Proceedings of the 21st European Conference on Information Systems (ECIS 2013), Utrecht, the Netherlands.*
http://aisel.aisnet.org/ecis2013_materials

Eilon, S. (1969). Prescription in management decisions. *Journal of Management Studies, 6*(2), 181–197.
https://doi.org/10.1111/j.1467-6486.1969.tb00590.x

Einhorn, H. J. (1970). The use of nonlinear, noncompensatory models in decision making. *Psychological Bulletin, 73*(3), 221.

Elahi, G., & Yu, E. (2012). Comparing alternatives for analyzing requirements trade-offs–In the absence of numerical data. *Information and Software Technology, 54*(6), 517–530.

Elliot, S. (2011). Transdisciplinary perspectives on environmental sustainability: A resource base and framework for IT-enabled business transformation. *MIS Quarterly, 35*(1), 197–236.

Elving, W. J. L. (2005). The role of communication in organisational change. *Corporate Communications: An International Journal, 10*(2), 129–138.

Emery, F. E., & Trist, E. L. (1965). The causal texture of organizational environments. *Human Relations, 18*, 21–31.

Emery, F. E., & Trist, E. L. (1973). *Towards a social ecology: Contextual appreciations of the future in the present.* Melbourne, Australia: Plenum Publishing.

Eoyang, G., & Holladay, R. (2013). *Adaptive action: Leveraging uncertainty in your organization.* Stanford, CA: Stanford Business Books, Stanford University Press.

Espinoza, F. (2007). Enterprise architecture and change management. *Journal of Enterprise Architecture, 3*(2), 27–35.

Falkenberg, E. D., Verrijn–Stuart, A. A., Voss, K., Hesse, W., Lindgreen, P., Nilsson, B. E., et al. (Eds.). (1998). *A Framework of Information Systems Concepts.* IFIP WG 8.1 Task Group FRISCO, IFIP, Laxenburg, Austria. ISBN 3-901-88201-4.

Faller, H., & de Kinderen, S. (2014). The impact of cultural differences on enterprise architecture effectiveness: A case study. In *Proceedings of the 8th Mediterranean Conference on Information Systems (MCIS 2014)*, Paper 37. AIS Electronic Library. Last checked on July 15, 2016.
http://aisel.aisnet.org/mcis2014/37

Feldman, M. S. (2000). Organizational routines as a source of continuous change. *Organization Science, 11*(6), 611–629.
https://doi.org/10.1287/orsc.11.6.611.12529

Feltus, C., Dubois, E., Proper, H. A., Band, I., & Petit, M. (2012). Enhancing the ArchiMate standard with a responsibility modeling language for access rights management. In M. Singh Gaur, A. Elçi, O. B. Makarevich, M. A. Orgun, & V. Singh (Eds.), *Proceedings of the 5th International Conference of Security of Information and Networks (SIN 2012), Jaipur, India*, (pp. 12–19). New York, NY: ACM Press. ISBN 978-1-450-31668-2.

Fettke, P., & Loos, P. (2003). Classification of reference models – A methodology and its applications. *Information Systems and E-Business Management, 1*(1), 35–53.
https://doi.org/10.1007/bf02683509

Fettke, P., & Loos, P. (2007). Perspectives on reference modeling. In P. Fettke & P. Loos (Eds.), *Reference Modeling for Business Systems Analysis* (pp. 1–20). Hershey, PA: Idea Group.

Finkelstein, A., Kramer, J., Nuseibeh, B., Finkelstein, L., & Goedicke, M. (1992). Viewpoints: A framework for integrating multiple perspectives in system development. *International Journal on Software Engineering and Knowledge Engineering, Special Issue on Trends and Research Directions in Software Engineering Environments, 2*(1), 31–58.

Fischer, C., Winter, R., & Aier, S. (2010). What is an enterprise architecture design principle? Towards a consolidated definition. In *Proceedings of the 2nd International Workshop on Enterprise Architecture Challenges and Responses*, Yonezawa, Japan.

Fishbein, M., & Ajzen, I. (1975). *Belief, attitude, intentions and behavior: An introduction to theory and research*. Boston, MA: Addison-Wesley.

Flyvbjerg, B., & Budzier, A. (2012). Why your IT project may be riskier than you think. *Harvard Business Review, 89*(9), 23–25.

Ford, J. D., & Ford, L. W. (1995). The role of conversations in producing intentional change in organizations. *Academy of Management Review, 20*(3), 541–570.

Franckson, M., & Verhoef, T. F. (Eds.). (1999). *Managing risks and planning deliveries*. Information Services Procurement Library. Den Haag, the Netherlands: Ten Hagen & Stam. ISBN 9-076-30483-1.

Fredenberger, W. B., Lipp, A., & Watson, H. J. (1997). Information requirements of turnaround managers at the beginning of engagements. *Journal of Management Information Systems, 13*(4), 167–192.

Fry, L. W., Vitucci, S., & Cedillo, M. (2005). Spiritual leadership and army transformation: Theory, measurement, and establishing a baseline. *The Leadership Quarterly, 16*(5), 835–862.

Furneaux, B., Janasz, T., Schild, T., & Klimmek, R. (2012). Risk management. In A. Uhl & L. A. Gollenia (Eds.), *A handbook of business transformation management methodology* (pp. 85–107). Farnham, UK: Gower.

Galbraith, J. R. (1974). Organization design: An information processing view. *Interfaces, 4*(3), 28–36.

Galbraith, J. R. (1977). *Organization design* (1st ed.). Reading, MA: Addison-Wesley.

Gardner, D., Fehskens, L., Naidu, M., Rouse, W. B., & Ross, J. W. (2012). Point-counterpoint: Enterprise architecture and enterprise transformation as related but distinct concepts. *Journal of Enterprise Transformation, 2*(4), 283–294.

GEA (2011). GEA Groeiplatform. In Dutch. Last checked on July 6, 2014. http://www.groeiplatformgea.nl

Gersick, C. J. G. (1991). Revolutionary change theories: A multilevel exploration of the punctuated equilibrium paradigm. *Academy of Management Review, 16*(1), 10–36.

Ghanavati, S., Amyot, D., & Peyton, L. (2009). Compliance analysis based on a goal-oriented requirement language evaluation methodology. In *Proceedings of the 7th IEEE International Requirements Engineering Conference (RE 2009)* (pp. 133–142). Los Alamitos, CA: IEEE Computer Society.

Giddens, A. (1984). *The constitution of society: Outline of the theory of structuration.* Cambridge, UK: Polity Press. ISBN 0-520-05728-7.

Gilsdorf, J. W. (1998). Organizational rules on communicating: How employees are – and are not – Learning the ropes. *The Journal of Business Communication, 35*(2), 173–201.

Gordon, L. A., & Miller, D. (1976). A contingency framework for the design of accounting information systems. *Accounting, Organizations and Society 1*(1), 59–69.

Gorry, G. A., & Scott Morton, M. S. (1971). A framework for management information systems. *Sloan Management Review, 13*(1), 55–70.

Government of the United States of America. (2002). *Sarbanes-Oxley Act of 2002.* Technical Report H. R.3763, Government of the United States of America.

Greefhorst, D., & Proper, H. A. (2011). *Architecture principles – The cornerstones of enterprise architecture.* Enterprise Engineering Series. Heidelberg, Germany: Springer. ISBN 978-3-642-20278-0.

Greefhorst, D., Proper, H. A., & Plataniotis, G. (2013). The Dutch State of the practice of architecture principles. *Journal of Enterprise Architecture, 9*(4), 20–25.

Greenhalgh, T., Robert, G., MacFarlane, F., Bate, P., & Kyriakidou, O. (2004). Diffusion of innovations in service organizations: Systematic review and recommendations. *The Milbank Quarterly, 82*(4), 581–629.

Greenwood, R., & Hinings, C. R. (1996). Understanding radical organizational change: Bringing together the old and the new institutionalism. *The Academy of Management Review, 21*(4), 1022–1054.

Greenwood, R., Oliver, C., Suddaby, R., & Sahlin-Andersson, K. (2008). *The SAGE handbook of organizational institutionalism.* London, UK: Sage Publications.

Greenwood, R., Raynard, M., Kodeih, F., Micelotta, E. R., & Lounsbury, M. (2011). Institutional complexity and organizational responses. *The Academy of Management Annals, 5*(1), 317–371.

Gregor, S. (2006). The nature of theory in information systems. *MIS Quarterly, 30*(3), 611–642.

Gregor, S., & Hevner, A. (2013). Positioning and presenting design science research for maximum impact. *MIS Quarterly, 37*(2), 337–355.

Gregor, S., & Jones, D. (2007). The anatomy of a design theory. *Journal of the Association for Information Systems, 8*(5), 312–335.

Gregor, S., Müller, O., & Seidel, S. (2013). Reflection, abstraction and theorizing in design and development research. In *ECIS 2013*, Paper 74. http://aisel.aisnet.org/ecis2013_materials

Gryning, M., Mertz, M., Khan, A., & Staack, J. (2010). Improve cooperation and alignment by involving the enterprise in the architectural development. *Journal of Enterprise Architecture, 6*(4), 19–26.

Guiltinan, J. P. (1987). The price bundling of services: A normative framework. *Journal of Marketing, 51*(2), 74–85.

Gutman, J. (1997). Means–end chains as goal hierarchies. *Psychology and Marketing, 14*(6), 545–560.

Hall, J. A. (1990). Seven myths of formal methods. *IEEE Software, 7*(5), 11–19.

Hall, P. A., & Taylor, R. C. R. (1996). Political science and the three new institutionalisms. *Political Studies, 44*(5), 936–957.

Hamel, G., & Prahalad, C. K. (1994). *Competing for the future*. Boston: Harvard Business Press.

Hammer, M., & Champy, J. (1993). *Reengineering the corporation: A manifesto for business revolution*. New York, NY: Harper Business.

Harmsen, A. F., Grahlmann, K., & Proper, H. A. (Eds.). (2011). *Proceedings of the 3rd Working Conference on Practice-Driven Research on Enterprise Transformation (PRET 2010), Delft, the Netherlands* (Vol. 89). Lecture Notes in Business Information Processing. Heidelberg, Germany: Springer. ISBN 978-3-642-23387-6.

Harmsen, A. F., Proper, H. A., & Kok, N. (2009). Informed governance of enterprise transformations. In H. A. Proper, A. F. Harmsen, & J. L. G. Dietz (Eds.), *Proceedings of the 1st NAF Academy Working Conference on Practice-Driven Research on Enterprise Transformations (PRET 2009), Held at the 21st International Conference on Advanced Information Systems Engineering (CAiSE 2009), Amsterdam, the Netherlands* (Vol. 28, pp. 155–180). Lecture Notes in Business Information Processing. Heidelberg, Germany: Springer. ISBN 978-3-642-01858-9. https://doi.org/10.1007/978-3-642-01859-6_9

Harmsen, F., & Molnar, W. A. (2013). Perspectives on enterprise transformation: Approaching transforming enterprises with a conceptual meta-model. In *Keynotes of the 15th IEEE Conference on Business Informatics (CBI 2013), Vienna, Austria*. Last checked on July 15, 2016. http://tinyurl.com/h6vk5me

Hawkins, M. A., & Rezazade Mehrizi, M. H. (2012). Knowledge boundary spanning process: Synthesizing four spanning mechanisms. *Management Decision, 50*(10), 1800–1815.

Head, B. W., & Alford, J. (2015). Wicked problems: Implications for public policy and management. *Administration & Society, 47*(6). https://doi.org/10.1177/0095399713481601

Henderson, J. C., & Venkatraman, N. (1993). Strategic alignment: Leveraging information technology for transforming organizations. *IBM Systems Journal, 32*(1), 4–16.

Henderson, K. (1991). Flexible sketches and inflexible data bases: Visual communication, conscription devices, and boundary objects in design engineering. *Science, Technology, & Human Values, 16*(4), 448–473.

Henderson-Sellers, B., & Ralyté, J. (2010). Situational method engineering: State-of-the-art review. *Journal of Universal Computer Science, 16*(3), 424–478.

Hess, T. J., McNab, A. L., & Basoglu, K. A. (2014). Reliability generalization of perceived ease of use, perceived usefulness, and behavioral intentions. *MIS Quarterly, 31*(1), 1–28.

Hevner, A. R., March, S. T., Park, J., & Ram, S. (2004). Design science in information systems research. *MIS Quarterly, 28*, 75–106.

Hjort-Madsen, K. (2006). Enterprise architecture implementation and management: A case study on interoperability. In *Proceedings of the 39th Annual Hawaii International Conference on System Sciences (HICSS 2006)* (Vol. 4). Washington, DC: IEEE.

Hjort-Madsen, K. (2007). Institutional patterns of enterprise architecture adoption in government. *Transforming Government: People, Process And Policy, 1*(4), 333–349.

Hock-Hai Teo, B., Tan, C. Y., & Wei, K.-K. (1997). Organizational transformation using electronic data interchange: The case of Tradenet in Singapore. *Journal of Management Information Systems, 13*(4), 139–165.

Hoebeke, L. (1994). *Making work systems better: A practitioner's reflections.* Chichester, UK: Wiley.

Hofstede, G. H. (1998). Identifying organizational subcultures: An empirical approach. *Journal of Management Studies, 35*(1), 1–12.

Hofstede, G. H. (2001). *Culture's consequences: Comparing values, behaviors, institutions, and organizations across nations* (2nd ed.). London, UK: Sage Publications. ISBN 0-8039-7323-3.

Hofstede, G. H., Hofstede, G. J., & Minkov, M. (2010). *Cultures and organizations: Software of the mind : Intercultural cooperation and its importance for survival* (3rd ed.). New York, NY: McGraw-Hill. ISBN 0071664181.

Holt, A. W. (1988). Diplans: A new language for the study and implementation of coordination. *ACM Transactions on Information Systems, 6*(2), 109–125. ISSN 1046-8188. https://doi.org/10.1145/45941.45942

Hoogervorst, J. A. P. (2004). Enterprise architecture: Enabling integration, agility and change. *International Journal of Cooperative Information Systems, 13*(3), 213–233.

Hoogervorst, J. A. P. (2009). *Enterprise governance and enterprise engineering*. Enterprise Engineering Series. Heidelberg, Berlin, Germany: Springer. ISBN 978-3-540-92670-2.

Horkoff, J., & Yu, E. (2013). Comparison and evaluation of goal-oriented satisfaction analysis techniques. *Requirements Engineering, 18*(3), 199–222. https://link.springer.com/article/10.1007/s00766-011-0143-y.

Hu, Q., Hart, P., & Cooke, D. (2007). The role of external and internal influences on information systems security – A neo-institutional perspective. *The Journal of Strategic Information Systems, 16*(2), 153–172.

Huy, Q. N. (1999). Emotional capability, emotional intelligence, and radical change. *Academy of Management Review, 24*(2), 325–345.

Iacob, M.-E., Jonkers, H., Lankhorst, M. M., & Proper, H. A. (2009). *ArchiMate 1.0 specification*. The Open Group. ISBN 978-9-087-53502-5.

Iacob, M.-E., Jonkers, H., Lankhorst, M. M., Proper, H. A., & Quartel, D. A. C. (2012). *ArchiMate 2.0 specification*. The Open Group. ISBN 1-937-21800-3.

IEEE. (1990). *IEEE Standard Glossary of Software Engineering Terminology*. Technical Report ANSI/IEEE Std 610.12, IEEE Standards Department, Los Alamitos, CA.

IEEE. (2000). *Recommended Practice for Architectural Description of Software Intensive Systems*. Technical Report IEEE P1471:2000, ISO/IEC 42010:2007, IEEE Explore, Los Alamitos, CA, Piscataway, NJ. The Architecture Working Group of the Software Engineering Committee, Standards Department, IEEE. ISBN 0-738-12518-0.

IEEE. (2011). Systems and software engineering – Architecture description. *ISO/IEC/IEEE 42010:2011(E) (Revision of ISO/IEC 42010:2007 and IEEE Std 1471-2000)* (pp. 1–46). https://doi.org/10.1109/IEEESTD.2011.6129467

IFIP-IFAC Task Force on Architectures for Enterprise Integration. (2003). GERAM – The generalised enterprise reference architecture and methodology. In P. Bernus, L. Nemes, & G. Schmidt (Eds.) *Handbook on enterprise architecture* (pp. 21–63), International Handbooks on Information Systems. Heidelberg, Germany: Springer. ISBN 978-3-540-00343-4.

Inmon, W. H. (2000). *Creating the Data Warehouse Data Model from the Corporate Data Model*. Technical Report, Inmon Consulting Services, Castle Rock, CO.

iStar. (2016). i* – An agent- and goal-oriented modelling framework. Last checked on July 27, 2016. http://www.cs.toronto.edu/km/istar/

Iyamu, T. (2009). The factors affecting institutionalisation of enterprise architecture in the organisation. In *Proceedings of the 11th IEEE Conference on Commerce and Enterprise Computing (CEC 2009)*, (pp. 221–225).

Jaffe, E. D. (1979). Multinational marketing intelligence: An information requirements model. *Management International Review, 19*(2), 53–60.

Jansen, A., & Bosch, J. (2005). Software architecture as a set of architectural design decisions. In *Proceedings of the 5th IEEE/IFIP Working Conference on Software Architecture (WICSA 2005)* (pp. 109–120). Washington, DC: IEEE.

Jaques, E. (1998). *Requisite organization: A total system for effective managerial organization and managerial leadership for the 21st century* (2nd ed.). Gloucester, MA: Cason Hall & Co.

Jenkins, J. C. (1977). Radical transformation of organizational goals. *Administrative Science Quarterly, 22*(4), 568–586.

Jepperson, R. L. (1991). Institutions, institutional effects, and institutionalism. In W. W. Powell & P. J. DiMaggio (Eds.), *The new institutionalism in organizational analysis* (pp. 143–163). Chicago: University of Chicago Press.

Johnston, J., & Madura, J. (2000). Valuing the potential transformation of banks into financial service conglomerates: Evidence from the Citigroup merger. *The Financial Review, 35*(2), 17–36.

Jones, M. R., & Karsten, H. (2008). Giddens's structuration theory and information systems research. *MIS Quarterly, 32*(1), 127–157.

Jonkers, H., Band, I., & Quartel, D. (2012). *The ArchiSurance case study*. White Paper Y121. San Francisco, CA: The Open Group.

Jonkers, H., Lankhorst, M. M., Doest, H. t., Arbab, F., Bosma, H., & Wieringa, R. (2006). Enterprise architecture: Management tool and blueprint for the organisation. *Information Systems Frontiers, 8*(2), 63–66.

Jung, R., & Reichert, M. (Eds.). (2013). *Proceedings of the 5th International Workshop on Enterprise Modelling and Information Systems Architectures (EMISA 2013), St. Gallen, Switzerland*, (Vol. 222). Lecture Notes in Informatics. Bonn, Germany: Gesellschaft für Informatiek. ISBN 978-3-88579-616-9.

Kaplan, R. S., Norton, D. P., & Barrows, E. A. (2008). Developing the strategy: Vision, value gaps, and analysis. *Balanced Scorecard Review*. https://hbr.org/product/developing-the-strategy-vision-value-gaps-and-analysis/B0801A-PDF-ENG.

Karsten, H., Lyytinen, K., Hurskainen, M., & Koskelainen, T. (2001). Crossing boundaries and conscripting participation: Representing and integrating knowledge in a paper machinery project. *European Journal of Information Systems, 10*(2), 89–98.

Keidel, R. W. (1994). Rethinking organizational design. *Academy of Management Executive, 8*(4), 12–28.

Keller, S., & Price, C. (2011). *Beyond performance: How great organizations build ultimate competitive advantage* (1st ed.). Hoboken, NJ: Wiley.

Kilmann, R. (1995). A holistic program and critical success factors of corporate transformation. *European Management Journal, 13*(2), 175–186.

King, J. L., Gurbaxani, V., Kraemer, K. L., McFarlan, F. W., Raman, K. S., & Yap, C. S. (1994). Institutional factors in information technology innovation. *Information Systems Research, 5*(2), 139–169.

Kleinmuntz, D. N., & Schkade, D. A. (1993). Information displays and decision processes. *Psychological Science, 4*, 221–227. https://doi.org/10.1111/j.1467-9280.1993.tb00265.x

Korhonen, J. J., & Hiekkanen, K. (2013). Doing IT better: An organization design perspective. In *Proceedings of the 9th European Conference on Management, Leadership and Governance (ECMLG 2013), Klagenfurt, Austria*.

Korhonen, J. J., & Molnar, W. A. (2014). Enterprise architecture as capability: Strategic application of competencies to govern enterprise transformation. In H. A. Proper & J. Ralyté (Eds.), *16th IEEE Conference on Business Informatics*. ISBN 978-1-4799-5779-8.

Korhonen, J. J., & Poutanen, J. (2013). Tripartite approach to enterprise architecture. *Journal of Enterprise Architecture, 9*(1), 28–38.

Kosanke, K. (1995). CIMOSA – Overview and status. *Computers in Industry, 27*(2), 101–109.

Kotlarsky, J., van den Hooff, B., & Houtman, L. (2012). Are we on the same page? Knowledge boundaries and transactive memory system development in cross-functional teams. *Communication Research*, Advance online publication. https://doi.org/10.1177/0093650212469402

Kotler, P. (2000). *Marketing management*. Upper Saddle River, NJ: Prentice Hall.

Kotter, J. P. (1995). Leading change: Why transformation efforts fail. *Harvard Business Review, 73*(2), 59–67.

Kotter, J. P. (1996). *Leading change*. Boston, MA: McGraw-Hill Professional.

Kraus, G., Becker-Kolle, C., & Fischer, T. (2006). *Handbuch change-management: Steuerung von Veränderungsprozessen in Organisationen. Einflussfaktoren und Beteiligte. Konzepte, Instrumente und Methoden* (2nd ed.). Berlin, Germany: Cornelsen. ISBN 978-3-589-23635-0.

Kruchten, P. (2004). An ontology of architectural design decisions in software intensive systems. In *2nd Groningen Workshop on Software Variability* (pp. 54–61).

Kruchten, P., Lago, P., & van Vliet, H. (2006). Building up and reasoning about architectural knowledge. In C. Hofmeister, I. Crnkovic, & R. Reussner (Eds.), *Quality of software architectures* (Vol. 4214, pp. 43–58). Lecture Notes in Computer Science. Heidelberg, Germany: Springer. ISBN 978-3-540-48819-4. https://doi.org/10.1007/11921998_8

Kunz, W., & Rittel, H. W. J. (1970). *Issues as Elements of Information Systems*. Technical Report, Studiengruppe für Systemforschung, Heidelberg, Germany. Last checked on July 27, 2016. http://tinyurl.com/zf2rmxv

Kurpjuweit, S., & Winter, R. (2007). Viewpoint-based meta model engineering. In M. Reichert, S. Strecker, & K. Turowski (Eds.), *Proceedings of EMISA 2007 - 2nd International Workshop on Enterprise Modelling and Information Systems Architectures, St. Goar, Germany* (pp. 143–161).

Labusch, N. (2015). *Information requirements in enterprise transformations: An enterprise architecture management perspective*. PhD thesis, University of St. Gallen, St. Gallen, Switzerland.

Labusch, N., & Aier, S. (2014). Information provision as a success factor in the architectural support of enterprise transformations. In Aveiro et al. (Eds.), *Proceedings of the 16th IEEE Conference on Business Informatics* (pp. 141–148). ISBN 978-1-4799-5779-8. https://doi.org/10.1109/CBI.2014.31

Labusch, N., Aier, S., Rothenberger, M., & Winter, R. (2014a). Architectural support of enterprise transformations: Insights from corporate practice. In D. Kundisch, L. Suhl, & L. Beckmann (Eds.), *Proceedings of the 12th International Conference on Wirtschaftsinformatik (WI 2014)*, (pp. 1048–1060). Universität Paderborn.

Labusch, N., Aier, S., & Winter, R. (2013). Beyond enterprise architecture modeling – What are the essentials to support enterprise transformations? In R. Jung & M. Reichert (Eds.), *Enterprise Modelling and Information Systems Architectures (EMISA 2013)* (pp. 13–26). ISBN 978-3-88579-616-9.

Labusch, N., Aier, S., & Winter, R. (2014b). A reference model for the information-based support of enterprise transformations. In M. C. Tremblay, D. v. d. Meer, M. Rothenberger, A. Gupta, & V. Yoon (Eds.), *Proceedings of the 9th International Conference on Design Science Research in Information Systems and Technology (DESRIST 2014), Miami, FL* (Vol. 8463, pp. 194–208) Lecture Notes in Computer Science. Heidelberg, Germany: Springer.

Labusch, N., & Winter, R. (2013). Towards a conceptualization of architectural support for enterprise transformation. In *ECIS 2013*, Paper 116. http://aisel.aisnet.org/ecis2013_cr/116

Lahrmann, G., Labusch, N., Winter, R., & Uhl, A. (2012). Management of large-scale transformation programs: State of the practice and future potential. In S. Aier et al. (Eds.), *Trends in Enterprise Architecture Research and Practice-Driven Research on Enterprise Transformation* (pp. 253–267). ISBN 978-3-642-34162-5. https://doi.org/2010.1007/978-3-642-34163-2_15

Landry, S. J., Levin, K., Rowe, D., & Nickelson, M. (2009). Enabling collaborative work across different communities of practice through boundary objects: Field studies in air traffic management. *International Journal of Human-Computer Interaction, 26*(1), 75–93.

Lange, M. (2012). *Evaluating the realization of benefits from enterprise architecture management: Construction and validation of a theoretical model: Dissertation.* Wirtschaftsinformatik. München, Germany: Verlag Dr. Hut. ISBN 978-3-8439-0558-9.

Lankhorst, M. M. (Ed.). (2012). *Enterprise architecture at work: Modelling, communication and analysis* (3rd ed.). Enterprise Engineering Series. Heidelberg, Germany: Springer. ISBN 978-3-642-29650-5.

Lankhorst, M. M., Proper, H. A., & Jonkers, H. (2010). The anatomy of the Archi-Mate language. *International Journal of Information System Modeling and Design (IJISMD), 1*(1), 1–32. https://doi.org/10.1007/978-3-642-01862-6_30

Laudon, K. C., & Laudon, J. P. (2006). *Management information systems: Managing the digital firm* (10th ed.). Englewood Cliffs, NJ, Upper Saddle River, NJ: Prentice Hall.

Lee, J. (1991). Extending the Potts and Bruns model for recording design rationale. In *Proceedings of the 13th International Conference on Software Engineering, 1991* (pp. 114–125). Los Alamitos, CA: IEEE.

Lee, J., & Lai, K.-Y. (1991). What's in design rationale? *Human–Computer Interaction, 6*(3–4), 251–280.

Levendovszky, T., Karsai, G., Maroti, M., Ledeczi, A., & Charaf, H. (2002). Model reuse with metamodel-based transformations. *Software Reuse: Methods, Techniques, and Tools, 2319,* 166–178.
https://link.springer.com/chapter/10.1007/3-540-46020-9_12

Levina, N., & Vaast, E. (2005). The emergence of boundary spanning competence in practice: Implications for implementation and use of information systems. *MIS Quarterly, 29*(2), 335–363.

Lewis, W., Agarwal, R., & Sambamurthy, V. (2003). Sources of influence on beliefs about information technology use: An empirical study of knowledge workers. *MIS Quarterly, 27*(4), 657–678.

Liaskos, S., McIlraith, S. A., Sohrabi, S., & Mylopoulos, J. (2011). Representing and reasoning about preferences in requirements engineering. *Requirements Engineering, 16*(3), 227–249.

Likert, R. (1932). A Technique for the measurement of attitudes. *Archives of Psychology, 22*(140), 1–55.

Lindström, A. (2006). On the syntax and semantics of architectural principles. In *Proceedings of the 39th Hawaii International Conference on System Sciences (HICSS 2006).*

Lineweaver, C. H., Davies, P. C. W., & Ruse, M. (2013). What is complexity? Is it increasing? In C. H. Lineweaver, P. C. W. Davies, & M. Ruse (Eds.) *Complexity and the arrow of time.* Cambridge, UK: Cambridge University Press.

Loh, L., & Venkatraman, N. (1992). Diffusion of information technology outsourcing: Influence sources and the Kodak effect. *Information Systems Research, 3*(4), 334–358.

Lohman, F. A. B., Sol, H. G., & de Vreede, G. (2003). The illusion of effective management information: A critical perspective. In *Proceedings of the 36th Hawaii International Conference on System Sciences (HICSS 2003).*

Luiten, G., Cooper, G., Froese, T., Junge, R., Björk, B. C., Karstila, K., et al. (1993). An information reference model for architecture, engineering, and construction. In *First International Conference on the Management of Information Technology for Construction* (pp. 1–10).

Lyytinen, K., & Damsgaard, J. (2001). What's wrong with the diffusion of innovation theory? In M. A. Ardis, & B. L. Marcolin (Eds.), *Diffusing software product and process innovations* (pp. 173–190). Heidelberg, Germany: Springer.

Macdonald, I., Burke, C., & Stewart, K. (2006). *Systems leadership: Creating positive organisations.* Burlington, VT: Gower.

MacLean, A., Young, R. M., Bellotti, V. M. E., & Moran, T. P. (1991). Questions, options, and criteria: Elements of design space analysis. *Human–computer interaction, 6*(3–4), 201–250.

Magalhães, R., & Proper, H. A. (2017). Model-enabled design and engineering of organisations. *Organisational Design and Enterprise Engineeering, 1*(1), 1–12.
http://dx.doi.org/10.1007/s41251-016-0005-9.

Maglio, P. P., & Spohrer, J. (2008). Fundamentals of service science. *Journal of the Academy of Marketing Science, 36*(1), 18–20. https://doi.org/10.1007/s11747-007-0058-9

Malone, T. W., & Crowston, K. (1990). What is coordination theory and how can it help design cooperative work systems? In *Proceedings of the 1990 ACM Conference on Computer-Supported Cooperative Work (CSCW 1990).*

Malone, T. W., & Crowston, K. (1994). The interdisciplinary study of coordination. *ACM Computing Surveys, 26*(1), 87–119. ISSN 0360-0300. https://doi.org/10.1145/174666.174668

Mandis, S. G. (2013). *What happened to Goldman Sachs: An insider's story of organizational drift and its unintended consequences.* Boston, MA: Harvard Business Review Press. ISBN 978-1422194195. http://www.marchmenthill.com/qsi-online/2011-06-19/organisational-drift

March, J. G., & Simon, H. A. (1958). *Organizations.* New York, NY: Wiley.

March, S. T., & Smith, G. F. (1995). Design and natural science research on information technology. *Decision Support Systems, 15*(4), 251–266.

Marchand, D. A., & Peppard, J. (2008). *Designed to Fail: Why IT Projects Under-Achieve and What To Do About It.* Technical Report IMD 2008-11, IMD International.

Markus, M. L., & Robey, D. (1988). Information technology and organizational change – Causal structure in theory and research. *Management Science, 34*(5), 583–598.

Marosin, D., & Ghanavati, S. (2015). Measuring and managing the design restriction of enterprise architecture (EA) principles on EA models. In *Eighth IEEE International Workshop on Requirements Engineering and Law, RELAW 2015, Ottawa, ON, Canada, August 25, 2015* (pp. 37–46). Washington, DC: IEEE Computer Society. ISBN 978-1-5090-0104-0. https://doi.org/10.1109/RELAW.2015.7330210

Marosin, D., Ghanavati, S., & van der Linden, D. J. T. (2014). A principle-based goal-oriented requirements language (GRL) for enterprise architecture. In F. Dalpiaz & J. Horkoff (Eds.), *Proceedings of the 7th International i* Workshop Co-located with the 26th International Conference on Advanced Information Systems Engineering (CAiSE 2014), Thessaloniki, Greece* (Vol. 1157). CEUR-WS.org. http://ceur-ws.org/Vol-1157/paper4.pdf

Marosin, D., van Zee, M., & Ghanavati, S. (2016). Formalizing and modeling enterprise architecture (EA) principles with goal-oriented requirements language (GRL). In S. Nurcan, P. Soffer, M. Bajec, & J. Eder (Eds.), *Proceedings of the 28th International Conference on Advanced Information Systems Engineering (CAiSE 2016), Ljubljana, Slovenia* (Vol. 9694, pp. 205–220). Lecture Notes in Computer Science. Heidelberg, Germany: Springer. ISBN 978-3-319-39695-8. https://doi.org/10.1007/978-3-319-39696-5_13

Martinez, J. I., & Jarillo, J. C. (1989). The evolution of research on coordination mechanisms in multinational corporations. *Journal of International Business Studies, 20*(3), 489–514.

Matthes, F., Buckl, S., Leitel, J., & Schweda, C. M. (2008). *Enterprise Architecture Management Tool Survey 2008*. Chair for Informatics 19 (sebis), Technische Universität München, Munich, Germany.

McAdam, R. (2003). Radical change: A conceptual model for research agendas. *Leadership & Organization Development Journal, 24*(4), 226–235.

McCann, J., & Selsky, J. (1984). Hyperturbulence and the emergence of type 5 environments. *Academy of Management Review, 9*(3), 460–470.

McGinnis, L. F. (2007). Enterprise modeling and enterprise transformation. *Information, Knowledge, Systems Management, 6*(1–2), 123–143.

McMorland, J. (2005). Are you big enough your job? Is your job big enough for you? Exploring levels of work in organisations. *University of Auckland Business Review, 7*(2), 75–83.

Meertens, L. O., Iacob, M. E., Nieuwenhuis, L. J. M., van Sinderen, M. J., Jonkers, H., & Quartel, D. (2012). Mapping the business model canvas to ArchiMate. In *Proceedings of the 27th Annual ACM Symposium on Applied Computing (SAC 2012), Trento, Italy* (pp. 1694–1701). New York, NY: ACM. ISBN 978-1-4503-0857-1.
https://doi.org/10.1145/2245276.2232049

Mentzer, J. T., Rutner, S. M., & Matsuno, K. (1997). Application of the means-end value hierarchy model to understanding logistics service value. *International Journal of Physical Distribution & Logistics Management, 27*(9/10), 630–643.

Meriam–Webster. (2003). Meriam–Webster Online, Collegiate Dictionary.

Mernik, M., Heering, J., & Sloane, A. M. (2005). When and how to develop domain-specific languages. *ACM Computing Surveys, 37*(4), 316–344.

Meyer, J. W., & Rowan, B. (1977). Institutionalized organizations: Formal structure as myth and ceremony. *American Journal of Sociology, 83*(2), 340–363.

Mignerat, M., & Rivard, S. (2009). Positioning the institutional perspective in information systems research. *Journal of Information Technology, 24*(4), 369–391.

Mintzberg, H. (1983). *Power in and around organizations*. Englewood Cliffs, NJ: Prentice Hall.

Mintzberg, H., Ahlstrand, B. W., & Lampel, J. (2001). *Strategy Safari: The Complete guide through the wilds of strategic management*. New York, NY: Free Press.

Mintzberg, H., Raisingham, D., & Théorêt, A. (1976). The structure of unstructured decision processes. *Administrative Science Quarterly, 2*(21), 246–275.
http://www.jstor.org/stable/2392045

Moen, R., & Norman, C. (2006). Evolution of the PDCA cycle. Last checked on February 17, 2017.
http://www.pkpinc.com/files/NA01MoenNormanFullpaper.pdf

Molnar, W. A., & Korhonen, J. J. (2014). Research paradigms and topics in enterprise engineering – Analysis of recent conferences and workshops. In *Eigth IEEE International Conference on Research Challenges in Information Science (RCIS 2014), Marrakesh, Morocco*. Los Alamitos, CA: IEEE Explore.

Moody, D. L. (2009). The "Physics" of notations: Toward a scientific basis for constructing visual notations in software engineering. *IEEE Transactions on Software Engineering Software Engineering, 35*(6), 756–779. https://doi.org/10.1109/TSE.2009.67

Mykhashchuk, M., Buckl, S., Dierl, T., & Schweda, C. M. (2011). Charting the landscape of enterprise architecture management. In A. Bernstein & G. Schwabe (Eds.), *Proceedings of the 10th International Conference on Wirtschaftsinformatik (WI 2011)* (Vol. 1, pp. 570–577).

Nabukenya, J. (2005). Collaboration engineering for policy making: A theory of good policy in a collaborative action. In *Proceedings of the 15th European Conference on Information Systems (ECIS 2005), Regensburg, Germany* (pp. 54–61).

Nabukenya, J. (2009). *Improving the quality of organisational policy making using collaboration engineering.* PhD thesis, Radboud University, Nijmegen, the Netherlands.

Nabukenya, J., van Bommel, P., & Proper, H. A. (2007). Collaborative IT Policymaking as a means of achieving Business-IT Alignment. In B. Pernici & J. A. Gulla (Eds.), *Proceedings of the Workshop on Business/IT Alignment and Interoperability (BUSITAL 2007), Held in Conjunction with the 19th Conference on Advanced Information Systems (CAiSE 2007), Trondheim, Norway* (pp. 461–468. Trondheim, Norway: Tapir Academic Press. ISBN 978-8-251-92245-6.

Nabukenya, J., van Bommel, P., & Proper, H. A. (2009). A theory-driven design approach to collaborative policy making processes. In *Proceedings of the 42nd Hawaii International Conference on System Sciences (HICSS-42), Los Alamitos, Hawaii.* Los Alamitos, CA: IEEE Computer Society Press.

Nakakawa, A. (2012). *A collaboration process for enterprise architecture creation.* PhD thesis, Radboud University, Nijmegen, the Netherlands. ISBN 978-90-8891496-6.

Nakakawa, A., van Bommel, P., & Proper, H. A. (2010a). Challenges of involving stakeholders when creating enterprise architecture. In B. F. v. Dongen & H. A. Reijers (Eds.), *Proceedings of the 5th SIKS/BENAIS Conference on Enterprise Information Systems (EIS 2010), Eindhoven, the Netherlands* (pp. 43–55). Last checked on July 15, 2016. http://tinyurl.com/hhzqz7c

Nakakawa, A., van Bommel, P., & Proper, H. A. (2010b). Towards a theory on collaborative decision making in enterprise architecture. In R. Winter, J. L. Zhao, & S. Aier (Eds.), *Proceedings on the International Conference on Design Science Research in Information Systems and Technology (DESRIST 2010), St. Gallen, Switzerland* (Number 6105, pp. 538–541). Lecture Notes in Computer Science. Heidelberg, Germany: Springer.

Nakakawa, A., van Bommel, P., & Proper, H. A. (2011a). Applying soft systems methodology in enterprise architecture creation workshops. In M. Nüttgens, O. Thomas, & B. Weber (Eds.), *Proceedings of the 4th International Workshop on Enterprise Modelling and Information Systems Architectures (EMISA 2011), Hamburg, Germany* (Number 190, pp. 37–50). Lecture Notes in Informatics. Bonn, Germany: Gesellschaft für Informatiek. ISBN 978-3-885-79284-0.

Nakakawa, A., van Bommel, P., & Proper, H. A. (2011b). Definition and validation of requirements for collaborative decision-making in enterprise architecture creation. *International Journal of Cooperative Information Systems, 20*(1), 83–136. https://doi.org/10.1142/S021884301100216X

Nakakawa, A., van Bommel, P., & Proper, H. A. (2013). Supplementing enterprise architecture approaches with support for executing collaborative tasks – A case of TOGAF ADM. *International Journal of Cooperative Information Systems, 22*(2), 1350007. https://doi.org/10.1142/S021884301100216X

Nakakoji, K. (1996). Beyond language translation: Crossing the cultural divide. *IEEE Software, 13*(6), 42–46.

NBS. (1993). *Integrated Definition for Information Modeling (IDEF0)* (Vol. 183). National Bureau of Standards, Washington, DC, USA. Last checked on July 15, 2016. http://www.idef.com/idefo-function_modeling_method/

Neyer, A.-K., & Maicher, L. (2013). Understanding the role of objects in interactive innovation. In R. Alt & B. Franczyk (Eds.), *Proceedings of the 11th International Conference on Wirtschaftsinformatik (WI2013)* (pp. 756–778).

Nicolini, D., Mengis, J., & Swan, J. (2012). Understanding the role of objects in cross-disciplinary collaboration. *Organization Science, 23*(3), 612–629.

Nielsen, J. A., Mathiassen, L., & Newell, S. (2014). Theorization and translation in information technology institutionalization: Evidence from Danish home care. *MIS Quarterly, 38*(1), 165–186.

Niemann, K. D. (2005). IT governance and enterprise architecture - Impact of IT cost reduction on innovation power. *Journal of Enterprise Architecture, 1*(1), 31–40.

Niemietz, H., de Kinderen, S., & Constantinidis, C. (2013). Understanding the role of subcultures in the enterprise architecture process. In *ECIS 2013* (pp. 298–305). Last checked on July 15, 2016. http://aisel.aisnet.org/ecis2013_cr/129/

Normann, R. (2001). *Reframing business: When the map changes the landscape.* Chichester, UK: Wiley.

OCIO. (1996). *Summary of Major Provisions of the Clinger-Cohen Act of 1996.* Technical Report, U.S. Department of Commerce – Office of the Chief Information Officer.

OECD. (2002). *The Greek Social Security System.* Technical Report, Ministry of Labour and Social Security, General Secretariat for Social Security.

Okhuysen, G. A., & Bechky, B. A. (2009). Coordination in organizations: An integrative perspective. *The Academy of Management Annals, 3*(1), 463–502.

Oliver, C. (1991). Strategic responses to institutional processes. *Academy of Management Review, 16*(1), 145–179.

Oliver, R. L. (1977). Effect of expectation and discontinuation on postexposure product evaluations: An alternative interpretation. *Journal of Applied Psychology, 62*(4), 480–486.

Oliver, R. L. (1980). A cognitive model of the antecedents and consequences of satisfaction decisions. *Journal of Marketing Research, 17*(4), 460–469.

Olivier, A. (2013). *Organisational design: What your university forgot to teach you.* München, Germany: Xlibris.

OMG. (2003). *UML 2.0 Superstructure Specification – Final Adopted Specification.* Technical Report ptc/03–08–02, Object Management Group, Needham, MA.

OMG. (2007). *OMG Unified Modeling Language (OMG UML), Infrastructure, V2.1.2.* Technical Report, The Object Management Group, Needham, MA. http://www.omg.org/spec/UML/2.1.2/Infrastructure/PDF

OMG. (2011). *Business Process Modeling Notation, V2.0.* Technical Report OMG Document Number: formal/2011-01-03, Object Management Group, Needham, MA.

Op 't Land, M., & Proper, H. A. (2007). Impact of principles on enterprise engineering. In H. Österle, J. Schelp, & R. Winter (Eds.), *Proceedings of the 15th European Conference on Information Systems* (pp. 1965–1976). St. Gallen, Switzerland: University of St. Gallen.

Op 't Land, M., Proper, H. A., Waage, M., Cloo, J., & Steghuis, C. (2008). *Enterprise architecture – Creating value by informed governance.* Enterprise Engineering Series. Heidelberg, Germany: Springer. ISBN 978-3-540-85231-5.

Orlikowski, W. J., & Barley, S. R. (2001). Technology and institutions: What can research on information technology and research on organizations learn from each other? *MIS Quarterly, 25*(2), 145–165.

Otto, B., & Österle, H. (2012). Principles for knowledge creation in collaborative design science research. In *Proceedings of the 33rd International Conference on Information Systems (ICIS 2012), Orlando, FL* (pp. 2408–2423).

Pache, A.-C., & Santos, F. (2013). Embedded in hybrid contexts: How individuals in organizations respond to competing institutional logics. In M. Lounsbury & E. Boxenbaum (Eds.), *Research in the sociology of organizations* (pp. 3–35). Bingley, UK: Emerald Group Publishing Limited.

Pareto, L., Eriksson, P., & Ehnebom, S. (2010). Architectural descriptions as boundary objects in system and design work. In D. C. Petriu, N. Rouquette, & Ø. Haugen (Eds.), *Model driven engineering languages and systems* (pp. 406–419). Berlin, Heidelberg, Germany: Springer.

Parsons, J. (2003). Effects of local versus global schema diagrams on verification and communication in conceptual data modeling. *Journal of Management Information Systems, 19*(3), 155–183.

Parsons, T. (1960). *Structure and process in modern societies.* New York, NY: Free Press.

Pawlowski, S. D., & Robey, D. (2004). Bridging user organizations: Knowledge brokering and the work of information technology professionals. *MIS Quarterly, 28*(4), 645–672.

Payne, J. W. (1976). Task complexity and contingent processing in decision making: An information search and protocol analysis. *Organizational Behavior and Human Performance, 16*(2), 366–387.

Peffers, K., Rothenberger, M., & Kuechler, B. (Eds.). (2012). *Proceedings of the 7th International Conference on Design Science Research in Information Systems and Technology (DESRIST 2012), Las Vegas, NV* (Vol. 7286). Lecture Notes in Computer Science. Heidelberg, Germany: Springer. ISBN 978-3-642-29862-2. https://doi.org/10.1007/978-3-642-29863-9

Peffers, K., Tuunanen, T., Rothenberger, M. A., & Chatterjee, S. (2007). A design science research methodology for information systems research. *Journal of Management Information Systems, 24*(3), 45–77.

Peppard, J., & Ward, J. (2004). Beyond strategic infromation systems: Towards an IS capability. *Journal of Strategic Information Systems, 13*,167–194.

Peristeras, V., & Tarabanis, K. (2000). Towards an enterprise architecture for public administration using a top-down approach. *European Journal of Information Systems, 9*,252–260.

Phang, C. W., Kankanhalli, A., & Ang, C. (2008). Investigating organizational learning in eGovernment projects: A multi-theoretic approach. *The Journal of Strategic Information Systems, 17*(2), 99–123.

Pijpers, V., De Leenheer, P., Gordijn, J., & Akkermans, H. (2012). Using conceptual models to explore business-ICT alignment in networked value constellations. *Requirements Engineering, 17*(3), 203–226. ISSN 0947-3602. https://doi.org/10.1007/s00766-011-0136-x

Plataniotis, G., de Kinderen, S., Ma, Q., & Proper, H. A. (2015a). A conceptual model for compliance checking support of enterprise architecture decisions. In *Proceedings of the 17th IEEE Conference on Business Informatics (CBI 2015), Lisbon, Portugal* (Vol. 1, pp. 191–198). https://doi.org/10.1109/CBI.2015.46

Plataniotis, G., de Kinderen, S., & Proper, H. A. (2013a). Relating decisions in enterprise architecture using decision design graphs. In D. Gasevic, M. Hatala, H. R. Motahari Nezhad, & M. Reichert (Eds.), *Proceedings of the 17th IEEE International Enterprise Distributed Object Computing Conference (EDOC 2013), Vancouver, Canada* (pp. 139–146). Los Alamitos, CA: IEEE Explore. https://doi.org/10.1109/EDOC.2013.23

Plataniotis, G., de Kinderen, S., & Proper, H. A. (2014a). A computational approach for design rationalization in enterprise architecture. In *Proceedings of the 8th IEEE International Conference on Research Challenges in Information Science (RCIS 2014), Marrakesh, Morocco.*

Plataniotis, G., de Kinderen, S., & Proper, H. A. (2014b). Capturing design rationales in enterprise architecture: A case study. In *Proceedings of the 7th IFIP WG 8.1 Working Conference on the Practice of Enterprise Modeling (PoEM 2014).*

Plataniotis, G., de Kinderen, S., & Proper, H. A. (2014c). Challenges of capturing design rationales in enterprise architecture: A case study. In *Proceedings of the 8th Transformation & Engineering of Enterprises Workshop (TEE 2014), Held in Conjunction with the 16th IEEE Conference on Business Informatics (CBI 2014), Geneva, Switzerland.* CEUR-WS.org. http://ceur-ws.org/Vol-1182/

Plataniotis, G., de Kinderen, S., & Proper, H. A. (2014d). EA anamnesis: An approach for decision making analysis in enterprise architecture. *International Journal of Information System Modeling and Design (IJISMD)*, *5*(3), 75–95. ISSN 1947-8186.
https://doi.org/10.4018/ijismd.2014070104

Plataniotis, G., de Kinderen, S., van der Linden, D. J. T., Greefhorst, D., & Proper, H. A. (2013b). An empirical evaluation of design decision concepts in enterprise architecture. In J. Grabis, M. Kirikova, J. Zdravkovic, & J. Stirna (Eds.), *Proceedings of the 6th IFIP WG 8.1 Working Conference on the Practice of Enterprise Modeling (PoEM 2013), Riga, Latvia* (Vol. 165, pp. 24–38). Lecture Notes in Business Information Processing. Heidelberg, Germany: Springer. ISBN 978-3-642-41640-8.
https://doi.org/10.1007/978-3-642-41641-5_3

Plataniotis, G., Ma, Q., Proper, H. A., & de Kinderen, S. (2015b). Traceability and modeling of requirements in enterprise architecture from a design rationale perspective. In *Proceedings of the 9th IEEE International Conference on Research Challenges in Information Science (RCIS 2015), Athens, Greece* (pp. 518–519).
https://doi.org/10.1109/RCIS.2015.7128916

PMI. (2001). *Project Management Body of Knowledge*. Technical Report, The Project Management Institute.

PMI. (2008). *A guide to the project management body of knowledge* (4th ed.). Newtown Square, PA: Project Management Institute.

Poole, M., & DeSanctis, G. (2003). Structuration theory in information systems research: Methods and controversies. In M. Whitman & A. Woszczynski (Eds.), *The handbook for information systems research*. Hershey, PA: Idea Group Publishing.

Powell, W. W. (1991). Expanding the scope of institutional analysis. In W. W. Powell & P. J. DiMaggio (Eds.), *The new institutionalism in organizational analysis* (pp. 183–203). Chicago, IL: The University of Chicago Press.

Powell, W. W., & Colyvas, J. A. (2008). Microfoundations of institutional theory. In R. Greenwood, C. Oliver, R. Suddaby, & K. Sahlin (Eds.), *The SAGE handbook of organizational institutionalism* (pp. 276–298). London, UK: Sage Publications.

Prakken, B. (2000). *Information, organization and information systems design: An integrated approach to information problems*. Heidelberg, Germany: Springer. ISBN 978-1461369905.

Premkumar, G., Ramamurthy, K., & Saunders, C. S. (2005). Information processing view of organizations: An exploratory examination of fit in the context of interorganizational relationships. *Journal of Management Information Systems, 22*(1), 257–294.

Proper, H. A. (2001). *ISP for large–scale migrations*. Information Services Procurement Library. Den Haag, the Netherlands: Ten Hagen & Stam. ISBN 9-076-30488-2.

Proper, H. A. (2014). Enterprise architecture – Informed steering of enterprises in motion. In *Proceedings of the 15th International Conference (ICEIS 2013),*

Angers, France – Revised Selected Papers (Vol. 190, pp. 16–34). Lecture Notes in Business Information Processing. Heidelberg, Germany: Springer. https://doi.org/10.1007/978-3-319-09492-2_2

Proper, H. A., & Lankhorst, M. M. (2014). Enterprise architecture – Towards essential sense-making. *Enterprise Modelling and Information Systems Architectures (EMISA), 9*(1), 5–21.

Proper, H. A., & Op 't Land, M. (2010). Lines in the water – The line of reasoning in an enterprise engineering case study from the public sector. In A. F. Harmsen, H. A. Proper, F. Schalkwijk, J. Barjis, & S. J. Overbeek (Eds.), *Proceedings of the 2nd Working Conference on Practice-Driven Research on Enterprise Transformation (PRET 2010), Delft, the Netherlands* (Vol. 69, pp. 193–216). Lecture Notes in Business Information Processing. Heidelberg, Germany: Springer. ISBN 978-3-642-16769-0.

Proper, H. A., & Ralyté, J. (Eds.). (2014). *Proceedings of the 16th IEEE Conference on Business Informatics (CBI 2014), Geneva, Switzerland* (Vol. 1). Los Alamitos, CA: IEEE Computer Society Press. ISBN 978-1-4799-5779-8.

Proper, H. A., Verrijn–Stuart, A. A., & Hoppenbrouwers, S. J. B. A. (2005). Towards utility–based selection of architecture–modelling concepts. In S. Hartmann & M. Stumptner (Eds.), *Proceedings of the Second Asia–Pacific Conference on Conceptual Modelling (APCCM 2005), Newcastle, NSW, Australia* (Vol. 42, pp. 25–36). Conferences in Research and Practice in Information Technology Series, Sydney, NSW, Australia. Sydney: Australian Computer Society. ISBN 1-920-68225-2.

Prosci. (2014). *Best practices in change management* (2014th ed.). Loveland, CO: Prosci Inc.

Pulkkinen, M., Naumenko, A., & Luostarinen, K. (2007). Managing information security in a business network of machinery maintenance services business - enterprise architecture as a coordination tool. *Journal of Systems and Software, 80*(10), 1607–1620.

Purchase, V., Parry, G., Valerdi, R., Nightingale, D., & Mills, J. (2011). Enterprise transformation: Why are we interested, what is it, and what are the challenges? *Journal of Enterprise Transformation, 1*(1), 14–33.

Purvis, R. L., Sambamurthy, V., & Zmud, R. W. (2001). The assimilation of knowledge platforms in organizations: An empirical investigation. *Organization Science, 12*(2), 117–135.

Ralyté, J., Brinkkemper, S., & Henderson–Sellers, B. (Eds.). (2008). *Proceedings of the IFIP WG 8.1 Working Conference on Situational Method Engineering (SME 2008), Geneva, Switzerland.* Heidelberg, Germany: Springer. ISBN 978-0-387-73946-5.

Ramsay, J. (2005). The real meaning of value in trading relationships. *International Journal of Operations & Production Management, 25*(6), 549–565. https://doi.org/10.1108/01443570510599719

Ran, A., & Kuusela, J. (1996). Design decision trees. In *Proceedings of the 8th International Workshop on Software Specification and Design* (p. 172). Los Alamitos, CA: IEEE Computer Society.

Razo-Zapata, I. S., De Leenheer, P., Gordijn, J., & Akkermans, H. (2012). Fuzzy verification of service value networks. In J. Ralyte & X. Franch (Eds.), *Proceedings of the 24th International Conference on Advanced Information Systems Engineering (CAiSE 2012), Gdansk, Poland.* Heidelberg, Germany: Springer.

Razo-Zapata, I. S., Gordijn, J., De Leenheer, P., & Akkermans, H. (2011). Dynamic cluster-based service bundling: A value-oriented framework. In *Proceedings of the 13th IEEE Conference on Commerce and Enterprise Computing (CEC 2011), Luxembourg.* Last checked on July 15, 2016.
http://tinyurl.com/zesr25l

Reichert, M., Strecker, S., & Turowski, K. (Eds.). (2007). *Proceedings of the 2nd International Workshop on Enterprise Modelling and Information Systems Architectures (EMISA 2007), St. Goar am Rhein, Germany* (Number 119). Lecture Notes in Informatics. Bonn, Germany: Gesellschaft für Informatik.

Reitsma, E., Jansen, P., van der Werf, E., & van den Steenhoven, H. (2004). Wat is de beste veranderaanpak? *Management Executive.* In Dutch.
http://www.managementexecutive.nl/artikel/2956/
Wat-is-de-beste-veranderaanpak.

Richardson, G. L., Jackson, B. M., & Dickson, G. W. (1990). A principles-based enterprise architecture: Lessons from Texaco and Star Enterprise. *MIS Quarterly, 14*(4), 385–403. ISSN 0276-7783.
http://www.jstor.org/stable/249787

Rittel, H. W. J., & Webber, M. M. (1973). Dilemmas in a general theory of planning. *Policy Sciences, 4*,155–169.

Rodrigues, L. S., & Amaral, L. (2010). Issues in enterprise architecture value. *Journal of Enterprise Architecture, 6*(4), 27–32.

Rogers, E. M. (2003). *Diffusion of innovations* (5th ed.). New York, NY: Free Press.

Rosenkranz, C., Vraneši, H., & Holten, R. (2014). Boundary interactions and motors of change in requirements elicitation: A dynamic perspective on knowledge sharing. *Journal of the Association for Information Systems, 15*(6), 306–345.

Ross, J. W. (2003). Creating a strategic IT architecture competency: Learning in stages. *MIS Quarterly Executive, 2*(1), 31–43.

Ross, J. W., & Beath, C. M. (2006). Sustainable IT outsourcing success: Let enterprise architecture be your guide. *MIS Quarterly Executive, 5*(4), 181–192.

Ross, J. W., & Quaadgras, A. (2012). Enterprise architecture is not just for architects. *CISR Research Briefings, 7*(9).
http://cisr.mit.edu/blog/documents/2012/09/19/2012_0901_
architecturelearning_rossquaadgras.pdf/.

Ross, J. W., Weill, P., & Robertson, D. C. (2006). *Enterprise architecture as strategy: Creating a foundation for business execution.* Boston, MA: Harvard Business School Press. ISBN 1-591-39839-8.

Rossi, M., Ramesh, B., Lyytinen, K., & Tolvanen, J. P. (2004). Managing evolutionary method engineering by method rationale. *Journal of the Association for Information Systems, 5*(9), 356–391.

Rothrock, L., & Yin, J. (2008). Integrating compensatory and noncompensatory decision-making strategies in dynamic task environments. In T. Kugler,

J. C. Smith, T. Connolly, & Y. J. Son (Eds.), *Decision modeling and behavior in complex and uncertain environments. Springer optimization and its applications* (Vol. 21, pp. 125–141). New York: Springer.
http://dx.doi.org/10.1007/978-0-387-77131-1_6.

Rouse, W. B. (2005). A theory of enterprise transformation. *Systems Engineering, 8*(4), 279–295. ISSN 1520-6858.
https://doi.org/10.1002/sys.20035

Rouse, W. B. (2006). *Enterprise transformation: Understanding and enabling fundamental change*. Hoboken, NJ: Wiley.

Rouse, W. B., & Baba, M. (2006). Enterprise transformation – Fundamental enterprise changes begin by looking at the challenges from technical, behavioral, and social perspectives. *Communications of the ACM, 49*(7), 67–72.

Rowbottom, R., & Billis, D. (1987). *Organisational design: The work-levels approach*. Aldershot, UK: Gower.

Roy, S., & Kitching, E. (2013). 70% of transformation programs fail. Last checked on August 9, 2016.
http://tinyurl.com/zjp9mmx

Rüegg-Stürm, J. (2004). *Einführung in die Managementlehre*. Bern, Switzerland: Haupt Verleg. ISBN 3-258-06999-9.

Rüegg-Stürm, J. (2005). *The new St. Gallen management model: Basic categories of an approach to integrated management*. Basingstoke, New York: Palgrave Macmillan.

Safrudin, N., Rosemann, M., Recker, J., & Genrich, M. (2014). A typology of business transformations. *360° – The Business Transformation Journal, 2014*(10), 25–41.

Sarker, S., & Lee, A. S. (1999). IT-enabled organizational transformation: A case study of BPR failure at TELECO. *The Journal of Strategic Information Systems, 8*(1), 83–103.

SCC. (2009). *SCOR Frameworks*. Technical Report, Supply Chain Council. Last checked on June 15, 2009.
http://www.supply-chain.org/resources/scor

Schaeffer, J., Szafron, D., Lobe, G., & Parsons, I. (1993). The enterprise model for developing distributed applications. *IEEE Parallel and Distributed Technology, 1*(3), 85–96.

Scheer, A.-W. (2000). *ARIS – Business process modeling*. Heidelberg, Germany: Springer. ISBN 3-540-65835-1.

Schein, E. H. (2004). *Organizational culture and leadership* (3rd ed.). San Francisco: Jossey-Bass. ISBN 0-7879-6845-5.

Schein, E. H. (2010). *Organizational culture and leadership* (4th ed.). San Francisco, CA: Wiley.

Schelp, J., & Winter, R. (2009). Language communities in enterprise architecture research. In V. Vaishanvi & R. Baskerville (Eds.), *Proceedings of the 4th Conference on Design Science Research in Information Systems and Technology (DESRIST 2009), Philadelphia, PA* (pp. 1–10). New York, NY: ACM.

Schmidt, C., & Buxmann, P. (2011). Outcomes and success factors of enterprise IT architecture management: Empirical insight from the international financial services industry. *European Journal of Information Systems, 20*(2), 168–185.

Schönherr, M. (2009). Towards a common terminology in the discipline of enterprise architecture. In G. Feuerlicht & W. Lamersdorf (Eds.), *3rd Workshop on Trends in Enterprise Architecture Research (TEAR 2008) at the 6th International Conference on Service Oriented Computing (ICSOC 2008)* (Vol. 5472, pp. 400–413). Lecture Notes in Computer Science. Heidelberg, Germany: Springer.

Schrader, U., & Hennig-Thurau, T. (2009). VHB-JOURQUAL 2: Method, results, and implications of the German academic association for business research's journal ranking. *BuR - Business Research, 2*(2), 180–204.

Schützenberger, M. P. (1954). A tentative classification of goal-seeking behaviours. *Journal of Mental Science, 100*, 97–102.

Scott, W. R. (2008). Lords of the dance: Professionals as institutional agents. *Organization Studies, 29*(2), 219–238.

Scott, W. R. (2013). *Institutions and organizations: Ideas, interests, and identities* (4th ed.). London, UK: Sage Publications.

Scott, W. R., & Meyer, J. W. (1991). The organization of societal sectors: Propositions and early evidence. In W. W. Powell & P. J. DiMaggio (Eds.), *The new institutionalism in organizational analysis* (pp. 108–140). Chicago, IL: The University of Chicago Press.

Sein, M. K., Henfridsson, O., Purao, S., Rossi, M., & Lindgren, R. (2011). Action design research. *MIS Quarterly, 35*(1), 37–56.

Senge, P. M. (1990). *The fifth discipline – The art and practice of the learning organization.* New York, NY: Doubleday. ISBN 978-0-385-51725-6.

Sidorova, A., & Kappelman, L. A. (2011). Better business-IT alignment through enterprise architecture: An actor-network theory perspective. *Journal of Enterprise Architecture, 7(1)*, 39–47.

Simon, D., Fischbach, K., & Schoder, D. (2013). An exploration of enterprise architecture research. *Communications of the Association for Information Systems, 32*(1), 1–72.

Simons, R. (1994). *Levers of control: How managers use control systems to drive strategic renewal.* Boston, MA: Harvard Business School Press. ISBN 978-0-875-84559-3.

Singh, R., Mathiassen, L., Stachura, M. E., & Astapova, E. V. (2011). Dynamic capabilities in home health: IT-enabled transformation of post-acute care. *Journal of the Association for Information Systems, 12*(2), Article 2.

Sledgianowski, D., & Luftman, J. (2005). IT-business strategic alignment maturity: A case study. *Journal of Cases on Information Technology, 7*(2), 102–120.

Soh, C., & Sia, S. K. (2004). An institutional perspective on sources of ERP package–organisation misalignments. *The Journal of Strategic Information Systems, 13*(4), 375–197.

Sousa, P., Gabriel, R., Tadao, G., Carvalho, R., Sousa, P. M., & Sampaio, A. (2011). Enterprise transformation: The Serasa Experian case. In F. Harmsen, K. Grahlmann, & E. Proper (Eds.), *Practice-Driven Research on Enterprise*

Transformation. PRET 2011 (pp. 134–145). Berlin: Springer. ISBN 978-3-642-23387-6.
https://doi.org/10.1007/978-3-642-23388-3_7

Sousa, P., Lima, J., Sampaio, A., & Pereira, C. (2009). An approach for creating and managing enterprise blueprints: A case for IT blueprints. In A. Albani, J. Barjis, & J. L. G. Dietz (Eds.), *Advances in enterprise engineering III* (Vol. 34, pp. 70–84). Lecture Notes in Business Information Processing. Heidelberg, Germany: Springer. ISBN 978-3-642-01914-2.
https://doi.org/10.1007/978-3-642-01915-9_6

Sowa, J., & Zachman, J. A. (1992). Extending and formalizing the framework for information systems architecture. *IBM Systems Journal, 31*(3), 590–616.

Star, S. L., & Griesemer, J. R. (1989). Institutional ecology, 'Translations' and boundary objects: Amateurs and professionals in Berkeley's Museum of Vertebrate Zoology 1907-39. *Social Studies of Science, 19*(4), 387–420.
https://doi.org/10.1177/030631289019003001

Steenbergen, M. v. (2011). *Maturity and effectiveness of enterprise architecture.* PhD thesis, University of Utrecht, Utrecht, the Netherlands. ISBN 978-90-393-5554-1.

Stensaker, I., Falkenberg, J., & Grønhaug, K. (2008). Implementation activities and organizational sensemaking. *The Journal of Applied Behavioral Science, 44*(2), 162–185.

Stiles, P., Uhl, A., & Stratil, P. (2012). Meta management. In A. Uhl & L. A. Gollenia (Eds. 2012), *A handbook of business transformation management methodology* (pp. 13–29). Farnham: Gower.

Stirna, J., & Persson, A. (2012). Purpose driven competency planning for enterprise modeling projects. In J. Ralyté, X. Franch, S. Brinkkemper, & S. Wrycza (Eds.), *Proceedings of the 24th International Conference on Advanced Information Systems Engineering (CAiSE 2012), Gdansk, Poland* (Vol. 7328, pp. 662–677). Lecture Notes in Computer Science. Heidelberg, Germany: Springer. ISBN 978-3-642-31094-2.
https://doi.org/10.1007/978-3-642-31095-9_43

Strano, C., & Rehmani, Q. (2007). The role of the enterprise architect. *International Journal of Information Systems and e-Business Management, 5*(4), 379–396.

Stremersch, S., & Tellis, G. J. (2002). Strategic bundling of products and prices: A new synthesis for marketing. *Journal of Marketing, 66*(1), 55–72.

Suchman, M. C. (1995). Managing legitimacy: Strategic and institutional approaches. *Academy of Management Review, 20*(3), 571–610.

Svenson, O. (1979). Process descriptions of decision making. *Organizational Behavior and Human Performance, 23*(1), 86–112.

Swanson, E. B., & Ramiller, N. C. (1997). The organizing vision in information systems innovation. *Organization Science, 8*(5), 458–474.

Tamm, T., Seddon, P. B., Shanks, G., & Reynolds, P. (2011a). Delivering business value through enterprise architecture. *Journal of Enterprise Architecture, 7*(2), 17–30.

Tamm, T., Seddon, P. B., Shanks, G., & Reynolds, P. (2011b). How does enterprise architecture add value to organisations? *Communications of the Association for Information Systems, 28*(1), 141–168.

Tang, A., Babar, M. A., Gorton, I., & Han, J. (2006). A survey of architecture design rationale. *Journal of Systems and Software, 79*(12), 1792–1804. ISSN 0164-1212. https://doi.org/10.1016/j.jss.2006.04.029

Tang, A., Jin, Y., & Han, J. (2007). A rationale-based architecture model for design traceability and reasoning. *Journal of Systems and Software, 80*(6), 918–934. ISSN 0164-1212. https://doi.org/10.1016/j.jss.2006.08.040

Teo, H. H., Wei, K. K., & Benbasat, I. (2003). Predicting intention to adopt interorganizational linkages: An institutional perspective. *MIS Quarterly, 27*(1), 19–49.

The Open Group. (2009). *TOGAF version 9*. Zaltbommel, the Netherlands: Van Haren Publishing. ISBN 978-9-087-53230-7.

The Open Group. (2011). *TOGAF version 9.1* (10th ed.). Zaltbommel, the Netherlands: Van Haren Publishing. ISBN 978-9-087-53679-4.

Thenmozhi, M. (2009). *Module 9 - Strategic Management*. Lecture Notes, Department of Management Studies, Indian Institute of Technology, Madras, India.

Thomas, O. (2005). Understanding the term reference model in information systems research: History, literature analysis and explanation. In C. J. Bussler & A. Haller (Eds.), *BPM 2005 International Workshops, BPI, BPD, ENEI, BPRM, WSCOBPM, BPS* (Vol. 3812, pp. 484–496). Lecture Notes in Computer Science. Heidelberg, Germany: Springer.

Thompson, J. D. (1967). *Organizations in action: Social science bases of administrative theory*. New York, NY: McGraw-Hill.

Tolbert, P. S., & Zucker, L. G. (1996). The institutionalization of institutional theory. In S. R. Clegg, C. Hardy, & W. R. Nord (Eds.), *Handbook of organization studies* (pp. 175–190). London: Sage Publications Ltd.

Tolman, E. C., & Brunswik, E. (1935). The organism and the causal texture of the environment. *Psychological Review, 42*, 43–77.

Trist, E. (1977). A concept of organizational ecology. *Australian Journal of Management, 2*(2), 161–175.

Tropos. (2016). Tropos. Last checked on July 27, 2016. http://www.troposproject.org

Tushman, M. L., & Nadler, D. A. (1978). Information processing as an integrating concept in organizational design. *The Academy of Management Review, 3*(3), 613–624.

Tyree, J., & Akerman, A. (2005). Architecture decisions: Demystifying architecture. *Software, IEEE, 22*(2), 19–27.

Uhl, A., & Gollenia, L. A. (Eds.). (2012). *A handbook of business transformation management methodology*. Farnham, UK: Gower.

Valorinta, M. (2011). IT alignment and the boundaries of the IT function. *Journal of Information Technology, 26*(1), 46–59.

van Aken, J. E. (2004). Management research based on the paradigm of the design sciences: The quest for field-tested and grounded technological rules. *Journal of Management Studies, 41*(2), 219–246.

van Aken, J. E., & Nagel, A. P. (2004). *Organising and Managing the Fuzzy Front End of New Product Development*. Technical Report, Eindhoven University of Technology.
https://pure.tue.nl/ws/files/1826685/585732.pdf

van Bommel, P., Buitenhuis, P. G., Hoppenbrouwers, S. J. B. A., & Proper, H. A. (2007). Architecture principles – A regulative perspective on enterprise architecture. In M. Reichert, S. Strecker, & K. Turowski (Eds.), *EMISA 2007* (pp. 47–60). Bonn: Gesellschaft fuer Informatik.

van Buuren, R., Gordijn, J., & Janssen, W. (2005). Business case modelling for E-services. In *Proceedings of the 18th Bled eConference – eIntegration in Action*. AIS.

van der Aalst, W. M. P. (2011). *Process mining: Discovery, conformance and enhancement of business processes*. Heidelberg, Germany: Springer. ISBN 978-3642193446.

van der Hoek, A., & Wolf, A. L. (2003). Software release management for component-based software. *Software—Practice & Experience, 33*(1), 77–98.

van der Raadt, B., Bonnet, M., Schouten, S., & van Vliet, H. (2010). The relation between EA effectiveness and stakeholder satisfaction. *The Journal of Systems and Software, 83*(10), 1954–1969.

van der Raadt, B., Schouten, S., & van Vliet, H. (2008). Stakeholder perception of enterprise architecture. In R. Morrison, D. Balasubramaniam, & K. Falkner (Eds.), *Software architecture* (Vol. 5292, pp. 19–34). Lecture Notes in Computer Science. Heidelberg, Germany: Springer. ISBN 978-3-540-88029-5.

van Deursen, A., Klint, P., & Visser, J. (2000). Domain-specific languages: An annotated bibliography. *Sigplan Notices, 35*(6), 26–36.

van Zee, M. (2016). eGovernment – GRL Extension. Last checked on July 27, 2016.
https://github.com/RationalArchitecture/eGovernment

van Zee, M., Bex, F., & Ghanavati, S. (2015). Rationalization of goal models in GRL using formal argumentation. In D. Zowghi, V. Gervasi, & D. Amyot (Eds.), *Proceedings of the 23rd IEEE International Requirements Engineering Conference (RE 2015), Ottawa, Canada*.
https://doi.org/10.1109/RE.2015.7320426

van Zee, M., Marosin, D., Ghanavati, S., & Bex, F. (2016). RationalGRL: A framework for rationalizing goal models using argument diagrams. In I. Comyn-Wattiau, K. Tanaka, I.-l. Song, S. Yamamoto, & M. Saeki (Eds.), *Proceedings of the 35th International Conference on Conceptual Modeling (ER 2016), Gifu, Japan* (pp. 553–560). ISBN 978-3-319-46396-4.

van Zee, M., Plataniotis, G., Marosin, D., & van der Linden, D. J. T. (2014). Formalizing enterprise architecture decision models using integrity constraints. In Proper and Ralyté (Eds.), *16h IEEE Conference on Business Informatics (CBI)* (pp. 143–150). ISBN 978-1-4799-5779-8.
https://doi.org/10.1109/CBI.2014.27

van't Wout, J., Waage, M., Hartman, H., Stahlecker, M., & Hofman, A. (2010). *The integrated architecture framework explained*. Heidelberg, Germany: Springer. ISBN 978-3-642-11517-2.

Vargo, S. L., & Akaka, M. A. (2009). Service-dominant logic as a foundation for service science: Clarifications. *Service Science, 1*(1), 32–41.

Vargo, S. L., Maglio, P. P., & Akaka, M. A. (2008). On value and value co-creation: A service systems and service logic perspective. *European Management Journal, 26*(3), 145–152.

Vellani, K. (2007). *Strategic security management - A risk assessment guide for decision makers*. Oxford: Butterworth Heinemann. ISBN 978-0-12-370897-7. Last checked on July 15, 2016. http://tinyurl.com/jlm97w5

Venable, J., Pries-Heje, J., & Baskerville, R. (2012). A comprehensive framework for evaluation in design science research. In K. Peffers, M. Rothenberger, & B. Kuechler (Eds.), *Proceedings of the 7th International Conference on Design Science Research in Information Systems: Advances in Theory and Practice* (pp. 423–438). Berlin: Springer. ISBN 978-3-642-29862-2. https://doi.org/10.1007/978-3-642-29863-9_31

Venable, J., Pries-Heje, J., & Baskerville, R. (2016). FEDS: A framework for evaluation in design science research. *European Journal of Information Systems, 25*(1), 77–89.

Venkatesh, V., & Bala, H. (2008). Technology acceptance model 3 and a research agenda on interventions. *Decision Sciences, 39*(2), 273–315.

Venkatesh, V., & Davis, F. D. (2000). A theoretical extension of the technology acceptance model: Four longitudinal field studies. *Management Science, 46*(2), 186–204.

Venkatesh, V., Morris, M. G., Davis, G. B., & Davis, F. D. (2003). User acceptance of information technology: Toward a unified view. *MIS Quarterly, 27*(3), 425–478.

Venkatesh, V., Thong, J. Y. L., & Xu, X. (2012). Consumer acceptance and use of information technology: Extending the unified theory of acceptance and use of technology. *MIS Quarterly, 36*(1), 157–178.

Vennix, J. A. M. (1996). *Group model building: Facilitating team learning using systems dynamics*. New York, NY: Wiley.

Verband der Hochschullehrer für Betriebswirtschaft. (2011). VHB-JOURQUAL 2.1 (2011) – Alphabetische Übersicht JQ 2.1.

Versteeg, G., & Bouwman, H. (2006). Business architecture: A new paradigm to relate business strategy to ICT. *Information Systems Frontiers, 8*, 91–102.

vom Brocke, J., Petry, M., & Gonser, T. (2012). Business process management. In A. Uhl & L. Gollenia (Eds.), *The handbook of business transformation management* (pp. 109–139). Farnham: Gower.

vom Brocke, J., Simons, A., Niehaves, B., Riemer, K., Plattfaut, R., & Cleven, A. (2009). Reconstructing the giant: On the importance of rigour in documenting the literature search process. In S. Newell, E. A. Whitley, N. Pouloudi, J. Wareham, & L. Mathiassen (Eds.), *Proceedings of the 17th European Conference on*

Information Systems (ECIS 2009), Verona, Italy (pp. 2206–2217). ISBN 978-8-861-29391-5. Last checked on July 15, 2010.
http://is2.lse.ac.uk/asp/aspecis/20090183.pdf

Wagter, R. (2009). *Sturen op samenhang op basis van GEA – Permanent en event driven*. Zaltbommel, the Netherlands: Van Haren Publishing. In Dutch. ISBN 978-9-087-53406-6.

Wagter, R. (2013). *Enterprise coherence governance*. PhD thesis, Radboud University, Nijmegen, the Netherlands.

Wagter, R., Nijkamp, G., & Proper, H. A. (2007). *Overview 1th phase - General enterprise architecturing*. White Paper GEA-1. Utrecht, the Netherlands: Ordina. In Dutch.

Wagter, R., Proper, H. A., & Witte, D. (2011). Enterprise coherence assessment. In F. Harmsen, K. R. Grahlmann, & E. Proper (Eds.), *Practice-driven research on enterprise transformation* (pp. 28–52). Berlin: Springer. ISBN 978-3-642-23387-6.

Wagter, R., Proper, H. A., & Witte, D. (2012a). A practice-based framework for enterprise coherence. In H. A. Proper, A. F. Harmsen, K. Gaaloul, & S. Wrycza (Eds.), *Proceedings of the 4th Working Conference Practice-Driven Research on Enterprise Transformation (PRET 2012), Gdansk, Poland* (Vol. 120). Lecture Notes in Business Information Processing. Heidelberg, Germany: Springer. ISBN 978-3-642-31133-8.
https://doi.org/10.1007/978-3-642-31134-5

Wagter, R., Proper, H. A., & Witte, D. (2012b). Enterprise coherence in the Dutch Ministry of Social Affairs and Employment. In C. Huemer, G. Viscusi, I. Rychkova, & B. Andersson (Eds.), *Proceedings of the 7th International Workshop on Business/IT-Alignment and Interoperability (BUSITAL 2012)*. Lecture Notes in Business Information Processing. Heidelberg, Germany: Springer.

Wagter, R., Proper, H. A., & Witte, D. (2012c). On the use of GEA at the Dutch Ministry of Social Affairs and Employment. In S. Rinderle-Ma, J. Sanz, & X.-Y. Bai (Eds.), *Proceedings of the 14th IEEE Conference on Commerce and Enterprise Computing (CEC2012), Hangzhou, China* (pp. 115–119). Los Alamitos, CA: IEEE Computer Society Press. ISBN 978-0-769-54857-9.
https://doi.org/10.1109/CEC.2012.26

Wagter, R., Proper, H. A., & Witte, D. (2012d). The extended enterprise coherence-governance assessment. In S. Aier, M. Ekstedt, F. Matthes, E. Proper, J. L. Sanz (Eds.), *Trends in enterprise architecture research and practice-driven research on enterprise transformation* (pp. 218–235). Berlin: Springer. ISBN 978-3-642-34162-5.
https://doi.org/10.1007/978-3-642-34163-2

Wagter, R., Proper, H. A., & Witte, D. (2013a). A theory for enterprise coherence governance. In P. Saha (Ed.), *A systematic perspective to managing complexity with EA*. Hershey, PA: IGI Publishing.

Wagter, R., Proper, H. A., & Witte, D. (2013b). Enterprise coherence governance in the public sector. In *Proceedings of the 15th IEEE Conference on Business*

Informatics (CBI 2013), Vienna, Austria (pp. 117–124). Los Alamitos, CA: IEEE Computer Society Press. https://doi.org/10.1109/CBI.2013.25.

Wagter, R., van den Berg, M., Luijpers, J., & van Steenbergen, M. E. (2005). *Dynamic enterprise architecture; how to make it work.* New York, NY: Wiley. ISBN 978-0-471-68272-1.

Walgenbach, P., & Meyer, R. E. (2008). *Neoinstitutionalistische Organisationstheorie.* Stuttgart, Germany: W. Kohlhammer.

Ward, J., & Daniel, E. (2006). *Benefits management: Delivering value from IS and IT investments.* New York, NY: Wiley.

Ward, J., Rennebaum, T., & Amling, S. (2012). Value Management. In A. Uhl & L. A. Gollenia (Eds.), *A handbook of business transformation management methodology* (pp. 57–81). Farnham: Gower.

Ward, J., & Uhl, A. (2012). Success and failure in transformation – Lessons from 13 case studies. *360° – The Business Transformation Journal, 2012*(3), 30–38.

Watson, H. J., & Frolick, M. N. (1993). Determining information requirements for an EIS. *MIS Quarterly, 17*(3), 255–269.

Webster, J., & Watson, R. T. (2002). Analyzing the past to prepare for the future: Writing a literature review. *MIS Quarterly, 26*(2), 13–23.

Wegmann, A. (2003). On the systemic enterprise architecture methodology (SEAM). In *International Conference on Enterprise Information Systems (ICEIS 2003).*

Weick, K. E., & Quinn, R. E. (1999). Organizational change and development. *Annual Review of Psychology, 50*, 361–86. https://doi.org/10.1146/annurev.psych.50.1.361

Weiss, M. (2010). APC forum: Chubb's enterprise architecture. *MIS Quarterly Executive, 9*(4), 261–262.

Weiss, M. (2012). APC forum: Carestream health's IT transformation. *MIS Quarterly Executive, 11*(1), 49–50.

Weiss, S., Aier, S., & Winter, R. (2013). Institutionalization and the effectiveness of enterprise architecture management. In *Proceedings of the 34th International Conference on Information Systems (ICIS 2013), Milano, Italy.* Association for Information Sytems.

Weiss, S., & Winter, R. (2012). Development of measurement items for the institutionalization of enterprise architecture management in organizations. In S. Aier, M. Ekstedt, F. Matthes, E. Proper, J. L. Sanz (Eds.), *Trends in enterprise architecture research and practice-driven research on enterprise transformation* (pp. 268–283), Berlin: Springer. ISBN 978-3-642-34162-5. https://doi.org/10.1007/978-3-642-34163-2

Wenger, E. (2000). Communities of practice and social learning systems. *Organization, 7*(2), 225–246. https://doi.org/10.1177/135050840072002

Wieringa, R. J. (2014). *Design science methodology for information systems and software engineering.* Heidelberg, Germany: Springer. ISBN 978-3-662-43838-1. https://doi.org/10.1007/978-3-662-43839-8

Wilkinson, M. (2006). Designing an 'Adaptive' enterprise architecture. *BT Technology Journal, 24*(4), 81–92. ISSN 1358-3948.
https://doi.org/10.1007/s10550-006-0099-5

Williams, C. K., & Karahanna, E. (2013). Causal explanation in the coordinating process: A critical realist case study of federated IT governance structures. *MIS Quarterly, 37*(3), 933–964.

Winter, R. (2010). Business Engineering – Betriebswirtschaftliche Konstruktionslehre und ihre Anwendung im Gesundheitswesen. In P. Rohner & R. Winter (Eds.), *Patientenidentifikation und Prozessorientierung - wesentliche Elemente des vernetzten Krankenhauses und der integrierten Versorgung* (pp. 33–55). Heidelberg, Germany: Springer.

Winter, R. (2012). Construction of situational information systems management methods. *International Journal of Information System Modeling and Design (IJISMD), 3*(4), 67–85.

Winter, R. (2014). Architectural thinking. *Business & Information Systems Engineering, 6*(6), 361–364.

Winter, R., & Aier, S. (2011). How are enterprise architecture design principles used? In *The 6h Workshop on Trends in Enterprise Architecture Research (TEAR 2011) at the 15th IEEE International Enterprise Distributed Object Computing Conference (EDOC 2011), Helsinki, Finland* (pp. 314–321). Los Alamitos, CA: IEEE Computer Society.

Winter, R., Bucher, T., Fischer, R., & Kurpjuweit, S. (2007). Analysis and application scenarios of enterprise architecture – An exploratory study (reprint). *Journal of Enterprise Architecture, 3*(3), 33–43.

Winter, R., & Fischer, R. (2006). Essential layers, artifacts, and dependencies of enterprise architecture. In *Workshop on Trends in Enterprise Architecture Research (TEAR 2006), Held at the 10th IEEE International Enterprise Distributed Object Computing Conference (EDOC 2006), Hong Kong, China* (p. 30). Los Alamitos, CA: IEEE Computer Society Press.
https://doi.org/10.1109/EDOCW.2006.33

Winter, R., & Fischer, R. (2007). Essential layers, artifacts, and dependencies of enterprise architecture. *Journal of Enterprise Architecture, 3*(2), 7–18.

Winter, S. J., & Butler, B. S. (2011). Creating bigger problems: Grand challenges as boundary objects and the legitimacy of the information systems field. *Journal of Information Technology, 26*(2), 99–108.

Woodruff, R. B. (1997). Customer value: The next source for competitive advantage. *Journal of the Academy of Marketing Science, 25*(2), 139–153.

Yadav, S. B. (1985). Classifying an organization to identify its information requirements: A comprehensive framework. *Journal of Management Information Systems, 2*(1), 39–60.

Yin, R. K. (2009). *Case study research – Design and methods* (4th ed.). London, UK: Sage Publications. ISBN 978-1-412-96099-1.

Zachman, J. A. (1987). A framework for information systems architecture. *IBM Systems Journal, 26*(3), 276–292.

Zeitz, G., Mittal, V., & McAulay, B. (1999). Distinguishing adoption and entrenchment of management practices: A framework for analysis. *Organization Studies, 20*(5), 741–776.

Zimmermann, H. (1980). OSI reference model – The ISO model of architecture for open systems interconnection. *IEEE Transactions on Communications, 28*(4), 425–432.

Zimmermann, O., Koehler, J., Leymann, F., Polley, R., & Schuster, N. (2009). Managing architectural decision models with dependency relations, integrity constraints, and production rules. *Journal of Systems and Software, 82*(8), 1249–1267. https://doi.org/10.1016/j.jss.2009.01.039

Zuboff, S. (1985). Automate/informate: The two faces of intelligent technology. *Organizational Dynamics, 14*(2), 5–18.

Zucker, L. G. (1977). The role of institutionalization in cultural persistence. *American Sociological Review, 42*(5), 726–743.

Zucker, L. G. (1987). Institutional theories of organization. *Annual Review of Sociology, 13*, 443–464.

Zucker, L. G. (1991). The role of institutionalization in cultural persistence. In W. W. Powell & P. J. DiMaggio (Eds.), *The new institutionalism in organizational analysis* (pp. 83–107). Chicago, IL: The University of Chicago Press.

Printed in the United States
By Bookmasters